THE FIRST URBAN CHURCHES 1

METHODOLOGICAL FOUNDATIONS

Society of Biblical Literature

Writings from the Greco-Roman World Supplement Series

Ronald F. Hock, Editor

Number 7

THE FIRST URBAN CHURCHES 1
METHODOLOGICAL FOUNDATIONS

Edited by
James R. Harrison and L. L. Welborn

SBL Press
Atlanta

Copyright © 2015 by SBL Press

All rights reserved. No part of this work may be reproduced or transmitted in any form or by any means, electronic or mechanical, including photocopying and recording, or by means of any information storage or retrieval system, except as may be expressly permitted by the 1976 Copyright Act or in writing from the publisher. Requests for permission should be addressed in writing to the Rights and Permissions Office, SBL Press, 825 Houston Mill Road, Atlanta, GA 30329 USA.

Library of Congress Cataloging-in-Publication Data

First urban churches / edited by James R. Harrison and L. L. Welborn.
 volumes cm. — (Society of Biblical Literature. Writings from the Greco-Roman world Supplement series ; Number 7)
 Includes bibliographical references.
 Contents: 1. Methodological foundations.

 ISBN 978-1-62837-102-4 (v. 1 : pbk. : alk. paper) — ISBN 978-1-62837-104-8 (v. 1 : ebook) — ISBN 978-1-62837-103-1 (v. 1 : hardcover : alk. paper)
 1. City churches. 2. Church history—Primitive and early church, ca. 30–600. 3. Cities and towns—Religious aspects—Christianity. I. Harrison, James R., 1952– editor.
 BV637.F57 2015
 270.109173'2—dc23   2015021858

Printed on acid-free paper.

Contents

Abbreviations vii

The First Urban Churches: Introduction
  James R. Harrison 1

Assessing the Potential of Archaeological Discoveries for the
  Interpretation of New Testament Texts: The Case of a Gladiator
  Fragment from Colossae and the Letter to the Colossians
  Alan Cadwallader..41

The City in Roman Egypt: The Evidence of the Papyri
  Malcolm Choat..67

Epigraphy and the Study of Polis and *Ekklēsia* in the Greco-
  Roman World
  Paul Trebilco...89

Gaia, Polis, and *Ekklēsia* at the Miletus Market Gate: An Eco-
  critical Reimagination of Revelation 12:16
  Brigitte Kahl..111

Coinage and Colonial Identity: Corinthian Numismatics and
  the Corinthian Correspondence
  Bradley J. Bitner..151

The Polis and the Poor: Reconstructing Social Relations from
  Different Genres of Evidence
  L. L. Welborn 189

Methodological Considerations in Using Epigraphic Evidence to
   Determine the Socioeconomic Context of the Early Christians
   Julien M. Ogereau 245

Urban Portraits of the "Barbarians" on the Fringes of the Roman
   Empire: The Archaeological, Numismatic, Epigraphic, and
   Iconographic Evidence
   James R. Harrison 277

Contributors...319
Index of Primary Texts 321
Index of Modern Authors...335

Abbreviations

Ancient Sources

Aen.	Virgil, *Aeneid*
Ann.	Tacitus, *Annales*
Att.	Cicero, *Epistulae ad Atticum*
Aug.	Suetonius, *Augustus*
Bell. civ.	Appian, *Bella civilia*; Caesar, *Bellum civile*
Bell. gall.	Caesar, *Bellum gallicum*
Bell. jug.	Sallust, *Bellum jugurthinum*
Carm.	Horace, *Carmina*
Cat.	Cicero, *In Catalinam*
Cic.	Plutarch, *Cicero*
Civ.	Augustine, *De civitate Dei*
Claud.	Suetonius, *Claudius*
Clem.	Seneca the Younger, *De clementia*
Controv.	Seneca the Elder, *Controversiae*
De or.	Cicero, *De oratore*
Deipn.	Athenaeus, *Deipnosophistae*
Diag.	Tacitus, *Dialogus de oratoribus*
Diatr.	Epictetus, *Diatribai (Dissertationes)*
Dom.	Cicero, *De domo suo*
Dysk.	Menander, *Dyskolos*
Ep.	Horace, *Epistulae*; Martial, *Epigrams*; Pliny the Younger, *Epistulae*
Epod.	Horace, *Epodi*
Fab. Aes.	Phaedrus, *Fabulae Aesopiae*
Geogr.	Strabo, *Geographica*
Har. resp.	Cicero, *De haruspicum responso*
Hermot.	Lucian, *Hermotimus (De sectis)*
Hist.	Sallust, *Historiae*; Tacitus, *Historiae*

Inst.	Quintilian, *Institutio oratoria*
J.W.	Josephus, *Jewish War*
Leg. man.	Cicero, *Pro Lege manilia* (*De imperio Cn. Pompeii*)
Merc. cond.	Lucian, *De mercede conductis*
Metam.	Apuleius, *Metamorphoses*
Mor.	Plutarch, *Moralia*
Mur.	Cicero, *Pro Murena*
Nat.	Pliny the Elder, *Naturalis historia*
Nec.	Lucian, *Necyomantia*
Noct. att.	Gellius, *Noctes atticae*
Or.	Demosthenes, *Orationes*
Pauper. amand.	Gregory of Nyssa, *De pauperibus amandis*
Phaedr.	Plato, *Phaedrus*
Pisc.	Lucian, *Piscator*
Plut.	Aristophanes, *Plutus*
Poet.	Aristotle, *Poetica*
Pol.	Aristotle, *Politica*
Pont.	Ovid, *Epistulae ex Ponto*
Rep.	Cicero, *De republica*
Resp.	Plato, *Respublica*
Saec.	Horace, *Carmen saeculare*
Sat.	Juvenal, *Satirae*
Saturn.	Lucian, *Saturnalia*
Sest.	Cicero, *Pro Sestio*
Somn.	Lucian, *Somnium* (*Vita Luciani*); Philo, *De somniis*
Theaet.	Plato, *Theaetatus*
Theog.	Hesiod, *Theogonia*
Tib.	Suetonius, *Tiberius*
Tr.	Ovid, *Tristia*
Val.	Tertullian, *Adversus Valentinianos*
Virt.	Philo, *De virtutibus*
Vit. Aesop.	*Vita Aesopi*
Vit. Mos.	Philo, *Vita Mosis*

Secondary Sources

ABSA	*Annual of the British School at Athens*
AE	*L'Année épigraphique*. Edited by René Cagnat et al. Paris: Presses universitaires de France, 1888–.

AGJU	Arbeiten zur Geschichte des Antiken Judentums und des Urchristentums
AHR	*American Historical Review*
AJA	*American Journal of Archaeology*
AJP	*American Journal of Philology*
ANRW	*Aufstieg und Niedergang der römischen Welt: Geschichte und Kultur Roms im Spiegel der neueren Forschung.* Part 2, Principat. Edited by Hildegard Temporini and Wolfgang Haase. Berlin: de Gruyter, 1972–.
AnSt	*Anatolian Studies*
APF	*Archiv für Papyrusforschung*
AuOr	*Aula Orientalis*
BASP	*Bulletin of the American Society of Papyrologists*
BBR	*Bulletin for Biblical Research*
BCH	*Bulletin de correspondance hellénique*
BCHSupp	Supplements to Bulletin de correspondance hellénique
BDAG	Danker, Frederick W., Walter Bauer, William F. Arndt, and F. Wilbur Gingrich. *Greek-English Lexicon of the New Testament and Other Early Christian Literature*. 3rd ed. Chicago: University of Chicago Press, 2000.
BE	Bulletin épigraphique
BGU	*Aegyptische Urkunden aus den Königlichen Staatlichen Museen zu Berlin, Griechische Urkunden*. Berlin: Weidmann, 1895–.
Bib	*Biblica*
BibInt	Biblical Interpretation Series
BR	*Biblical Research*
BTB	*Biblical Theology Bulletin*
BWANT	Beiträge zur Wissenschaft vom Alten und Neuen Testament
BZNW	Beihefte zur Zeitschrift für die neutestamentliche Wissenschaft
CBET	Contributions to Biblical Exegesis and Theology
CBQ	*Catholic Biblical Quarterly*
CIG	*Corpus Inscriptionum Graecarum*. Edited by August Boeckh. 4 vols. Berlin, 1828–1877
CIL	*Corpus Inscriptionum Latinarum*. Berlin, 1862–.
CJ	*Classical Journal*

ABBREVIATIONS

ConBNT	Coniectanea Neotestamentica or Coniectanea Biblica: New Testament Series
CRAI	Comptes rendus de l'Académie des inscriptions et belles-lettres
CRINT	Compendia Rerum Iudaicarum ad Novum Testamentum
DocsAug	Documents Illustrating the Reigns of Augustus and Tiberius. Edited by V. Ehrenberg and A. H. M. Jones. Oxford: Clarendon, 1963.
DocsGaius	Documents Illustrating the Principates of Gaius, Claudius and Nero. Edited by E. M. Smallwood. Cambridge: Cambridge University Press, 1967.
EDNT	Exegetical Dictionary of the New Testament. Edited by Horst Balz and Gerhard Schneider. 3 vols. Grand Rapids: Eerdmans, 1990–1993.
GR	Greece and Rome
GRBS	Greek, Roman, and Byzantine Studies
HTR	Harvard Theological Review
HTS	Harvard Theological Studies
IEph	Wankel, Hermann, et al., eds. Die Inschriften von Ephesos. 8 vols. Bonn: Habelt, 1979–1984.
IG	Inscriptiones Graecae. Editio Minor. Berlin: de Gruyter, 1924–
IGRR	Inscriptiones graecae ad res romanas pertinentes
IK	Inschriften griechischer Städte aus Kleinasien. Edited by Helmut Engelmann. Bonn: Habelt: 1972–.
IKorinthKent	Kent, John Harvey. The Inscriptions 1926–1950. Vol. 8.3 of Corinth: Results of Excavations. Cambridge, MA: Harvard University Press, 1966.
IMT	Barth, Matthias, and Josef Stauber. Inschriften Mysia und Troas. Munich: Leopold Wenger-Institut, 1993.
Int	Interpretation
IstMitt	Istanbuler Mitteilungen
JAC	Jahrbuch für Antike und Christentum
JBL	Journal of Biblical Literature
JEA	Journal of Egyptian Archaeology
JGRChJ	Journal of Greco-Roman Christianity and Judaism
JHS	Journal of Hellenic Studies
JNAA	Journal of the Numismatic Association of Australia

JÖAI	Jahreshefte des Österreichischen Archäologischen Institutes
JRA	Journal of Roman Archaeology
JRH	Journal of Religious History
JRS	Journal of Roman Studies
JSNT	Journal for the Study of the New Testament
JSNTSup	Journal for the Study of the New Testament Supplement Series
KEK	Kritisch-exegetischer Kommentar über das Neue Testament (Meyer- Kommentar)
LBW	Le Bas, Philippe, and William Henry Waddington, eds. *Inscriptions grecques et latines recueillies en Grèce et en Asie Mineure*. Paris: Didot, 1870.
LCL	Loeb Classical Library
LGPN	*A Lexicon of Greek Personal Names*. Edited by P.M. Fraser and Elaine Matthews. 5 vols. Oxford: Clarendon, 1987–2010.
LSJ	Liddell, Henry George, Robert Scott, Henry Stuart Jones. *A Greek-English Lexicon*. 9th ed. with revised supplement. Oxford: Clarendon, 1996
LSTS	The Library of Second Temple Studies
MAMA	*Monumenta Asiae Minoris Antiqua*. Edited by W. M. Calder et al. London: Manchester University Press; Longmans, Green, 1928–.
MDAI	Mitteilungen des Deutschen archäologischen Instituts
MEFR	Mélanges d'archéologie et d'histoire de l'école français de Rome
NewDocs	*New Documents Illustrating Early Christianity*. Edited by G. H. R. Horsley et al. North Ryde, NSW: The Ancient History Documentary Research Centre, Macquarie University, 1981–.
NICOT	New International Commentary on the Old Testament
NovT	Novum Testamentum
NovTSup	Supplements to Novum Testamentum
NTOA	Novum Testamentum et Orbis Antiquus
NTS	New Testament Studies
NumC	Numismatic Chronicle
ÖAI	Österreichischen archäologischen Instituts

OCD	*Oxford Classical Dictionary*. Edited by Simon Hornblower and Antony Spawforth. 4th ed. Oxford: Oxford University Press, 2012
OEANE	*The Oxford Encyclopedia of Archaeology in the Near East*. Edited by Eric M. Meyers. 5 vols. New York: Oxford University Press, 1997
OGI	*Orientis Graeci Inscriptiones Selectae*. Edited by Wilhelm Dittenberger. 2 vols. Leipzig: Hirzel, 1903–1905.
OTL	Old Testament Library
P.Bas.	Rabel, Ernst, and Wilhelm Spiegelberg, eds. *Papyrusurkunden der Öffentlichen Bibliothek der Universität zu Basel*. 2 vols. Berlin: Weidmann, 1917.
P.Berl.Bork.	Borkowski, Zbigniew, ed. *Une description topographique des immeubles à Panopolis*. Warsaw: Państwowe Wydawnictwo Naukowe, 1975.
P.Mich.	*Michigan Papyri*. Ann Arbor: University of Michigan Press, 1931–.
P.Oslo	Eitrem, Samson, and Leiv Amundsen, eds. *Papyri Osloenses*. 3 vols. Oslo: Dybwad, 1925–1936.
P.Oxy.	Grenfell, Bernard P., et al., eds. *The Oxyrhynchus Papyri*. London: Egypt Exploration Fund, 1898–.
P.Ryl.	Hunt, Arthur S., et al., eds. *Catalogue of the Greek and Latin Papyri in the John Rylands Library, Manchester*. 4 vols. Manchester: Manchester University Press, 1911–1952.
PG	*Patrologia Graeca* [= *Patrologiae Cursus Completus: Series Graeca*]. Edited by Jacques-Paul Migne. 162 vols. Paris: Migne, 1857–1886.
PHI	Packhard Humanities Institute
PW	*Paulys Real-Encyclopädie der classischen Altertumswissenschaft*. New edition by Georg Wissowa and Wilhelm Kroll. 50 vols. in 84 parts. Stuttgart: Metzler & Druckenmüller, 1894–1980
RechPap	*Recherches de Papyrologie*
RevPhil	*Revue de philologie*
RIC	*The Roman Imperial Coinage*. Edited by Harold Mattingly. 10 vols. London: Spink, 1923–1994.
RIDA	*Revue Internationale des Droits de l'Antiquité*
RGRW	Religions in the Graeco-Roman World

RPC	*Roman Provincial Coinage*
RTR	*Reformed Theological Review*
SB	*Sammelbuch griechischer Urkunden aus Aegypten.* Edited by Friedrich Preisigke et al. Wiesbaden: Harrassowitz, 1915–.
SBLDS	Society of Biblical Literature Dissertation Series
SBLTT	Society of Biblical Literature Texts and Translations
SEG	Supplementum epigraphicum graecum
SIG	*Sylloge Inscriptionum Graecarum.* Edited by Wilhelm Dittenberger. 4 vols. 3rd ed. Leipzig: Hirzel, 1915–1924
SNTSMS	Society of New Testament Studies Monograph Series
ST	*Studia Theologica*
Studia Pontica	Anderson, J. G. C., Franz Cumont, and Henri Grégoire. *Studia Pontica.* 3 vols. Brussels: Lamertin, 1903–1910.
TANZ	Texte und Arbeiten zum neutestamentlichen Zeitalter
TAPA	*Transactions and Proceedings of the American Philological Association*
TENTS	Texts and Editions for New Testament Study
TextMin	Textus Minores
TNTC	Tyndale New Testament Commentaries
TSAJ	Texte und Studien zum antiken Judentum
TynBul	*Tyndale Bulletin*
USQR	*Union Seminary Quarterly Review*
WBC	Word Biblical Commentary
WUNT	Wissenschaftliche Untersuchungen zum Neuen Testament
ZNW	*Zeitschrift für die neutestamentliche Wissenschaft und die Kunde der älteren Kirche*
ZPE	*Zeitschrift für Papyrologie und Epigraphik*

The First Urban Churches: Introduction

James R. Harrison

1. Introduction

1.1. The Rationale of The First Urban Churches Series

The series The First Urban Churches investigates the expansion of early Christianity as an urban phenomenon from Jerusalem to Rome. This will be explored primarily from the perspective of Paul's letters and the books of Acts and Revelation against the backdrop of the local documentary and archaeological evidence. The rationale for this approach is that two blind spots have traditionally vitiated the scholarly study of the corporate and civic life of the first urban believers in the eastern and western Mediterranean basin. First, scholars have focused on the literary evidence of the literate upper classes throughout the empire at the expense of the local documentary, numismatic, archaeological, and iconographic evidence of the Mediterranean cities in which the early churches flourished. Second, almost by way of reaction to the upper-class bias of our literary sources, the first Christians have been caricatured as a "lower-class" phenomenon, though significant scholars such as Edwin Judge, Abraham Malherbe, and Gerd Theissen have challenged this stereotype of Christian origins.[1]

---

1. For a brief overview of the scholarship, supportive and critical of Judge's approach, see James R. Harrison, introduction to *The First Christians in the Roman World: Augustan and New Testament Essays*, by E. A. Judge, ed. James R. Harrison, WUNT 229 (Tübingen: Mohr Siebeck, 2008), 17–20. Contra Justin J. Meggitt, *Paul, Poverty and Survival* (Edinburgh: T&T Clark, 1998). Most recently, see Bruce W. Longenecker, *Remember the Poor: Paul, Poverty, and the Greco-Roman World* (Grand Rapids: Eerdmans, 2010), passim; L. L. Welborn, *An End to Enmity: Paul and the "Wrongdoer" of Second Corinthians*, BZNW 185 (Berlin: de Gruyter, 2011), 230–81.

Adolf Deissmann's conclusion regarding the "lower-class" social position of the early Christians, however, emerged historically by his narrow focus on the papyrus evidence as the formative background for the understanding early Christianity, though Deissmann's position on the social location of the first believers is more nuanced than has been generally recognized.[2] Additionally, New Testament researchers have failed to bring the full range of documentary and archaeological evidence into sympathetic dialogue with the upper-class literary evidence and the writings of the New Testament. Wayne Meeks's sociological approach to the urban environment of the early Christians has posed the right questions regarding the social location of the New Testament texts, but it has failed to generate the detailed city-by-city approach, based on a close analysis of the local civic evidence, that is required to understand the experiences of the first urban Christians and their writings.[3] Only recently are we starting to see the emergence of such an approach in the publications of New Testament scholars.

The series The First Urban Churches seeks to redress this imbalance by (1) launching a city-by-city study of the key centers of the urban expansion of early Christianity, and (2) reinvigorating the study of specific cities in which the first believers lived through the relevant literary and New Testament sources being brought into dialogue with the local documentary, archaeological, iconographic, and numismatic evidence. It seeks to bring together New Testament and classical scholars in the study of the New Testament writings as primary evidence for the understanding of civic and religious life in the first-century Mediterranean world. It is hoped that

---

Thanks are expressed to Julien M. Ogereau, who read this essay, gave helpful feedback, and suggested extra literature at stages.

2. Adolf Deissmann, "Primitive Christianity and the Lower Classes," *Expositor* 7 (1909): 208–24; Deissmann, *Light from the Ancient East: The New Testament Illustrated by Recently Discovered Texts from the Graeco-Roman World*, 2nd ed. (1927; repr., Grand Rapids: Baker, 1978). For a helpful correction of popular misrepresentations of Deissmann's views regarding the early Christians' social location, see Longenecker, *Remember the Poor*, 255 n. 13.

3. Wayne A. Meeks, *The First Urban Christians: The Social World of the Apostle Paul*, 2nd ed. (New Haven: Yale University Press, 2003). For an insightful critique of Meeks's sociological methodology in relation to ancient cities, see Richard L. Rohrbaugh, "The City in the Second Testament," *BTB* 21 (1991): 67–75, esp. 68. More recently, see Reinhard von Bendemann and Markus Tiwald, eds., *Das frühe Christentum und die Stadt*, BWANT 198 (Stuttgart: Kohlhammer, 2012).

the wide range of methodologies and disciplines employed in this investigation would ensure a more holistic approach than has been the case in the past. The first volume of The First Urban Churches, therefore, investigates the methodology of responsibly handling the nonliterary evidence in reconstructing the political, social, and religious life of ancient cities.

1.2. Defining the Ancient Polis: Methodological Issues

Several comments on the methodology of defining polis in the ancient world are warranted. We must let our ancient sources speak in their own terms about what constitutes the polis, taking into account the genre of writing employed and allowing for their diversity of approach. First, in the philosophical literature, Aristotle famously speaks of humans as "political" animals by nature because they find their perfection in the self-sufficiency of the polis, which, in his view, is also "among the things by nature" (*Pol.* 1253a2–3). The "village" represents the partnership arising from the union of several "households" (*Pol.* 1255b19–20), whereas the polis is composed of several villages that attain full self-sufficiency for their inhabitants (*Pol.* 1252b28–29, 31–53a1).[4] The New Testament also maintains the distinction between "village" and "city," though without explaining the grounds for the distinction (Matt 9:35; 10:11; Mark 6:56; Luke 8:1; 13:22).[5] One presumes that the distinction was axiomatic for the auditors and did not require any amplification.

However, Aristotle admits that there were (presumably monarchic) alternatives to the polis (*Pol.* 1252b19–20), but he dismisses them as prepolitical.[6] But the historical reality was that the New Testament polis of the postclassical world was situated within larger entities of "empire" that also sponsored their own versions of "self-sufficiency," whether they were the Hellenistic monarchies of the past or the current Roman provincial system. The classical ideal of the *autarkeia* ("self-sufficiency": Aristotle, *Pol.* 1321b; cf. 2 Cor 9:8) and autonomy of the polis may have been very occasionally part of the civic rhetoric,[7] but it was no longer the political reality.

---

4. For full discussion, see Thomas L. Pangle, *Aristotle's Teaching in the* Politics (Chicago: University of Chicago Press, 2013).
5. Rohrbaugh, "City in the Second Testament," 67.
6. Pangle, *Aristotle's Teaching*, 33.
7. Note the possible restoration of "[αὐτάρ]κειαν of the Colossian people" (l. 5)

Second, according to the second-century CE geographer and ethnographer Pausanias, a "village" was distinguished, in comparison to the polis, by there being "no government buildings, no theatre, no agora, no water conducted to a fountain, and ... the people live in hovels like mountain cabins on the edge of a ravine" (10.4.1).[8] Here the polis is understood in terms of its civic, political, cultural, and infrastructural activities carried on within the boundaries of its precincts. Clearly, in the understanding of Pausanias, the "civilizing" role of the polis for its inhabitants and its hinterland is symbolized by its substantial civic structures within the city itself.[9] Conversely, from the Roman perspective of Cicero, when early human beings gathered together "they called such a collocation of buildings a town or a city, being punctuated with shrines and common spaces" (Cicero, *Har. resp.* 1.41). As Richard Jenkyns pithily observes, "Worship and public area—these are the basics."[10]

Third, the polis is also defined in terms of its mythological origins, actions, and accomplishments.[11] The Ephesian inscriptions are a helpful

---

in a decree (first–second century CE) honoring the repairer of the baths at Colossae (Alan Cadwallader, "Honouring the Repairer of the Baths at Colossae," *NewDocs* 10:110–13). If Cadwallader's restoration is correct, the city asserts both self-sufficiency and (implicitly) autonomy from any rquirement of imperial patronage because of the beneficence extended to the city by its wealthy elite citizens. However, a factor counting against Cadwallader's very cautious and guarded restoration of αὐτάρκεια, which is certainly possible, is the the rarity of the word in the inscriptional corpora. A web search of the Packard Humanities Institute Greek Epigraphy program only furnished one case of its occcurence (*SEG* 26.121 [Attica: 10/9–3/2 BCE]), itself heavily restored.

8. See M. I. Finley, "The Ancient City: From Fustel de Coulanges to Max Weber and Beyond," *Comparative Studies in Society and History* 19 (1977): 305–27.

9. On the hinterland as part of the polis, see IEph 1a.7.2, l. 11 ("the Ephesians who live in Ephesus or in the countryside;" cf. l. 15) and IEph 1a.8, ll. 16–17 ("the protection, safety and salvation both of the temple of Artemis and of the city and its countryside"). The strong nexus between the hinterland and polis is seen in the civilizing of the barbarians as they settled down to agriculture and, consequently, to urban life (Strabo, *Geogr.* 4.1.5). See John Rich and Andrew Wallace-Hadrill, eds., *City and Country in the Ancient World* (London: Routledge, 1991).

10. Richard Jenkyns, *God, Space, and City in the Roman Imagination* (Oxford: Oxford University Press, 2013), 114.

11. Rohrbaugh, "City in the Second Testament," 67. Note Ovid's comments regarding the relation of Rome's imperial identity to her god/gods: "Rome, which looks around the whole globe from its seven hills, the site of empire and the gods" (*Tr.*

source for providing this perspective on "polis." The polis of Ephesus is spoken of in terms of its divine origins. An inscription celebrating the power of Artemis over a sorcerer's art announces at the outset the relation of Artemis to Ephesus: "she is the leader of the entire city from (its) origin (being the) midwife and increaser of mortals and giver of produce."[12] The "antiquity of the god's cult" is emphasized (IEph 1a.18b, l. 4), as well as the fact that the impact of Artemis's divine manifestations (IEph 1a.24B, ll. 8–14), has made Ephesus internationally famous.

> Since the goddess Artemis, leader of our city, is honoured not only in her homeland, which she has made the most illustrious of all cities through her own divine nature, but also among the Greeks and also the barbarians, the result is that everywhere her shrines and sanctuaries have sprung up, and temples have been founded for her and altars dedicated to her because of the visible manifestations effected by her.

The status of the city is also enhanced by its status of being a "twice" (IEph 1a.22; 1a.23; 2.728; 3.730; 5.1606) or "thrice" *neokoros* (IEph 2.212), referring to its privileged position as a warden of multiple temples of the imperial cult.[13] In other words, the illustrious status of a polis in the Greek East was increasingly determined by its *fides* to Rome and the reciprocation of honor to the ruler for his patronage. By contrast, the *neokoros* reference in Acts 19:35 refers to Ephesus as warden of the illustrious civic cult of Artemis alone.[14] The earliest inscriptional *neokoros* occurrence occurs in the Domitianic inscription that refers to the "the *neokoros* city of the Augusti of the Ephesians" (IEph 6.2034).[15] However, the rivalry between

---

1.5.69–70); "Rome, the city of Mars, shall look forth victorious from its hill upon the conquered globe" (*Tr.* 1.3.7.51–52).

12. James R. Harrison, "Artemis Triumphs over a Sorcerer's Evil Art," *NewDocs* 10:37–47, §8, ll. 3–4. Note IEph 1a.27, l. 13: "the greatest goddess Artemis, from whom the most beautiful things come to all."

13. For discussion, see Steven J. Friesen, *Twice Neokoros: Ephesus, Asia and the Cult of the Flavian Imperial Family*, Religions in the Graeco-Roman World 116 (Leiden: Brill, 1993); Barbara Burrell, *Neokoroi: Greek Cities and Roman Emperors*, Cincinnati Classical Studies 2/9 (Leiden: Brill, 2004), 58–85.

14. This interpretation is confirmed by a Neronian coin with the legend Ἐφεσίων νεωκόρον on the reverse (Friesen, *Twice Neokoros*, 53).

15. Friesen (ibid., 56–57) has posited that the numismatic evidence of the Domitianic period reveals two "twice *neokoros*" coins, announcing the innovation of a cult of Artemis and of the Sebastoi. However, the epigraphic evidence, which is highly

Ephesus, Smyrna, and Pergamum as *neokoroi* meant that each city aspired for the status of being called a "metropolis,"[16] an honorific that Ephesus flaunted in the face of its rivals (IEph 1a.22, ll. 34–42).

> Because of these things even now, for good fortune, it was decided by the world's artists under the patronage of Dionysius and imperator T. Aelius Hadrianus Antoninus Augustus Pius, victors of sacred games, crowned victors and their competitors who meet at the quinquennial contest (held) in the *greatest* and *first* metropolis of Asia, and the twice-neokoros-of-the-Augusti city of the great Ephesians.[17]

In short, the differing genres of evidence and styles of rhetoric relating to "polis" have to be respected. We are provided with a variety of apertures through which we can look at what a city was (or was perceived to be) in the minds of the ancients. We must therefore resist the temptation to view the ancient polis from our industrial and postindustrial perspectives, or reduce our understanding of the city to a single concept,[18] or assume, given the diversity of the ancient evidence, that a sociological approach will generate a better conceptual understanding of what constitutes a polis.[19]

---

sensitive to these issues, is unequivocally clear in refuting this position: the appearance of "twice *neokoros*" only appeared in the period of Hadrian, transitioning from a reference to *neokoros* alone in 130/131 CE (IEph 2.430: τῷ νεωκόρῳ Ἐφεσίω[ν]) to "twice *neokoros*" in 132 CE (*IG* II² 3297). See Barbara Burrell, "Temples of Hadrian, not Zeus," *GRBS* 43 (2003): 31–50, esp. 44. As Burrell has argued, the Domitianic coin evidence to which Friesen appeals in order to establish a "twice *neokoris*" legend has been shown to have been recut later, with the result that these falsified Ephesian coins deceived early numismatic interpreters, as well their followers who have relied on their arguments (Burrell, *Neokoroi*, 65). In reality, the legends of these falsified coins were based on the post-Hadrianic coinage.

16. IEph 1a.23, ll. 4–5: "the greatest metropolis of Asia, and all but for the (whole) world."

17. For the Ephesian *neokoros* coins, see Barclay Vincent Head, *A Catalogue of the Greek Coins of the British Museum: Greek Coins of Ionia* (London: British Museum, 1892), 79–93, §§233–34, 235, 242, 254, 259, 262, 264–265, 268, 270–72, 276–77, 280–81, 291, 298–99, 301–3, 306, 308–9.

18. Finley ("Ancient City," 327) states: "allowing for exceptions, Graeco-Roman towns did not all have common factors of sufficient weight to warrant both their inclusion in a single category and their differentiation from both the oriental and the medieval town."

19. See the classic discussion of Gideon Sjoberg, *The Preindustrial City: Past and Present* (New York: Free Press, 1960).

Finally, another important aspect of research—sometimes overlooked—that should be seriously considered is the investigation of the hinterlands of city life, focusing on the nearby small villages where archaeological and epigraphic evidence might be available. In particular, the funerary inscriptions, if present, would be crucial for investigating the populace over a period of time. Given that the New Testament maintains the distinction between "village" and "city," a totally "urban" lens to our research might oversimplify the social, parochial, and geographical complexities of ancient life.

1.3. The Ancient City in Modern Scholarship

A brief overview of the main scholarly works on the ancient city is apposite. The foundational work is Fustel de Coulanges's 1864 French classic, which studies the religion, laws, and institutions of Greek and Roman city-states.[20] While the work provides an invaluable collection of literary sources for modern researchers, its scholarship is vitiated by its Aryan evolutionary assumptions and simplistic treatment of the causes of urban development.[21] The polemical nature of de Coulanges's thesis, therefore, should give the reader reason for caution. The works of Mason Hammond and Lewis Mumford cover in broad brushstrokes the urban development of the major ancient civilizations,[22] whereas the two books of A. H. M. Jones are exemplary in their meticulous use of the literary, documentary,

---

20. Fustel de Coulanges, *The Ancient City: A Study on the Religion, Laws, and Institutions of Greece and Rome* (Garden City, New York: Doubleday, 1955). The French work of Gustave Glotz, *La cité grecque* (Paris: La Renaissance du Livre, 1928: ET, *The Greek City and Its Institutions* [London: Kegan Paul, Trench, Trubner, 1929]) follows de Coulanges's thesis in considering the polis to be the result of the orderly or evolutionary development from the patrician gens. However, Glotz posits that the ancient polis culminates in Athenian democracy and then declines with the advent of the Macedonian conquest. See, however, the appreciative discussion of A. D. Momigliano, "The Ancient City of Fustel de Coulanges (1970)," in *Studies on Modern Scholarship*, ed. G. W. Bowersock and Timothy J. Cornell (Berkeley: University of California Press, 1994), 162–78.
21. Rohrbaugh, "City in the Second Testament," 70.
22. Lewis Mumford, *The City in History: Its Origins, Its Transformations, and Its Prospects* (New York: Harcourt, Brace & World, 1961); Mason Hammond, *The City in the Ancient World* (Cambridge, MA: Harvard University Press, 1972). See V. Gordon Childe, "The Urban Revolution," *The Town Planning Review* 21 (1950): 3–17. See also Joyce Marcus and Jeremy A. Sabloff, eds., *The Ancient City: New Perspectives on Urbanism in the Old and New Worlds* (Santa Fe: School for Advanced Research Press, 2008).

archaeological, and numismatic evidence to establish the nature of provincial urban culture.[23] In terms of Roman cities, John E. Stambaugh's book provides an excellent coverage of the variegated aspects of urban life in Rome, including an overview of the capital's development and Roman urbanism in other areas.[24] As far as western Asia Minor, a collection of essays on the urbanism of several of the biblical cities located there, among others, is valuable.[25] Finally a series of specialist studies on benefaction, cultic officials, civic elites, municipal virtues, magistrates and city government, and the local associations have added great riches to our understanding of the urbanized regions of the Mediterranean basin.[26]

---

23. A. H. M. Jones, *Cities of the Eastern Roman Provinces* (Oxford: Oxford University Press, 1971 [orig. 1937]); Jones, *The Greek City from Alexander to Justinian* (Oxford: Clarendon, 1940).

24. John E. Stambaugh, *The Ancient Roman City* (Baltimore: Johns Hopkins University Press, 1988). See also Peter Connolly and Hazel Dodge, *The Ancient City: Life in Classical Athens and Rome* (Oxford: Oxford University Press, 1998); Helen M. Parkins, ed., *Roman Urbanism: Beyond the Consumer City* (London: Routledge, 1997).

25. David Parrish, ed., *Urbanism in Western Asia Minor: New Studies on Aphrodisias, Ephesos, Hierapolis, Pergamon, Perge and Xanthos* (Portsmouth, RI: Journal of Roman Archaeology, 2001). See also Edwin M. Yamauchi, *The Archaeology of New Testament Cities in Western Asia Minor* (London and Glasgow: Pickering & Inglis, 1980); Charles Gates, *Ancient Cities: The Archaeology of Urban Life in the Ancient Near East and Egypt, Greece and Rome* (London: Routledge, 2011).

26. **Benefaction:** Philippe Gauthier, *Les cités grecques et leur bienfaiteurs (IVe–Ier s. av. J-C): Contribution à l'histoire des institutions*, Suppléments au Bulletin de Correspondance Hellénique 12 (Athens: École française d'Athènes, 1985); Léopold Migeotte, *L'emprunt public dans les cités grecques: recueil des documents et analyse critique* (Québec: Les Editions du Sphinx, Les Belles Lettres, 1984); Migeotte, *Les souscriptions publiques dans les cités grecques* (Geneva: Droz, 1992); Migeotte, *Les finances des cités grecques* (Paris: Les Belles Lettres, 2014); Arjan Zuiderhoek, *The Politics of Munificence in the Roman Empire: Citizens, Elites and Benefactors in Asia Minor* (Cambridge: Cambridge University Press, 2009). **Cultic officials:** Gabrielle Frija, *Les prêtres des empereurs: Le culte impérial civique dans la province romaine d'Asie. Histoire* (Rennes: Presses Universitaires de Rennes, 2012); Marietta Horster and Anja Klöckner, eds., *Cities and Priests: Cult Personnel in Asia Minor and the Aegean Islands from the Hellenistic to the Imperial Period* (Berlin: de Gruyter, 2013). **Civic elites:** Mireille Cébeillac-Gervasoni and Laurent Lamoine, eds., *Les élites et leurs facettes: Les élites locales dans le monde hellénistique et romain* (Rome: École française de Rome; Clermont-Ferrand: Presses universitaires Blaise-Pascal, 2003); Laurent Capdetrey and Yves Lafond, eds., *La cité et ses élites: Pratiques et représentation des formes de domination et de contrôle social dans les cités grecques; Actes du colloque de Poitiers, 19–20 octobre 2006* (Pessac, France: Ausonius, 2010). **Municipal virtues:** Elizabeth Forbis, *Municipal Virtues in*

We turn now to a brief study of select cities of the early Christian churches, following the Acts narrative and their intersection with (primarily) the Pauline Epistles. Several of the cities of Rev 2–3 are omitted in what follows (Smyrna, Pergamum, Thyatira, Sardis, Philadelphia), but Colin Hemer's work on the cities provides a good starting point.[27] How are researchers positioned in coming to grips with the intersection of the archaeological, documentary, and numismatic evidence of the major cities of the early Christians? How does it contribute to our understanding of the biblical texts?

2. From Jerusalem to Rome: Investigating the Major Cities of Early Christianity

2.1. Jerusalem, Caesarea Maritima, and the Cities of Ancient Palestine

In comparison to previous generations of scholars, we stand in a privileged position in discussing the epigraphic realia of the cities of ancient Pales-

---

the Roman Empire (Stuttgart: Teubner, 1996). **Magistrates and city government:** David Magie, *Roman Rule in Asia Minor: To the End of the Third Century after Christ*, 2 vols. (Princeton: Princeton University Press, 1950); Pierre Fröhlich, *Les cités grecques et le contrôle des magistrates (IVe–Ier siècle avant J.-C.)* (Geneva: Droz, 2004); Sviatoslav Dmitriev, *City Government in Hellenistic and Roman Asia Minor* (Oxford: Oxford University Press, 2005). **Local associations:** John S. Kloppenborg and Stephen G. Wilson, eds., *Voluntary Associations in the Graeco-Roman World* (London: Routledge, 1996); Onno M. van Nijf, *The Civic World of Professional Associations in the Roman East* (Amsterdam: Gieben, 1997); Philip A. Harland, *Associations, Synagogues, and Congregations: Claiming a Place in Ancient Mediterranean Society* (Minneapolis: Fortress, 2003); Ilias Arnaoutoglou, *Thusias heneka kai sunousias: Private Religious Associations in Hellenistic Athens* (Athens: Academy of Athens, 2003); Jinyu Liu, *Collegia Centonariorum: The Guilds of Textile Dealers in the Roman West* (Leiden: Brill, 2009); John S. Kloppenborg and Richard S. Ascough, eds., *Attica, Central Greece, Macedonia, Thrace*, vol. 1 of *Greco-Roman Associations: Texts, Translations, and Commentary* (Berlin: de Gruyter 2011); Monique Dondin-Payre and Nicolas Tran, eds., *Collegia: Le phénomène associative dans l'Occident romain* (Bordeaux: Ausonius, 2012); Richard S. Ascough et al., eds., *Associations in the Greco-Roman World: A Sourcebook* (Waco, TX: Baylor University Press, 2012); Pierre Fröhlich and Patrice Hamon, eds., *Groupes et associations dans cités grecques (IIIe siècle av. J.-C.–IIe siècle ap. J.-C.). Actes de la table ronde de Paris, INHA, 19–20 juin 2009* (Geneva: Droz, 2013).

27. Colin J. Hemer, *The Letters to the Seven Churches of Asia in their Local Setting*, JSNTSup 11 (Sheffield: JSOT Press, 1986). See Friesen's critique of Hemer: Steven J. Friesen, "Revelation, Realia, and Religion: Archaeology in the Interpretation of the Apocalypse," *HTR* 88 (1995): 291–314.

tine. The inscriptions of Palestine and Caesarea Maritima have long been available in French and English translation for researchers.[28] But with the advent of the *Corpus Inscriptionum Iudaeae/Palestinae*, the projected nine-volume series edited by the celebrated German epigraphist Werner Eck and the prominent Israeli papyrologist Hannah Cotton, scholars will now have an abundance of Palestinian epigraphic evidence in Latin, Greek, Hebrew, Samaritan, Aramaic, and Phoenician to examine. From 2010 to 2014, three volumes had been published, providing scholars with indispensible insight into the people, conventions, politics, and institutions of Jerusalem, Caesarea and the Middle Coast, and the South Coast.[29] We are witnessing here a generational change in the epigraphic scholarship on Judaea and Palestine that will transform the discipline for decades to come. The inscriptional evidence of the synagogues from the first century onward has also been collected,[30] allowing investigation of their honorific and benefaction culture.[31]

---

28. Jean-Baptiste Frey, *Europe*, vol. 1 of *Corpus Inscriptionum Judaicarum: Jewish Inscriptions from the Third Century BC to the Seventh Century AD* (New York: Ktav, 975 [Fr. orig. 1936]); Clayton Miles Lehmann and Kenneth G. Holum, *The Joint Expedition to Caesarea Maritima. Excavation Reports: The Greek and Latin Inscriptions of Caesarea Maritima* (Boston: ASOR, 2000).

29. Hannah M. Cotton et al., eds., *Jerusalem, Part 1: 1–704*, vol. 1.1 of *Corpus Inscriptionum Iudaeae/Palestinae* (Berlin: de Gruyter, 2010); Hannah M. Cotton et al., eds., *Jerusalem, Part 2: 705–1120*, vol. 1.2 of *Corpus Inscriptionum Iudaeae/Palestinae* (Berlin: de Gruyter, 2012); Walter Amerling et al., eds., *Caesarea and the Middle Coast 1121–2160*, vol. 2 of *Corpus Inscriptionum Iudaeae/Palestinae* (Berlin: de Gruyter, 2011); Walter Amerling et al., eds., *South Coast 2161–2648*, vol. 3 of *Corpus Inscriptionum Iudaeae/Palestinae* (Berlin: de Gruyter, 2014).

30. Anders Runesson, Donald D. Binder, and Birger Olsson, eds., *The Ancient Synagogue from Its Origins to 200 C.E.: A Source Book*, Ancient Judaism and Early Christianity 72 (Leiden: Brill, 2008). For the archaeological evidence, see Lee I. Levine, *Ancient Synagogues Revealed* (Jerusalem: Israel Exploration Society, 1981); Dan Urman and Paul V. M. Flesher, eds., *Ancient Synagogues: Historical Analysis and Archaeological Discovery* (Leiden: Brill, 1995); Ze'ev Weiss and Ehud Netzer, *Promise and Redemption: A Synagogue Mosaic from Sepphoris*, 2nd ed. (Jerusalem: Israel Museum, 1998); Donald D. Binder, *Into the Temple Courts: The Place of the Synagogues in the Second Temple Period*, SBLDS (Atlanta: Society of Biblical Literature, 1999).

31. Baruch Lifshitz, *Donateurs et fondateurs dans les synagogues juives* (Paris: Gabalda 1967); Susan Sorek, *Remembered for Good: A Jewish Benefaction System in Ancient Palestine* (Sheffield: Sheffield Phoenix Press, 2010).

Moreover, there is detailed scholarly coverage of the archaeology and history of Jerusalem and Caesarea Maritima.[32] The numismatic evidence, too, is readily available in two collections.[33] Future researchers will be able continue to build on this solid base of scholarly work, helped by the explosion of archaeological work being undertaken in Israel. This will enable the gospel narratives of Jesus's ministry and the depiction of the Jerusalem church in Acts to be brought into profitable dialogue with Josephus's narrative of Herodian and Roman power, as well as Philo's brief forays into the area (*De legatione ad Gaium; In Flaccum*). Hopefully this may also throw a more nuanced light on the elements of continuity and discontinuity between the New Testament, first-century Judaism, and the (later) rabbinic sources.

---

32. W. C. Van Unnik, *Tarsus or Jerusalem: The City of Paul's Youth* (London: Epworth, 1962); Joachim Jeremias, *Jerusalem in the Time of Jesus* (London: SCM, 1973); Lee I. Levine, *Roman Caesarea: An Archaeological Topical Study* (Jerusalem: Institute of Archaeology, Hebrew University of Jerusalem, 1975); Michael Avi-Yonah, *Encyclopedia of Archaeological Excavations in the Holy Land* (London: Oxford University Press, 1975–1978), vols. 1–4; Eliat Mazar and Benjamin Mazar, *Qedem, Excavations in the South of the Temple Mount—The Ophel of Biblical Jerusalem* (Jerusalem: Israel Exploration Society, 1989), vol. 29; Kenneth G. Holum et al., eds., *King Herod's Dream: Caesarea on the Sea* (New York: Norton, 1988); Ephraim Stern, ed., *New Encyclopedia of Archaeological Excavations in the Holy Land*, vols. 1–4 (Jerusalem: Israel Exploration Society and Carta, 1993); Stern, *Supplementary Volume*, vol. 5 of *New Encyclopedia of Archaeological Excavations in the Holy Land* (Jerusalem: Israel Exploration Society and Carta, 2008); Hillel Geva, ed., *Ancient Jerusalem Revealed* (Jerusalem: Israel Exploration Society, 1994); Jerome Murphy-O'Connor, *The Holy Land* (Oxford: Oxford University Press, 1998); Ariel Lewin, *The Archaeology of Ancient Judea and Palestine* (Los Angeles: J. Paul Getty Museum, 2005); Ehud Netzer, *Architecture of Herod, the Great Builder* (Grand Rapids: Baker Academic, 2008); Eric M. Meyers and Mark A. Chancey, *Alexander to Constantine*, vol. 3 of *Archaeology of the Land of the Bible* (New Haven: Yale University Press, 2012).

33. Ya'aḳov Meshorer, *A Treasury of Jewish Coins: From the Persian Period to Bar Kokhba* (New York: Amphora, 2001); David Hendin, *Guide to Biblical Coins*, 5th ed. (New York: Amphora, 2010). On the coins of Caesarea Maritima in the late empire, see Robert L. Hohlfelder, "Caesarea Maritima in Late Antiquity: An Introduction to the Numismatic Evidence," in *Ancient Coins of the Graeco-Roman World: The Nickle Numismatic Papers*, ed. Waldemar Heckel and Richard Sullivan (Waterloo, ON: Wilfred Laurier University Press, 1984), 261–86.

2.2. Pisidian Antioch, Ankara, and the Cities of First-Century Galatia

Whether one subscribes to a Northern or Southern Galatian hypothesis for the addressees of Paul's letter to the Galatians, we have substantial archaeological and epigraphic background relevant to the letter, whatever its destination might be. In this regard Galatians commentators, strangely, have ignored Stephen Mitchell's English translation of Northern Galatian inscriptions from the district of Ankyra,[34] as well as the Pisdian Antioch collection of Barbara Levick and W. M. Ramsay.[35] In 2012 the collection of the inscriptions from the city of Ankara were also published in English translation, including the most up-to-date rendering of the Res Gestae.[36] It is worth remembering in this regard that an inscription in the inner area of the portico of the Temple of Rome and Augustus at Ankara lists the names of the annually appointed priests of the god Augustus and of the goddess Roma as well as their benefactions.[37] Significantly, the vast majority of the high priests have Celtic names, indicating that the imperial priesthoods were pathways for the acquisition of civic status, providing opportunities for the competitive provincial elites to demonstrate their personal wealth and their faithfulness (*fides*) as clients to the Roman ruler. Because of the outstanding work of Gabrielle Frija in collecting the inscriptions of the imperial priests in the Roman province of Asia, scholars can now search the entire corpus on the worldwide web site by site, with original texts and French translations, charting the imperial priestly elites of the Greek East.[38]

---

34. Stephen Mitchell, *Regional Epigraphic Catalogues of Asia Minor II: The Ankara District; The Inscriptions of North Galatia* (Oxford: B.A.R., 1982).

35. W. M. Ramsay, "Colonia Caesarea (Pisidian Antioch) in the Augustan Age," *JRS* 6 (1916): 84–134; Ramsay, "Studies in the Roman Province Galatia: VI. Some Inscriptions of Colonia Caesarea Antiochea," *JRS* 14 (1924): 172–205; Barbara Levick, "An Honorific Inscription from Pisidian Antioch," *AnSt* 8 (1958): 219–22; Levick, "Unpublished Inscriptions from Pisidian Antioch," *AnSt* 17 (1967): 101–21; Maurice A. Byrne and Guy Labarre, *Nouvelles inscriptions d'Antioche de Pisidie d'après les Notebooks de W. M. Ramsay* (Bonn: Habelt, 2006).

36. Stephen Mitchell and David French, eds., *From Augustus to the End of the Third Century AD*, vol. 1 of *The Greek and Latin Inscriptions of Ankara (Ancyra)* (Munich: Beck, 2012). A second volume is forthcoming.

37. Ibid., 138–50.

38. Frija, *Les Prêtres des empereurs*. See Frija's webiste, *Prêtres civiques*, http://www.pretres-civiques.org/.

Considerable study of Pisidian Antioch and Phrygian/Anatolian culture has been undertaken,[39] with many elements of this research being highly profitable for New Testament exegesis.[40] Other cities of South Galatia could also be explored for their cultural relevance to the New Testament. For example, in South Galatia, the cities of Iconium, Lystra, and Derbe should be more thoroughly investigated,[41] along with Pessinus and Germa in North Galatia.[42] In sum, there is considerable inscriptional and archaeological evidence to be sifted for the valuable exegetical insights that could be brought to the study of Galatians and Acts 13:1–14:24.

---

39. W. M. Ramsay, *The Cities and Bishoprics of Phrygia, Being an Essay of the Local History of Phrygia from the Earliest Times to the Turkish Conquest*, 2 vols. (Oxford: Clarendon, 1895–1897); David M. Robinson, "Roman Sculptures from colonia Caesarea (Pisidian Antioch)," *Art Bulletin* 9 (1926): 5–69; Cilliers Breytenbach, *Paulus und Barnabas in der Provinz Galatien: Studien zu Apostelgeschichte 13f.; 16,6; 18, 32 und den Adressaten des Galaterbriefes*, AGJU (Leiden: Brill, 1996), 160–62; Stephen Mitchell and Marc Waelkens, *Pisidian Antioch: The Site and Its Monuments* (London: Duckworth/Classical Press of Wales, 1998); Robert L. Mowery, "Paul and Caristanius at Pisidian Antioch," *Bib* 87 (2006): 223–42; B. B. Rubin, "(Re)presenting Empire: The Roman Imperial Cult in Asia Minor, 31 BC–AD 63" (PhD diss., University of Michigan, 2008); Adrian J. Ossi, "The Roman Honorific Arches of Pisidian Antioch: Reconstruction and Contextualization" (PhD. diss., University of Michigan, 2010); Elaine K. Gazda and Diana Y. Ng, eds., *Building a New Rome: The Imperial Colony of Pisidian Antioch (25 BC–AD 700)* (Ann Arbor: Kelsey Museum Publication, 2011).

40. Clinton E. Arnold, "'I Am Astonished That You Are So Quickly Turning Away!' (Gal 1:6): Paul and Anatolian Folk Belief," *NTS* 51 (2005): 429–49; Mowery, "Paul and Caristanius"; Justin K. Hardin, *Galatians and the Imperial Cult: A Critical Analysis of the First-Century Social Context of Paul's Letter*, WUNT 2/237 (Tübingen: Mohr Siebeck, 2008); James R. Harrison, "'More Than Conquerors' (Rom 8:37): Paul's Gospel and the Augustan Triumphal Arches of the Greek East and Latin West," *Buried History* 47 (2011): 3–21.

41. Breytenbach, *Paulus und Barnabas*, 162–67; Cilliers Breytenbach and Carola Zimmermann, *Early Christianity in Lycaonia and Adjacent Areas* (Leiden: Brill, forthcoming). See also the epigraphic data base for Asia Minor at P. Toalster and C. Zoller, "Epigraphic Database for Ancient Asia Minor," http://www.epigraphik.uni-hamburg.de/database. Note also the (forthcoming) epigraphic database of early Christian inscriptions of Greece and Asia Minor (ICAM/ICG), which is currently being developed by the Berlin Cluster of Excellence TOPOI/Humboldt University (Berlin), to be completed in 2016. For details, see "Authorization of Early Christian Knowledge Claims Research Project: B-5-3," Topoi, http://www.topoi.org/project/b-5-3/.

42. Breytenbach, *Paulus und Barnabas*, 121–24; Toalster and Zoller, *Epigraphic Database for Ancient Asia Minor*.

2.3. Philippi

The inscriptional corpus of Philippi has been well served for several years now by Peter Pilhofer's monumental collection of the extant inscriptions.[43] But Cédric Brélaz's recent collection of the Philippian collections relating to the public life of the colony and of the Roman state places us in an even stronger position in terms of our understanding of imperial Philippi; another collection of the classical and Hellenistic inscriptions relating to the Greek and Macedonian period of the city by Angelos Zannis and Chaido Koukouli-Chrysanthaki is also forthcoming.[44] Several recent studies on Philippi have considerably expanded our knowledge of its historical, cultural, religious, and administrative evolution of the city,[45] adding to the earlier classic publications of Paul Collart and Philippe Lemerle,[46] though Lemerle's exhaustive coverage

---

43. Peter Pilhofer, *Katalog der Inschriften von Philippi*, vol. 2 of *Philippi*, 2nd ed., WUNT 1/119 (Tübingen: Mohr Siebeck, 2009). Before Pilhofer, we were indebted to Paul Collart, "Inscriptions de Philippes (I)," *BCH* 56 (1932): 192–231; Collart, "Inscriptions de Philippes (II)," *BCH* 57 (1933): 313–79. For the Christian inscriptions, see Denis Feissel, *Recueil des inscriptions chrétiennes de Macédoine du IIIe au VIe siècle* (Athens: École Française d'Athènes, 1983).

44. Cédric Brélaz, *Inscriptions relatives à la vie publique de la colonie et de l'Etat romains*, vol. 2.1 of *Corpus des inscriptions grecques et latines de Philippes* (Athens: École française d'Athènes 2014); Angelos G. Zannis and Chaido Koukouli-Chrysanthaki, *La cité grecque et macédonienne (inscriptions classiques et hellénistiques)*, vol. 2.2 of *Corpus des inscriptions grecques et latines de Philippes* (Athens: École française d'Athènes, forthcoming). A third volume of Philippian inscriptions, edited by Cédric Brélaz and Clément Sarrazanas (= *CIPh* 2.3), will review the inscriptions from the paleo-Christian and proto-Byzantine period.

45. Lilian Portefaix, *Sisters Rejoice: Paul's Letter to the Philippians and Luke-Acts as seen by First-Century Women*, ConBNT 20 (Stockholm: Almqvist & Wiksell, 1988); Valerie Ann Abrahamsen, *Women and Worship at Philippi: Diana/Artemis and Other Cults in the Early Christian Era* (Portland: Astarte Shell Press, 1995); Lukas Bormann, *Philippi: Stadt und Christengemeinde zur Zeit des Paulus*, NovTSup 78 (Leiden: Brill, 1995); Peter Pilhofer, *Die erste christliche Gemeinde Europas*, vol. 1 of *Philippi*, WUNT 1/87 (Tübingen: Mohr Siebeck, 1995); Charalambos Bakirtzis and Helmut Koester, eds., *Philippi at the Time of Paul and after His Death* (Harrisburg, PA: Trinity Press International, 1998); Peter Oakes, *Philippians: From People to Letter*, SNTSMS 110 (Cambridge: Cambridge University Press, 2001).

46. Paul Collart, *Philippes ville de Macédoine de ses origines jusqu'à la fin de l'époque romaine* (Paris: Boccard, 1937); Philippe Lemerle, "Palestre Romaine a Phillippes," *BCH* 61 (1937): 86–102; Lemerle, *Philippes et la Macédoine orientale*

of the archaeological evidence has never really been superseded. The most recent English studies of the archaeology of Philippi are those of Geōrgios G. Gounarēs and Eduard Verhoef,[47] as well as a French guide to the Forum.[48] In terms of the numismatic evidence, there is Paulos Lambros's study of the Philippian gold coins, originally published in Greek in 1854.[49] Michel Amandry has also written a definitive essay on the operations of the city's provincial mint in the imperial period, focusing on the coin issues from the reign of Gallienus that were marked with the letters RPCP (*Res Publica Coloniae Philippensium*).[50]

The exegetical dividends arising from Pilhofer's publication of the Philippian inscriptions in a readily accessible volume is becoming increasingly apparent. Joseph Hellerman, for example, has investigated the ascent of honor articulated in the Philippian military and civic inscriptions against the backdrop of Christ's shameful descent to cruciform dishonor (Phil 2:5–8), richly illustrating the rewards of a documentary approach to

---

à l'époque chrétienne et byzantine. Recheches d'histoire et d'archéologie: Contents: 1 Textes; 2 Album (Paris: Boccard, 1945). See also Étienne Lapaulus, "Sculptures de Philippes," *BCH* 59 (1935): 175–92; Jacques Coupry, "Sondage à l'ouest du forum de Philippes," *BCH* 62 (1938): 42–50; Paul Collart and Pierre Ducrey, *Philippes I: Les reliefs rupestres* (Paris: Boccard, 1975).

47. Geōrgios G. Gounarēs and Emmanouela G. Gounarē, *Philippi: Archaeological Guide* (Thessaloniki: University Studio Press, 2004); Eduard Verhoef, *Philippi: How Christianity Began in Europe. The Epistle to the Philippians and the Excavations at Philippi* (London: Bloomsbury, 2013).

48. Michel Sève and Patrick Weber, *Guide du forum de Philippes* (Athens: École Française d'Athènes, 2012).

49. Paulos Lambros, *Gold Coins of Philippi* (Chicago: Obol International, 1975 [Gk orig. 1854]).

50. Michel Amandry, "Le monnayage de la *Res Publica Coloniae Philippensium*," in *Sonderdruck aus Edith Schönert-Geiss zum 65. Geburtstag*, ed. Stephanos Nomismatikos (Berlin: Akademie, 1998), 23–30. For the coinage of the cities in the Roman provinces, see especially the publications of Andrew Burnett and Michel Amandry, eds., *From the Death of Caesar to the Death of Vitellius (44 BC–AD 69)*, vol. 1 of *Roman Provincial Coinage* (London: British Museum Press; Paris: Bibliothèque Nationale, 1992 [rev. 2006]); Burnett and Amandry, *Supplement I* (1999), only available electronically in PDF; Burnett and Amandry, *From Vespasian to Domitian (AD 69–96)*, vol. 2 of *Roman Provincial Coinage* (London: British Museum Press; Paris: Bibliothèque Nationale, 1999). Additionally, see Christopher J. Howgego, Volker Heuchert, and Andrew Burnett, eds., *Coinage and Identity in the Roman Provinces* (Oxford: Oxford University Press, 2005).

Pauline exegesis.⁵¹ Richard Ascough's study of the Philippian association inscriptions has also provided an important springboard for helping us understand better the dynamics and social location of the Pauline house churches.⁵² Additionally, the book of Julien Ogereau represents an exhaustive and authoritative analysis of the contemporary documentary evidence of *koinōnia* language in its economic and legal context.⁵³ Ogereau has meticulously opened up a new vista in Philippians scholarship, reinvigorating the earlier (but largely dismissed) hunch of J. Paul Sampley on the issue.⁵⁴ Paul's financial relationships in his missionary outreach at Philippi, Ogereau argues, reflected the rituals and language of ancient Roman *societas* contracts. These testify to the apostle's engagement with Roman legal practice in this instance, though in the process Paul transformed the expression of these traditional financial conventions though his apostolic gospel.

Last, the archaeological site of Philippi is extensive and initially challenging because of the minimal information provided at the site for the convenience of modern visitors. Furthermore, the vast majority of its evidence postdates the New Testament. Thus new studies that demystify the layout, monuments, culture, and activities of the city in its various periods, as well as spelling out their chronological interrelation, would be of enormous help to New Testament researchers.⁵⁵

---

51. Joseph Hellerman, *Reconstructing Honor in Roman Philippi: Carmen Christi as Cursus Pudorum*, SNTSMS 132 (Cambridge: Cambridge University Press, 2005).

52. Richard S. Ascough, *Paul's Macedonian Associations: The Social Context of Philippians and 1 Thessalonians*, WUNT 2/161 (Tübingen: Mohr Siebeck, 2003), 110–61. For the epigraphic and archaeological evidence for Philippian associations, see Ascough et al., *Associations in the Greco-Roman World*, 39–42 §§41–44, 222 §B3.

53. Julien M. Ogereau, *Paul's Κοινωνία with the Philippians: A Socio-historical Investigation of a Pauline Economic Partnership*, WUNT 2/377 (Tübingen: Mohr Siebeck, 2014); Ogereau, "Paul's Κοινωνία with the Philippians: Societas as a Missionary Funding Strategy," *NTS* 60 (2014): 360–78.

54. J. Paul Sampley, *Pauline Partnership in Christ* (Philadelphia: Fortress, 1980).

55. Laura S. Nasrallah, "Spacial Perspectives: Space and Archaeology in Roman Philippi," in *Studying Paul's Letters: Contemporary Perspectives and Methods*, ed. Joseph A. Marchal (Minneapolis: Fortress, 2012), 54–74.

2.4. Thessalonica and Athens

In spite of the sparse first-century archaeological evidence available at Thessalonica,[56] a host of publications have recently appeared on the city,[57] including discussions of the first-century imperial context of the Thessalonian epistles (most recently, James Harrison).[58] Notwithstanding the paucity of material evidence in comparison to the other cities being discussed, the inscriptional evidence is voluminous,[59] with, for example, decrees honoring Roman and association benefactors, as well as a (late) inscription from a synagogue at Thessalonica (see Acts 17:2).[60] The Thessalonian

---

56. However, the archaeological artifacts at the museum of Thessaloniki are substantial. See the popular book of Manolēs Andronikos, *Thessalonike Museum: A New Guide to the Archeological Treasures* (Athens: Ekditike Hellados, 1982). Consequently, important works on the museum's holdings are periodically published: Note the (projected) four-volume series of Giōrgos Despinēs, Theodosia Stefanidou-Tiveriou, and Emm Voutyras, eds., *Katalogos glypton tou Archaiologikou Mouseiou Thessalonikis* (an English translation exists as well: *Catalogue of Sculpture in the Archaeological Museum of Thessaloniki*); vol. 1: *Thessaloniki: Morphotiko Idryma Ethnikes Trapezes* (1997); vol. 2: *Thessaloniki: Morphotiko Idryma Ethnikes Trapezes* (2003; published only in Greek); vol. 3: *Thessaloniki: Morphotiko Idryma Ethnikes Trapezes* (2003, published only in Greek). Work has already begun on volume 4, which will bring the series to conclusion. The series collects and discusses a broad spectrum of Greek and Roman marble sculptures from ancient Macedonia.

57. Christoph Vom Brocke, *Thessaloniki, Stadt des Kassander und Gemeinde des Paulus: Eine frühe christliche Gemeinde in ihrer heidnischen Umwelt*, WUNT 2/125 (Tübingen; Mohr Siebeck, 2001); Richard S. Ascough, *Paul's Macedonian Associations: The Social Context of Philippians and 1 Thessalonians*, WUNT 2/161 (Tübingen: Mohr Siebeck, 2003); Cilliers Breytenbach, *Frühchristliches Thessaloniki*, Studien und Texte zu Antike und Christentum 44 (Tübingen: Mohr Siebeck, 2007); Laura Nasrallah et al., eds., *From Roman to Early Christian Thessalonikē: Studies in Religion and Archaeology*, HTS 64 (Cambridge, MA: Harvard University Press, 2010).

58. James R. Harrison, *Paul and the Imperial Authorities at Thessalonica and Rome: A Study in the Conflict of Ideology*, WUNT 1/273 (Tübingen: Mohr Siebeck, 2011).

59. Charles F. Edson, *Inscriptiones Thessalonicae et viciniae*, vol. 10, pt. 2, fasc. 1 of *Inscriptiones Graecae Epiri, Macedoniae, Thraciae, Scythia* (Berlin: de Gruyter, 1972). Since the publication of Edson's *IG* volume, over five hundred new Thessalonian inscriptions, published and unpublished, have been collected by Pantelis Nigdelis, Aristotle University of Thessaloniki, for a further *IG* 10.2.1 Supplement, to be published in 2016–2017.

60. Holland L. Hendrix, *Thessalonicans Honor Romans* (ThD diss., Harvard University, 1984); Hendrix, "Benefactor/Patron Networks in the Urban Environment: Evidence from Thessalonica," *Semeia* 56 (1992): 39–58; Pantelis Nigdelis, "Synagoge(n)

inscriptions have not been translated (as opposed to those of Aphrodisias, Corinth, and Philippi, for example), so considerable light could be shed on the Thessalonian epistles by concentrating on the epigraphic evidence of this corpus. In this regard, Pantelis Nigdelis (see n. 64) has recently assembled some 140 Thessalonian inscriptions, additional to Charles Edson's collection, from the imperial period.[61] Nigdelis's selection, which provides a commentary on each individual inscription, focuses on the public life of the city, its private associations and professional life, as well as its funerary practices and demographic composition.[62] It is likely that this rich collection of inscriptions will throw considerable light on the social relations and Greco-Roman cultural conventions and belief systems that form the backdrop to Paul's Thessalonian correspondence.

In the case of Athens, even though New Testament scholars have predictably concentrated on Paul's Areopagus address (Acts 17:16–34), there is an abundance of Athenian association decrees that would provide insight into the similarities and differences of the house churches with the ancient clubs,[63] as well as the honorific rituals of a significant Mediterranean city.[64] In sum, a focus on the inscriptions places us at the cutting edge of engagement with recent historical and New Testament scholarship on both cities.

---

und Gemeinde der Juden in Thessaloniki: Fragen aufgrund einer neuen jüdischen Grabinschrift der Kaiserzeit," *ZPE* 102 (1994): 297–306; Ascough, *Paul's Macedonian Associations*, 162–90; Nigdelis, "Voluntary Associations in Roman Thessalonikê: In Search of Identity and Support in a Cosmopolitan Society," in Nasrallah, *From Roman to Early Christian Thessalonikê*, 13–47. For the epigraphic and archaeological evidence for associations at Athens and Thessalonica, see Ascough, *Associations in the Greco-Roman World*, 9–16 §§1–7, 221–22 B2; 45–53 §§47–59.

61. Pantelis Nigdelis, *Epigraphika Thessalonike, Symvole sten politike kai koinonike historia tes archaias Thessalonikes* (*Epigraphica Thessalonicensia: A Contribution to the Political and Social History of Ancient Thessaloniki*) (Thessaloniki: University Studio Press, 2006).

62. See Paraskevi Martzavou, review of *Epigraphika Thessalonike, Symvole sten politike kai koinonike historia tes archaias Thessalonikes*, by Pantelis Nigdelis, *Bryn Mawr Classical Review* (July 25, 2008), http://bmcr.brynmawr.edu/2008/2008-07-25.html.

63. Nicholas F. Jones, *The Associations of Classical Athens* (Amsterdam: Gieben, 1997).

64. Geoffrey C. R. Schmalz, *Augustan and Julio-Claudian Athens: A New Epigraphy and Prosopography*, Mnemosyne Supplementum 302 (Leiden: Brill, 2009).

2.5. Corinth, Isthmia, and Cenchreae

The American School of Classical Studies at Athens (ASCSA) began excavations at ancient Corinth in 1896. Initially the archaeological focus was topographical, but excavations soon began to concentrate on the center of the city. From the period of 1925–1940 a vast metropolis was unearthed that constituted one of the great cities of the Roman East. Excavations continue to this day. The Corinth Monograph Series, published by the ASCSA since 1932, currently comprises some forty-three publications as part of a twenty-one-volume series and is regularly supplemented by new monographs.[65] Every conceivable aspect of Corinthian material culture (pottery, sculpture, lamps, etc.) and civic life (the agora, stoas, basilicas, springs, villas, acrocorinth, cemeteries, asclepion, baths, potter's quarter, theater, sanctuary of Demeter and Kore, etc.) has been discussed. Reports on archaeological and inscriptional finds at Corinth are also published in *Hesperia*.[66]

In terms of the inscriptions, three volumes of Latin and Greek inscriptions from Corinth were published last century and have recently been supplemented with a new volume of inscriptions.[67] Older collections of Corinthian inscriptions have also been republished.[68] However, there is need for investigation of the new inscriptions published by *Hesperia*, *SEG*, and *ZPE* and for these to inform the exegesis of the Corinthian epistles

---

65. On the website of the American School of Classical Studies at Athens, one may view the vast range of ASCSA publications on Corinth, spanning 1932 to 2013: http://www.ascsa.edu.gr/index.php/publications/browse-by-series/corinth. See also the ASCSA publication of Elizabeth R. Gebhard and Timothy E. Gregory, eds., *"The Bridge of the Untiring Sea": The Corinthian Isthmus from Prehistory to Late Antiquity*, Hesperia Supplement 48 (Princeton: American School of Classical Studies at Athens, 2014).

66. See also the excellent Corinthian archaeological updates of David K. Pettegrew (Messiah College) on "Corinthian Matters: A Resource for the Study of the Corinthia, Greece" (http://corinthianmatters.com/).

67. B. D. Meritt, *Greek Inscriptions, 1896–1927*, vol. 8, part 1 of *Corinth* (Cambridge, MA: ASCSA, 1931); A. B. West, *Latin Inscriptions, 1896–1926*, vol. 8, part 2 of *Corinth* (Cambridge, MA: ASCSA, 1931); J. H. Kent, *The Inscriptions, 1926–1950*, vol. 8, part 3 of *Corinth* (Princeton: ASCSA, 1966); R. S. Stroud, *The Sanctuary of Demeter and Kore: The Inscriptions*, vol. 18, part 6 of *Corinth* (Princeton: ASCSA, 2013).

68. L. R. Dean, *Latin Inscriptions from Corinth* (Piscataway, NJ: Analecta Gorgiana, 2009); K. Smith, *Greek Inscriptions from Corinth II* (Piscataway, NJ: Analecta Gorgiana, 2009).

where appropriate. Two examples will suffice. First, a Corinthian inscription honoring the *retiarius* Draukos could throw light on Paul's arena imagery in 1 Cor 4:9, as well as the Corinthian lamp evidence relating to gladiators.[69] Second, the publication of a new Corinthian inscription referring to individual named Erastus (*SEG* 29.301) was discussed by Andrew Clarke many years later after its publication in 1991.[70] This new inscription contributed to reviving the ongoing scholarly discussion regarding the "Erastus" of Rom 16:23 (ὁ οἰκονόμος τῆς πόλεως ["the treasurer of the city"]) and the treasurer's relation to the earlier famous Erastus inscription found at Corinth and published by Kent in 1966 (IKorinthKent 232). The focus of the ensuing heated debate has been the social location of the Corinthian believers (1 Cor 1:26–29) and of Erastus himself.[71] In the most recent article on the issue, Timothy Brookins has examined the 105 datable inscriptional references to Erastus up to the fifth century CE, arguing that only two (possibly three) individuals bear this name in first-century Greece and that, significantly, in each case they have an elite profile.[72] In the first-century world, where social mobility was widespread, it is not inconceivable that one of these individuals went on to hold the prestigious position of οἰκονόμος at Corinth.

---

69. Michael Carter, "A Doctor Secutorum and the *Retiarius* Draukos from Corinth," *ZPE* 126 (1999): 262–68. For a *retiarius* on an unglazed Corinthian lamp, clad in a loin cloth, left, with sword and trident, see Oscar Broneer, *Terracotta Lamps*, vol. 4, part 2 of *Corinth* (Cambridge, MA: ASCSA, 1930), §633. See Cavan W. Concannon, "'Not for an Olive Wreath, but Our Lives': Gladiators, Athletes, and Early Christian Bodies," *JBL* 133 (2014): 193–214; James R. Unwin, "'Thrown Down but Not Destroyed': Paul's Use of a Spectacle Metaphor in 2 Corinthians 4:7–15," *NovT* (forthcoming).

70. Andrew D. Clarke, "Another Corinthian Erastus Inscription," *TynBul* 42 (1991): 146–51. See also his excellent monograph, with its attention to epigraphic evidence: Clarke, *Secular and Christian Leadership in Corinth: A Socio-historical and Exegetical Study of 1 Corinthians 1–6*, AGJU 18 (Leiden: Brill, 1993).

71. See Welborn, *An End to Enmity*, 260–82, for a balanced summary of the recent debate. See also in the current volume Paul Trebilco, "Epigraphy and the Study of *Polis* and *Ekklēsia* in the Greco-Roman World," §3.6. On the issue of "honor" conflicts in the Corinthian epistles, see Harry A. Stansbury, "Corinthian Honor, Corinthian Conflict: A Social History of Early Roman Corinth and Its Pauline Community" (PhD diss., University of California Irvine, 1990).

72. Timothy A. Brookins, "The (In)frequency of the Name 'Erastus' in Antiquity: A Literary, Papyrological, and Epigraphic Catalogue," *NTS* 59 (2013): 496–516.

The potential for bringing the inscriptions into fruitful dialogue with the Corinthian epistles has been amply demonstrated, to cite just three examples, by the works of Bruce Winter, L. L. Welborn, and Bradley Bitner.[73] Winter, through his careful use of the inscriptions and his exploration of their intersection with the literary evidence, has opened up our eyes to the sociocultural issues affecting the first-century believers at Corinth,[74] as well as unpacking the rhetorical expectations that the Corinthians and interloping "super-apostles" were demanding from their apostle.[75] Welborn, in an innovative monograph, has insightfully brought together the literary evidence regarding the consolatory rhetorical genre and the Corinthian epigraphic and archaeological evidence in trying to identify the shadowy figure of the "wrongdoer" in 2 Cor 2:5–8 and 7:12.[76] Bitner, in a forthcoming book, examines how the Corinthian constitution continued after the colonial foundation to shape the form of civic life, arguing analogously from the epigraphic record of other such constitutions in antiquity (e.g., the Spanish Charters) in the absence of the original constitution at Corinth. After reconstructing how Corinth's constitution would probably have appeared to its citizens, Bitner adeptly brings this material into dialogue with Paul's establishment of Christ's covenantal community for his house churches in the city. In this seminal and highly original work, Bitner explores the extent to which Paul's covenantal construction of Christian identity would have interacted with the civic constitution at Corinth, showing how Paul sensitively responded to the local colonial resonances of Roman law in his alternate understanding of the believer's status in Christ.[77]

---

73. Reference should also be made to Cavan W. Concannon's excellent monograph (*"When You Were Gentiles": Specters of Ethnicity in Roman Corinth and Paul's Corinthian Correspondence*, Synkrisis [New Haven: Yale University Press, 2014]), which constructs a portrait of the ancient Corinthians, with whom Paul interacts, based on the literary, numismatic, and archaeological evidence.

74. Bruce W. Winter, *After Paul Left Corinth: The Influence of Secular Ethics and Social Change* (Grand Rapids: Eerdmans, 2001).

75. Bruce W. Winter. *Philo and Paul among the Sophists*, SNTSMS 96 (Cambridge: Cambridge University Press, 1997).

76. Welborn, *An End to Enmity*.

77. Bradley J. Bitner, *Paul's Political Strategy in 1 Corinthians 1–4: Constitution and Covenant*, SNTSMS 163 (Cambridge: Cambridge University Press, 2015).

Last, the numismatic evidence of Corinth, too, has been well serviced by the older works of Barclay Vincent Head and Katharine May Edwards,[78] with the recent numismatic updates of Amandry and Mary Hoskins Walbank adding considerably to our knowledge of Corinth.[79] Furthermore, there are excellent monographs and articles on the city of Corinth, both as the wealthy Greek polis pre-146 BCE and the Roman colony post-44 CE.[80] In sum, modern scholars have a wealth of Corinthian documentary, numismatic, and archaeological evidence to bring to bear on aspects of "local" exegesis of the Corinthian epistles.

However, the archaeological and epigraphic evidence of nearby Isthmia and the harbor city of Corinth, Cenchreae, produces even further opportunities for intersections with the Corinthian epistles. In the case of Isthmia, the archaeology of the city has been well documented in the nine volumes published by the American School of Classical Studies at Athens,[81] though, disappointingly, there are so far no publications on the coinage and inscriptions.[82] Once again, it is crucial that the Isthmian inscriptions published by *Hesperia*, *SEG*, and *ZPE* are brought into the service of the exegesis of the Corinthians epistles. For example, an inscribed lead tablet associated with the games, found at the bottom of a reservoir in the West Water Works at Isthmia, says this: "I, Marius Tyrannos, disqualify

---

78. Barclay Vincent Head, *A Catalogue of the Greek Coins: Corinth, Colonies of Corinth, etc.* (London: British Museum, 1889), 1–93; Katharine May Edwards, *Coins, 1896–1929*, vol. 6 of *Corinth* (Cambridge, MA: ASCSA, 1933).

79. Michel Amandry, *Le Monnayage des Duovirs Corinthiens*, BCHSupp (Athens: École française d'Athènes, 1988); Mary E. Hoskins Walbank, "Image and Cult: The Coinage of Roman Corinth," in *Corinth in Context: Comparative Studies on Religion and Society*, ed. Steven J. Friesen, Daniel N. Schowalter, and James C. Walters (Leiden: Brill, 2011), 151–98. See the essay of Bradley J. Bitner in this volume for an authoritative critique of New Testament scholarly usage of numismatic evidence in Corinthian studies.

80. J. R. Wiseman, "Corinth and Rome I: 228 BC–AD 267," *ANRW* 7.1:438–548; Donald W. Engels, *Roman Corinth: An Alternative Model for the Classical City* (Chicago: University of Chicago Press, 1990); J. B. Salmon, *Wealthy Corinth: A History of the City to 338 BC* (Oxford: Clarendon, 1997).

81. On the website of the American School of Classical Studies at Athens nine ASCSA publications on Isthmia, spanning 1973 to 2012, may be accessed at http://www.ascsa.edu.gr/index.php/publications/browse-by-series/isthmia.

82. See, however, Marietta Sasel-Kos, "The Latin Inscriptions from Isthmia," *Vestnik (Ljubljana)* 29 (1978): 346–53.

Semakos."[83] Along with ancient visual evidence touching on disqualification in the ancient games,[84] this inscription throws light on Paul's fear of "disqualification" as an apostle at Corinth in 1 Cor 9:27b, illustrating contextually the riveting metaphor that culminates his athletic imagery in 9:24–27a.[85]

As far as Cenchreae, six volumes have appeared covering the archaeological evidence,[86] one of which deals with the numismatic evidence, but there is no similar volume devoted to the inscriptions. As noted before in relation to other cities, a search of the Cenchreae inscriptions in *Hesperia*, *SEG*, and *ZPE* would produce valuable exegetical results. For example, a lead curse tablet found in the Koutsongila cemetery at Roman Cenchreae (*SEG* 57.332: mid-first century CE, or late third century CE) is an intriguing find. It is a prayer against a thief who had stolen an item of clothing, with the result that the author of the curse summons the chthonic deities for assistance. The supernatural power of Lord Abrasax is invoked: "take revenge and completely mow down the son of Caecil(i)us, O Lord Chan Sêreira Abrasax!"[87] Possibly we see here something of the conceptual back-

---

83. D. Jordan and A. J. S. Spawforth, "A New Document from the Isthmian Games," *Hesperia* 51 (1982): 65–68.

84. James R. Harrison, "Paul and the Athletic Ideal in Antiquity: A Case Study in Wrestling with Word and Image," in *Paul's World*, ed. Stanley E. Porter, Pauline Studies 4 (Leiden, Brill, 2007), 81–109.

85. For discussion of the deliberate defacing of an Isthmian honorific inscription (Oscar Broneer, "Excavations at Isthmia: Fourth Campaign, 1957–1958," *Hesperia* 28.4 (1959): 298–343, esp. 324–26 §5) and its significance thematically to 2 Cor 6:8 ("in honor and dishonor"), see James R. Harrison, "Paul and Ancient Civic Ethics: Redefining the Canons of Honour in the Graeco-Roman World," in *Paul in Graeco-Roman Context*, ed. Cilliers Breytenbach, BETL 277 (Leuven: Peeters, 2015), 75–118, esp. 97–98.

86. Robert Scranton, Joseph W. Shaw, and Leila Ibrahim, eds., *Topography and Architecture*, vol. 1 of *Kenchreai, Eastern Port of Corinth* (Leiden: Brill, 1978); Leila Ibrahim, ed., *The Panels of Opus Sectile in Glass*, vol. 2 of *Kenchreai, Eastern Port of Corinth* (Leiden: Brill, 1976); Robert Hohlfelder, ed., *The Coins*, vol. 3 of *Kenchreai, Eastern Port of Corinth* (Leiden: Brill, 1978); Beverley Adamsheck, ed., *The Pottery*, vol. 4 of *Kenchreai, Eastern Port of Corinth* (Leiden: Brill, 1979); Hector Williams, ed., *The Lamps*, vol. 5 of *Kenchreai, Eastern Port of Corinth* (Leiden: Brill, 1981); Wilma Olch Stein, ed., *Ivory, Bone, and Related Wood Finds*, vol. 6 of *Kenchreai, Eastern Port of Corinth* (Leiden: Brill, 2007). See also Robert Scranton and Edwin S. Ramage, "Investigations at Corinthian Kenchreai," *Hesperia* 36.2 (1987): 124–86.

87. See Christopher A. Faraone and Joseph L. Rife, "A Greek Curse against a Thief

drop to Paul's warning to the Corinthians, including those living in the port city of Cenchreae, about being led astray by idols, as they had been in their preconversion days (1 Cor 12:2; cf. 10:7, 14–22). Believers who are led by the Spirit of God, Paul avers, can never say, "Let Jesus be cursed!" Rather they will always confess "Jesus is Lord" (1 Cor 12:3). Two texts on a rectangular lead tablet, found in the debris of the southeast quarter of the sanctuary of Demeter and Kore at Corinth (fourth century CE), also address the gods of the underworld, either Katachthonois Hermes or Hades, with "lordship" language: "Lord gods of the underworld—"; "Lord, expose them and—cut their hearts, Lord, by means of the gods of the underworld. THE [- - -]."[88] Paul was well aware of the various counterfeits of spiritual power available in the ancient world and wanted the Corinthian believers to be absolutely clear about the consequences of their confessional and experiential commitment to the risen Christ. Once again, we see here the riches that a *local* understanding of the inscriptional evidence brings to the exegesis of (what is to a modern audience) a puzzling text.

2.6. Ephesus

The British engineer John Turtle Wood was the director of the first archaeological excavation of Ephesus from 1864 onward, which was carried out under the auspices of the British Museum. Wood published two seminal works on Ephesus in 1877 and 1890, with the former containing a substantial appendix of Ephesian inscriptions.[89] David George Hogarth continued Wood's work on the temple of Artemis, supervising the archaeological

---

from the Koutsongila Cemetery at Roman Kenchreai," *ZPE* 160 (2007): 141–57. Curse tablets were widespread in the cities and regions visited by Paul. See the classic work of Adolf Kirchhoff et al., eds., *Corpus inscriptionum Atticarum. Appendix: Defixionum tabellae Atticae* (Berlin: Reimer, 1897). A new volume of *IG* 16: *Corpus defixionum Graecarum. Pars I: Defixiones Atticae* is being prepared for future publication as part of the Berlin Excellence Cluster TOPOI.

88. R. S. Stroud, ed., *The Sanctuary of Demeter and Kore: The Inscriptions*, vol. 18.6 of *Corinth* (Princeton: ASCSA, 2013), §127.

89. John Turtle Wood, *Discoveries at Ephesus, Including the Site and Remains of the Great Temple of Diana* (London: Longmans, Green, 1877); Wood, *Modern Discoveries on the Site of Ancient Ephesus* (London: Longmans, Green, 1890). The British Museum (E. L. Hicks, *The Collection of Ancient Greek Inscriptions in the British Museum Part III: Priene, Iasos and Ephesos* [Oxford: Clarendon, 1890], 67–292) published exact representations of the Ephesian inscriptions collected by Wood at Ephe-

THE FIRST URBAN CHURCHES: INTRODUCTION   25

expedition at the site from 1904 onward. Hogarth wrote on the temple of Artemis, setting out the literary evidence regarding the Artemesion and cataloging its finds with commentary.[90] Further excavations of the Austrian Archaeological Institute began in 1895 under Otto Benndorf, and the work continues to this day.[91] Thirty-seven monographs have been published from 1906 to 2013 in the Forshungen in Ephesos series (FiE), covering thoroughly each archeological structure at Ephesus and their associated finds.[92] Articles on Ephesus, among many other ancient sites, are also published in its annual journal.[93]

Excavations were interrupted from 1913 onward by World War I, but Adolf Deissmann worked tirelessly to get international funding for their resumption, participating in the renewed digs at Ephesus from 1926 to 1929 and unleashing a stream of articles on Ephesus.[94] Inexplicably, Deissmann's role is totally ignored on the ÖAI centenary publication in its discussion of the period 1926–1935, notwithstanding the fact that he made a fundamental contribution to the work of the ÖAI during the period.[95] From 1954 onward, the archaeologists of the Ephesus Museum commenced excavations and restorations of the site of Ephesus and continue to do so until this day.[96]

---

sus during 1863–1874, supplemented in each case with commentaries, and including many further uncopied inscriptions (67).

90. David George Hogarth, *Excavations at Ephesus: The Archaic Artemesia* (London: British Museum, 1908).

91. See Gilbert Wiplinger and Gudrun Wlach, *Ephesus: 100 Years of Austrian Research* (Vienna: Österreichische Archäoligisches Institut, 1996). See also the three-volume centenary collection of the ÖAI celebrating its archaeological work: Herwig Friesinger and Fritz Krinzinger, eds., *100 Jahre Österreichische Forschungen in Ephesos: Akten des Symposions Wien 1995* (Vienna: Austrian Academy of Sciences, 1999).

92. For the publications, see http://www.oeaw.ac.at/antike/index.php?id=159.

93. The journal is *Jahreshefte des Österreichischen Archäologischen Institutes in Wien* (= *JÖAI*: *Annual Notebooks of the Austrian Archaeological Institute at Vienna*).

94. For Deissmann's work at Ephesus, see Albrecht Gerber, *Deissmann the Philologist* (Berlin: de Gruyter, 2010), 155–206. Deissmann wrote a stream of articles on Ephesus in 1918, 1923, 1925, 1927 (four articles), 1930, and 1931. For the details, see *Deissmann the Philologist*, 595–97; for his work on the Ephesian inscriptions, 180–81, 189, 194, 198.

95. Wiplinger and Wlach, *Ephesus*, 42–57.

96. For the official publication of the Ephesus Museum detailing its exhibits, see Meltem Cansever, ed., *Ephesus Museum Selçuk* (Beyoğlu-Istanbul: BKG, 2010).

In 1948 the colossus of Greek epigraphy, Louis Robert, began to publish a series of penetrating articles on the epigraphy of Ephesus,[97] but Robert did not surpass the vast arsenal of articles on the Ephesian inscriptions written before him by Josef Keil.[98] In the 1970s the University of Köln, as part of the IK series headed up by Reinhold Merkelbach,[99] began to collect the vast Ephesian inscriptional corpus (IEph) in an eight-volume publication that appeared over the period 1979–1984.[100] Other noteworthy publications on the Ephesian inscriptions also appeared in the early 1980s.[101] There are, to be sure, some deficiencies with the production of the IEph corpus. First, the editors of IEph did not attempt to date the vast majority of the Ephesian inscriptions. By contrast, the online Packhard Humanities Institute (PHI) Greek Epigraphy program of the Ephesian inscriptions,[102] edited by Donald McCabe, offers dates for most of the inscriptions, but readers are nevertheless advised to consult the original published edition of the inscription in order to check the editor's commentary in this regard. Second, the helpful commentaries that accompanied the first volume (IEph 1a) peter out by the second volume, undoubtedly in order to expedite the production of the ensuing volumes. In short,

---

97. Louis Robert, "Les hellénodiques à Éphèse," *Hellenica* 5 (1948): 59–63; Robert, "Epitaphes juives d'Éphèse et de Nicomédie," *Hellenica* 11–12 (1960): 90–111; Robert, "Sur des inscriptions d' Éphèse: fêtes, athletes, empereurs, épigrammes," *RevPhil* 41 (1967): 7–84; Robert, "Sur des inscriptions d' Éphèse: 6. Lettres impériales à Éphèse," *RevPhil* 41 (1967): 44–64; Robert, "Les femmes théores à Éphèse," *CRAI* (1974): 176–81; Robert, "Sur des inscriptions d' Éphèse: II. Sur une lettre d'un proconsul d'Asie," *RevPhil* 51 (1977): 7–14; Robert, "Sur des inscriptions d' Éphèse 12. Deux inscriptions pseudo-Éphésiennes," *RevPhil* 55 (1981): 9–13; Robert, "Dans une maison d' Éphèse, un serpent et une chiffre," *CRAI* (1982): 126–32.

98. For the seventy-five publications of Josef Keil, see Richard Oster, *A Bibliography of Ancient Ephesus* (Philadelphia: American Theological Library Association; Metuchen, NJ: Scarecrow, 1987), 60–66 §§657–731.

99. The series of the University of Köln, Inschriften griechischer Städte aus Kleinasien, sought to publish city by city the epigraphic texts for the regions of Asia Minor, even if the "finished edition" status was not achievable for some (or many) of the texts.

100. Hermann Wankel, *Die Inshcriften von Ephesos*, 8 vols. in 11 (Bonn: Habelt, 1979–1984).

101. Dieter Knibbe, *Der Staatsmarkt: Die Inschriften des Prytaneions I: Die Kureteninschriften und sonstige religiöse Texte* (Vienna: Österreichisches Archäologisches Institut, 1981); Dieter Knibbe and Sıtkı İsa Bülent Iplikçioğlu, *Ephesos im Spiegel seiner Inschriften* (Vienna: Schlindler, 1984).

102. See http://www.epigraphy.packhum.org/.

the collection of IEph does not reflect the precision of production that Robert would have expected. But Merkelbach was very rightly concerned to make the vast Ephesian corpus available to researchers as quickly as possible so that scholars *themselves* could take up the challenge of bringing the precision of Robert and Keil to their study of the inscriptional documents.[103] Researchers of Ephesus, therefore, stand in an enviable position, with all the resources of IEph and PHI at their disposal, in reconstructing the social, institutional, religious, and political history of the city from its epigraphy, in comparison to the more limited resources of other cities in Asia Minor.

Moreover, the epigraphy needs to be brought into dialogue with the archaeological record of the city. It is therefore surprising that Jerome Murphy-O'Connor did not draw at all from this invaluable corpus of documentary evidence—around 3,600 inscriptions at least—in collecting the primary sources relating to Ephesus, a total that excludes newly published Ephesian inscriptions in *SEG* and *ZPE* from 1985 onward and other unpublished inscriptions. Though a valuable work, Murphy-O'Connor's approach is entirely literature- and archaeology-based, apart from one fleeting inscriptional reference.[104] By contrast, the intense value of the documentary and archaeological evidence is readily seen in the publications of G. H. R. Horsley, Guy Rogers, Steven Friesen, Rick Strelan, *NewDocs*, Helmut Koester, Michel Cottier, and Norbert Zimmermann and Sabine Ladstätter, to name but a few.[105] Finally, the coinage of Ephesus, both in

---

103. See the criticisms of G. H. R. Horsley, "The Inscriptions of Ephesos and the New Testament," *NovT* 34 (1992): 119–20.

104. Jerome Murphy-O'Connor, *St. Paul's Ephesus: Texts and Archaeology* (Collegeville, MN: Liturgical Press, 2008), 175.

105. G. H. R. Horsley, "A Fishing Cartel in First-Century Ephesos," *NewDocs* 5:95–114; Horsley, "Inscriptions of Ephesos," 105–68; Guy MacLean Rogers, *The Sacred Identity of Ephesos* (London: Routledge, 1991); Rogers, *The Mysteries of Artemis: Cult, Polis, and Change in the Graeco-Roman World*, Synkrisis (New Haven: Yale University Press, 2013); Friesen, *Twice Neokoros*; Rick Strelan, *Paul, Artemis, and the Jews in Ephesus* (Berlin: de Gruyter, 1996); G. H. R. Horsley, "The Silversmiths at Ephesos," *NewDocs* 4:7–10; R. A. Kearsley, "Some Asiarchs in Ephesos," *NewDocs* 4:46–55; Richard Oster, "Holy Days in Honour of Artemis," *NewDocs* 4:74–82; G. H. R. Horsley, "Giving Thanks to Artemis," *NewDocs* 4:127–29; Horsley, "Fishing Cartel"; R. A. Kearsley, "The Mysteries of Artemis at Ephesos," *NewDocs* 6:196–202; Kearsley, "Ephesus: *Neokoros* of Artemis," *NewDocs* 6:203–5; James R. Harrison, "Family Honour of a Priestess of Artemis," *NewDocs* 10:31–38; Harrison, "Artemis Triumphs

the Hellenistic and imperial periods, has been intensively discussed in the scholarly literature.[106]

The enormity of the Ephesian epigraphic corpus, therefore, allows researchers to use its evidence not only for the urban world of Ephesus[107] but also for the cultural conventions and elitist ideology pervading social life in Asia Minor more generally.[108] Furthermore, the Ephesian

---

Over a Sorcerer's Evil Art," *NewDocs* 10:39–47; Harrison, "The 'Grace' of Augustus Paves a Street at Ephesus," *NewDocs* 10:61–66; Helmut Koester, ed., *Ephesos: Metropolis of Asia. An Interdisciplinary Approach to Its Archaeology, Religion and Culture* (Cambridge, MA: Harvard University Press, 2004); M. Cottier et al., eds., *The Customs Law of Asia* (Oxford: Oxford University Press, 2008); Norbert Zimmermann and Sabine Ladstätter, *Wall Painting in Ephesos from the Hellenistic to the Byzantine Period* (Istanbul: Ege Yayinlari, 2011).

Note also the following works on Ephesus itself: Anton Bammer, *Ephesos: Stadt an Fluss und Meer* (Graz: Akademische Druck- u. Verlagsanstalt, 1988); Richard E. Oster, "Ephesus as a Religious Center under the Principate, I. Paganism before Constantine," *ANRW* 18.3:1661–1728; Friedmund Hueber, *Ephesos Gebaute Geschichte* (Mainz: von Zabern, 1997); Peter Scherrer, *Ephesus: The New Guide*, rev. ed. (Istanbul: Ege Yayinlari, 2000); John K. Davies, "The Well Balanced *Polis*: Ephesos," in *The Economies of Hellenistic Societies, Third to First Century BC*, ed. Zosia H. Archibald, John K. Davies, and Vincent Garielsen (Oxford: Oxford University Press, 2011), 176–206. For a magisterial discussion of early Christianity in Ephesus, see Paul Trebilco, *The Early Christians in Ephesus from Paul to Ignatius* (Grand Rapids: Eerdmans, 2004).

106. Barclay V. Head, *A Catalogue of the Greek Coins of Ionia* (London: British Museum, 1892), 47–115; Edward Robinson, "The Coins from the Ephesian Artemision Reconsidered," *JHS* 71 (1951): 156–67; Gilbert K. Jenkins, "Hellenistic Gold Coins of Ephesus," *Anadolu* (1980): 183–88; Richard Oster, "Numismatic Windows into the Social World of Early Christianity: A Methodological Inquiry," *JBL* 101 (1982): 195–223; Stefan Karwiese, "The Artemisium Coin Hoard and the First Coins of Ephesus," *Revue belge de numismatique* 137 (1991): 1–28; John Paul Lotz, "The *Homonoia* Coins of Asia Minor and Ephesians 1:21," *TynBul* 50 (1999): 173–88; Lyn Kidson, "Minting in Ephesus: Economics and Self-Promotion in the Early Imperial Period," *JNAA* 23 (2013): 27–36.

107. Philip Harland, "Honours and Worship: Emperors, Imperial Cults, and Associations at Ephesus (First to Third Centuries CE)," *Studies in Religion* 25 (1996): 319–34. For the epigraphic and archaeological evidence for Ephesian associations, see Ascough, *Associations in the Greco-Roman World*, 99–108 §§159–75, 222–24 §§B4–B5.

108. For two fine samples of such an approach, see R. Saunders, "Attalus, Paul and PAIDEIA: The Contribution of *I. Eph.* 202 to Pauline Studies," in *Early Christianity, Late Antiquity, and Beyond*, vol. 2 of *Ancient History in a Modern University*, ed. T. W. Hillard et al. (Grand Rapids: Eerdmans 1998), 175–83; E. A. Judge, "Ethical Terms in

epigraphic evidence should be brought to bear on the exegetical study of Ephesians.[109] The theory that Ephesians is a "circular" letter has probably militated against the idea that local epigraphic evidence might throw light on exegetical, historical, and literary puzzles of the epistle, irrespective of whether the author is considered pseudonymous or the apostle himself. The rich contribution that the honorific inscriptions makes to our understanding of the genre of the notoriously long sentence in Eph 1:3–14 is a case in point.[110]

2.7. Colossae, Hierapolis, and Laodicea

At the outset, mention must be made of Ulrich Huttner's magisterial monograph that deals with the expansion of early Christianity in the Lycus Valley.[111] With meticulous attention to the archeological, inscriptional, and literary evidence, Huttner incisively discusses Colossians and Philemon, the evidence of Revelation, as well as the evidence of the church fathers regarding the bishops of Hierapolis, ecclesiastical institutions, persecutions, and legends. It is methodologically an excellent example of what needs to be done in our discipline. But what studies have been devoted to each of the Lycus Valley cities themselves?

St Paul and the Inscriptions of Ephesus," in *The First Christians in the Roman World*, 368–77.

109. However the comment of Peter T. O'Brien (*The Letter to the Ephesians*, Pillar New Testament Commentary [Grand Rapids: Eerdmans, 2009], 49) demonstrates the resistance of exegetes to our position: "a specific knowledge of the ancient city of Ephesus, in spite of the increasing amount of information available to us, especially through the inscriptions, does not assist us a great deal in interpreting the letter." The untested assumption implicit in O'Brien's statement is made clear when one remembers there are more than 3,600 Ephesian inscriptions. How can we claim that no difference will be made to the interpretation of Ephesians if we refuse from the outset to engage with such a vast corpus of inscriptions? I am grateful to Isaac Soon for drawing my attention to this reference. However, the *Papyrologische Kommentare zum Neuen Testament* (Göttingen: Vandenhoeck & Ruprecht) is a significant exegetical step forward in this regard. A similar project employing the inscriptions is imperative.

110. Holland Hendrix, "On the Form and Ethos of Ephesians," *USQR* 42 (1988): 3–15.

111. Ulrich Huttner, *Early Christianity in the Lycus Valley*, Early Christianity in Asia Minor (Leiden: Brill, 2013). See, in the same series, Cilliers Breytenbach and Carola Zimmermann, *Early Christianity in Lycaonia and Adjacent Areas* (Leiden: Brill, forthcoming).

Although the mound of Colossae remains to be excavated, scholars have been able to pursue studies of the site, as the Alan Cadwallader and Michael Trainor volume has shown.[112] Not only have new Colossian inscriptions been recently found in situ and translated by Cadwallader,[113] but also pottery shards from the mound itself and various funerary stelae from the neighboring area have provided revealing insights into Colossian culture and personalities.[114] Rosalinde Kearsley's article in the volume, on the inscriptions of Hierapolis and Laodicea, shows in miniature the riches to be mined by incisive epigraphic research.[115] The recent work of Rosemary Canavan employs the iconography of clothing found on the Lycus Valley statuary, stelae, and coins to throw light on the clothing imagery behind Col 3:1–17.[116] Canavan's highly original scholarship illustrates the great potential of "visual" exegesis. Last, although Colossae remains an "ugly stepsister" in this scenario, yet to be excavated and bypassed by the new Turkish highway on the tourist track, the recent finds of Colossian inscriptions published by Cadwallader underscore the riches remaining to be unearthed should excavation begin sometime in the future.[117] Cadwallader's rich discussion of the relevance to Colossians

---

112. Alan H. Cadwallader and Michael Trainor, eds., *Colossae in Space and Time: Linking to an Ancient City*, NTOA/SUNT 94 (Göttingen: Vandenhoeck & Ruprecht, 2011).

113. Alan H. Cadwallader, "Refuting an Axiom of Scholarship on Colossae: Fresh Insights from New and Old Inscriptions," in Cadwallader and Trainor, *Colossae in Space and Time*, 170–75; Cadwallader, "Honouring the Repairer of the Baths at Colossae," *NewDocs* 10:110–13.

114. Michael Trainor, "Excavating Epaphras of Colossae," 232–46, and Bahadir Duman and Erim Konakçi, "The Silent Witness of the Mound of Colossae: Pottery Remains," 247–81, both in Cadwallader and Trainor, *Colossae in Space and Time*.

115. Rosalinde A. Kearsley, "Epigraphic Evidence for the Social Impact of Roman Government in Laodicea and Hierapolis," in Cadwallader and Trainor, *Colossae in Space and Time*, 130–50.

116. Rosemary Canavan, *Clothing the Body of Christ at Colossae*, WUNT 2/334 (Tübingen: Mohr Siebeck, 2012).

117. Cadwallader "Refuting an Axiom," 170–74; Alan Cadwallader, "A New Inscription, A Correction and a Confirmed sighting from Colossae," *Epigrapha Anatolia* 40 (2007): 109–18; Cadwallader, "Honouring the Repairer of the Baths: A New Inscription from Kolossai," *Antichthon* 46 (2012): 150–83. See also Cadwallader's semi-popular book, *Fragments of Colossae* (Adelaide: ATF Press, forthcoming). Cadwallader has also edited two Colossian epitaphs in *SEG* 57.1384–85. Cadwallader has mentioned to me in private email correspondence (March 22, 2014) that he is

of a fragment of a Colossian gladiator stele, recently pointed out to him by a local on a trip to Colossae, is a case in point.[118]

The Italian epigraphist Tullia Ritti has long since collected and published the Greek inscriptions of Hierapolis.[119] Ritti has recently published an English collection of these inscriptions, with commentary, relevant to specific archaeological sites of Hierapolis.[120] Both of these works build on the vast corpus of inscriptions from Hierapolis collected by Walther Judeich at the end of the nineteenth century.[121] Moreover, Hierapolis is also a very important archaeological site in the Lycus Valley. It is famous for its vast necropolis and accompanying inscriptions (revealing a Jewish presence in the city), its theater with its famous mythological relief, and seating for the civic elites and dignitaries, local associations, and gladiator reliefs,[122] to name a few attractions. As recently as 2010 an Italian monograph on the coinage of Hierapolis from extensive archaeological campaigns has been published.[123] It is therefore a curiosity of Colossians scholarship, given that

---

preparing two other Colossian inscriptions for publication: (1) a pedestal noted in an obscure 2005 Turkish publication and (2) an epitaph from the necropolis where a man, his wife, and the wife of another man are mentioned as occupying the grave ("a rare but not unique reference, although usually an allocation to another man [friend etc.] is the norm").

118. The paper of Alan Cadwallader ("Russell Crowe at Colossae? A Gladiatorial Fragment and the Letter to the Colossians") was presented at the Fellowship of Biblical Studies conference, September 29, 2014, Mandelbaum House, Sydney, Australia, and is now included in expanded form in this volume ("Assessing the Potential of Archaeological Discoveries for the Interpretation of New Testament Texts: The Case Study of a Gladiator Fragment from Colossae and the Letter to the Colossians").

119. Tullia Ritti, *Hierapolis, scavi e ricerche I: Fonti letterarie ed epigrafiche* (Rome: Bretschneider, 1985).

120. Tullia Ritti, *An Epigraphic Guide to Hierapolis (Pamukkale)* (Istanbul: Ege Yayinlari, 2006). On the archaeology of Hierapolis, see Francesco D'Andria, *Hierapolis of Phrygia (Pamukkale): An Archaeological Guide*, 2nd ed. (Istanbul: Ege Yayinlari, 2010).

121. See Carl Humann et al., eds., *Altertümer von Hierapolis* (Berlin: Reimer, 1898), 67–202.

122. See Ritti, *An Epigraphic Guide*. For the "association" inscriptions of Hierapolis, see Ascough, *Associations in the Greco-Roman World*, 94–99 §§147–58. On the Hierapolis theater relief, see Francesco D'Andria and Tullia Ritti, *Hierapolis, scavi e ricerche II: Le sculture del Teatro. I rilievi con i cicli di Apollo e Artemide* (Rome: Bretschneider, 1985). On gladiators at Hierapolis, see Tullia Ritti and Salim Yilmaz, *Gladiatori e venationes a Hierapolis di Frigia* (Rome: Accademia Naz. dei Lincei, 1998).

123. Adriana Travaglini and Valeria Giulia Camilleri, *Hierapolis di Frigia, le monete: campagne di seavo 1957–2004* (Istanbul: Ege Yayinlari, 2010).

Epaphras was also a pastor to believers at nearby Hierapolis and Laodicea (Col 4:13), that the abundant epigraphic, numismatic, and archaeological evidence of each city has not been brought into dialogue with the epistle, especially in view of our meager material evidence from Colossae.

Laodicea is another important archaeological site, with its inscriptions recently published,[124] as well as a massive two-volume study, published in Turkish, of the necropolis surrounding the city in all directions, comprising some 283 tombs.[125] In the case of the necropolises of Hierapolis and Laodicea, the hierarchical and agonistic values of the civic elites are revealed in the mortuary ostentation of the postclassical polis. Such ostentation became even more prolific as the civic elites moved increasingly into the center of the polis with their grandiose monuments and inscriptions. Here we have the opportunity to study, from the perspective of the Lycus Valley cities (Col 1:2; 4:13, 15–16; Rev 3:14), the social outworking of the values promulgated by the early Christians (e.g., Col 3:1–4:6; Rev 3:14–22), as well as Paul's use of the gladiatorial imagery of the arena (e.g., 1 Cor 4:8–13; 2 Cor 4:8–9; 6:3–10), to cite two examples. Furthermore, Trainor has brought into play the evidence of funerary stelae in discussing the network of social relations fostered by Epaphras in his house churches in the Lycus Valley.[126] Although the study of these cities by New Testament scholars is in its infancy,[127] the explosion of archaeological work being carried out at Laodicea and Hierapolis, along with the study of their inscriptions, will reveal further insights into the urban culture of the Lycus Valley and its house churches.

---

124. Thomas Corsten, ed., *Die Inschriften von Laodikeia am Lykos* (Bonn: Habelt, 1997). Before the volume of Corsten, we were indebted to Louis Robert's discussion of the Laodicean inscriptions: "Inscriptions," in *Laodicée du Lycos: Le Nymphée (campagne 1961-1963)*, ed. Jean des Gagniers et al. (Québec: L'Université Laval, 1969), 247–389.

125. C. Selal, M. Okunak, and M. Bilgin, *Laodikeia Nekropulü (2004-2010 Yillari)*: vol. 1: *Laodikeia çalismalari. Metin*, vol. 2: *Laodikeia çalismalari* (Istanbul: Ege Yayinlari, 2011).

126. Trainor, "Excavating Epaphras of Colossae," 232–46; Trainor, *Epaphras: Paul's Educator at Colossae* (Collegeville, MN: Liturgical Press, 2008).

127. Cadwallader and Trainor, *Colossae in Space and Time*; see Larry Kreitzer, *Hierapolis in the Heavens: Studies in the Letter to the Ephesians* (London: T&T Clark, 2008).

THE FIRST URBAN CHURCHES: INTRODUCTION 33

2.8. Rome and Ostia

Recently, in a methodologically innovative book, Peter Oakes has helpfully brought the evidence of Romans into dialogue with the archaeological evidence of Pompeii.[128] Oakes culled demographic information and data from Pompeii to depict daily life in a typical *insula*, or apartment complex, similar to those that some of Paul's auditors might have lived in at Rome. [129] Oakes suggested that these analogous materials point to the likelihood of a Christian meeting occurring in a craftsman's workshop in an apartment block in Transtiberim in Rome.[130] Although the evidence for Pompeii and Herculaneum is extensive, one wonders why Oakes did not bring the (admittedly more meager) archaeological evidence of Rome into dialogue with Romans. This is not meant in any way to diminish Oakes's very considerable achievement: rather it is simply a reminder that we must prioritize the local evidence, even where it is ambiguous, fragmentary, or inconclusive.

In the case of Rome, the archaeological remains of an early second-century-BCE *insula* were found at base of the Capitoline Hill, close to the nearby Roman Forum.[131] We also have four *CIL* inscriptions mentioning *insulae* at Rome (*CIL* 6.67, 10250, 29791, 9824), as well as further inscriptional (e.g., *AE* 1971.45) and literary references (Tertullian, *Val.* 7) attesting to their presence in the city.[132] While we must not play down the

---

128. Peter Oakes, *Reading Romans in Pompeii: Paul's Letter at Ground Level* (Minneapolis: Fortress, 2010).

129. Ibid., 1–97. See also James Packer, "Inns at Pompeii: A Short Survey," *Cronache Pompeiane* 4 (1978): 5–53; Andrew D. Wallace-Hadrill, "Elites and Trade in the Roman Town," in *City and Country in the Ancient World*, ed. John Rich and Andrew D. Wallace-Hadrill (London: Routledge, 1991), 241–72; Marisa Ranieri Panetta, ed., *Pompeii: The History, Life, and Art of the Buried City* (Vercelli: White Star, 2004); John Joseph Dobbins and Pedar William Foss, eds., *The World of Pompeii* (London: Routledge, 2007); Mary Beard, *Pompeii: The Life of a Roman Town* (London: Profile, 2008); Gregory S. Aldrete, *Daily Life in the Roman City: Rome, Pompeii and Ostia* (Norman: University of Oklahoma Press, 2009).

130. Oakes, *Romans in Pompeii*, 98–126. Note Oakes's comment (91): "Jewett is undoubtedly correct that most of the groups met in apartment blocks rather than houses. Apartment blocks were too prevalent at Rome for this to be otherwise."

131. Amanda Claridge, *Rome: An Oxford Archaeological Guide* (Oxford: Oxford University Press, 2010), 262–64 fig. 110.

132. Lawrence Richardson, *A New Topographical Dictionary of Ancient Rome* (Baltimore: Johns Hopkins University Press, 1992), 208.

unequivocal New Testament evidence for the *domus* of socially advantaged believers being initially the primary site for house church meetings, Robert Jewett's argument that the early Christians at Thessalonica and Rome also met in *insulae* merits consideration.[133] Moreover, there were other options for meeting places for the early Roman believers.[134] Given the presence of slaves—including some from the *familia Caesaris* (Phil 4:22)—in the early Christian community at Rome, an inscription (*CIL* 6.6215, 6216) from a socially prominent Julio-Claudian family in the city helps us to imagine how Christian slaves in a well-off *domus* might have had access to apartment blocks for their meetings.[135] In a tombstone from the Statilius household at Rome, we hear of slaves such as "Cerdo, caretaker (ins[ul(arius)]) of the apartment block" and "Eros, the other caretaker (ins(ularius)) of the apartment block."[136] Would a trusted believing slave (see Eph 5:5–8; Col 3:22–25; 1 Pet 2:18) have been able to persuade his master about the use of a room for a "meeting place" in an apartment block, or would the use of a space by a non-Roman "cult" have been socially unthinkable for a Roman apartment owner? What would have happened if the master were a Christian? While this scenario is speculative and the social ramifications are unclear, this type of evidence allows us to see that, as the early Christian movement grew rapidly, alternatives to the *domus* as a meeting place must have been required. This is now confirmed by the important new work of Edward Adams on the issue, referred to above.[137] He has set out all the evidence for the wide range of nonhouse meeting places adopted by Christians in the early centuries for their worship and teaching, placing in question

---

133. Robert Jewett, "Tenement Churches and Communal Meals in the Early Church: The Implications of a Form-Critical Analysis of 2 Thessalonians 3:10," *BR* 38 (1993): 23–43; Jewett, "Are There Allusions to the Love Feast in Rom 13:8–10?," in *Common Life in the Early Church: Essays Honoring Graydon F. Snyder*, ed. Julian Victor Hills (Harrisburg, PA: Trinity Press International, 1998), 265–78; Jewett, *Romans: A Commentary*, Hermeneia (Minneapolis: Fortress, 2007).

134. Edward Adams, *The Earliest Christian Meeting Places: Almost Exclusively Houses?* (London: T&T Clark, 2013).

135. See, however, Oakes's cautionary comments about not overstating the case for the "upward social mobility" of slaves from a limited sample of slaves in the *family Caesaris* (*Romans in Pompeii*, 78–79).

136. Brian K. Harvey, trans., *Roman Lives: Ancient Roman Life as Illustrated by Latin Inscriptions* (Newburyport MA: Focus, 2004), 89 §55.

137. Adams, *Earliest Christian Meeting Places*, 138–97.

the scholarly assumption that the *domus* remained the primary (or only) meeting place for believers. The issue acutely raises the question of the social location of believers at Rome. Readers are referred to the different conclusions of Peter Lampe and Edwin Judge on the topic, each appealing to the Latin inscriptional evidence.[138]

In terms of the capital itself, many scholars have meticulously discussed the archaeological sites of Rome and its harbor town Ostia,[139] with others collecting the inscriptions and primary-source literature relating to

---

138. Peter Lampe, *From Paul to Valentinus: Christians at Rome in the First Two Centuries* (Minneapolis: Fortress, 2003), 153-95; Edwin A. Judge, "The Roman Base of Paul's Mission," in *The First Christians in the Roman World*, 553-67.

139. For Rome, see especially Margareta Steinby, ed., *Lexicon Topographicum Urbis Romae*, 5 vols. (Rome: Edizioni Quasar, 1993-2000). Additionally, see Samuel Ball Platner and Thomas Ashby, *A Topographical Dictionary of Ancient Rome* (London: Oxford University Press, 1929); Ernest Nash, *A Pictorial Dictionary of Ancient Rome* (London: Thames & Hudson, 1968); James E. Packer, "Housing and Population in Imperial Ostia," *JRS* 57 (1967): 80-99; Packer, *The Insulae of Imperial Ostia* (Rome: Memoirs of the American Academy in Rome, 1971); Russell Meiggs, *Roman Ostia*, 2nd ed. (Oxford: Clarendon, 1973); Giovanna Vitelli, "Grain Storage and Urban Growth in Imperial Ostia: A Quantitative Study," *World Archaeology* 12 (1980): 54-68; Claridge, *Rome: An Archaeological Guide*; Richardson, *Topographical Dictionary*; Jan Theo Bakker, *Living and Working with Gods: Studies of Evidence for Private Religion and its Material Environment in the City of Ostia (100-500 AD)* (Leiden: Brill, 1994); Bakker, *The Mills-Bakeries of Ostia: Description and Interpretation* (Amsterdam: Gieben, 1999); Jon Coulston and Hazel Dodge, *Ancient Rome: The Archaeology of the Eternal City* (Oxford: Oxford University Committee for Archaeology, 2000); Birger Olsen, Dieter Mitternacht, and Olof Brandt, eds., *The Synagogue of Ancient Ostia and the Jews of Rome: The Building and Its History from the First to the Fifth Century* (Stockholm: Åström, 2001); Catharine Edwards and Greg Woolf, eds., *Rome the Cosmopolis* (Cambridge: Cambridge University Press, 2003); Filippo Coarelli, *Rome and Environs: An Archaeological Guide* (Berkeley: University of California Press, 2007); Aldrete, *Daily Life*; Hannah Stöger, "Roman Ostia: Space Syntax and the Domestication of Space," in *Layers of Perception. CAA 2007. Proceedings of the 35th International Conference on Computer Applications and Quantitative Methods in Archaeology, April 2-6, 2007, Berlin, Germany*, ed. Axel Posluschny, Karsten Lambers, and Irmela Herzog (Bonn: Habelt, 2007), 322-27; http://archiv.ub.uni-heidelberg.de/propylaeumdok/516/1/10_03_stoeger_ostia.pdf; Stöger, "Clubs and Lounges at Roman Ostia: The Spatial Organisation of a Boomtown Phenomenon," *Proceedings of the Seventh Space Syntax Symposium*, ed. Daniel Koch, Lars Marcus, and Jesper Steen (Stockholm: KTH, 2009), http://hdl.handle.net/1887/14297; Björn Christian Ewald and Carlos F. Noreña, eds., *The Emperor and Rome: Space, Representation, and Ritual* (Cambridge: Cambridge University Press, 2010). On the epigraphic and archaeologi-

the various buildings of the city.[140] While the imperial context of Romans has been well covered in New Testament studies,[141] the symbolic messages conveyed by the sacred space of monuments at Rome, their relation to each other, and their ideological significance in relation to the motifs of Romans need to be discussed, especially in terms of "audience reception" of Paul's message.[142]

In sum, this intersection of the inscriptional evidence with the archaeological record at Rome helps us to venture into largely untraveled territory in scholarship on Romans, a journey that would perhaps help us hear Paul's text with the ears of a resident of early imperial Rome.

3. Conclusion

The series The First Urban Churches comes at an important stage for New Testament scholars. Significant strides have been made in the archaeological exploration of our biblical cities, with the lamentable exception

---

cal evidence for associations in Ostia, see Ascough, *Associations in the Greco-Roman World*, 199–202 §§317–18, 228–36 §§B11–B21.

140. Donald Dudley, *Urbs Romana: A Source Book of Classical Texts on the City and Its Monuments* (London: Phaidon, 1967); Peter J. Aicher, *Rome: A Source-Guide to the Ancient City*, vol. 1 (Wauconda: Bolchazy-Carducci, 2004). On the epigraphic and archaeological evidence for associations in Rome, see Ascough, *Associations in the Greco-Roman World*, 205–15 §§319–29, 238–40 §§B25–B28.

141. Jewett, *Romans*; Neil Elliot, *The Arrogance of the Nations: Reading Romans in the Shadow of Empire* (Minneapolis: Fortress, 2008); Harrison, *Paul and the Imperial Authorities*; Harrison, "More Than Conquerors"; Harrison, "Augustan Rome and the Body of Christ: A Comparison of the Social Vision of the *Res Gestae* and Paul's Letter to the Romans," *HTR* 106 (2013): 1–36. See also Peter Oakes, ed., *Rome in the Bible and the Early Church* (Carlisle: Paternoster, 2002).

142. James R. Harrison, "Paul among the Romans," in *All Things to All Cultures: Paul among Jews, Greeks and Romans*, ed. Mark Harding and Alanna Nobbs (Grand Rapids: Eerdmans, 2013), 143–76, esp. 143–47. See, however, the excellent work of Jenkyns, *God, Space and City*. More generally, see Peter Richardson, *City and Sanctuary: Religion and Architecture in the Roman East* (London: SCM, 2002). The restoration of Augustus's mausoleum, gated off in the 1960s, was recently commenced with government funding in 2014 for a 2016 opening. See Tom Kington, "Augustus Rules Again as Rome Acts to Restore Lost Mausoleum," *The Guardian*, March 29, 2014, http://www.theguardian.com/world/2014/mar/29/augustus-rome-lost-mausoleum/. For photographs of the mausoleum from 1921 to 1941, see Fabio Betti et al., ed., *Mausoleo di Augusto Demolizioni e scavi* (Rome: Electa, 2011).

of Colossae, as well as in the collection of the inscriptional texts in various translated volumes (French, German, modern Greek, and English) for most of the cities. The time has come for New Testament exegetes to listen more closely than they have ever before to the early Christian writings in their first-century urban context. The exegetical dividends will be rich and unexpected.

GENERAL BIBLIOGRAPHY ON THE CITY IN ANTIQUITY

Arnaoutoglou, Ilias. *Thusias heneka kai sunousias: Private Religious Associations in Hellenistic Athens*. Athens: Academy of Athens, 2003.

Ascough, Richard S., Philip A. Harland, and John S. Kloppenborg, ed. *Associations in the Greco-Roman World: A Sourcebook*. Waco, TX: Baylor University Press, 2012.

Bendemann, Reinhard von, and Markus Tiwald, eds. *Das frühe Christentum und die Stadt*. BWANT 198. Stuttgart: Kohlhammer, 2012.

Burrell, Barbara. *Neokoroi: Greek Cities and Roman Emperors*. Cincinnati Classical Studies 2/9. Leiden: Brill, 2004.

Capdetrey, Laurent, and Yves Lafond, eds. *La cité et ses élites: Pratiques et représentation des formes de domination et de contrôle social dans les cités grecques; Actes du colloque de Poitiers, 19–20 octobre 2006*. Pessac, France: Ausonius, 2010.

Cébeillac-Gervasoni, Mireille, and Laurent Lamoine, eds. *Les élites et leurs facettes: Les élites locales dans le monde hellénistique et romain*. Rome: École française de Rome; Clermont-Ferrand: Presses universitaires Blaise-Pascal, 2003.

Childe, V. Gordon. "The Urban Revolution." *The Town Planning Review* 21 (1950): 3–17.

Connolly, Peter, and Hazel Dodge. *The Ancient City: Life in Classical Athens and Rome*. Oxford: Oxford University Press, 1998.

De Coulanges, Fustel. *The Ancient City: A Study on the Religion, Laws, and Institutions of Greece and Rome*. Garden City, NY: Doubleday, 1955.

Danker, Frederick W. *Benefactor: Epigraphic Study of a Graeco-Roman and New Testament Field*. St Louis: Clayton, 1982.

Deissmann, Adolf. "Primitive Christianity and the Lower Classes." *Expositor* 7 (1909): 208–24.

———. *Light from the Ancient East: The New Testament Illustrated by Recently Discovered Texts from the Graeco-Roman World*. 2nd ed. London: Hodder & Stoughton, 1927.

Dmitriev, Sviatoslav. *City Government in Hellenistic and Roman Asia Minor.* Oxford: Oxford University Press, 2005.

Dondin-Payre, Monique, and Nicolas Tran, eds. *Collegia: Le phénomène associative dans l'Occident romain.* Bordeaux: Ausonius, 2012.

Finley, M. I. "The Ancient City: From Fustel de Coulanges to Max Weber and Beyond." *Comparative Studies in Society and History* 19 (1977): 305–27.

Forbis, Elizabeth. *Municipal Virtues in the Roman Empire.* Stuttgart: Teubner, 1996.

Frija, Gabrielle. *Les prêtres des empereurs: Le culte impérial civique dans la province romaine d'Asie. Histoire.* Rennes: Presses Universitaires de Rennes, 2012.

Fröhlich, Pierre. *Les cités grecques et le contrôle des magistrates (IVe–Ier siècle avant J.-C.).* Geneva: Droz, 2004.

Fröhlich, Pierre, and Patrice Hamon, eds. *Groupes et associations dans cités grecques (IIIe siècle av. J.-C.–IIe siècle ap. J.-C.). Actes de la table ronde de Paris, INHA, 19–20 juin 2009.* Geneva: Droz, 2013.

Gates, Charles. *Ancient Cities: The Archaeology of Urban Life in the Ancient Near East and Egypt, Greece and Rome.* London: Routledge, 2011.

Gauthier, Philippe. *Les cités grecques et leur bienfaiteurs (IVe–Ier s. av. J-C): Contribution à l'histoire des institutions.* Suppléments au Bulletin de Correspondance Hellénique 12. Athens: École française d'Athènes, 1985.

Glotz, Gustave. *La cité grecque.* Paris: La Renaissance du Livre, 1928. ET: *The Greek City and Its Institutions.* London: Kegan Paul, Trench, Trubner, 1929.

Harland, Philip A. *Associations, Synagogues, and Congregations: Claiming a Place in Ancient Mediterranean Society.* Minneapolis: Fortress, 2003.

Horster, Marietta, and Anja Klöckner, eds. *Cities and Priests: Cult Personnel in Asia Minor and the Aegean Islands from the Hellenistic to the Imperial Period.* Berlin: de Gruyter, 2013.

Jenkyns, Richard. *God, Space and City in the Roman Imagination.* Oxford: Oxford University Press, 2013.

Judge, E. A. *The First Christians in the Roman World: Augustan and New Testament Essays.* Edited by James R. Harrison. WUNT 229. Tübingen: Mohr Siebeck, 2008.

Jones, A. H. M. *Cities of the Eastern Roman Provinces.* Oxford: Oxford University Press, 1971 (orig. 1937).

———. *The Greek City from Alexander to Justinian*. Oxford: Clarendon, 1940.
Kloppenborg, John S., and Richard S. Ascough, eds. *Attica, Central Greece, Macedonia, Thrace*. Vol. 1 of *Greco-Roman Associations: Texts, Translations, and Commentary*. Berlin: de Gruyter 2011.
Kloppenborg, John S., and Stephen G. Wilson, eds. *Voluntary Associations in the Graeco-Roman World*. London: Routledge, 1996.
Liu, Jinyu. *Collegia Centonariorum: The Guilds of Textile Dealers in the Roman West*. Leiden: Brill, 2009.
Longenecker, Bruce W. *Remember the Poor: Paul, Poverty, and the Greco-Roman World*. Grand Rapids: Eerdmans, 2010.
Magie, David. *Roman Rule in Asia Minor: To the End of the Third Century after Christ*. 2 vols. Princeton: Princeton University Press, 1950.
Marcus, Joyce, and Jeremy A. Sabloff, eds. *The Ancient City: New Perspectives on Urbanism in the Old and New Worlds*. Santa Fe: School for Advanced Research Press, 2008.
Meeks, Wayne A. *The First Urban Christians: The Social World of the Apostle Paul*. 2nd ed. New Haven: Yale University Press, 2003.
Meggitt, Justin J. *Paul, Poverty and Survival*. Edinburgh: T&T Clark, 1998.
Migeotte, Léopold. *L'emprunt public dans les cités grecques: Recueil des documents et analyse critique*. Québec: Les Editions du Sphinx, Les Belles Lettres, 1984.
———. *Les finances des cités grecques*. Paris: Les Belles Lettres, 2014.
———. *Les souscriptions publiques dans les cités grecques*. Geneva: Droz, 1992.
Momigliano, A. D. "The Ancient City of Fustel De Coulanges (1970)." Pages 162–78 in *Studies on Modern Scholarship*. Edited by G. W. Bowersock and T. J. Cornell. Berkeley: University of California Press, 1994.
Nijf, Onno M. van. *The Civic World of Professional Associations in the Roman East*. Amsterdam: Gieben, 1997.
Parkins, Helen M., ed. *Roman Urbanism: Beyond the Consumer City*. London: Routledge, 1997.
Parrish, David, ed. *Urbanism in Western Asia Minor: New Studies on Aphrodisias, Ephesos, Hierapolis, Pergamon, Perge and Xanthos*. Portsmouth, RI: Journal of Roman Archaeology, 2001.
Price, S. R. F. *Rituals and Power: The Roman Imperial Cult in Asia Minor*. Cambridge: Cambridge University Press, 1984.
Rich, John, and Andrew Wallace-Hadrill, eds. *City and Country in the Ancient World*. London: Routledge, 1991.

Rohrbaugh, Richard L. "The City in the Second Testament." *BTB* 21 (1991): 67–75.
Sjoberg, Gideon. *The Preindustrial City: Past and Present.* New York: Free Press, 1960.
Stambaugh, John E. *The Ancient Roman City.* Baltimore: Johns Hopkins University Press, 1988.
Welborn, L. L. *An End to Enmity: Paul and the "Wrongdoer" of Second Corinthians.* BZNW 185. Berlin: de Gruyter, 2011.
Yamauchi, Edwin M. *The Archaeology of New Testament Cities in Western Asia Minor.* London and Glasgow: Pickering & Inglis, 1980.
Zanker, Paul. *The Power of Images in the Age of Augustus.* Translated by Alan Shapiro. Ann Arbor: University of Michigan Press, 1988.
Zuiderhoek, Arjan. *The Politics of Munificence in the Roman Empire: Citizens, Elites and Benefactors in Asia Minor.* Cambridge: Cambridge University Press, 2009.

Assessing the Potential of Archaeological Discoveries for the Interpretation of New Testament Texts: The Case of a Gladiator Fragment from Colossae and the Letter to the Colossians

Alan Cadwallader

The nature and intent of allusions to gladiatorial and athletic imagery in the Pauline corpus has received ongoing forays by scholars from Vic Pfitzner to, most recently, Cavan Concannon. To some extent the focus of such studies has been on the authorial parameters of meaning and usage. Less attention has been directed toward the wider literary appropriation of such imagery, especially following the Augustan harnessing of gladiatorial shows as a strategy of muscular imperialization. The putative audiential appropriation of such imagery in each specific addressed local community has been almost completely absent from such studies, Colossae most particularly. The issue redirects attention to the cultural currency in the particularities of time and space, period and location, available to an audience to "think with,"[1] and therefore provides an essential comparative grid for Pauline literary usage.[2] Critical reference to the material and visual context shaping the imaginative and linguistic field of reference of hearers of Pauline letters affords considerable expansion of how such writings could be understood to function. The recent discovery of a gladiatorial relief at Colossae provides an opportunity to investigate the

---

1. See Cavan W. Concannon, *"When You Were Gentiles": Specters of Ethnicity in Roman Corinth and Paul's Corinthian Correspondence* (New Haven: Yale University Press, 2014), 49–50.

2. "Pauline" in this usage makes no judgment about authentic and disputed letters unless and until issues of interpretative adjustment and accent become critical.

agonistic consciousness of its civic populace and the key locations where such consciousness was developed, and to postulate how a small group within that populace might respond to the receipt of a letter that utilizes imagery from gladiatorial contests.

This essay explores the significance of the discovery of the relief first by assessing its artistic, architectural, and cultural significance; second by setting it into the context of a cultural and literary appropriation of gladiatorial imagery and language; and third by exploring the potential of an agonistic consciousness in Colossian society for the reception of the Epistle to the Colossians.

1. The Colossian Gladiator Relief

In February 2012, a small number of Turkish newspapers and websites carried a report of a large fragment of a gladiatorial relief found at Honaz.[3] The brief article credited a member of the Denizli Naturalists Association, Ümit Şıracı, with referring his discovery to Professor Celal Şimşek, though he had ensured that he had taken a photograph for online posting.[4] Şimşek, the director of excavations at the site of Laodikeia, promptly announced that the artifact would be removed to the Denizli Müze at Pamukkale, located in the old Roman baths complex of Hierapolis. The relief had been installed in a newly constructed retaining wall in a southern street of the town of Honaz. My colleague Michael Trainor and I had been shown this relief in 2005 by a local Honaz inhabitant whose farm covers much of the ancient höyük and surrounds of Colossae.

There was no formal indication of the specific find location of the relief, though the Colossae höyük (tell) shows considerable evidence of unauthorized digging, especially at the northern perimeter of the theater *cavea*. There have been some dramatic local news items about the capture of thieves with their contraband intended for the global antiquities

---

3. See the *Denizli News*, February 8, 2012, http://www.denizlihaber.com/turizm/oren-yerleri/tarihi-eserden-duvar-ormusler/; *Archaeology News*, February 8, 2012, http://arkeolojihaber.net/tag/laodikeia-antik-kenti/page/4/. The report was also carried by the Rapid Delivery news service February 8, 2012, http://hizlihaberler.blogspot.com.au/2012/02/tarihe-saygszlk.html.

4. See http://aktuel.mynet.com/galeri/haber/tarihe-saygisizlik-tarihe-saygisizlik/9567/242896/.

market.[5] However, in the area, the exchange of artifacts is a long-established custom that strengthens kin and friendship bonds and cultivates the ties of patronage that are part of Turkish society. Mehmet Özdoğan, the renowned Turkish archaeologist, calls this "atavistic patrimony" and recognizes that it is one of the tiers of preservation and storage that has operated from Ottoman times,[6] albeit often in tension with local and national museum officials. This piece appears to have functioned much in this way and underscores the importance for archaeologists and biblical scholars respectfully to establish connections with local people for whom ancient sites are part of their situational inheritance.[7]

The size of the limestone fragment is approximately 45 cm high by 40 cm wide and was originally part of a more extensive frieze. It shows some signs of wear, but belts, straps, *cardiophylax*, loincloths, and leggings are clearly visible. Two tiers, or registers of action, divided by a simple band molding, are visible, though a third tier cannot be ruled out.[8] Two tiers of action is the regular artistic schema in friezes and often in mosaics, with single concentrations the norm on lamps and, usually, funerary monuments for gladiators themselves. The damage to the top of the Colossian piece interrupts the carving below, where an upper border would be expected, thus precluding absolute certainty. It is likely, though this is yet to be confirmed, that the back of the relief was left rough, to aid its fixture (as here in its modern reassignment) into another structure. By comparison with such reliefs found at other cities in Asia, the most likely candidates for that structure are the theater (or stadium), the mausoleum of the priest of the imperial cult who owned or leased a gladiator troupe, or a gladiatorial school barracks.

---

5. One report of illegal pilfering of artifacts near the site of Colossae details how dangerous the pursuit of thieves can be. See http://www.todayszaman.com/anasayfa_gendarmerie-sergeant-killed-while-chasing-artifact-thieves_390365.html.

6. See Mehmet Özdoğan, "Ideology and Archaeology in Turkey" in *Archaeology Under Fire: Nationalism, Politics and Heritage in the Eastern Mediterranean and Middle East*, ed. Lynn Meskell (London: Routledge, 1988), 11–23 (14).

7. See James Cuno, *Who Owns Antiquity? Museums and the Battle over Our Ancient Heritage* (Princeton: Princeton University Press, 2008), 67–87.

8. The fine marble example from Lycia of a gladiator relief (now in the Royal Ontario Museum) has three tiers. A four-tiered tombstone fragment from the Appian Way is now held at the Musei Capitolini in Rome.

Figure 1. The Colossae gladiator relief mortared into a modern wall. Photograph by the author.

It contains a distinct pair of gladiators in each tier with one member of another pair in the lower register at left. The upper register also has a standing shield at the left, featuring an *umbo* (a boss) centered in a horizontal rib of a slightly curvilinear shield, with a figure's foot at its bottom left. Rarely for such friezes, there is a herm edging the right border that both marks the limit of the presentation of the action (with the legs of the vanquished crooked against it) and yet also draws attention because of the turned face of the victor. There is no border at the left, indicating that the frieze communicated an extended portrayal of gladiator (or possibly including *venator*) combat, perhaps similar to such panels known from Selçuk, Istanbul, and many other museums in the Mediterranean. Whether this relief delivered a typological or narrative sequence cannot be determined, though it conforms with many such reliefs by ending at the lower right with a defeated gladiator, prostrate on the ground.

In this fragment a number of different gladiator types are visible, in combat with one another, probably as members of different squads (*pali*). From upper left to bottom right, these are, with some degree of certainty in spite of the abraded and fragmentary state of the stone, a *provocator*, a *retiarius*, a *thraex*, a fallen *secutor*, and triumphant *retiarius*. Gladiators were armed and armored in different ways, each conferring particular advantages and disadvantages, to add spice to the display and the manner of defeat/death.

In the top register, the *provocator* (at the left), sports an angled-brim helmet and heavy armor (especially apparent in the greave on his leading leg). He was the gladiator usually charged to initiate the action. The straps across his back that held a breastplate (the *cardiophylax*) in position can also be seen, and perhaps the leather binding that was wrapped around his right knee. His right arm is heavily strapped with a dense cloth *manica*. The combatant appears to have been a *retiarius* going by the heavily bandaged left arm and the band across his back to hold his shoulder and neck protection (the *galerus*) in place. His leggings also seem shorter and lighter, exactly what was needed for this quick-moving fighter. Though normally given from a crouched position, his raised right arm (and finger?) may indicate surrender—quite advisable given that he seems to have lost his trident, although the *provocator* also appears to have surrendered his shield (at the left?).

The upright shield at the left of the *provocator* may have been claimed by the referee (the *rudis*), whose foot alone remains in the fragment at the extreme left. There were rules governing the gladiatorial contests, administered by these referees, who wore distinctive clothing (usually a purple-banded white tunic). Needless to say, they maintained a discrete distance from the flurry of the event, exercising their interventions with a suitably lengthy wand.

There may also have been some conventions of honor between combatants, erratically applied, it seems, if a declamation credited to the rhetorician Quintilian is any indication, where one man stood in as gladiator for a friend only to meet his death in the stadium (Quintilian, *Major Declamation* 9).[9] But of the detail of regulations and customs we know little.[10]

In the lower register, at the left, there is only one partial gladiator remaining. He is probably a *thraex* type, going by the helmet that retains an indication of a crest bending back at the top (intruding into the molding) and a possible hint of a small convex shield (the *parmula*). Whoever he is fighting is lost from the piece. But the next section along retains the stock pair of combatants, both wearing the standard thick belts above their loincloths.

The *retiarius* sports no helmet and has a heavily manacled left arm topped with the remains of the shoulder deflector (the *galerus*). He exalts over a fallen *secutor*, who has honored his vow—the *sacramentum gladiatorium*[11]—and lies prostrate. He still wears his longer-finned brim helmet,

---

9. Gerot Krapinger, ed., *[Quintilian] Der Gladiator (Grössere Deklamationen, 9)* (Cassino: Università degli Studi di Cassino, 2007).

10. See Michael Carter, "Gladiatorial Combat: The Rules of Engagement," *CJ* 102 (2006/2007): 97–113; see also Kathleen M. Coleman, "Valuing Others in the Gladiatorial Barracks," in *Valuing Others in Classical Antiquity*, ed. Ralph M. Rosen and Ineke Sluiter, Mnemosyne Supplements (Leiden: Brill, 2010), 419–45.

11. *Uri, vinciri, verberari, ferroque necari patior*, "I submit to be burned, to be bound, to be beaten and killed by an iron weapon." See Seneca, *Epistle* 4.37.1 (omit-

belt, and thick quilted wrapping (his *manica*) on his right arm and perhaps shows his greave legging (*ocrea*) on his left leg slightly elevated above his right. But he is "nude," that is, without his weaponry, which has been seized and raised victoriously by his conqueror.

A rare element in this fragment is the herm, toward which the victor turns. Such an element in a gladiator relief is known from a highly fragmentary section from Aphrodisias,[12] but without the features found in this example from Colossae. The herm was an honorific sculpture, a long stone, squared around its perimeter, containing a head at the top and, if male, genitalia protruding at the middle (indicating dignity and virility).[13] Under Roman improvisation, the herm structure was applied to portraiture, as in dedications to a patron, but the usual focus was to a god. The particular god of the gladiatorial contest was Nemesis, and there appears to be a hint of a wheel protruding onto the relief molding.[14] In the photograph this is accented somewhat by the seepage of pigment from the black mortar used in the modern embedding. The use of a herm for a female god or attendant is rare, though not unknown,[15] but I have not found a clear

---

ting *verberari*); cf. 7.4–5; 71.23; Petronius, *Satyricon* 117.5–6. (Unless otherwise stated, editions of ancient texts are from the LCL.) On the gladiator oath, see Georges Ville, *La gladiature en occident des origins à la mort de Domitien* (Rome: École française de Rome, 1981), 246–55.

12. See A. C. Hrychuk Kontokosta, "Gladiatorial Reliefs and Élite Funerary Monuments," in *Aphrodisias Papers 4: New Research on the City and Its Monuments*, ed. by Christopher Ratté and R. R. R. Smith (Portsmouth, RI: Journal of Roman Archaeology, 2008), 190–229 (200, 222–23) (taken to be a herm of Hermes Engonios).

13. Hermes Enagonios ("of the games") was sometimes adopted by gladiators from his patronage of athletic contests (Pindar, *Pythian Ode* 2.10; Pausanias, *Travels* 5.14.9; Athenaeus, *Deipnosophists* 11.490–491 [quoting Simonides]; P.Oxy. 1015) and would, if intended, have invited the genitalia here. But Nemesis, the goddess of inevitability (see *BE* 1963.278 for a striking dual dedication to Καιρὸς Κάλος and Nemesis; this captures Nemesis better than the myopic accent on "Vengeance"), appears to have been the dominant divine arbiter of the arena combat. See Louis Robert, *Les gladiateurs dans l'Orient grec* (Amsterdam: Hakkert, 1971 [Fr. orig. 1940]), 64.

14. On the wheel as a marker of Nemesis, see Michael B. Hornum, *Nemesis, the Roman State and the Games* (Leiden: Brill, 1993), 24–28, 322–25.

15. See Yulia Ustinova, *The Supreme Gods of the Bosporan Kingdom: Celestial Aphrodite and the Most High God* (Leiden: Brill, 1999), 33–38. Some of the herms from the famous sanctuary of Nemesis in Rhamnous have sometimes been identified as female though this is contested: see Olga Palagia and David Lewis, "The Ephebes of Erechtheis, 333/2 BC and Their Dedication," *ABSA* 84 (1989): 333–44 at 337–39.

parallel to its support for Nemesis.[16] However, Nemesis *is* one of the gods familiarly patronizing activities at a theater, stadium, or amphitheater. A sanctuary of some type, a Nemeseion, actually formed part of the theater building complex at Ephesos, Side, Perge, and Mylasa.[17] Certainly one finds dedications to Nemesis at theaters that have undergone some modification so that spectacles can be staged.[18] More pertinently, gladiators are recorded as offering dedications to Nemesis at Aphrodisias, Harlicarnassos, and, by association, at Ephesos or Smyrna.[19]

Because gladiatorial games were a development of Roman rule in Asia Minor, the contests appear to have become a crucial display of the imperial cult even though the games themselves were already well-entrenched by the late Republic.[20] Although the absence of a specific location for this relief from Colossae compounds the difficulty of dating, the religious accent in the fragment indicated by the *retiarius*'s turn to the herm comports with

---

16. Michael Hornum (*Nemesis, the Roman State*) carries no mention of a herm, though the study is not exhaustive.

17. Hrychuk Kontokosta, "Gladiatorial Reliefs," 194.

18. For example, at the theaters at Thasos (*SEG* 57.818) and at Pessinus (*SEG* 47.1699); see at Lappa on Crete (*SEG* 59.1059). Nemesis is mentioned in second-century-CE alphabetical oracles at Hierapolis, one of Colossae's close neighbours in the Lycus Valley. See Tullia Ritti, "Oracoli alfabetici a Hierapolis di Frigia," *Miscellanea greca e romana* 14 (1989): 245–86, though such oracle forms were quite standardized with occasional local variations. Compare the similar form from Tymbriada in Pisidia (*SEG* 38.1328), which affirms (in a paronomasial play on words) that apportioning justice for human beings lies completely in her hands: Ἡ Νέμεσις ἀνθρώποισι τὴν δίκην νέμει (l.7). Nemesis therefore enjoyed devotion in a sweep from Macedonia to the East and was frequently found in the context of the performance of spectacles. See E. Bouley, "Le culte de Nemesis et les jeux de l'amphithéâtre dans les provinces balkaniques et danubiennes" in *Spectacula I: Gladiateurs et amphitheatres*, ed. Claude Domergue, Christian Landes, and Jean-Marie Pailler (France: Aimgo, 1990), 241–51; Hornum, *Nemesis, the Roman State*, supra.

19. For Aphrodisias, see Angelos Chaniotis, "Aphrodite's Rivals: Devotion to Local and Other Gods at Aphrodisias," *Cahiers Glotz* 21 (2010): 235–48 at 240–41, though the connection of the votive with Nemesis is Chaniotis's deduction. For Halicarnassos, see Robert, *Gladiateurs*, 182–83 (§179, and p. 42. For Ephesos or Smyrna, see Christopher P. Jones, "A Statuette of Nemesis," *Epigraphica Anatolica* 33 (2001): 45–47. The statuette was a dedicatory gift for the association of *philoploi*—what today we might call gladiator groupies or cheer squads!

20. See generally Tullia Ritti and Salim Yılmaz, *Gladiatori e venationes a Hierapolis di Frigia* (Rome: Accademia nazionale dei Lincei, 1998); Michael Carter, "*Archiereis* and Asiarchs: A Gladiatorial Perspective," *GRBS* 44 (2004): 41–68.

the characteristic of so much of social and cultural life in the Roman imperial period. Religion cannot be divorced from the world of gladiators, the more particularly because religion was interwoven with the setting in which many cities housed gladiatorial performances—the theater.[21] This, combined with *comparanda* from other cities in the province, is highly suggestive of a first- to third-century date for the relief. But in addition to the principle of comparison with evidence from other sites, it is important to place the artifact in the context of other known material from the same site. Though in the case of Colossae the pickings are slim,[22] the beginnings of the civic context for gladiatorial shows can be offered.

We know of two agonothetes of the third century CE who would likely have had some responsibility for the games,[23] as also, from coins, three holders of the office of stephanophoros.[24] In the second century, a certain brother of one Heliodoros appears to have had a crucial leadership position in Colossae.[25] Among an array of civic offices that he held, he led the Colossian delegation "in the sacrifices at the second temple" (συνθύσας τῷ δευτέρῳ να[ῷ], 1.10), which Louis Robert takes as a reference to an imperial sanctuary.[26] It is probably a reference to the second neokorate temple at Ephesos (131/132 CE) rather than that of Pergamon (113/114 CE) or Smyrna (124 CE) given the notable emphasis on Artemis in Colossae's coinage[27] and a further office mentioned in the same inscription that

---

21. See Alison Futrell, *Blood in the Arena: The Spectacle of Roman Power* (Austin: University of Texas Press, 1997), 79, though her accent is the amphitheater. Additionally, see John Arthur Hanson, *Roman Theater-Temples* (Princeton: Princeton University Press, 1959), 85–89; and Richard C. Beacham, *Spectacle Entertainments of Early Imperial Rome* (New Haven: Yale University Press, 1999), 27, 32.

22. The call for the survey and excavation of Colossae goes back at least to William Buckler and William Calder, *Monumenta Asiae Minoris Antiqua*, vol. 6, *Monuments and Documents from Phrygia and Caria* (Manchester: Manchester University Press, 1939), xi.

23. Heracleon (*MAMA* 6.41) and Tatianos (*MAMA* 6.40).

24. Hans Silvius von Aulock, *Münzen und Städte Phrygiens* (Tübingen: Wasmuth, 1980, 1987), vol. 2, §§586–88, 594–95, for Menekles, Nigros, and Aurelius Makrianos.

25. LBW 1693b = IGRR 4.870 as corrected by Louis Robert, "Les Inscriptions," in Gagniers, *Laodicée du Lycos*, 247–389 (269, 277–78).

26. *BE* 1970.584.

27. In the extant imperial coins of Colossae, now numbering about 190 coins (with auctioned coins added to the list in von Aulock), almost one-third carry some manifestation of Artemis, whether Ephesiaca or the hunter. The fullest published list is in von Aulock, *Münzen und Städte Phrygiens*, 2:83–94.

pushes the date toward the middle of the second century.[28] The inscription mentions the important provision that Heliodoros's brother delivered at the time of "the/a grain shortage" (ἐν σειτοδείᾳ, l.8) for civic and imperial needs. The fact that this is listed among the various offices the honorand held, along with a notation that grain was supplied at "favorable rates" (ἐπὶ τὸ εὐωνότερον, l.9) indicates how significant a shortage it was. The most pressing instance of famine known in the region appears to come from the time of Lucius Verus, around 162 CE.[29] Last, there is an inscription honoring the emperor Trajan that was erected by Apphia, daughter of Heracleon, the priestess of Zeus[30]—probably the patron god of the city of Colossae. The interconnection of honors for the emperor and the religious focus of Colossae would suggest that she may have had some responsibility for the provision of gladiatorial games.[31] So from the time of Trajan (98–117 CE) to that of Trebonianus Gallus (251–53 CE) there is evidence from Colossae of those officials in place so that gladiatorial games could be mounted. Of course, none of this evidence mentions gladiators, just as our overall evidence from Colossae is meager. The most that can be deduced is that the civic infrastructure in place was capable of providing for such games. The visit of Hadrian to the city on his pan-Hellenic tour in 129 CE[32]

---

28. William Ramsay contented himself with an "uncertain date" (*Cities and Bishoprics of Phrygia* [Oxford: Clarendon, 1895–1897], 1:212). David Magie combined "the imperial period" with "second or third centuries" (*Roman Rule in Asia Minor: To the End of the Third Century after Christ* [Princeton: Princeton University Press, 1950], 986 n. 22).

29. See Clinton E. Arnold, *The Colossian Syncretism: The Interface between Christianity and Folk Belief at Colossae* (Grand Rapids: Baker, 1996), 129.

30. *IGRR* 4.868. Some ambiguity has been noted for the reconstruction of the text, with the possibility that instead of the τοῦ Διὸς Κο[λοσσηνοῦ, Zeus of the Kolossians, or τοῦ Διοσκο[υρίδου (Heracleon) son of Dioskorides. (Διοσκορίδου is a possible variant on the name); see Robert, "Inscriptions," 278–79, followed perhaps too confidently by Ulrich Huttner, *Early Christianity in the Lycus Valley* (Leiden: Brill, 2013), 44 n. 123. However, one would expect the ἱέ]ρεια at the end of the inscription (though succeeded by a sign) to bear some explicatory designation (see *SEG* 25.118; 28.848; *CIG* 2900; *SEG* 59.237 for a few of many examples of both antecedent and subsequent qualifiers).

31. The responsibility of a high priestess for gladiatorial contests is clear in *IMT* 1498 (Cyzikus).

32. The key inscription is *IGRR* 4.869, an honorific dedication to Hadrian Olympios. See Wilhelm Weber, *Untersuchungen zur Geschichte des Kaisers Hadrianus* (Leipzig: Teubner, 1907), 223; H.-G. Pflaum, *Les Carrières Procuratoriennes Équestres sous le Haut-Empire romain* (Paris: Geuthner, 1960), 1:263; Anna S. Benjamin, "The

is strongly suggestive that such a Roman mark of loyalty would be on display. But precisely because of this array of implicit evidence, wedded with the discovery of the relief itself, the presence of gladiators in the civic life of Colossae is likely to have been in place at least by the first century CE.

2. Romanization and/or Appropriation

Gladiator and *venator* contests became a feature in most of the cities across the Roman world from the last decades of the Republic. Amphitheaters, one of the main venues for the performances,[33] range from Isurium in the north of England to Dura Europos on the eastern boundary. Gladiators infiltrate almost every artistic and not-so-artistic medium, from coins to lamps, from glassware to jewelry, from bronze statuettes to terracotta figurines, from mosaics to funerary reliefs, from frescoes to roughly executed graffiti sketches.

One of the transformations of space that gladiatorial and venatorial spectacles wrought was in the architecture of the theater. Although amphitheaters and stadia were sometimes built in Asia,[34] such as we find at Priene and Laodikeia, existing Greek-style theaters were frequently transformed so as to accommodate the spectacles while ensuring the safety of the spectators.[35] This meant an expansion of the *scaena*, a raising of the platform supporting the front seats along with a construction of a parapet

---

Altars of Hadrian in Athens and Hadrian's Panhellenic Program," *Hesperia* 32 (1963): 57–86 at 82; Helmut Halfmann, *Itinera principum: Geschichte und Typologie der Kaiserreisen im Römischen Reich* (Stuttgart: Steiner, 1986), 206. To this should be added the restoration of the city's authority to mint its own coins during the rule of Hadrian. Olympian Hadrian was also honored in a Colossian coin (von Aulock, *Münzen und Städte Phrygiens*, §547). Von Aulock's listing of a coin from the reign of Caligula (§545) has been rejected: Andrew Burnett, Michel Amandry, and Pau Ripollès, *Roman Provincial Coinage: Supplement 1* (London: British Museum Press, 1998), 35 §2891.

33. The amphitheater was perhaps derived from the shape of the forum, which seems to have been the original venue. See Katherine E. Welch, *The Roman Amphitheatre from Its Origins to the Colosseum* (Cambridge: Cambridge University Press, 2007), 30–71.

34. Jesper Carlsen lists only three: at Cyzicus, Pergamon, and Nysa: "Gladiators in Ancient Halikarnassos," in ΛΑΒΡΥΣ: *Studies Presented to Pontus Hellström*, ed. Lars Karlsson, Susanne Carlsson, and Jesper Blid Kullberg (Uppsala: Uppsala Universitet, 2014), 441–50 (441).

35. Welch, *Roman Amphitheatre*, 164–78.

wall, greater control over ingress and egress especially in and around the *ima* (lower) *cavea* and elaboration of the rooms, stalls, and conduits of protagonists.[36]

Given that there is no indication of a stadium at Colossae, it is likely that the theater received extensive modification some time in the first century BCE to first century CE.[37] The shape of the *cavea* as presently visible has a slightly ovular extension, consistent with some Greek theaters. It has been estimated that a further bank of twelve to fifteen rows of seats lie beneath the surface.[38] By calculation from the diameter of the theater and comparison with other similar-sized theaters (such as Iguvium in Italy and Priene on the coast of Asia), it can be estimated that the capacity of Colossae's theatre was five to seven thousand people. The theater was the prime venue for a range of social gatherings, from dramatic and comic performances to the honors accorded leading athletes.[39] And it would have been the venue for the welcome extended to the emperor Hadrian on his pan-Hellenic tour, a welcome that, for all the Hellenistic coloring that Hadrian was cultivating, yet looked for marks of fidelity to and imitation of Rome. The theater and baths were prime candidates for such visual impressions.

But there was an added component to such Romanizing practices. The theater was one of the major places of reinforcement of social stratification. Seating places were carefully allocated, fanning out and up from the privileged seats for the agonothetes, other civic leaders, and esteemed visitors.

---

36. Louise Revell suggests that the architectural restructuring was also a form of social engineering to maintain the distinctions between the honorable and the shameful: *Roman Imperialism and Local Identities* (Cambridge: Cambridge University Press, 2009), 170–72.

37. The multiple functions of a theater are succinctly described by Frank Sear, *Roman Theatres: An Architectural Study* (Oxford: Oxford University Press, 2006), 40–42.

38. H. H. Baysal, "Le antiche città della valle del Lykos/Lykos Vadisindeki antik kentler," in *Ricerche Archeologiche Turche nella Valle del Lykos/Lykos Vadisi Türk Arkeoloji Arastirmalari*, ed. Francesco d'Andria and Francesca Silvestrelli (Lecce: Congredo Editore, 2000), 19–41 (24–25).

39. Such as Markos Aurelios Zenon, a Colossian athlete, who in the third century CE was successful at the games held at neighboring Tripolis *MAMA* 6.40 = *BCH* 11 (1887): 353 §11. For an overview of the theater, see my *Fragments of Colossae* (Adelaide: ATF Press, 2015), ch. 4.

Figure 2. A bema and lion-clawed seat edge from the theater at Colossae.

The *Lex Julia Theatralis* of Augustus reflected the emperor's concerns to enforce rigidly social distinctions, a significant change from the demic pattern of the Greek theater,[40] even as Augustus promoted the use of the theater for such events (Suetonius, *Augustus* 23). Slaves were confined to standing positions at the back of the theater. Women were separated from men. Special places were set aside for young men in training, for returned veterans, for guilds or "voluntary associations" such as the one called "The Friends" (οἱ ἑταῖροι) that we know had a group in Colossae.[41]

---

40. Arjan Zuiderhoek, "On the Political Sociology of the Imperial Greek City," *GRBS* 48 (2008): 417–45 (425); see, generally, Elizabeth Rawson, "Discrimina Ordinum: The Lex Julia Theatralis," *Papers of the British School at Rome* 55 (1987): 83–114.

41. *MAMA* 6.47. Ulrich Huttner (*Lycus Valley*, 31) suggests that another inscription from Colossae (*MAMA* 6.48) that credits an epitaph to the συγγενικὸν νειώτερον may indicate another association or phratry.

With regard to the individual named in figure 3, there is some dispute over the name of the honorand. Buckler and Calder took the name as masculine—Γλύκων (implying the right hand figure in the frame: *MAMA* 6.154); Tullia Ritti thinks similarly but takes the name as Γλυκωνᾶς (Tullia Ritti, H. H. Baysal, E. Miranda, and F. Guizza, *Museo archeologico di Denizli-Pamukkale: Catalogo delle iscrizioni latine e greche. Distretto di Denizli* [Naples: Università degli Studi, 2008], 198). Philip Harland takes the honor to be for a woman (implying the lefthand figure) (Γλύκωνα "Funerary Honors by Companions for Glykona [I–II CE]," *Associations in the Greco-Roman World: A Companion to the Sourcebook*, http://www.philipharland.com/greco-roman-associations/?p=12300). However, neither Γλυκωνᾶς nor Γλύκωνα is found in *LGPN* 5A and 5B. The usual feminine form is Γλυκωνίς. In addition, the standard iconography of such funerary epitaphs privileges the person on the right (in the perspective of the viewer). The masculine form is Doric.

While doubt may be entertained as to how far and how intensely the imperial edict influenced the East,[42] it is clear that seats were demarcated for various individuals and groups. Thus not only did the appeal of gladiatorial contests infuse Roman *virtus* into popular consciousness, but the social engineering that came as part of the package was clearly and markedly orchestrated as well.

But there is one critical component of the promotion of gladiator contests in the East that gives an insight into how closely tied to Rome these were. The groups of gladiators, the *familia gladiatorum* (φαμιλία μονομάχων), were usually owned and the contests arranged by the high priests/priestesses of the imperial cult in both province and local city, though private benefactions and even shows for profit-making occurred.[43] But the connection between the theater and the religious life of the city and region was pronounced, not only with altars and iconographic statues in position in the theater itself but also in the thoroughfare lines between temple and theater that combined festivities with ritual.[44]

Figure 3. The epitaph from "The Friends" that honors Gluko.

A two-hundred-year gap separates the first report of gladiatorial contests in Rome and in Asia. In Rome, the contests were part of the funeral

---

42. It clearly gained approval from some in the West, an indication perhaps of its implementation; see Suetonius, *Augustus* 44.

43. Guy Chamberland, "A Gladiatorial Show produced *in sordidam mercedem* (Tacitus *Ann.* 4.62)," *Phoenix* 61 (2007): 136–49 (137). It is too exacting to claim that "gladiatorial games and animal hunts were an exclusive feature of the emperor cult" as does Huttner, *Lycus Valley*, 66.

44. A close examination of Georg Weber's late nineteenth-century sketch of Colossae reveals a temple (now no longer visible) on the artificial acropolis of the biconical höyük approximately 160 m northwest of the theater: Georg Weber, "Der unterirdische Lauf des Lykos bei Kolossai," *MDAI, Athenische Abteilung* 16 (1891): 194–99 (195).

honors provided for Decimus Iunius Brutus Scaeva/Pera in 264 BCE;[45] in Ephesos, the context was extensive performances celebrating the Roman general Lucius Licinius Lucullus in 69 BCE (Plutarch, *Life of Lucullus* 23.1), apparently as part of the reestablishment of Roman authority in Asia toward the end of the Mithridatic Wars.[46] Plutarch's eulogizing notice is worth quoting in full:

> Λούκουλλος δὲ τὴν Ἀσίαν πολλῆς μὲν εὐνομίας, πολλῆς δ' εἰρήνης ἐμπεπληκὼς οὐδὲ τῶν πρὸς ἡδονὴν καὶ χάριν ἠμέλησεν, ἀλλὰ πομπαῖς καὶ πανηγύρεσιν ἐπινικίοις καὶ ἀγῶσιν ἀθλητῶν καὶ μονομάχων ἐν Ἐφέσῳ καθήμενος ἐδημαγώγει τὰς πόλεις, αἱ δ' ἀμειβόμεναι Λουκούλλειά τε ἦγον ἐπὶ τιμῇ τοῦ ἀνδρός, καὶ τῆς τιμῆς ἡδίονα τὴν ἀληθινὴν εὔνοιαν αὐτῷ παρεῖχον.

> Lucullus, after filling Asia to the brim with good order and peace, did not neglect the things which procure pleasure and favour, but during his stay at Ephesus won over the cities by means of processions and victory festivals and contests of athletes and gladiators. In exchange, the cities celebrated festivals which they called Lucullea, to do honour to the man, and bestowed upon him what is sweeter than honour, their genuine good-will.[47]

Although it must be acknowledged that Plutarch frequently uses a life simply as an arena in which to play out his own preferred values, there is more here than Jerome Murphy-O'Connor's dismissive assessment: "Circuses were a crude bribe to win loyalty, but if it worked in Rome, why not elsewhere?"[48] Plutarch is writing a little after the time that a letter to the Colossians is also being penned. His rendition reflects the imperial cast on

---

45. Livy, *Periochae* 16; Servius, *Commentary on the Aeneid* 3.67; Valerius Maximus 2.4.7 (trans H. J. Walker); Ausonius, *Griphus ternarii numeri* 36–37. See the discussion in Futrell, *Blood in the Arena*, 20–22.

46. There is also the notice of Polybius that Antiochus IV Epiphanes introduced a huge number of gladiators into the festivities at Daphne, near Antioch, in 166/165 BCE. See Rolf Strootman, "The Hellenistic Royal Courts: Court Culture, Ceremonial and Ideology in Greece, Egypt and the Near East, 336–30 BCE" (PhD diss., University of Utrecht 2007), 309–13.

47. Translation from Manuel Tröster, *Themes, Character and Politics in Plutarch's Life of Lucullus: The Construction of a Roman Aristocrat* (Stuttgart: Steiner, 2008), 38.

48. Jerome Murphy-O'Connor, *St. Paul's Ephesus: Texts and Archaeology* (Collegeville, MN: Liturgical Press, 2008), 126. In some ways, this is but a reiteration of some ancient attitudes; see, for example, Pseudo-Quintilian, *Minor Declarations* 260.13, 24.

empire, not the republican. These contests were laced with political, social, and cultic elements.[49]

It may sound obvious, but these "circuses" gained literary notice. Literary works rather than inscriptions are the sources for the early accounts. Modern Europeans have felt somehow confirmed in their own cultural values by hauling out those literary sources that are critical of gladiator contests.[50] But whether it be Pliny, Polybius, or Plutarch, the gladiatorial games were viewed as reinforcing Roman values; the foundation is distinctly Roman; it drives architectural developments; and it enhances the aristocratic rule of Roman society in a reciprocal exchange, where benefactors gain a prized return of confirmation of their social position and influence. The games were a *munus*, a duty that devolved on those who held significant rank and office in Roman society.

There is one element in Plutarch's description that stands out because it appears to touch on what has been noted, especially by Christian Mann, as a point of distinction between Western and Eastern perspectives on gladiators.[51] Plutarch writes of Lucullus increasingly exercising sway over the cities of Asia "by means of processions and victory festivals and contests of athletes and gladiators" (πομπαῖς καὶ πανηγύρεσιν ἐπινικίοις καὶ ἀγῶσιν ἀθλητῶν καὶ μονομάχων).[52] The total combination is significant: processions through to gladiator contests are all deemed to be part of what holds the polity together. But, in particular, the agonistic contests *combine* athletes and gladiators. It does not mean that athletics and combat were combined in the same program, but it does point to the *agones* having a range of constituents. And this is precisely one of the main distinguishing marks that Christian Mann discerns in the reception and perception of gladiators in the East. He notes that epitaphal formulae for gladiators in the East are longer than those in the West and draw on athletic evocations to extol the deceased.[53] Of special significance is the work of Dieter

---

49. See Elizabeth A. Castelli, *Martyrdom and Memory: Early Christian Culture Making* (New York: Columbia University Press, 2004), 112–17.

50. For example, Seneca, *Ep.* 7; Dio Chrysostom, *Or.* 31.121; Musonius Rufus, *Apollonius* (Philostratus, *Vit. Apoll.* 4.22); Lucian, *Demon.* 57.

51. Christian Mann, "Gladiators in the Greek East: A Case Study in Romanization," *International Journal of the History of Sport* 26 (2009): 272–97.

52. The language of "winning over" is very similar to that used by Suetonius of Julius Caesar's use of gladiator contests; see Suetonius, *Julius* 11 (*conciliato populi favore*).

53. Mann, "Gladiators in the Greek East," 284–87.

Knibbe, Wolfgang Pietsch, Fabian Kanz, and Karl Grossschmidt in Ephesus.[54] Knibbe had discovered in 1993 a gladiator cemetery (dated second-third century CE) 300 m from the stadium just outside the Northern/Koressos Gate and in a prominent position in the landscape of the city, at the north foot of Panayırdağ.[55] It was located close to the processional way linking the city to the main temple, that of great Artemis of the Ephesians. Every two or three weeks during the early Roman imperial period, a procession would pass along that processional way,[56] and while Artemis might be the formal focus, the gladiator cemetery was located so as to be in full view. Given that young men, ephebes, were expressly mentioned in the Salutaris inscription (IEph 1a.27, dated 104 CE)[57] as involved in the procession to enhance their education in civic responsibilities,[58] gladiators, even or especially in death, became part of the lesson.[59] One wonders whether gladiators could form part of the procession, however, given that in Roman law they were banned from entry into temples (Seneca, *Controversies* 1.2.4).[60] Moreover, the analysis of the exhumed bones of the

---

54. W. Pietsch and E. Trinkl, "Grabungsbericht der Kampagnen 1992/93," *Bericht und Materialien Österreichisches Archäologisches Institut* 6 (1995): 19–48; W. Pietsch, "Außerstädtische Grabanlagen von Ephesos," in *100 Jahre Österreichische Forschung in Ephesos, Akten des Symposions Wien 1999*, ed. Herwig Friesinger and Fritz Krinzinger (Vienna: Österreichische Akademie der Wissenschaften, 1999), 455–60; Fabian Kanz and Karl Grossschmidt, "Stand der anthropologischen Forschung zum Gladiatorenfriedhof in Ephesos," *Jahresheft des Österreichischen Archäologischen Institutes* 74 (2005): 103–23; and Kanz and Grossschmidt, "Head injuries of Roman gladiators," *Forensic Science International* 160 (2006): 207–16.

55. 20 m² were excavated. Panayırdağ means "festival mountain."

56. Guy MacLean Rogers, *The Sacred Identity of Ephesus: Foundation Myths of a Roman City* (London: Routledge, 1991).

57. 250 ephebes were intended to form part of the procession.

58. Jason König, *Athletics and Literature in the Roman Empire* (Cambridge: Cambridge University Press, 2013), 67–68.

59. Just such a lesson on death, incorporating the example of gladiators, is in Seneca, *Ep.* 37. Seneca is, however, particularly concerned to use the example for an a fortiori argument, privileging the willing engagement with death that is the requirement of the philosopher. On Seneca's use of gladiator imagery, see Mireille Armisen-Marchetti, Sapientiae facies: *étude sur les images de Sénèque* (Paris: Belles Lettres, 1989), 124–26; Christine Richardson-Hay "*Mera homicidia*: A Philosopher Draws Blood—Seneca and the Gladiatorial Games," *Prudentia* 36 (2004): 87–146.

60. Such a ban continued into Christian times, with gladiators prevented, at least in some parts of the empire, from being baptized; see Hippolytus, *Apostolic Tradition* 16.

sixty-seven gladiators has revealed not only the quality of the diet and intensity of training of their regimen, but also, from the injuries received, the regulatory control exercised by the *rudis*, the referee.[61] It is clear from the position, the cost and attention given to gladiators and their burials and the sometimes expansive and decorated funerary inscriptions, that gladiators could gain an esteemed position. They were in their manner of death, in Thomas Wiedemann's words, "great Romans,"[62] even if in life they remained *infames*.[63]

It may be true that there is a paradox of mimicry here where those whose status is that of the outcast in Roman society—criminals, slaves, and captives of war—yet exemplify Roman *virtus* in the face of death.[64] There are two notable exchanges that pass in the other direction. The first has already been mentioned briefly. Romanization in the East was not untrammelled and unidirectional.[65] That is, the adoption of gladiator contests, with all its impact on architecture and cult, nevertheless was viewed differently. This is a period of massive cultural upheaval. The advent of imperial rule not only meant nuanced distinction between East and West (provincial currency mintings are a clear indication of this) but also provided the opportunity for significant cultural adjustments—the so-called second sophistic is simply a broad, unwieldy classification for this.[66] Gladiatorial contests may have become widespread throughout Asia (as elsewhere), but the way they were viewed by the various local audiences was not necessarily identical. Gladiators may not have been incorporated into Olympics,[67] but the language of such contests, *agones*, was appropriated. Their epitaphs can be festooned with laurel crowns and palm fronds, given lengthy, even metrical inscriptions—all appeals to the agonistic traditions traditionally associated with athletes.[68] Such allusions were sometimes

---

61. Kanz and Grossschmidt, "Head Injuries," 216.
62. Thomas Weidemann, *Emperors and Gladiators* (London: Routledge, 1992), 35.
63. Theodosian, *Digest* 28.2.3 pr.
64. Cavan W. Concannon, "'Not for an Olive Wreath, but Our Lives': Gladiators, Athletes and Early Christian Bodies," *JBL* 133 (2014): 193–214 (197).
65. See Mann, "Gladiators in the Greek East," passim; Concannon, "Gladiators, Athletes," 195 n. 4.
66. See the criticism of the "second sophistic" in König, *Athletics and Literature*, 15.
67. Mann, "Gladiators in the Greek East," 279.
68. See, for example, the metrical inscription for Diodorus from Amisos mentioned below. Though not gladiatorial, at Colossae there is a metrical inscription honoring Kastor the pugilist from Colossae (*JHS* 18 [1898]: 90 §26; Reinhold Merkelbach

strengthened by connection with ancient heroes, by use of the term itself (ἥρων),[69] by the names adopted by the gladiators,[70] by reference to grandiose Homeric or military associations, by use of the boxing word πύξ as the word for the contest, and/or by the honor brought to the gladiator's homeland/city. As Concannon observes, "Greek gladiators, in their own self-presentation, sought to construct an image of themselves and their craft that was thoroughly rooted in Greek heroic and athletic traditions."[71] In this sense, even though the gladiator phenomena can be tracked to Roman cultivation, in the cities of Asia it assumed not a Roman but a Greek identity, though with sufficiently close proximation as to satisfy the demand for *fides*. And that identity made gladiators an agonistic example within society rather than at the margins seeking integration.[72] This is where the second aspect of exchange becomes important.

From the first century, a curious literary motif begins to be discerned, even among those Roman *literati* who otherwise sniff at gladiators.[73] Quite apart from borrowing gladiators as trainers for soldiers or as personal bodyguards,[74] imagery derived from the gladiatorial contest is found in Roman writers. This goes beyond the use of gladiators in positing an excruciating problem for Roman legal debate, such as we find in Pseudo-Quintilian's *Major Declamation* 9.[75] Rather the very act of oratory and training as an orator is sometimes compared with that of gladiators. Oratory, one of the avenues of agonistic struggle, called on metaphors

---

and Josef Stauber, *Steinepigramme aus dem griechischen Osten*, vol. 1, *Die Westküste Kleinasiens von Knidos bis Ilion* [Leipzig: Teubner, 1998], 1.02.15.01).

69. The use of "hero" (like the use of crowning) became widespread in Asia in the imperial period, covering a wide range of recipients. One, a certain well-named Herakles, is known from Colossae: *MAMA* 6.42.

70. Though not all gladiators took the names of heroes. An example from Apollonia in Pisidia names a gladiator as "Barbaros" (*MAMA* 4.168), though Robert wondered if it should be counted among gladiator monuments (*Gladiateurs*, 61 n. 1).

71. Concannon, "Gladiators, Athletes," 203.

72. See Mann, "Gladiators in the Greek East," 287.

73. For example, Seneca, *Ep.* 7; see the general comments of Thomas Scanlon, "Contesting Ancient Mediterranean Sport," in *Sport in the Cultures of the Ancient World: New Perspectives*, ed. Zinon Papakonstantinou (London: Routledge, 2013), 1–12 (3).

74. See, for example, Suetonius, *Julius* 39.

75. See, generally, Krapinger, *Der Gladiator*; G. Brescia, "Gladiatori per 'caso': Modelli antropologici in [Quintiliano], Declamazioni maggiori, IX," *Rhetorica* 27 (2009): 294–311. Compare Pseudo-Quintilian, *Minor Declarations* 287.8; 302.

from gladiatorial contest.[76] Thus Seneca compares the toughness required of an orator to that of a fighter;[77] the school for training orators took as its metaphor the gladiator school with *tiro*, the word for inexperienced gladiators, used of novice orators.[78] The orator's craft readily drew in metaphors to spice up the argument—so the image of a wounded, terminal gladiator could be deployed for a stepmother.[79] The somewhat petulant Polemo compares his own activity, at least according to his biographer, to that of a gladiator-and-some, and he weights the description of his oratory with agonistic language that he regards as the fitting point of comparison with gladiatorial contest (Philostratus, *Vit. soph.* 25). Polemo's erstwhile oratorical antagonist Favorinus is reputed to have written an entire declamation known as "For the Gladiators" (Philostratus, *Vit. soph.* 8). What is most significant, however, is that even when making use of gladiator imagery, in the majority of instances the literary metaphor is used to contrast the exemplary with the less exemplary, even if it be grudgingly admired.[80] In this sense, the Eastern inscriptions may testify to greater success in the status-raising of gladiators than that of literary texts.

All this suggests, first, that the gladiatorial phenomenon had encroached not just on popular imagination but on the literary; second, that gladiatorial contests had become part of the suite of cultural practices that were viewed as serving the reinforcement of the fabric of social integration; third, that imagery by which to think about and present gladiators had blurred considerably with that of athletes, heroes, and even the military; and fourth, that such imagery was seen as pertinent if not fitting for metaphorical use in other spheres, such as oratory. Given that there is now evidence that the cultural phenomena and realia of gladiators was pres-

---

76. This may align with the cultural shift discerned by Carlin Barton (*The Sorrows of the Ancient Romans: The Gladiator and the Monster* [Princeton: Princeton University Press, 1993], 28), but it provides an indication that members of the aristocracy were enabled to transfer displays of *virtus* from the battlefield to oratory, in part using the imagery of gladiators to achieve that objective.

77. Seneca, *Controversies* 2 pref. 2: *deerat illi oratorium robur et ille pugnatorius mucro*. Compare also Pseudo-Quintilian, *Minor Declarations* 305.8, 16; 317.11.

78. Seneca, *Controversies* 3 pref. 12–13. The word *tiro* had been used of an army recruit but had passed into gladiator service (Suetonius, *Jul.* 26).

79. Seneca, *Controversies* 9.6.1. The imagery comes in a speech of Fulvius Sparsus. Compare Pseudo-Quintilian, *Minor Declarations* 382.2

80. So, for example, Seneca, *Ep.* 22.1; 30.8; 70.20; Pseudo-Quintilian, *Minor Declamations*, 260.24; 279.8; 305.16; 382.2.

ent in and known to Colossae, there is warrant to make some suggestions about one of the few writings associated with Colossae.

3. The Letter to the Colossians in Performance and Reception Register

Even though a venatorial metaphor is clearly in view in 1 Cor 15:32, commentators have been loath to tread the gladiatorial path in interpretation. The legacy of an age of denial that gladiators were a feature of the Eastern, Greek provinces and a more recent abhorrence of the violence of the arena have worked to isolate Pauline metaphors from a gladiatorial, or more generally, a spectatorial perspective, except when cast passively as in 1 Cor 15. Vic Pfitzner in "Was St Paul a Sports Enthusiast?" concentrates on the athletic dimensions of Pauline metaphors. He acknowledges that there may be a gap between authorial intention and audiential reception and, further, that at times there is some doubt as to whether military or athletic terminology is intended.[81] By placing the options in such a dichotomy, the particular contribution of gladiators and, more generally, spectacles is elided from consideration, although he admits into consideration, at least as part of the debate, the recent argument of Robert Seesengood that elements in the Pastoral Letters are sufficiently hybrid as to admit the gladiatorial dimension.[82] Alternately, gladiator imagery is occasionally worked into analysis by blurring the distinction between gladiators and athletics.[83] It is clear, I hope, from the analysis thus far that there is a tension in the degree of approval for gladiators between West and East and between higher and lower orders in society. What is significant, however, is that the Pauline corpus does not appear to carry any of the disdain or a fortiori structure that we find in the rhetoricians.[84] This observation requires fur-

---

81. Vic Pfitzner, "Was St Paul a Sports Enthusiast? Realism and Rhetoric in Pauline Athletic Metaphors," in *Sports and Christianity: Historical and Contemporary Perspectives*, ed. Nick J. Watson and Andrew Parker (London: Routledge, 2012), 89–111 (90–91).

82. Robert Paul Seesengood, *Competing Identities: The Athlete and the Gladiator* (London: T&T Clark, 2006). Seesengood finds a blending of soldier, athlete, and prisoner/gladiator in 1 Tim 4:7–10; 6:11–12; and 2 Tim 4:6–8 (pp. 50–52).

83. See, for example, Edgar Krentz, "Paul, Games and the Military," in *Paul in the Graeco-Roman World: A Handbook*, ed. J. Paul Sampley (Harrisburg, PA: Trinity Press International, 2003), 344–83 (347, 353).

84. So Krentz, "Paul, Games," 353.

ther consideration than can be given here, though I am inclined to see the intertwining of slavery, suffering, and display of *virtus* as a way forward.

Given that Colossae can now be shown, albeit incompletely, to have an array of festivities and games (including gladiator contests) like many Asian cities, then the assumption is warranted that this is part of the cultural atmosphere of those who live there. Colossae is not like Rhodes, for example, which was distinguished positively (in some perspectives) from those hedonistic, blood-baying "others" through eschewing such spectacles in its midst (Dio Chrysostom, *Oration* 31.121). Even without straining the concentration too hard, therefore, recipients of a letter in Colossae would likely "hear" certain metaphors in this register.

Plutarch's description of the mutually reinforcing array of provisions that the Roman general Lucullus underwrote for Ephesos and cities in the region provides a convenient general classification for elements in the Letter to the Colossians: "processions and victory festivals and contests of athletes and gladiators" (πομπαῖς καὶ πανηγύρεσιν ἐπινικίοις καὶ ἀγῶσιν ἀθλητῶν καὶ μονομάχων). Space prevents exploration of the detail here, but a number of sections in Colossians invite further consideration against such a background. I would mention Col 2:15, with its references to disarming (ἀπεκδύομαι), publicly displaying (δειγματίζω), and triumphing (θριαμβεύω);[85] 2:5, with references to "order" (τάξις) and "solidity" (στερέωμα);[86] and, perhaps most interestingly, 2:18, with its rudic reference to disqualification (καταβραβεύω) (cf. 3:15 βραβεύω). The poignant inscription from Amisos (modern Samsun, on the Pontus) captures the role that a rudis or an agonothete might play in an intervention into a contest, that lead to the overturning of a victory.[87] Jerome saw in the Colossians verse a reference to just such an intervention, stemming from the imagery of theater contest (Jerome, *Ep.* 121). The use of βαβρεύω in 3:15 also conveys the sense of a prize or victory.

---

85. This would be more so if the section is seen as an extension of Col 1:15–20: so James D. G. Dunn, *The Epistles to the Colossians and to Philemon* (Grand Rapids: Eerdmans, 1996), 167.

86. Compare 1 Macc 9:14.

87. *Studia Pontica* 3.7; see Michael Carter, "Blown Call? Diodorus and the Treacherous Summa Rudis," *ZPE* 177 (2011): 63–69.

Conclusion

Read against the backdrop of the various spectacles that were designed to ensure the cohesiveness of Colossian society, for which evidence in a small fragment now adds to our appreciation of those dynamics, imagery in the Letter to the Colossians takes on new significance. That gladiator metaphors were acceptable fodder for literary works reinforces the a priori foundation warranting investigation of their use in the Letter to the Colossians. Further testing of these dimensions remains to be done, awaiting not only a thorough treatment of the textual evidence both in and beyond the Letter to the Colossians but also the hope that further material testimony will come to light. The discovery of a fragment of a gladiator relief has at least provided the impetus for a reconsideration of the letter, now allowing for more than military or athletic imagery as an acceptable backdrop. The archaeological evidence therefore has prompted the beginnings of a review of at least the audiential reception of the letter, if not a reappraisal of authorial intent.

Bibliography

Armisen-Marchetti, Mireille. *Sapientiae facies: Étude sur les images de Sénèque*. Paris: Les belles lettres, 1989.
Arnold, Clinton E. *The Colossian Syncretism: The Interface between Christianity and Folk Belief at Colossae*. Grand Rapids: Baker, 1996.
Aulock, Hans Silvius von. *Münzen und Städte Phrygiens*. 2 vols. Tübingen: Wasmuth, 1980–1987.
Barton, Carlin A. *The Sorrows of the Ancient Romans: The Gladiator and the Monster*. Princeton: Princeton University Press, 1993.
Baysal, H. H. "Le antiche cittá della valle del Lykos/Lykos Vadisindeki antik kentler." Pages 19-41 in *Ricerche Archeologiche Turche nella Valle del Lykos/Lykos Vadisi Türk Arkeoloji Arastirmalari*. Edited by Francesco d'Andria and Francesca Silvestrelli. Lecce: Congredo Editore, 2000.
Benjamin, Anna S. "The Altars of Hadrian in Athens and Hadrian's Panhellenic Program." *Hesperia* 32 (1963): 57–86.
Bouley, E. "Le culte de Nemesis et les jeux de l'amphithéâtre dans les provinces balkaniques et danubiennes." Pages 241–51 in *Spectacula I: Gladiateurs et amphithéâtres*. Edited by Claude Domergue, Christian Landes, and Jean-Marie Pailler. France: Aimgo, 1990.

Burnett, Andrew, Michel Amandry, and Pau Ripollès. *Roman Provincial Coinage: Supplement 1*. London: British Museum Press, 1998.
Brescia, G. "Gladiatori per 'caso': modelli antropologici in [Quintiliano], Declamazioni maggiori, IX." *Rhetorica* 27 (2009): 294–311.
Cadwallader, Alan H. *Fragments of Colossae*. Adelaide: ATF Press, 2015.
Carlsen, Jesper. "Gladiators in Ancient Halikarnassos." Pages 441–50 in ΛΑΒΡΥΣ: *Studies Presented to Pontus Hellström*. Edited by Lars Karlsson, Susanne Carlsson, and Jesper Blid Kullberg. Uppsala: Uppsala Universitet, 2014.
Carter, Michael. "*Archiereis* and Asiarchs: A Gladiatorial Perspective." *GRBS* 44 (2004): 41–68.
———. "Blown Call? Diodorus and the Treacherous Summa Rudis." *ZPE* 177 (2011): 63–69.
———. "Gladiatorial Combat: The Rules of Engagement." *CJ* 102 (2006/2007): 97–113.
Castelli, Elizabeth A. *Martyrdom and Memory: Early Christian Culture Making*. New York: Columbia University Press, 2004.
Chamberland, Guy. "A Gladiatorial Show Produced *in sordidam mercedem* (Tacitus *Ann*. 4.62)." *Phoenix* 61 (2007): 136–49.
Chaniotis, Angelos. "Aphrodite's Rivals: Devotion to Local and Other Gods at Aphrodisias." *Cahiers Glotz* 21 (2010): 235–48.
Coleman, Kathleen M. "Valuing Others in the Gladiatorial Barracks." Pages 419–45 in *Valuing Others in Classical Antiquity*. Edited by Ralph M. Rosen and Ineke Sluiter. Mnemosyne Supplements. Leiden: Brill, 2010.
Concannon, Cavan W. " 'Not for an Olive Wreath, but Our Lives': Gladiators, Athletes and Early Christian Bodies." *JBL* 133 (2014): 193–214.
———. *"When you were Gentiles": Specters of Ethnicity in Roman Corinth and Paul's Corinthian Correspondence*. New Haven: Yale University Press, 2014.
Cuno, James. *Who Owns Antiquity? Museums and the Battle over Our Ancient Heritage*. Princeton: Princeton University Press, 2008.
Dunn, James D. G. *The Epistles to the Colossians and to Philemon*. Grand Rapids: Eerdmans, 1996.
Futrell, Alison. *Blood in the Arena: The Spectacle of Roman Power*. Austin: University of Texas Press, 1997.
Halfmann, Helmut. *Itinera principum: Geschichte und Typologie der Kaiserreisen im Römischen Reich*. Stuttgart: Steiner, 1986.

Hornum, Michael B. *Nemesis, the Roman State and the Games.* Leiden: Brill, 1993.

Hrychuk Kontokosta, A. C. "Gladiatorial Reliefs and Élite Funerary Monuments." Pages 190–229 in *Aphrodisias Papers 4: New Research on the City and Its Monuments.* Edited by Christopher Ratté and R. R. R. Smith. Portsmouth, RI: Journal of Roman Archaeology, 2008.

Huttner, Ulrich. *Early Christianity in the Lycus Valley.* Leiden: Brill, 2013.

Jones, Christopher P. "A Statuette of Nemesis." *Epigraphica Anatolica* 33 (2001): 45–47.

Kanz, Fabian, and Karl Grossschmidt. "Stand der anthropologischen Forschung zum Gladiatorenfriedhof in Ephesos." *Jahresheft des Österreichischen Archäologischen Institutes* 74 (2005): 103–23.

———. "Head Injuries of Roman Gladiators." *Forensic Science International* 160 (2006): 207–16.

König, Jason. *Athletics and Literature in the Roman Empire.* Cambridge: Cambridge University Press, 2013.

Krapinger, Gernot, ed. *[Quintilian] Der Gladiator (Grössere Deklamationen, 9).* Cassino: Università degli Studi di Cassino, 2007.

Krentz, Edgar. "Paul, Games and the Military." Pages 344–83 in *Paul in the Graeco-Roman World: A Handbook.* Edited by J. Paul Sampley. Harrisburg, PA: Trinity Press International, 2003.

Mann, Christian. "Gladiators in the Greek East: A Case Study in Romanization." *International Journal of the History of Sport* 26 (2009): 272–97.

Murphy-O'Connor, Jerome. *St. Paul's Ephesus: Texts and Archaeology.* Collegeville, MN: Liturgical Press, 2008.

Özdoğan, Mehmet. "Ideology and Archaeology in Turkey." Pages 111–23 in *Archaeology Under Fire: Nationalism, Politics and Heritage in the Eastern Mediterranean and Middle East.* Edited by Lynn Meskell. London: Routledge, 1988.

Palagia, Olga, and David Lewis. "The Ephebes of Erechtheis, 333/2 BC and Their Dedication." *ABSA* 84 (1989): 333–44.

Pfitzner, Vic. "Was St Paul a Sports Enthusiast? Realism and Rhetoric in Pauline Athletic Metaphors." Pages 89–111 in *Sports and Christianity: Historical and Contemporary Perspectives.* Edited by Nick J. Watson and Andrew Parker. London: Routledge, 2012.

Pflaum, H.-G. *Les Carrières Procuratoriennes Équestres sous le Haut-Empire romain.* Paris: Geuthner, 1960.

Pietsch, W. "Außerstädtische Grabanlagen von Ephesos." Pages 455–60 in *100 Jahre Österreichische Forschung in Ephesos, Akten des Symposions*

Wien 1999. Edited by Herwig Friesinger and Fritz Krinzinger. Vienna: Österreichische Akademie der Wissenschaften, 1999.

Pietsch, W., and E. Trinkl. "Grabungsbericht der Kampagnen 1992/93." *Bericht und Materialien Österreichisches Archäologisches Institut* 6 (1995): 19–48.

Rawson, Elizabeth. "Discrimina Ordinum: The Lex Julia Theatralis." *Papers of the British School at Rome* 55 (1987): 83–114.

Revell, Louise. *Roman Imperialism and Local Identities.* Cambridge: Cambridge University Press, 2009.

Richardson-Hay, Christine. "*Mera homicidia*: A Philosopher Draws Blood—Seneca and the Gladiatorial Games." *Prudentia* 36 (2004): 87–146.

Ritti, Tullia. "Oracoli alfabetici a Hierapolis di Frigia." *Miscellanea greca e romana* 14 (1989): 245–86.

Ritti, Tullia, and Salim Yılmaz. *Gladiatori e venationes a Hierapolis di Frigia.* Rome: Accademia nazionale dei Lincei, 1998.

Ritti, Tullia, H. H. Baysal, E. Miranda, and F. Guizza. *Museo archeologico di Denizli-Pamukkale: Catalogo delle iscrizioni latine e greche. Distretto di Denizli.* Naples: Università degli Studi, 2008.

Robert, Louis. *Les gladiateurs dans l'Orient Grec.* Amsterdam: Hakkert, 1971 (French orig. 1940).

———. "Les Inscriptions." Pages 247–389 in *Laodicée du Lycos: Le Nymphée, Campagnes 1961–1963.* Edited by J. de Gagniers. Quebec: L'Université Laval, 1969.

Rogers, Guy MacLean. *The Sacred Identity of Ephesus: Foundation Myths of a Roman City.* London: Routledge, 1991.

Scanlon, Thomas. "Contesting Ancient Mediterranean Sport." Pages 1–12 in *Sport in the Cultures of the Ancient World: New Perspectives.* Edited by Zinon Papakonstantinou. London: Routledge, 2013.

Sear, Frank. *Roman Theatres: An Architectural Study.* Oxford: Oxford University Press, 2006.

Seesengood, Robert Paul. *Competing Identities: The Athlete and the Gladiator.* London: T&T Clark, 2006.

Strootman, Rudolf. "The Hellenistic Royal Courts: Court Culture, Ceremonial and Ideology in Greece, Egypt and the Near East, 336–30 BCE." PhD diss., University of Utrecht, 2007.

Tröster, Manuel. *Themes, Character and Politics in Plutarch's Life of Lucullus: The Construction of a Roman Aristocrat.* Historia 201. Stuttgart: Steiner, 2008.

Ustinova, Yulia. *The Supreme Gods of the Bosporan Kingdom: Celestial Aphrodite and the Most High God.* Leiden: Brill, 1999.

Ville, Georges. *La gladiature en occident des origins à la mort de Domitien.* Rome: École française de Rome, 1981.

Weber, Georg. "Der unterirdische Lauf des Lykos bei Kolossai." *MDAI, Athenische Abteilung* 16 (1891): 194–99.

Weber, Wilhelm. *Untersuchungen zur Geschichte des Kaisers Hadrianus.* Leipzig: Teubner, 1907.

Welch, Katherine E. *The Roman Amphitheatre from Its Origins to the Colosseum.* Cambridge: Cambridge University Press, 2007.

Weidemann, Thomas. *Emperors and Gladiators.* London: Routledge, 1992.

Zuiderhoek, Arjan. "On the Political Sociology of the Imperial Greek City." *GRBS* 48 (2008): 417–45.

to cities. For Richard Tomlinson, "Egypt remained largely immune to the system" of Roman urbanism, a statement he supports by noting a different mode of city use by the Ptolemies, stating, as do others, that there were only two "cities" in Ptolemaic Egypt.[7] It is true there were only three Greek *poleis* (including the pre-Ptolemaic foundation Naucratis) in Ptolemaic Egypt, but in the Roman period virtually all the nome *metropoleis* for which we have information had the cultural and administrative institutions which mark a Greco-Roman city: not only the machinery of the Roman administration[8] but also Hellenic cultural institutions such as *gymnasia* and theaters. It is true, however, that they did not levy their own taxes, though they became responsible for collecting them on behalf of the government through the liturgical system in the second century, and then with increasing local oversight via local councils in the third century.[9] Famously, they did not have their own town councils, *boulai*, until granted them by Septimius Severus in the early third century.[10]

---

pointing out in this connection that "the very flexibility of the [Roman] provincial administration ... causes one to doubt whether any province was typical" (4).

7. Richard Tomlinson, *From Mycenae to Constantinople: The Evolution of the Ancient City* (London: Routledge, 1992), xi (from where the quote is taken), 9 (on the Ptolemaic use of cities).

8. Alan K. Bowman and Dominic Rathbone, "Cities and Administration in Roman Egypt," *JRS* 82 (1992): 107–27; A. Jördens, "Der praefectus Aegypti und die Städte," in *Herrschaftsstrukturen und Herrschaftspraxis. Konzepte, Prinzipien und Strategien der Administration im römischen Kaiserreich. Akten der Tagung an der Universität Zürich, 18.–20.10.2004*, ed. Anne Kolb (Berlin: Akademie, 2006), 191–200; Jördens, "Das Verhältnis der römischen Amtsträger in Ägypten zu den 'Städten' in der Provinz," in *Lokale Autonomie und römische Ordnungsmacht in den kaiserzeitlichen Provinzen vom 1. bis 3. Jahrhundert*, ed. Werner Eck (Munich: Oldenbourg, 1999), 141–80; Jördens, "Government, Taxation, and Law," in *The Oxford Handbook of Roman Egypt*, ed. Christina Riggs (Oxford: Oxford University Press, 2012), 56–67.

9. On taxation in Roman Egypt, see Michael Sharp, "Shearing Sheep: Rome and the Collection of Taxes in Egypt, 30 BC–AD 200," in Eck, *Lokale Autonomie und römische Ordnungsmacht*, 213–41; Jördens, "Government, Taxation, and Law," 59–61; Sherman LeRoy Wallace, *Taxation in Egypt from Augustus to Diocletian* (Princeton: Princeton University Press, 1938). Alan K. Bowman, *The Town Councils of Roman Egypt* (Toronto: Hakkert, 1971), 69–77, discusses the involvement of town councils in tax collection in the third century; for the levying of minor taxes the proceeds of which were spent locally, see Sharp, "Shearing Sheep," 223.

10. Bowman, *Town Councils of Roman Egypt*, who deals with the situation before and after 200 CE at 11–19; see also Bowman and Rathbone, "Cities and Administration," 118–19; Jördens, "Der praefectus Aegypti," 164–69.

Technical definitions of "city" status could be adduced on the grounds of technical status (e.g., municipal), or denomination in contemporary documents (*urbs* or *polis*), or presence or absence of various institutions (a council, assembly, various officials), or size.[11] Rather than pronouncing on whether the cities of Roman Egypt were "cities" in the same way other settlements of similar size and urban complexity were in the Roman world, I would ask if the outcome to this question changes the way we use the evidence derived from and concerning them to help us understand early urban Christian communities. I would suggest that it does not materially effect this, and that the papyri from Egypt can thus play a useful role in helping us understand the urban contexts in which the first Christian communities developed. I would also stress the point that one cannot view the ancient city in isolation, or understand the city without investigating the symbiotic relationship of cities with their hinterland, and especially the villages and estates in their territory.[12] The wealth of urban elites, and indeed the very basis for their status as urban elites, was largely landholding in the countryside. And it is the papyri that allow us to chart this relationship between field, estate, village, and city.

Methodological caution is of course necessary. The papyri offer a wealth of detail. While the documentary evidence has some blind spots, most aspects of life in the Roman city can be illustrated, or at least illuminated. However, this evidential capital must be spent responsibly: the papyri provide such a wealth of evidence that heaping detail upon detail is not difficult. But a wealth of detail does not always make good history, especially as authors who use papyri in this series will be using them as comparative, not direct evidence. Anyone who uses papyrological evidence must decide what details to choose, and consider how to use them to build context.

Warnings about insecure provenance and difficulties of dating probably should not need stating, but completeness demands they are, and in

---

11. See the reflections of Jördens, "Der praefectus Aegypti," 141–42 and passim.

12. On the theme, see in general John Rich and Andrew Wallace-Hadrill, eds., *City and Country in the Ancient World* (London: Routledge 1991); Thomas S. Burns and John W. Eadie, eds., *Urban Centers and Rural Contexts in Late Antiquity* (East Lansing: Michigan State University Press, 2001); and on the medial area between urban and rural, Penelope J. Goodman, *The Roman City and Its Periphery* (London: Routledge, 2007); on Egypt, Bagnall's review of Alston, *The City in Roman and Byzantine Egypt*, cited above at n. 1.

any case it frequently appears that they *do* need restating. Many papyri have come to modern collections via the antiquities trade and have no secure provenance beyond "somewhere in Upper Egypt," but we are going to use them for comparative purposes anyway, so that matters less than if we were going to include one of the cities from Roman Egypt in this series. That the vast majority of papyri come from urban contexts is not a hindrance in the case of the present series, but that virtually no papyri survive from ancient Alexandria,[13] probably the only city in first-century Egypt that had a Christian community of any substance, should be kept in mind.

Of chief concern when assessing the use of the papyri in historical treatments is an all too common inclination to treat paleographic dating as a far more exact and precise science than it actually is: Who has not read a treatment of P.Ryl. 3.457 (or P52, as it is known to most New Testament scholars) that enthusiastically declares an early dating within a ten- to twenty-year range? We might note the oft-made assertion that Irenaeus's *Adversus heraeses* was being read in Egypt twenty years after its composition, because P.Oxy. 3.405 is paleographically dated to the early third century.[14] While it *could* be from twenty years after the composition of the work around 180, it could just as easily be from fifty years later, or even a bit more. It is to be hoped that the voices now pleading for a proper understanding of the nature of paleographical dating are heard.[15] In the case of the documentary papyri we are on slightly firmer footing: the cursive script in which most are written can be more readily dated than those commonly used for literary productions, many public documents are precisely dated, and examination of such aspects as prosopography or prices can provide extra precision in some cases.

---

13. There are of course papyri sent or taken from there in antiquity, but these are minor compared with the amount of papyri from other cities in the province.

14. See, e.g., Michael J. Kruger, *The Gospel of the Savior: An Analysis of P.Oxy. 840 and Its Place in the Gospel Traditions of Early Christianity* (Leiden: Brill, 2005), 246n151; Kruger, "Manuscripts, Scribes, and Book Production within Early Christianity," in *Christian Origins and Greco-Roman Culture: Social and Literary Contexts for the New Testament*, ed. Stanley E. Porter and Andrew W. Pitts, Early Christianity in Its Hellenistic Context 1, TENTS 9 (Leiden: Brill, 2012), 15–40, at 39.

15. See Brent Nongbri, "The Use and Abuse of P52: Papyrological Pitfalls in the Dating of the Fourth Gospel," *HTR* 98 (2005): 23–48; Nongbri, "Grenfell and Hunt on the Dates of Early Christian Codices: Setting the Record Straight," *BASP* 48 (2011): 149–62; Don Barker, "The Dating of New Testament Papyri," *NTS* 57 (2011): 571–82.

Egypt provides a useful case study of an urban Roman context, because most of the papyri were found in, and relate to, urban contexts.[16] It is also a relatively urbanized society. Roger Bagnall and Bruce Frier estimate a population for Roman Egypt of 4–5 million, with around 1.75 million living in cities that varied in size from around 20,000 to 40,000 inhabitants.[17] Alexandria was obviously much larger (ca. 500,000?);[18] these figures are somewhat elastic, but that around a third of Egypt's population was urban is probably not far wrong. For all the detail of Roman cities the papyri allow us to see, however, what we cannot find in this detail are Christians. We may imagine they behaved like the people we meet in the papyri, but we do not meet any in the papyri until the third century. In this, the documentary papyri are not like other documentary sources outside the New Testament, few of which can be securely anchored in Christianity's first century.

The editors of this book, and organizers of the panel from which it grew, not only wish to gather resources for the study of the first urban believers but also would like to offer a further correction to the conclusions drawn on the social position of the early Christians that followed on from the pioneering studies of Adolf Deissmann and, in the words of the organizers, his "overly narrow focus on the papyrological evidence as the formative background for the understanding early Christianity."[19] To the extent that future contributors to this series almost certainly will engage with this view of early Christianity, and the fact that papyrological evidence is directly related to this question both by the manner in which Deissmann allowed the "lower classes" to speak, and, consequently, the direct statements of the organizers, this requires attention here.

"By its social structure," Deissmann believed, "primitive Christianity points unequivocally to the lower and middle classes."[20] It is for others to discuss the social character of early Christianity, understandings of which

---

16. Bagnall, *Egypt in Late Antiquity*, 5.

17. Roger S. Bagnall and Bruce W. Frier, *The Demography of Roman Egypt*, 2nd ed. (Cambridge: Cambridge University Press, 2006), 53–56; see also Müller, "Urbanism," 222–23.

18. See Müller, "Urbanism," 221–22, with further references.

19. As stated in the description of the panel circulated to panelists in advance of the first year of its operation.

20. Adolf Deissmann, *Light from the Ancient East*, trans. Lionel Strachen, 4th ed. (New York: Harper, 1927), 7; see also the first edition, *Licht von Osten* (Tübingen: Mohr Siebeck, 1908), 4: "Die soziale Struktur des Urchristentums weist uns durchaus in die untere und in die mittlere Schicht."

have progressed considerably in the last century. Here, the point is worth making that the papyri themselves provide ample evidence for the contrary perspective. That is to say, when we position the "aristocratic literature" versus the "documentary evidence," as the organizers did in their initial description of the SBL program unit, we must recognize that the papyri frequently merely give us another insight into the "aristocratic" perspective. And this is the sort of people we expect to find in the papyri, because the majority of papyri document precisely the municipal class, landholders subject to liturgies. So we should not be at all surprised that when we start to find Christians among the papyri, they are among this class.

The earliest letter that securely features Christians (by a Christian to a Christian, I would argue[21]) is P.Bas. 1.16. It is without secure provenance (there seem no obvious grounds for van Haelst's assignment of it to the Great Oasis).[22] Mario Naldini's dating to the beginning of the third century is most commonly cited,[23] but the first editor's date of first half of the third century, bearing in mind Ulrich Wilcken's allowance of a mid-century dating,[24] seems safest. It may not be much earlier than any of our other third-century Christian letters; but be that as it may, it clearly proceeds from a municipal elite circle.

> Greetings, my incomparable [lord] brother Paul, I Arrian greet you, [pray]ing that the best things in life may accrue to you. Since [...]menibes

---

21. The scribe uses not only the Pauline "in the Lord" formula but also the *nomen sacrum* for κύριος; see Malcolm Choat, *Belief and Cult in Fourth-Century Papyri* (Turnhout: Brepols, 2006), 101–4, 119–25; that the use of these indicates that the recipient shares the beliefs of the sender seems a reasonable assumption.

22. J. van Haelst, "Les sources papyrologiques concernant l'église en Égypte à l'époque de Constantin," in *Proceedings of the Twelfth International Congress of Papyrology, Ann Arbor, 13–17 August 1968*, ed. Deborah H. Samuel (Toronto: Hakkert, 1970), 497–503, at 498; E. A. Judge and S. R. Pickering, "Papyrus Documentation of Church and Community in Egypt to the Mid-Fourth Century," *JAC* 20 (1977): 47–71 (48, 51).

23. Mario Naldini, *Il cristianesimo in Egitto: Lettere private nei papiri dei secoli ii–iv*, 2nd ed. (Florence: Nardini, 1998), no. 4.

24. See P.Bas 1.16, intro, quoting Wilcken's opinion, "III Jahrhundert—und zwar eher ins frühere oder mittlere." Wilcken noted in support of this the (still unpublished) text on the back, dating to Choiak 27 of a (presumably imperial) year 6, which reminded him of the Heroninos correspondence, the core of which dates 249–268 CE (see "Leuven Homepage of Papyrus Collections," *Trimegistos*, 2013, http://www.trismegistos.org/arch/archives/pdf/103.pdf).

> (?) was coming to you, I thought it necessary to greet you together with our lord father. And now I remind you [about] the gymnasiarchy, so that we here may not be burdened. For Herakleides cannot ... for he has been himself nominated for the council ... not anything therefore..., but also send me the fish sauce, but only if you judge it to be of good quality. Our lady mother is well and greets you together with your wives and sweetest children ... of the brothers and all our ... Greet our brother [...]genes and Xoides. All of us here greet you. I pray for your good health in the Lord.

Arrian reminds Paul about the gymnasiarchy, "so that we here may not be burdened": Herakleides cannot (do something, maybe help) for he has been himself nominated for the council. Nomination to the college who led the gymnasium—membership of which guaranteed a youth would graduate to the Hellenic elite of the city—was an honor; indeed, Arrian would have been one of his town's leading figures.[25] However, as the gymnasiarchs were required to share the not inconsiderable maintenance costs of the gymnasium for their year of office, it was also a financial burden, which Arrian sought to avoid. The point is, as with their friend Herakleides and his forthcoming role on their town's *boule*, that only those with sufficient means were liable for nomination to these offices.

Such is also the case, to a lesser extent, the first time we meet a Christian who is given that name in the papyri. This is Dioskoros in *SB* 16.12497, which probably dates to the second quarter of the third century,[26] and comes from Arsinoë, the capital of the Fayum.

> 40 For supervision of the water-tower and fountains of the metropolis [upon undertaking it, likewise]:
> 4 Sarapammon also called Arius of Nilus of Zoilus from [... (holding property worth) x drachmas].
>   He is the one (who works) with the new land-holder at(?) [...].
> 8 Isidorus also called Heracleides of Heron of Socrates[... (holding property worth) x drachmas].

---

25. On the gymnasiarchy, see Bowman, *Town Councils of Roman Egypt*, 28–29; Pieter Johannes Sijpesteijn, *Nouvelle liste des gymnasiarques des métropoles de l'Egypte romaine* (Zutphen: Terra, 1986), with earlier references at vii.

26. The fact that no one in the papyrus is given the nomen Aurelius, however, might be thought to suggest a date before the mass enfranchisement of the empire under Caracalla in 212.

He is Agathus, oil-manufacturer in(?) [...].
45 5 Theodorus son of Isidorus son of Ischyrion from [... (holding property worth) x drachmas].
He is the son of the Isidorus who lives in the [...].
6 Ammonius son of the Magnus also called Menouthes from the gymnasium (district) [... (holding property worth) x drachmas]
He is the garrulous Ammonius (who is) a workman [at ... ?].
2 Antonius Dioscorus son of Horigenes the Alexandrian [... (holding property worth) x drachmas].
50 He is the Dioscorus (who is a) Christian [at? ...].

"Antonius Dioscorus son of Horigenes the Alexandrian," whom a second hand—who adds notes that were probably intended to help identify those on the list[27]—identifies as a Christian, was probably a minor property owner. Not a rich man by any means, but sufficiently well off to be considered for the public service of "supervision of the water-tower and fountains of the metropolis."

While much of the action in the cities on which this series focuses takes place in public—in the agora, on the street, and in other public forums—much of it happens in private households, as integral a part of a city as its forum, theater, or gymnasium. If houses can be planned from the archaeological record, the documentary record allows us to chart the families who lived in them. Foremost among our records here is the census. Census declarations, attested from 12 to 259 and submitted at fourteen-year intervals after 33/34,[28] seem to have registered the entire population of Egypt regardless of legal status (i.e., citizenship), registered (usually) by house.

The census returns allow us an insight into household structures, and the sometimes idiosyncratic way the household was conceptualized, or at least presented to the authorities, in the Roman world. They show the Roman family in all its variety, from a sole occupant through to multiple, and sometime multigenerational, families living together. Here there is

---

27. Though see Peter van Minnen, "The Roots of Egyptian Christianity," *APF* 40 (1994): 71–85, at 74–77.

28. On the census, see Bagnall and Frier, *Demography of Roman Egypt*; Marcel Hombert and Claire Préaux, *Recherches sur le recensement dans l'Égypte romaine (P. Bruxelles Inv. E. 7616)*, Papyrologica Lugduno-Batava 5 (Leiden: Brill, 1952); *NewDocs* 6:112–32. There is evidence for a census in 11/12, and reasonable circumstantial evidence for a seven-year cycle back in time from there to 11/10 BCE.

much material for those who wish to understand the household unit in the Roman world. A typically complex household arrangement is revealed in a return filed in 175 CE in the village of Karanis in the Fayum.[29] Ptollas son of Sabinus registers not only himself but also his sister and wife Ptolemais, their daughter, his mother, twin sisters who are said to be relatives, one of whom has a child who is *apator* (without father), a freedwoman of these sisters' brother, who is a soldier and appears to be the ward of Ptollas,[30] and six slaves, themselves constituting three generations of a family. Alongside all of these people who live in the house, Ptollas lists someone who does not, his older brother Harpokras, who is in flight (ἐν ἀναχωρήσει), having apparently fled his village.

> To Potam[on, strategos of the Arsinoite nome, Herakleides] division and to Asklepiades, royal scribe of the same [division and] to the village scribe of the village of Karanis and to the laographoi of the same village from Pt[ollas, son of Sabinus, the son] of Ptolemaios, mother Vettia, daughter of Vettios from the village of Ka[ranis]. I register myself and my family for the house-by-house registration of the year 14 of Aurelius Anton[inus Caesar, the] lord. And I am Ptollas, 48 years old and (I register) [my] brother Harp[o]k[r]as, being in flight, 44 years old, and Ptolemais, [my] sister and wife, 38 years old and the daughter of both of us, Vetti[a, x years old] and my mother Vettia, daughter of Vettios, 72 years old and my kinswomen, Soeris and Taos, both daughters of Ptolemaios, son of Pnephero[s], mother [NN], daughter of Ptolemaios, twins, 38 years old, and Tha[k]iaris(?), [daughter] of Taos, father unknown, 12 years old and Sarapia[s], the freedwoman of the brother of [...], Valerius Aphrod[i]sios, soldier of the cohors I Ulpia Af[rorum], 30 years old. There belongs to me and [my] siblings half of the house and courtyard and oil press and vacant space inherited from our father and (there belongs) to [Ptol]emais alone a house [and] courtyard and other spaces and another courtyard with appurtenances and [... a(?)] courtyard and a house which has fallen

---

29. *BGU* 2.447 (Karanis, 11/27/175). The household is 173-Ar-9 in Bagnall and Frier, *Demography of Roman Egypt*, 250–51. The translation reproduced here is that produced for the Heidelberger Gesamtverzeichnis der griechischen Papyrusurkunden Ägyptens Enhancement Project, http://www.papy.uni-hd.de/trans/DFG/eng/9178eng.html. For numerous corrections to the text, which are reflected in this translation, see James M. Cowey and Daniel Kah, "Bemerkungen zu Texten aus BGU I–IV. Teil I: Zensusdeklarationen," *ZPE* 163 (2007): 147–82 (170–72).

30. φροντιζομ(ένῳ) ὑπ' ἐμ[οῦ, Ο]ὐαλε[ρίῳ] Ἀφροδεισίῳ στρ(ατιώτῃ), *BGU* 2.447.18–19.

into disrepair and a third and a fifteenth part of a house and courtyard and [of another courtyard] and other appurtenances and a vacant space and (there belongs) to Vettia a house and courtyard and another house and (there belongs) to Soe[r]is and Taos and their brother, my charge, Vale[r]i[us] Aphrodeisios, the above mentioned soldier, a quarter of a house and courtyard and other appurtenances and (there belongs) to [S]empronius Hermeinos, cavalryman of the ala Mauretana, [- - -], my charge, scrutinized by the ex-prefect Sempronius Liber[alis] in year 18 of the God Aelius Antonin[us], in Thoth, which according to the Roman calendar is [August the ...] a quarter of a house and courtyard and other appurtenances. And (I register) the slaves, Kopr[ia], 40 [years old] and Sarapias, her offspring, 20 years old and Dioskoros, another offspring of her, 6 years old and Polydeukes, nicknamed Eros, an offspring [of her], 4 years old [and D]id[yme], an offspring of Sarapias, 4 years old, and Kastor, an offspring of the same Sa[rapi]as, two months old. Therefore I submit (this registration).
Year 16 of Aurelius Anton[inus Ca]esar, the lord, Hathyr 30.
(Hand 2) I, Ptolemaios, [have received] a duplicate.
(Hand 3 ?) I, Pe[- - -]. (Hand 4 ?) I, Valeriusalias Heron, have signed.

A considerable array of property is declared by this household, owned by Ptollas, his wife, his mother, the siblings who live with them, and another cavalryman, Sempronius Hermeinos, who is also under the charge of Ptollas. Extended and multiple families in the one household[31] are more common in rural than urban areas.[32] At the other end of the scale, some returns record people living by themselves in the cities.[33]

> To Polydeukes, secretary in the metropolis and the harbour, from Semtheus, son of Hephaistas, son of Panasis, and the mother being Nemesous, daughter of Herakleios, who is one of the inhabitants of Herakleopolis, and registered in the formerly called amphodarchy of Areios. I register myself for the 16th year of our Lord Hadrianus Caesar in accordance with the instructions given by Flavius Titianus, the most excellent prefect, for the part I have of a house close to Arpsentesis: I am Semtheus, inhabitant, 39 years old and I swear by the Fortuna of Imperator Caesar

---

31. Recognizing that it is very difficult to tell exactly who in these households lived where from some of these returns, see Bagnall and Frier, *Demography of Roman Egypt*, 58.
32. Ibid., 66–67.
33. P.Oslo 3.98 (Herakleopolis, 132/133 CE) = Bagnall and Frier, *Demography of Roman Egypt*, 131-He-1 (p. 209); the translation is that of the editor.

Traianus Hadrianus Augustus and the god Herakles in health and truth that I have delivered this declaration and that I have not lied or given an incomplete picture or left out anyone who ought to have been declared by me—otherwise I would have been responsible according to the oath. In the 17th year of the emperor Caesar Traianus Hadrianus Augustus.

Within these households and between them, personal contracts of marriage and adoption, or notifications of divorce and death, allow us to map the construction and relationship of families;[34] a wealth of documentation informs us on patterns of landholding;[35] in the wills and testaments we see the mechanisms by which property is passed between generations.[36]

Stepping out from this family property, outside the houses, into the streets, the papyri allow us to map the city textually. Often this is a floating map, and even if we have a secure archaeological plan of an urban space (and this is somewhat of a rarity in Egypt, where settlement archaeology has received less attention than elsewhere[37]), we can have difficulty tallying it with what the papyri tell us, though villages such as Karanis offer possibilities.[38] Leaving to one side the wider methodological goal of properly integrating archaeological and papyrological sources, the papyri alone allow something of a reconstruction of local neighborhoods, giving a sense of how houses and buildings related to each other, and how urban residents conceptualized them as relating to one another. Contracts for the sale of houses routinely specify the position of the house relative to its neighbors, stepping through the points of the compass to describe the nearby buildings:

---

34. See, for instance, Uri Yiftach-Firanko, *Marriage and Marital Arrangements: A History of the Greek Marriage Document in Egypt; 4th Century BCE–4th Century CE* (Munich: Beck, 2003).

35. Jane Rowlandson, *Landowners and Tenants in Roman Egypt: The Social Relations of Agriculture in the Oxyrhynchite Nome* (Oxford: Clarendon, 1996).

36. L. Migliardi Zingale, *I testamenti romani nei papiri e nelle tavolette d'Egitto: Silloge di documenti dal I al IV secolo d.C.*, 3rd ed. (Torino: Giappichelli, 1997); Uri Yiftach-Firanko, "Deeds of Last Will in Graeco-Roman Egypt: A Case Study in Regionalism," *BASP* 39 (2002): 149–64.

37. See Müller, "Urbanism in Graeco-Roman Egypt," 217, who characterizes "the overall situation of settlement-archaeology in Egypt" as "rather dire."

38. See Peter van Minnen, "House-to-House Enquiries: An Interdisciplinary Approach to Roman Karanis," *ZPE* 100 (1994): 227–51.

Aurelius [...]apion, son of Heras and Alexandra, from the illustrious and most illustrious city of the Oxyrhynchites, to Aurelius [...]ion, son of Didymos and Thaesis, from the same city, greeting. I acknowledge that I have sold to you from the present time for ever (ll. 1–4) ... the empty[39] house, beneath which is a cellar, with all its appurtenances, belonging to me in the same city [i.e., Oxyrhynchus] of the North Quay quarter of which the boundaries are, on the south a public street, on the north a storeroom used by [...], on the east property of Dioskoros, oil-merchant, on the west a public street beyond which is the Augusteum (Σεβαστῖον) ... (ll. 9–11).[40]

Tryphon, son of Dionysius, about ... years old, of middle height, fair, with a long face and a slight squint, and having a scar on his right wrist, has bought from his mother Thamounis' cousin, Pnepheros son of Papontos, also an inhabitant of Oxyrhynchus, about 65 years old, of middle height, fair, having a long face and a scar above his ... eyebrow and another on his right knee, (the document being drawn up) in the street,[41] one half of a three-storied house inherited from his mother, together with all its entrances and exits and appurtenances, situated by the Serapeum at Oxyrhynchus in the southern part of the street called Temgenouthis to the west of the lane leading to Shepherds' Street, its boundaries being, on the south and east, public roads, on the north, the house of the aforesaid Thamounis, mother of Tryphon the buyer, on the west, the house of Tausiris, sister of Pnepheros the seller, separated by a blind alley, for the sum of 32 talents of copper... (ll. 2–9).[42]

Across these documents, one notices that the street itself onto which the house fronts is not always the first and most important data point, as it would be in a modern description of the location of a house: one normally starts by noting the suburb or neighborhood—*amphodos*, *kleros*, or similar—in which the property stands; twelve *phylai* containing between them at least thirty-four *amphodoi* are known for Roman Oxyrhynchus (a town whose population might have been in the vicinity of 30,000).[43] P.Oxy. 1.99,

---

39. Another word, perhaps another adjective, is lost between οἰκείαν (*l.* οἰκίαν) and [κε]νήν.

40. *SB* 10.10728 (Oxyrhynchus, 318 CE), trans. Revel A. Coles, "Two Papyri in the University of Michigan Collection," *TAPA* 97 (1966): 55–66, at 58.

41. Ἐν ἀγυιᾷ, a common phrase seemingly indicating scribal activity in the public street.

42. P.Oxy. 1.99 (Oxyrhynchus, 55 CE), translation is that of the editors.

43. See Krüger, *Oxyrhynchos in der Kaiserzeit*, 73–94; on the population size, see 68–69.

above, is unusual in its specificity. One might compare to the way one often describes the location of a house not by its street but by its quarter, such "addresses" that survive either on the backs of letters or, at times, on separate sheets of papyrus: these usually use landmarks to guide the letter carrier; P.Oxy. 34.2719 (Oxyrhynchus, third century)[44] is an elaborate example.

> Consignment of Rufus' letters: [From] the moon gate, walk as if towards the granaries and when you [come] to the first street, turn left behind the thermae where (there is) a [shrine], and go westwards. Go down the steps and up [the others] and turn right and after [the] precinct to the [temple] on the right side there [is] a seven-story house and on top of the gatehouse (a statue) of Fortune [and] opposite the basket-weaving shop. Enquire there or from the concierge and you will be informed. And shout yourself; Lucius will answer you.

No doubt street names were often not given because many streets simply did not have names: Julian Krüger is able to list the names of around twenty streets (variously ῥύμη, δρόμος, πλατεῖα, and λαύρα) in Roman-period Oxyrhynchite papyri.[45] The main unit of location was the town quarter. Within the quarter, it will presumably have been well known which house was at issue; if not, the description of the property, and more so the listing of the γείτονες, neighbors, will make this clear. Such descriptions frequently involve noting a road onto which the property faces; in the Fayum this is often the "royal road" (ῥύμη βασιλική), which formed the main street of many villages. In a village, the "neighbors" are often vacant lots, vineyards, or the plots of other farmers:[46] in contracts from cities, one starts to sense the built-up houses.

With the aid of these, one can map the spatial relationships between properties: in a reedition of three sales of houses from first-century Socnopaiou Nesos, a village in the Fayum, Nikos Litinas is able to reconstruct the relationship of the houses to one another and produce a map.[47] The

---

44. See *NewDocs* 7:31–32, the source of the translation given here.
45. Krüger, *Oxyrhynchos in der Kaiserzeit*, 94–100.
46. See, e.g., P.Mich. 2.121 (Tebtynis, 42 CE), in which the various contracts are preserved; P.Mich. 3.188 (Bacchias, 120 CE); P.Mich. 5.241 (Tebtynis, 46 CE); P.Mich. 5.250 (Talei, 18 CE), P.Mich. 5.251 (Talei, 19 CE).
47. Nikos Litinas, "Three Sales of Houses at Socnopaiou Nesos," *BASP* 39 (2002): 63–96, see 79.

same can be done for many settlements from Roman Egypt. On a grander scale, one can produce a map of Oxyrhynchus showing the major roads and main public buildings that are attested in the papyri.[48] This can be constructed via painstaking observation of buildings mentioned in many papyri in relation to each other, but it is made substantially easier by longer documents that take a more synoptic view of cities. A number of these are later than the first century, but they do serve to illustrate the relationship of Christian space to the city, so are worth mentioning here.

A list from Oxyrhynchus drawn up in the first half of the fourth century (P.Oxy. 1.43v.) records the guards assigned to various buildings around the city. It is again noticeable that the locations at which guards are to be stationed are normally given not by street[49] but by reference to a prominent landmark.

column 1
5   living at the house …
    of …thotos, oil merchant, …
    At the house of (the) fuller … ,
    Horos … stay-
    ing in the same place.
10 At the northern ekklesia,
    Apphous (son) of Theon,
    living in the stables of Aionia.
    And at the house of Chortaikos or
    (the) vaults and little well,
15 Hermeias (son) of Heras,
    staying nearby.

column 3
15 And in the Creticon,
    Claudius (son) of Stephanus through Nicetes.
    And at the southern gate,
    Paulus (son) of Onnophris.
    And at the southern ekklesia,
20 Amois (son) of Parammon, staying
    opposite the house of Epimachus (the) waxworker.

---

48. Krüger, *Oxyrhynchos in der Kaiserzeit*, figure 4.
49. *Pace* Grenfell and Hunt, who expanded ρ' as ρ(ύμη) rather than πρ(ός).

While a few streets are mentioned, most places noted are private houses, wells, temples, city gates, theaters, baths, gymnasia, tetrastyla, Nilometers. Among these are two *ekklesiae*, the north and south *ekklesiae*, at which guards are also stationed. The document is fascinating as it stands, as it gives an excellent example of the articulation of the city in the eyes of the public servants drawing up the list. The status of the *ekklesiae* has been debated: Grenfell and Hunt implied the text could be dated to soon after 295, the date of the military accounts on the front, and most commentators have simply repeated this. Yet the text could have been copied much later,[50] and in the absence of credible suggestions as to what these *ekklesiae* could be except churches, it seems likely that this text dates to the reign of Constantine or even his sons, when we can more easily imagine churches occupying prominent positions inside the main north and south gates of the city, on the main road that ran between them, staking out their claim for public prominence as easily identifiable landmarks.

Further data for a textual map of a Roman city in Egypt can be drawn from the lists of buildings that were periodically compiled. A particularly well-preserved example comes from Panopolis in the first quarter of the fourth century.[51] When the text commences (sometime after the lost start of the papyrus), we are with a group of civic officials, wandering the streets of Panopolis, noting in succession the buildings on each street, seemingly going down one side of a street at a time. The following selections show the character of the document.

column 2
28 [...] alongside (it) (the) linen-weaving shop of Besas, (the) *kemio*-seller.
New one-storeyed house, of Maria, off the alley.
Ano(ther), of (the) sons of Agamemnon.

column 3
24 We went up [such and such a] street.
House of (the) mother of Hyiotheos.

---

50. Bagnall, *Egypt in Late Antiquity*, 53 with n. 60.
51. P.Berl.Bork. (Panopolis, 315–330 CE?), now reprinted as *SB* 24.16000.

Ano(ther) house, of (the) sons of Serenus, (son) of Pasino[...].
House and *ekklesia* of(?) Se...
Ano(ther), on the corner, of Theodorus, (son) of [...]ps.

column 9
28 Ano(ther) old (one), on the corner, of Petetriphis, (son) of Coudion.
Ano(ther), of Nemesas, (the) *diakonos*.
Ano(ther), of Cyrus, (the) priest, and par(tners).

column 11
31 Ano(ther), on the north, of Cyrus, (the) priest.
Ano(ther), of Fortunatus, (the) *diakonos*.
Ano(ther), of Besas, (son) of Harbalaus.

column 13
22 Ano(ther), of Onnophris, (the) carpenter.
Ano(ther), collapsing, of Aquila, (son) of Theognostus, and of (his) par(tners).

Geneva A 4
9 Ano(ther), on the corner, of Petetriphis, (the) priest.
Ano(ther), of Apollo, (the) *diakonos*.
Vacant site, (declared) by Besas, (the) engineer.

Here, too, the lack of street names is noticeable, but this is in part an artifact of the preservation of the papyrus, as at one point (3.24) we read, "we went up the street...," and the name is lost. At times, however, we glimpse the actual lack of street names, when the surveyors refer to "Another (house) of Bassus with vacant land in an alley lying on another road" (1.13–14). If I seem to be overstressing this lack of street names, it is nonetheless important to recognize the ways in which the Greco-Roman city was articulated, and how it differed from our own in this regard.

A variety of types of houses are listed in the Panopolis list: old, new, ruined, uninhabited, and single-story, the rarity of the last indicating most houses were two or more stories. Vacant land is signaled, as are a number of other types of buildings. Two buildings of dual use are signaled with οἰκία ἤτοι: this does not mean "or," as the building at 18.13 is not likely to have been "a house or a storage chamber." Rather, ἤτοι here means "and also."⁵² So we can allow the οἰκία ἤτοι ἐκκλισία (l. ἐκκλησία) in 3.27 to be a "house and also an assembly." The sigma and epsilon that follow ἐκκλισία⁵³ may preserve a trace of the name of its founder, or the owner of the house from which the church (a function that at this date we may accept as probable) grew.

In this papyrus, we may follow the surveyors around the town: they turn up a street, whose name is of course lost (ἀνέβημεν εἰς ῥύμην [3.24]): they come in succession to the house of the mother of Uiotheos (which, interestingly given the later fame in this region and beyond of one bearer of the name, is the equivalent of Coptic Shenoute), the house of the sons of Serenos, the house church (if we may call it thus), then, "on the corner" (ἐπιγώνιος) as the text says, the house of Theodoros; around this turn they found the mill of Cyrus son of Araps (or perhaps Cyrus the Arab), the houses of Heron the potter (declared by Lysimachos and his partners, κοινωνοί), Sepnouthos, Claudius the bath attendant, Heron—whose house seems to have contained a goldsmith—then a new house, a single-story house, and a workshop on the corner, at which point the surveyors turned down an alley (εἴσοδος) to list its houses. Even if we cannot know where we are in the city, we can see the street on which this house church stands, surrounded by houses and workshops.

Here a Christian function for this building is highly likely; I am willing to listen to other explanations of what this "assembly" was but have not found any of those previously proffered persuasive.⁵⁴ Elsewhere this same papyrus teaches us caution. Six *diakonoi* are listed as owners of houses.⁵⁵ Christian deacons they could be, though the word occurs in pre-Constantinian papyri for undefined types of attendants,⁵⁶ and no other Christian clergy are listed here. Three live next door to non-Christian priests, ἱερεῖς; one lives two doors away from a temple of Ammon the great god: Can we rule out that these are temple attendants? As always in the papyri, terminology should be carefully studied in its own context.

---

52. P. Sijpesteijn, "The Meanings of ἤτοι in the Papyri," *ZPE* 90 (1992): 241–50.

53. If we accept this reading, allowed as possible by the editor; I prefer this to a genitive ἐκκλησίας.

54. Victor Martin, "Relevé topographique des immeubles d'une métropole (P.Gen. Inv. 108)," *RechPap* 2 (1962): 37–73 (= SB 8.9902), at 66, did not know what force the word should be given, except that it should not have a Christian one.

55. 1.19, 9.29, 11.7, 32, 14.30, Gen. A 4.10.

56. See Choat, *Belief and Cult*, 59.

Now we are out in the streets, among the public buildings of the city. We may witness the sort of public interactions that fill out the days of the Roman city; the business transactions between citizens, binding not only those within the city but also the villages and hinterland to the urban landowning class. Most importantly, perhaps, we see the administration. The papyri show us how the Roman administration worked at the level of the empire's cities; this basic articulation of the Roman city we are witness to, from the communication within the administration to the interaction of the populace with it, in records of proceedings before officials, for example. Slight differences in administrative practice, in names of officials and so on, exist around the Roman world; but Egypt was not some "wild west" that followed its own rules, and what we see there will provide us with a good basis for understanding how the cities that feature in this series articulated themselves in their public life.

BIBLIOGRAPHY

Alston, Richard. *The City in Roman and Byzantine Egypt*. London: Routledge, 2002.
Bagnall, Roger S. *Reading Papyri, Writing Ancient History*. London: Routledge, 1995.
———. Review of *The City in Roman and Byzantine Egypt*, by Richard Alston. *JEA* 89 (2003): 297–300.
———. "Models and Evidence in the Study of Religion in Late Roman Egypt." Pages 23–41 in *From Temple to Church: Destruction and Renewal of Local Cultic Topography in Late Antiquity*. Edited by Johannes Hahn, Stephen Emmel, and Ulrich Gotter. RGRW 163. Leiden: Brill 2008.
———, ed. *The Oxford Handbook of Papyrology*. Oxford: Oxford University Press, 2009.
Bagnall, Richard S., and Bruce W. Frier. *The Demography of Roman Egypt*. 2nd ed. Cambridge: Cambridge University Press, 2006.
Barker, Don. "The Dating of New Testament Papyri." *NTS* 57 (2011): 571–82.
Bowman, Alan K. *The Town Councils of Roman Egypt*. Toronto: Hakkert, 1971.
Bowman, Alan K., and Dominic Rathbone. "Cities and Administration in Roman Egypt." *JRS* 82 (1992): 107–27.

Burns, Thomas S., and John W. Eadie, eds. *Urban Centers and Rural Contexts in Late Antiquity.* East Lansing: Michigan State University Press, 2001.

Choat, Malcolm. *Belief and Cult in Fourth-Century Papyri.* Turnhout: Brepols, 2006.

———. "Christianity." Pages 474–89 in *The Oxford Handbook to Roman Egypt.* Edited by Christina Riggs. Oxford: Oxford University Press, 2012.

Coles, Revel A. "Two Papyri in the University of Michigan Collection." *TAPA* 97 (1966): 55–66.

Cowey James M., and Daniel Kah. "Bemerkungen zu Texten aus BGU I-IV. Teil I: Zensusdeklarationen." *ZPE* 163 (2007): 147–82.

Deissmann, Adolf. *Light from the Ancient East.* Translated by Lionel Strachen. 4th ed. New York: Harper, 1927.

Gates, Charles. *Ancient Cities: The Archaeology of Urban Life in the Ancient Near East and Egypt, Greece, and Rome.* 2nd ed. London: Routledge, 2011.

Goodman, Penelope J. *The Roman City and Its Periphery.* London: Routledge, 2007.

Haelst, J. van. "Les sources papyrologiques concernant l'église en Égypte à l'epoque de Constantin." Pages 497–503 in *Proceedings of the Twelfth International Congress of Papyrology, Ann Arbor, 13–17 August 1968.* Edited by Deborah H. Samuel. Toronto: Hakkert, 1970.

Hombert, Marcel, and Claire Préaux. *Recherches sur le recensement dans l'Égypte romaine (P. Bruxelles Inv. E. 7616).* Papyrologica Lugduno-Batava 5. Leiden: Brill, 1952.

Jördens, A. "Government, Taxation, and Law." Pages 56–67 in *The Oxford Handbook of Roman Egypt.* Edited by Christina Riggs. Oxford: Oxford University Press, 2012.

———. "Der praefectus Aegypti und die Städte." Pages 191–200 in *Herrschaftsstrukturen und Herrschaftspraxis: Konzepte, Prinzipien und Strategien der Administration im römischen Kaiserreich. Akten der Tagung an der Universität Zürich, 18.–20.10.2004.* Edited by Anne Kolb. Berlin: Akademie, 2006.

———. "Das Verhältnis der römischen Amtsträger in Ägypten zu den 'Städten' in der Provinz." Pages 141–80 in *Lokale Autonomie und römische Ordnungsmacht in den kaiserzeitlichen Provinzen vom 1. bis 3. Jahrhundert.* Edited by Werner Eck. Munich: Oldenbourg, 1999.

Judge, E. A., and S. R. Pickering. "Papyrus Documentation of Church and Community in Egypt to the Mid-Fourth Century." *JAC* 20 (1977): 47–71.
Krüger, Julian. *Oxyrhynchos in der Kaiserzeit: Studien zur Topographie und Literaturrezeption*. Frankfurt am Main: Lang, 1990.
Kruger, Michael J. *The Gospel of the Savior: An Analysis of P.Oxy.840 and Its Place in the Gospel Traditions of Early Christianity*. Leiden: Brill, 2005.
———. "Manuscripts, Scribes, and Book Production within Early Christianity." Pages 15–40 in *Christian Origins and Greco-Roman Culture: Social and Literary Contexts for the New Testament*. Edited by Stanley E. Porter and Andrew W. Pitts. Early Christianity in Its Hellenistic Context 1, TENTS 9. Leiden: Brill, 2012.
Litinas, Nikos. "Three Sales of Houses at Socnopaiou Nesos." *BASP* 39 (2002): 63–96.
Martin, Victor. "Relevé topographique des immeubles d'une métropole (P.Gen. Inv. 108)." *RechPap* 2 (1962): 37–73.
———. "The Roots of Egyptian Christianity." *APF* 40 (1994): 71–85.
Minnen, Peter van. "House-to-House Enquiries: An Interdisciplinary Approach to Roman Karanis." *ZPE* 100 (1994): 227–51.
Monson, Andrew. *From the Ptolemies to the Romans: Political and Economic Change in Egypt*. Cambridge: Cambridge University Press, 2012.
Müller, Wolfgang. "Urbanism in Graeco-Roman Egypt." Pages 217–56 in *Cities and Urbanism in Ancient Egypt: Papers from a Workshop in November 2006 at the Austrian Academy of Sciences*. Edited by Manfred Bietak, Ernst Czerny, and Irene Forstner-Müller. Vienna: Österreichische Akademie der Wissenschaften, 2010.
Naldini, Mario. *Il cristianesimo in Egitto: Lettere private nei papiri dei secoli ii–iv*. 2nd ed. Florence: Nardini, 1998.
Nonbri, Brent. "Grenfell and Hunt on the Dates of Early Christian Codices: Setting the Record Straight." *BASP* 48 (2011): 149–62.
———. "The Use and Abuse of P52: Papyrological Pitfalls in the Dating of the Fourth Gospel." *HTS* 98 (2005): 23–48.
Rapoport, Amos. "The Study of Spatial Quality." *Journal of Aesthetic Education* 4 (1970): 81–95.
Redford, Donald B. "The Ancient Egyptian 'City': Figment or Reality?" Pages 210–20 in *Urbanism in Antiquity: From Mesopotamia to Crete*.

Edited by Walter E. Aufrecht, Neil A. Mirau, and Steven W. Gauley. Sheffield: Sheffield Academic, 1997.

Rich, John, and Andrew Wallace-Hadrill, eds. *City and Country in the Ancient World*. London: Routledge 1991.

Routledge, Carolyn. "Temple as Center in Ancient Egyptian Urbanism." Pages 221–35 in *Urbanism in Antiquity: From Mesopotamia to Crete*. Edited by Walter E. Aufrecht, Neil A. Mirau, and Steven W. Gauley. Sheffield: Sheffield Academic, 1997.

Rowlandson, Jane. *Landowners and Tenants in Roman Egypt: The Social Relations of Agriculture in the Oxyrhynchite Nome*. Oxford: Clarendon, 1996.

Rupprecht, Hans-Albert. *Kleine Einführung in die Papyruskunde*. Darmstadt: Wissenschaftliche Buchgesellschaft, 1994.

Sharp, Michael. "Shearing Sheep: Rome and the Collection of Taxes in Egypt, 30 BC–AD 200." Pages 213–41 in *Lokale Autonomie und römische Ordnungsmacht in den kaiserzeitlichen Provinzen vom 1. bis 3. Jahrhundert*. Edited by Werner Eck. Munich: Oldenbourg, 1999.

Sijpesteijn, Pieter Johannes. "The Meanings of ἤτοι in the Papyri." *ZPE* 90 (1992): 241–50.

———. *Nouvelle liste des gymnasiarques des métropoles de l'Egypte romaine*. Zutphen: Terra, 1986.

Tomlinson, Richard. *From Mycenae to Constantinople: The Evolution of the Ancient City*. London: Routledge, 1992.

Yiftach-Firanko, Uri. "Deeds of Last Will in Graeco-Roman Egypt: A Case Study in Regionalism." *BASP* 39 (2002): 149–64.

———. *Marriage and Marital Arrangements: A History of the Greek Marriage Document in Egypt. 4th Century BCE–4th Century CE*. Munich: Beck, 2003.

Zingale, L. Migliardi. *I testamenti romani nei papiri e nelle tavolette d'Egitto: Silloge di documenti dal I al IV secolo d.C.* 3rd ed. Torino: Giappichelli, 1997.

Epigraphy and the Study of Polis and *Ekklēsia* in the Greco-Roman World

Paul Trebilco

One fundamental area of study in our investigations of the assemblies of Christ followers in the cities of the Greco-Roman world is epigraphy, the study of texts inscribed on durable materials.[1] These texts are inscriptions on stone or marble, and those found on metal, glass, or clay, or as part of mosaics, as well as graffiti.[2] They consist of a huge range of different types of texts: laws; decrees passed by city assemblies; royal and imperial letters and edicts; treaties; funerary, honorific, and building inscriptions; votive or dedicatory inscriptions in temples and synagogues; curse tablets; names of officeholders; winners in competitions; accounts of public expenditure; inscriptions about associations; manumission inscriptions; boundary markers; and so on. They provide original, firsthand sources about historical events, public administration, and social, political, economic, and religious life.[3] In a recent discussion, John Bodel suggests there are around

---

1. John Bodel, "Epigraphy and the Ancient Historian," in *Epigraphic Evidence: Ancient History from Inscriptions*, ed. John Bodel (London: Routledge, 2001), 2, follows the *OED* in defining epigraphy as "the science concerned with the classification and interpretation of inscriptions." For a discussion of the scope of epigraphy, see 2–5.

2. See William Tabbernee, "Epigraphy," in *The Oxford Handbook of Early Christian Studies*, ed. Susan Ashbrook Harvey and David G. Hunter (Oxford: Oxford University Press, 2008), 122.

3. See, for example, Richard Saller, "The Family and Society," in Bodel, *Epigraphic Evidence*, 95–117; James Rives, "Civic and Religious Life," in Bodel, *Epigraphic Evidence*, 118–36; Bradley Hudson McLean, *An Introduction to Greek Epigraphy of the Hellenistic and Roman Periods from Alexander the Great down to the Reign of Constantine* (Ann Arbor: University of Michigan Press, 2002), 181–299; Alison E. Cooley, *The Cambridge Manual of Latin Epigraphy* (Cambridge: Cambridge University Press, 2012), 1–116.

600,000 surviving Greek and Latin inscriptions dating from 800 BCE to 700 CE,[4] and of course more are found and published each year.

Here I will first give some of the advantages of the use of inscriptions in the study of the early groups of Christ followers. Second, I will note some of the limitations and disadvantages of epigraphy that must be borne in mind in any work. Third and finally, I will discuss some inscriptions that have significantly added to our understanding of the early groups of Christ followers in the Greco-Roman world, as well as studies that are exemplary in their use of inscriptions.

1. Advantages of the Use of Inscriptions in the Study of the Polis and Ekklēsia

First, inscriptions provide us with access to people in their contexts, to the language they used, to the cultures and social structures of which they were a part, as well as giving us unique glimpses into what they did, thought, and valued.[5] This is often information that we cannot gain from any other source.[6] As William Tabbernee notes:

> such unfiltered epigraphic glimpses, devoid of much of the editorial bias inherent in extant literary historical documents mainly written from the perspective of "the winners," often provide new, or hitherto not noticed, data regarding the "losers" (e.g. the Montanists) or the "powerless" (e.g. women). These, until now mainly overlooked, data have enabled recent scholars to provide a more accurate account of the social identity of early Christians.[7]

---

4. Bodel, "Epigraphy," 4.

5. See A. G. Woodhead, *The Study of Greek Inscriptions*, 2nd ed. (Cambridge: Cambridge University Press, 1981), 3-4; Fergus Millar, "Epigraphy," in *Sources for Ancient History*, ed. Michael Crawford (Cambridge: Cambridge University Press, 1983), 81-82.

6. On why people wrote inscriptions, and what he calls (246) "the rise and fall of the epigraphic habit," see Ramsay MacMullen, "The Epigraphic Habit in the Roman Empire," *AJP* 103 (1982): 233-46; Bodel, "Epigraphy," 6-15, and the literature discussed there.

7. Tabbernee, "Epigraphy," 133-34. He goes on to emphasize that epigraphy has particularly given insight into heretical groups and the role of women in the early church. On the latter see Ute E. Eisen, *Women Officeholders in Early Christianity: Epigraphical and Literary Studies* (Collegeville, MN: Liturgical Press, 2000); Kevin Madigan and Carolyn Osiek, *Ordained Women in the Early Church* (Baltimore: Johns

Second, inscriptions give evidence for people of a wider socioeconomic range than literary texts, which were generally written by the aristocratic elite and primarily give evidence for their perspectives and ideologies. By contrast, inscriptions—particularly funerary inscriptions—give voice to a much wider range of society, and to quite some extent show us "the ordinary person," their hopes and fears, their joys and aspirations.[8] Of course, some inscriptions clearly reflect elite perceptions and views, such as inscriptions in theaters, or some inscriptions in synagogues related to donations made by very wealthy people. And all inscriptions—like all texts—are ideological; what we have in funerary inscriptions, for example, is how people or their families *chose* to present themselves, rather than how they actually were. But it remains true that inscriptions represent a much broader socioeconomic range than literary texts.

Third, because of their wide-ranging nature, inscriptions are relevant to a whole multitude of topics in the study of the ancient world: the study of particular local communities or cities, of ancient institutions and customs, and of vocabulary and ideologies. As Fergus Millar notes, "there is almost infinite scope for exploring what the inscriptions do tell us, whether explicitly in what they report or implicitly in the fundamental structures of the values and assumptions which they embody."[9]

Finally, inscriptions continue to be discovered and published and so enable completely new areas of knowledge to develop, as well as giving fresh insight into old problems.

Hopkins University Press, 2005). Note also here the discovery of an inscription that has now led to the precise location of Tymion, which was an important center for the Montanists; see William Tabbernee, "The Discovery of the Tymion Inscription," in *Pepouza and Tymion: The Discovery and Archeological Exploration of a Lost Ancient City and an Imperial Estate*, ed. William Tabbernee and Peter Lampe (Berlin: de Gruyter, 2008), 49–74.

8. See Pieter Willem van der Horst, *Ancient Jewish Epitaphs: An Introductory Survey of a Millennium of Jewish Funerary Epigraphy (300 BCE–700 CE)* (Kampen: Kok Pharos, 1991), 11; Saller, "Family and Society," 95–117; MacMullen, "Epigraphic Habit," 244, notes that "the epigraphic habit ... was taken seriously, and by a large part of the population." Bodel, "Epigraphy," 30, writes: "Epitaphs account for perhaps two-thirds of all surviving Greek and Latin inscriptions and provide our most informative epigraphic evidence—indeed, overall our best ancient evidence—for the lives of persons below the upper levels of society." On wealth still being a factor in the production of inscriptions, see below.

9. Millar, "Epigraphy," 119.

2. Limitations and Disadvantages of Epigraphy

However, there are a number of limitations and disadvantages that arise from the nature of inscriptional evidence.

First, this evidence is only *partial*. Many inscriptions are formal, public documents of a limited nature, and generally inscriptions were not inexpensive,[10] so they contain information that those who commissioned them thought of sufficient importance that it should be commemorated on stone, or recorded in bronze. This means we are gaining insight only into what people *thought* was *significant* or *important*. Wealth remains something of a determining factor with some inscriptions at least, as Ramsay MacMullen points out when he notes: "the denser the population (most of all in cities compared to the countryside), and the richer, the more likely to produce inscriptions."[11] Thus a limited range of human activity and experience formed the subject matter of many inscriptions.

Further, whole areas of life do not appear at all in the inscriptions or do so only tangentially. For example, no inscription gives a summary of a synagogue sermon, and there are very few examples of biblical exegesis on stone. The nature of the epigraphical evidence, then, often leads us to study particular dimensions of a subject.[12] In addition, there is the problem too of the haphazard survival of inscriptions, and only some of what has survived has been found and published. Many of these inscriptions are fragmentary or damaged and so are incomplete. Restorations that are often very conjectural must be suggested, and so the problems of establishing the text can be substantial. Often vital information that would aid interpretation is simply missing. The evidence available to us, then, is a minute subcategory of the potential evidence regarding ancient life.

Related to this are the local cultural *customs* relating to what to inscribe on stone. Are particular virtues mentioned simply because they are customarily mentioned in epitaphs? An honorary decree tells us what the

---

10. There are exceptions of course, such as graffiti.
11. MacMullen, "Epigraphic Habit," 241. See McLean, *Greek Epigraphy*, 13–14, for details of costs.
12. With regard to Jewish epigraphy, the nature of the evidence leads us generally to study Jewish praxis and such areas as relationships with non-Jews rather than topics such as election, obedience, and atonement, which are generally inaccessible given the epigraphical evidence available. Thus the nature of the evidence determines what areas of study we can pursue through this evidence.

people concerned wanted to be read at the time—"spin" is clearly involved. If inscriptions are our principal source of information for a community or with regard to a particular custom, then we need to be aware of what Bodel calls the "epigraphic bias"[13] created by such customary practices and commemorative habits and ask if our evidence is actually representative and accurate—and so argue with caution.

Accordingly, the accidents of survival and discovery and the nature of what was inscribed mean that the results of epigraphic studies will always be partial and must be complemented by studying inscriptions alongside other sources of information: literary texts, papyri, coins, archaeological remains, iconography, and so on.

Second, inscriptions are often short and provide little by way of context for interpretation. Other evidence provided by archaeology and numismatics or literary sources must then be used to provide an intelligible cultural and historical framework of meaning. But when considering a particular understanding of an inscription, we must ask if the best interpretative framework has been chosen. A particular framework may be misleading or less suitable than another possibility. This is particularly the case when we do not have a substantial body of related literary documents. This also means that inscriptions are often best studied in groups, generally by locality or theme, in order to gain a sufficient concentration of evidence. In addition, we must ask appropriate questions of each type of inscription. As Bodel notes: "In order to yield useful information, the epigraphic corpus must be prodded into responsiveness by well-honed questions directed at appropriate points of its sprawling bulk: asking epitaphs about maritime commerce is less profitable than asking them about commemorative behavior or onomastic practices."[14]

Third, there is the problem of dating.[15] Some inscriptions contain a date given according to a known system or can be dated accurately through the mention of securely datable events or people; others can be dated approximately through letter forms, language or formulae, or from their archaeological context. However, dates are often uncertain or very wide (such as "the Roman imperial period"), and this makes discussion of

---

13. Bodel, "Epigraphy," 35; also 46–48.
14. Ibid., 5.
15. See Arthur E. Gordon, *Illustrated Introduction to Latin Epigraphy* (Berkeley: University of California Press, 1983), 38–42; Bodel, "Epigraphy," 49–52; McLean, *Greek Epigraphy*, 42–45, 149–78; Cooley, *Cambridge Manual*, 398–434.

chronology difficult. It also makes it complicated to draw on epigraphical insights to help interpret written texts, since the inscriptions may actually come from a very different time period from these texts.

Fourth, inscriptions are often very "local" in nature and contain no reference to the wider events of a period. This makes it difficult to determine how broader historical events and changing circumstances affected local communities.

Fifth, a particular problem is being able to identify inscriptions as Christian or Jewish; many such inscriptions often differed very little from those of non-Christians and non-Jews.[16] Christian inscriptions are identified as such by their content, or by Christian formulae or names or the use of distinctively Christian symbols, such as the cross, alpha and omega, the fish, palm branches, the anchor of hope, the dove.[17] As Tabbernee notes with regard to Christian inscriptions:

> The earliest Christians ... did not distinguish their tombstones with specifically Christian symbols, formulae, or words. Claims of identifiably Christian inscriptions from the first or early second centuries ... are overly optimistic. Only from the second half of the second century onward do we see clear evidence of Christianity on stelae (grave-markers) and, of course, on or near Christian graves in the catacombs at Rome or elsewhere.[18]

---

16. On this issue, see Ross S. Kraemer, "Jewish Tuna and Christian Fish: Identifying Religious Affiliation in Epigraphic Sources," *HTR* 84 (1991): 141–62; van der Horst, *Ancient Jewish Epitaphs*, 16–18; Walter Ameling, ed., *Kleinasien*, vol. 2 of *Inscriptiones Judaicae Orientis*, TSAJ 99 (Tübingen: Mohr Siebeck, 2004), 8–21; Jonathan J. Price and Haggai Misgav, "Jewish Inscriptions and Their Use," in *Midrash and Targum, Liturgy, Poetry, Mysticism, Contracts, Inscriptions, Ancient Science and the Languages of Rabbinic Literature*, part 2 of *The Literature of the Sages*, ed. Shmuel Safrai (Assen: Van Gorcum, 2006), 461–62.

17. See Michael P. McHugh, "Inscriptions," in *Encyclopedia of Early Christianity*, ed. Everett Ferguson et al. (New York: Garland, 1990), 463.

18. Tabbernee, "Epigraphy," 127. McLean, *Greek Epigraphy*, 279-80, writes: "No identifiably Christian tombstone has been found dating prior to the late second century A.D. Though there is no reason to doubt that many early Christians did have epitaphs, these lack any signs of Christian profession and so might be termed 'crypto-Christian.' As a result, many first- and second-generation Christian epitaphs survive in today's museums but cannot be differentiated from the mass of pagan inscriptions." A related issue is identifying inscriptions that relate to different groups of Christ followers; see, for example, the discussion in Elsa Gibson, *The "Christians for Christians"*

The same difficulty of identification occurs with Jewish inscriptions. Further, earlier writers were often overly dogmatic in asserting that an inscription was Christian, and were unaware that such texts could be Jewish. For pre-Constantinian inscriptions this is particularly difficult, and some inscriptions earlier thought to be Christian may in fact be Jewish.[19]

3. Examples of the Advances Made in the Study of the Early Christ Followers through Epigraphy

Epigraphy has of course been used in a multitude of ways to enhance the study of the New Testament and of the early Christ followers in general. Many, many examples could be cited of studies that have used inscriptions to shed much light on texts. Here I will highlight some inscriptions that have greatly aided New Testament studies, including the study of communities of Christ followers in the Greco-Roman world.

3.1. The Gallio Inscription and Pauline Chronology

In Acts 18:12–17 Paul appears in Corinth before Gallio, the proconsul of Achaia. An inscription discovered in Delphi (in a number of fragments) records a case in which Claudius decided in favor of Delphi and mentions L. Iunius Gallio as proconsul.[20] The document is dated after the

---

Inscriptions of Phrygia: Greek Texts, Translation and Commentary, HTS 32 (Missoula, MT: Scholars Press, 1978).

19. See Kraemer, "Jewish Tuna"; Paul R. Trebilco, "The Christian *and* Jewish Eumeneian Formula," in *Negotiating Diaspora: Jewish Strategies in the Roman Empire*, ed. John M. G. Barclay, LSTS 45 (Sheffield: Sheffield Academic, 2004), 66–88. Tabbernee, "Epigraphy," 127, writes: "The earliest dated recognizably Christian tombstone is probably that of a man named Eutyches (Calder 1955: 33–5 no. 2). The object which the deceased is shown holding in his right hand appears to be Eucharistic bread (the *panis quadratus*; compare *IMont* 3, 5–7), and the bunch of grapes in his left hand presumably represents eucharistic wine. Other (non-Christian) interpretations of these symbols, however, are possible." It is dated to 179–180 CE; see also McLean, *Greek Epigraphy*, 280. The earliest Christian use of ΙΧΘΥΣ is in the Aberkios inscription from the late second century; see Tabbernee, "Epigraphy," 127. For other early Christian inscriptions, see the helpful collection in Graydon F. Snyder, *Ante Pacem: Archaeological Evidence of Church Life before Constantine* (Macon, GA: Mercer University Press, 1985), 119–48.

20. The inscription is *SIG* 2.801; the most accessible edition, including all the fragments, is found in Jerome Murphy-O'Connor, *St. Paul's Corinth: Texts and*

twenty-sixth acclamation of Claudius as imperator (lines 1–2); from the evidence we have for other acclamations, we know this inscription was written before 1 August 52 CE,[21] and Rainer Riesner notes there is general agreement it was written between 1 April and 1 August 52.[22] This leads to the consensus that Gallio was proconsul of Achaia from 1 July 51 to 30 June 52[23] and hence that Paul appeared before Gallio in Corinth (Acts 18:12–17) at some point within this time range. It seems likely that the trial before Gallio was near the beginning of Gallio's term of office, which leads many scholars to suggest that Paul left Corinth in the summer of 51 CE, that is, between July and October.[24]

This is the only date in Pauline chronology for which we have evidence external to the New Testament. As Riesner notes, "all more recent commentaries to the Corinthian letters continue to take the Gallio-incident as the point of departure for their chronological reconstructions."[25] Clearly, this inscription is of great importance then.

3.2. The Erastus Inscription

An inscription that concerns the gift of a pavement for part of the city's marketplace was discovered in Corinth in 1929. It reads:

Erastus pro aedilit[at]e s(ua) p(ecunia) stravit
Erastus, in return for his aedileship paved (this) at his own expense.[26]

Archaeology (Wilmington, DE: Michael Glazier, 1983), 173–76; he gives a translation in on 141–42.

21. See Rainer Riesner, *Paul's Early Period: Chronology, Mission Strategy, Theology* (Grand Rapids: Eerdmans, 1998), 205–6.

22. See ibid., 206.

23. See ibid., 208.

24. See ibid., 208–9; Murphy-O'Connor, *St. Paul's Corinth*, 141–52; cf. Dixon Slingerland, "Acts 18:1–18, the Gallio Inscription, and Absolute Pauline Chronology," *JBL* 110 (1991): 439–49. Paul would then have arrived in Corinth in the winter of 49/50. Riesner, *Paul's Early Period*, 209–10, notes that the inscription and the evidence from Acts allow the "two most extreme possibilities of chronological reconstruction" (209) to be arrival in November 49 with the latest possible departure being at the end of 53 CE.

25. Riesner, *Paul's Early Period*, 211.

26. The inscription is in John Harvey Kent, *The Inscriptions 1926–1950*, vol. 8.3 of *Corinth: Results of Excavations* (Cambridge, MA: Harvard University Press, 1966), 99; see also David W. J. Gill, "Erastus the Aedile," *TynBul* 40 (1989): 293; Steven J. Friesen,

The two aediles in Corinth were elected annually and "were responsible for the maintenance of public streets and buildings, which included the market places, and they managed the revenues derived from such places, and they served as judges."[27]

In Rom 16, almost certainly written from Corinth,[28] Paul gives greetings from Erastus, who is called ὁ οἰκονόμος τῆς πόλεως (16:23). Many would argue that ὁ οἰκονόμος τῆς πόλεως was the equivalent of aedile,[29] or at least that "οἰκονόμος describes with reasonable accuracy the function of a Corinthian aedile."[30]

But are Erastus the aedile and Erastus the οἰκονόμος the same person?[31] Arguments that have been given in favor of the identification are that the cognomen Erastus was relatively uncommon,[32] the Erastus inscription was thought to be datable to the middle of the first century CE, and οἰκονόμος could correspond or be closely related to aedile.[33] But the identification is not certain,[34] and Justin Meggitt has convincingly shown that "these arguments are much weaker than has hitherto been recognised."[35] He concludes that it is "improbable that the Erastus of Rom. 16:23 is identifiable with the figure mentioned in the Corinthian inscription."[36] Steven Friesen has reconsidered the dating of the inscription, and suggests that "the probable date for the Erastus inscription is the mid-second century CE, which would make

---

"The Wrong Erastus: Ideology, Archaeology, and Exegesis," in *Corinth in Context: Comparative Studies on Religion and Society*, ed. Steven J. Friesen et al. (Leiden: Brill, 2010), 236; translation from Friesen. On dating, see Friesen, "The Wrong Erastus," 237–39.

27. Gill, "Erastus the Aedile," 294.

28. See Acts 18:7; Rom 16:1, 23; 1 Cor 1:14; Robert Jewett, *Romans: A Commentary*, Hermeneia (Minneapolis: Fortress, 2007), 21–22.

29. Gill, "Erastus the Aedile," 296–98.

30. Kent, *Inscriptions 1926–1950*, 99.

31. Justin J. Meggitt, "The Social Status of Erastus (Rom. 16:23)," *NovT* 38 (1996): 219 n. 10, gives a list of those who "have been quite bold about making this identification." He lists seven scholars.

32. See Andrew D. Clarke, "Another Corinthian Erastus Inscription," *TynBul* 42 (1991): 148–50.

33. See Gill, "Erastus the Aedile," 299, with discussion of those for and against the identification.

34. Ibid., 300: "The evidence does not allow us to be certain about the link between the two Erasti." See also Clarke, "Another Corinthian Erastus Inscription," 151.

35. Meggitt, "Social Status," 220; see also 220–23.

36. Ibid., 223.

it impossible for the *aedile* Erastus to be identical with Paul's Erastus."[37] On other grounds too he argues against the identification,[38] and also argues that Erastus the οἰκονόμος was not a believer.[39]

John Goodrich has recently argued that οἰκονόμος correlates best with *quaestor*,[40] which was "a high-ranking, honourable, and costly municipal position" with the holder of this office being "one of the city's wealthiest and most influential individuals."[41] On this view, Erastus the aedile and Erastus the οἰκονόμος are different people, but the Erastus of Rom 16 is still a person of significance. Goodrich has now also responded to Friesen's work, arguing, along with other points, that Erastus the οἰκονόμος should indeed be seen as a believer.[42]

This inscription clearly raises one of the issues with epigraphical studies: Is a person mentioned in an inscription to be identified with a person with the same name mentioned in a literary text? Often certainty is unobtainable, and caution is much the wiser path. The inscription also shows how significant issues of dating can be.

---

37. Friesen "Wrong Erastus," 243.
38. See ibid., 245–49.
39. See ibid., 249–55.
40. See John K. Goodrich, "Erastus, Quaestor of Corinth: The Administrative Rank of ὁ οἰκονόμος τῆς πόλεως (Rom 16.23) in an Achaean Colony," *NTS* 56 (2010): 90–115. He provides evidence for the *quaestor*-οἰκονόμος correlation with regard to Roman colonies. But see also the further contribution to this debate by Alexander Weiss, "Keine Quästoren in Korinth: Zu Goodrichs (und Theißens) These über das Amt des Erastos (Röm 16.23)," *NTS* 56 (2011): 576–81, and the reply by John K. Goodrich, "Erastus of Corinth (Romans 16.23): Responding to Recent Proposals on His Rank, Status, and Faith," *NTS* 57 (2011): 583–86, in which he argues (586) that "the municipal quaestorship remains a viable interpretation of Erastus' position."
41. Goodrich, "Erastus," 114.
42. See Goodrich, "Erastus of Corinth (Romans 16.23)" 587–93. Attention should also be drawn to the careful discussion of L. L. Welborn (*An End to Enmity: Paul and the "Wrongdoer" of Second Corinthians* [Berlin: de Gruyter, 2011], 260–83) on Erastus as a possible candidate for the socially powerful "wrongdoer" of 2 Corinthians 2 and 7, the figure who had opposed Paul while he was in Corinth. Welborn concludes that "the balance of evidence inclines towards identification of Paul's Erastus with the aedile of the inscription" (ibid., 279; cf. 267–73). Particularly valuable is Welborn's analysis of why New Testament scholars and classicists come to different conclusions about the Erastus inscription (273–79). He argues that divergent assumptions about the social status of the first Christians and the exclusivity of early Christianity are the crucial factors (278).

3.3. Augustus and the "Good News"

The well-known so-called Priene inscription contains the word εὐαγγέλιον.[43] Part of the inscription, which is the reply given by the provincial assembly of Asia to a letter written in 9 BCE by the proconsul of Asia, Paulus Fabius Maximus, reads:

> Providence has filled Augustus with divine power for the benefit of humanity, and in her beneficence has granted us and those who will come after us [a Savior] who has made war to cease and who shall put everything [in peaceful order].... And Caesar, [when he was manifest], transcended the expectations of [all who had anticipated the good news], not only by surpassing the benefits conferred by his predecessors but by leaving no expectation of surpassing him to those who would come after him, with the result that the birthday of our god signalled the beginning of good news for the world because of him [ἦρξεν δὲ τῶι κόσμωι τῶν δι' αὐτὸν εὐαγγέλι(ων ἡ γενέθλιος ἡμ)έρα τοῦ θεοῦ].[44]

The inscription was designed to introduce a new calendar, in which the emperor Augustus was honored by commencing the new year on his birthday, September 23. What is of interest here is the use of the word εὐαγγέλιον. As Graham Stanton notes, the inscription makes it clear that "the coming of the divine Augustus as 'good news' had been eagerly expected. He came as saviour and benefactor, bringing benefits for all. He has brought peace and will continue to do so. He was himself 'the good news.'"[45] This inscription—and others like it—provides a very important context that helps us to understand how the use of εὐαγγέλιον by Christ followers would have been heard.[46] As Stanton notes, "what is clear is that there were rival 'gospels.'"[47]

---

43. Graham N. Stanton, *Jesus and Gospel* (Cambridge: Cambridge University Press, 2004), 31, prefers to call it "the Calendar inscription."
44. Text and translation from ibid., 32. The text is found in *OGI* 2.458.
45. Stanton, *Jesus and Gospel*, 32.
46. See further ibid., 33–35, on whether Paul and others borrowed this term from the imperial cult. Whether or not they borrowed the term εὐαγγέλιον from the imperial cult, early Christ followers "adapted it radically and filled it with distinctively Christian content."
47. Ibid., 35. See also Craig A. Evans, "Mark's Incipit and the Priene Calendar Inscription: From Jewish Gospel to Greco-Roman Gospel," *JGRChJ* 1 (2000): 67–81.

3.4. The Salutaris Inscription from Ephesus

In 104 CE, C. Vibius Salutaris made a bequest to the boule and demos of Ephesus, the details of which are given in a 568-line inscription. From this text we learn that on procession days thirty-one gold and silver type-statues and images, nine of which were of Artemis,[48] were carried from the pronaos of the temple of Artemis outside the city wall to the Magnesian Gate, which was the main entrance to the city from the south; there the procession was joined by the ephebes. The procession then went to the theater, to the Koressos Gate, and back to the Artemisium.[49] The procession occurred on the days the city assembly met, on important festivals, and on a number of other occasions. Guy MacLean Rogers estimated that the procession would have occurred at least once every two weeks throughout the year,[50] and it is clear that Salutaris intended the procession to be a significant event in the city each time it occurred.[51] Further, since at least 260 individuals were involved in the procession through the streets, it "must have impeded, if not altogether halted traffic within the city at procession time."[52]

The inscription shows the vitality of the cult of Artemis in Ephesus in 104 CE. Further, Rogers has shown how Salutaris's foundation caused the people involved "to look (metaphorically) to the institutional structure of their city, to its Ionian foundation, and to the birth of the goddess Artemis, for their sense of social and historical identity in the complex and changing Roman world."[53] In particular, Salutaris's foundation, through focusing on the birth of the goddess, taught the people to look "to the birth of the goddess Artemis at Ephesos, for a theological sense of how Ephesian social and historical identity was grounded in a 'sacred reality,' which was

---

48. See the list of type-statues and images in Guy Maclean Rogers, *The Sacred Identity of Ephesos: Foundation Myths of a Roman City* (London: Routledge, 1991), 84–85.

49. For the route see ibid., 85–107. The whole procession would have lasted at least ninety minutes; see ibid., 110.

50. See ibid., 83.

51. IEph 1a.27, l. 91, makes it clear that the statues were to be carried at the front of the procession.

52. Rogers, *Sacred Identity*, 86; at least 250 ephebes were involved in the procession.

53. Ibid., 41. The inscription also shows that Salutaris wished to encourage reverence for Artemis among children in the city; see ibid., 59.

impervious to all humanly wrought challenges."⁵⁴ We can see then how central the goddess Artemis was to the identity of the city of Ephesus, and the intimate connection that existed between the city and her goddess.⁵⁵

The inscription greatly highlights the significance of Artemis for Ephesus and so helps us to understand the riot of Acts 19; it also sheds considerable light on the public nature of religion, and on the significance of the imperial cult—all important areas for New Testament study.

3.5. Horsley and Other Inscriptions from Ephesus

Greg Horsley has done a considerable amount of work that has highlighted the importance of inscriptions for the study of the New Testament, primarily through the series *New Documents Illustrating Early Christianity*.⁵⁶ One study he has undertaken has been of the association of fishermen and fishmongers of Ephesus. A stela with an inscription, dated to Nero's reign (54–59 CE), was set up by the association of fishermen and fishmongers of Ephesus in conjunction with the construction of a harbor tollhouse for the collection of custom dues relating to fishing.⁵⁷ Around one hundred members made contributions to the cost of the building.⁵⁸ Horsley analyzes the number of Latin and Greek names in the association; the figures are twenty-four Latin and fifty-five Greek names.⁵⁹ The ratio

---

54. Ibid., 69; see also 112–15, 145–47. The arrangements made by Salutaris were approved by the demos as a whole, so the foundation ultimately represented the attitude of the demos of Ephesus. It was also confirmed by Roman proconsuls.

55. The Salutaris inscription is dated in 104 CE, but it is likely that the practice of carrying the images of Artemis in procession on the festival of the goddess existed prior to this.

56. There are ten volumes to date, with volumes 1–5 being edited by G. H. R. Horsley, volumes 6–7 by Stephen R. Llewelyn with the collaboration of Rosalinde A. Kearsley, volumes 8–9 by Llewelyn, and volume 10 by Llewelyn and James R. Harrison.

57. The full text and translation is given in *NewDocs* 5:95–99.

58. *NewDocs* 5:107.

59. He also notes that nearly 50 percent of the members of the association are Roman citizens; he highlights "the large number of Roman citizens at a time when citizenship, especially in the East, was fairly rare, and therefore not only conferred formal rank but undoubtedly a certain status as well" (G. H. R. Horsley, "The Inscriptions of Ephesos and the New Testament," *NovT* 34 [1992]: 132). See *NewDocs* 5:108–9 for detailed analysis. In Horsley, "Inscriptions of Ephesos," 132, he notes: "those involved in this association of fish traders reflect the whole range in formal rank, from citizen to slave. This provides an intriguing analogy—that last word must be emphasized—for

is almost the same (23:45) for the names of those linked in some way to the Pauline churches in the New Testament. Horsley writes: "this group of fishermen and traders from Ephesos provides the first really comparable evidence known to me from a group contemporary with the NT in which we encounter a social 'mix' closely akin to that represented in the Pauline congregations."[60]

Of course, in their work on *New Documents* Horsley and others have shown what is to be gained for New Testament study from research on inscriptions in the areas of Greek lexicography, language, grammar, and social history in general.

3.6. Studying the Early Christ Followers in Rome

In *From Paul to Valentinus: Christians at Rome in the First Two Centuries*, Peter Lampe has demonstrated the great value of epigraphy for his topic. I note only two of the areas in which he uses inscriptions. First, analysis of archaeological and epigraphical evidence, along with detailed socioeconomic data from inscriptions (such as the number of bakeries in different areas), leads to the conclusion that groups of Christ followers flourished in the poorest and most densely populated districts of Rome.[61] Second, we know a number of the names of Christ followers in Rome from Romans 16; comparison of these names with those from inscriptions leads to the conclusion that "over two-thirds with a great degree of probability show

---

the similar spread attested in the Pauline congregations. We are encountering here a contemporary association with a social mix closely akin to the groups connected with Paul." Of course, there has been much discussion—notably by Steven Friesen and Bruce Longenecker—about the social level of Pauline Christ followers in recent years. See Steven J. Friesen, "Poverty in Pauline Studies: Beyond the So-Called New Consensus," *JSNT* 26 (2004): 323–61; Bruce W. Longenecker, "Exposing the Economic Middle: A Revised Economy Scale of the Study of Early Urban Christianity," *JSNT* 31 (2009): 243–78; Longenecker, *Remember the Poor: Paul, Poverty and the Greco-Roman World* (Grand Rapids: Eerdmans, 2010).

60. Horsley also notes a number of features of Acts 19 that are illustrated by Ephesian inscriptions—such as the prominence of Ephesus as "temple warden" of Artemis (Acts 19:35), the devotion to Artemis in the city, and the role of asiarchs; see Horsley, "Inscriptions of Ephesos," 136–38, 141–44, 153–56.

61. Peter Lampe, *From Paul to Valentinus: Christians at Rome in the First Two Centuries* (Minneapolis: Fortress, 2003), 65–66.

indications of slave origin."⁶² In his study, Lampe clearly demonstrates what can be gained when literary, epigraphical, and archaeological material is brought into conversation and analyzed together. Robert Jewett has then built on Lampe's insights in his commentary on Romans.⁶³

3.7. Other Topics

Many other topics and inscriptions could be discussed. Here I simply note some other areas of great interest to the study of the early groups of Christ followers:

- The associations and the rich evidence they provide as analogous groups to the early groups of Christ-followers.⁶⁴
- The study of named individuals in the Gospels and Richard Bauckham's study showing that they correspond well to Jewish names in use in Palestinian Jewish sources of the period.⁶⁵
- Several inscriptions and what has become called "the Palatine graffito," which help illuminate crucifixion in the first century CE.⁶⁶
- The Aphrodisias inscriptions, which list more than fifty people who are called "Theosebeis," or God worshipers, and their significance for discussions about God-fearers and the mission of the early groups of Christ followers to gentiles who had a place within the Diaspora Jewish communities.⁶⁷

---

62. Ibid., 183; see also 153–83; Jewett, *Romans*, 952–84.
63. See Jewett, *Romans*, 62–69, and passim.
64. See John S. Kloppenborg and Stephen G. Wilson, *Voluntary Associations in the Graeco-Roman World* (London: Routledge, 1996); John S. Kloppenborg and Richard S. Ascough, *Attica, Central Greece, Macedonia, Thrace*, vol. 1 of *Greco-Roman Associations: Texts, Translations, and Commentary*, BZNW 181 (Berlin: de Gruyter, 2011); Richard S. Ascough, Philip A. Harland, and John S. Kloppenborg, *Associations in the Greco-Roman World: A Sourcebook* (Waco, TX: Baylor University Press, 2012).
65. See Richard Bauckham, *Jesus and the Eyewitnesses: The Gospels as Eyewitness Testimony* (Grand Rapids: Eerdmans, 2006), 39–92.
66. See John Granger Cook, "Envisioning Crucifixion: Light from Several Inscriptions and the Palatine Graffito," *NovT* 50 (2008): 262–85.
67. The original publication is Joyce Maire Reynolds and Robert Tannenbaum, *Jews and God-Fearers at Aphrodisias: Greek Inscriptions with Commentary*, Proceedings of the Cambridge Philological Society Supplementary Volume 12 (Cambridge: Cambridge Philological Society, 1987). They thought the stelae contained one inscrip-

- The Theodotos inscription, with its emphasis on the study of the Torah, and the evidence it provides for synagogues in Jerusalem at the time of Jesus.[68] Here the question of dating is most acute.
- The contrasting ways in which the Old Testament is quoted in Jewish and in Christian epigraphy.[69]

4. Conclusions

I hope I have said enough to show that epigraphy has an invaluable contribution to make to study of the polis and *ekklēsia* in the Greco-Roman world. As Bodel comments, "there are few, if any, areas of ancient Greco-Roman culture that inscriptions do not somehow illuminate."[70]

Certainly epigraphy brings challenges: Is an inscription dated correctly, are we asking the right questions, or perhaps do we even need to consider if the inscription is authentic? Are we taking sufficient account of the epigraphical bias that has led to some things being inscribed and not others? Are we generalizing from too small a sample? In addition, often epigraphy can be frustrating: readings are unclear, or the meaning of particular inscriptions is ambiguous. Sometimes, too, we may be looking to inscriptions for insights that they simply cannot provide. But clearly epigraphy is a vital resource for our studies.

Bibliography

Ameling, Walter, ed. *Kleinasien*. Vol. 2 of *Inscriptiones Judaicae Orientis*. TSAJ 99. Tübingen: Mohr Siebeck, 2004.

---

tion from the third century CE, but subsequent discussion has shown that there are two separate inscriptions, one from the fourth and the other from the fifth centuries CE. On these inscriptions see also Dietrich-Alex Koch, "The God-Fearers between Facts and Fiction: Two Theosebeis-Inscriptions from Aphrodisias and Their Bearing for the New Testament," *ST* 60 (2006): 62–90.

68. See John S. Kloppenborg, "The Theodotos Synagogue Inscription and the Problem of First-Century Synagogue Buildings," in *Jesus and Archaeology*, ed. James H. Charlesworth (Grand Rapids: Eerdmans, 2006), 236–82.

69. See Pieter Willem van der Horst, "Biblical Quotations in Judaeo-Greek Inscriptions," in *The Scriptures of Israel in Jewish and Christian Tradition: Essays in Honour of Maarten J. J. Menken*, ed. Bart J. Koet et al. (Leiden: Brill, 2013), 363–76.

70. Bodel, "Epigraphy," xix.

Ascough, Richard S., Philip A. Harland, and John S. Kloppenborg. *Associations in the Greco-Roman World: A Sourcebook*. Waco, TX: Baylor University Press, 2012.
Bauckham, Richard. *Jesus and the Eyewitnesses: The Gospels as Eyewitness Testimony*. Grand Rapids: Eerdmans, 2006.
Bérard, François, Denis Feissel, Nicolas Laubry, Pierre Petitmengin, Denis Rousset, and Michel Sève. *Guide de L'Épigraphiste: Bibliographie choisie des épigraphies antiques et médiévales*. 3rd ed. Paris: Éditions Rue d'Ulms, 2000.
Bodel, John. "Epigraphy and the Ancient Historian." Pages 1–56 in *Epigraphic Evidence: Ancient History from Inscriptions*. Edited by John Bodel. London: Routledge, 2001.
Calder, W. M. "Early Christian Epitaphs from Phrygia." *AnSt* 5 (1955): 25–38.
Clarke, Andrew D. "Another Corinthian Erastus Inscription." *TynBul* 42 (1991): 146–51.
Cook, B. F. *Greek Inscriptions*. London: British Museum Publications, 1987.
Cook, John Granger. "Envisioning Crucifixion: Light from Several Inscriptions and the Palatine Graffito." *NovT* 50 (2008): 262–85.
Cooley, Alison E. *The Cambridge Manual of Latin Epigraphy*. Cambridge: Cambridge University Press, 2012.
Davies, John, and John Wilkes. *Epigraphy and the Historical Sciences*. Proceedings of the British Academy 177. Oxford: Oxford University Press, 2012.
Deissmann, Adolf. *Light from the Ancient East: The New Testament Illustrated by Recently Discovered Texts of the Graeco-Roman World*. Translated by Lionel Strachen. Rev. ed. London: Hodder & Stoughton: 1927.
Eisen, Ute E. *Women Officeholders in Early Christianity: Epigraphical and Literary Studies*. Collegeville, MN: Liturgical Press, 2000.
Evans, Craig A. "Mark's Incipit and the Priene Calendar Inscription: From Jewish Gospel to Greco-Roman Gospel." *JGRChJ* 1 (2000): 67–81.
Friesen, Steven J. "Poverty in Pauline Studies: Beyond the So-Called New Consensus." *JSNT* 26 (2004): 323–61.
———. "The Wrong Erastus: Ideology, Archaeology, and Exegesis." Pages 231–56 in *Corinth in Context: Comparative Studies on Religion and Society*. Edited by Steven J. Friesen, Daniel N. Schowalter and James C. Walters. NovTSup 135. Leiden: Brill, 2010.

Gathercole, Simon. "Jerusalem and Caesarea Inscriptions and New Testament Study: A Review Article." *JSNT* 35 (2013): 394–401.

Gibson, Elsa. *The "Christians for Christians" Inscriptions of Phrygia: Greek Texts, Translation and Commentary.* HTS 32. Missoula, MT: Scholars Press, 1978.

Gill, David W. J. "Erastus the Aedile." *TynBul* 40 (1989): 293–301.

Goodrich, John K. "Erastus, Quaestor of Corinth: The Administrative Rank of ὁ οἰκονόμος τῆς πόλεως (Rom 16.23) in an Achaean Colony." *NTS* 56 (2010): 90–115.

———. "Erastus of Corinth (Romans 16.23): Responding to Recent Proposals on His Rank, Status, and Faith." *NTS* 57 (2011): 583–93.

Gordon, Arthur E. *Illustrated Guide to Latin Epigraphy.* Berkeley: University of California Press, 1983.

Henten, Jan Willem van, and Pieter Willem van der Horst. *Studies in Early Jewish Epigraphy.* AGJU 21. Leiden: Brill, 1994.

Horsley, G. H. R. "The Inscriptions of Ephesos and the New Testament." *NovT* 34 (1992): 105–68.

Horst, Pieter Willem van der. *Ancient Jewish Epitaphs: An Introductory Survey of a Millennium of Jewish Funerary Epigraphy (300 BCE–700 CE).* CBET 2. Kampen: Kok Pharos, 1991.

———. "Biblical Quotations in Judaeo-Greek Inscriptions." Pages 363–76 in *The Scriptures of Israel in Jewish and Christian Tradition: Essays in Honour of Maarten J. J. Menken.* Edited by Bart J. Koet, Steve Moyise, and Joseph Verheyden. NovTSup 148. Leiden: Brill, 2013.

Jewett, Robert. *Romans: A Commentary.* Hermeneia. Minneapolis: Fortress, 2007.

Johnson, Gary J. *Early-Christian Epitaphs from Anatolia.* SBLTT 35. Early Christian Literature Series 8. Atlanta: Scholars Press, 1995.

Kant, Laurence H. "Jewish Inscriptions in Greek and Latin." *ANRW* 20.2:671–713.

Kent, John Harvey. *The Inscriptions 1926–1950.* Vol. 8.3 of *Corinth: Results of Excavations.* Cambridge, MA: Harvard University Press, 1966.

Keppie, Lawrence. *Understanding Roman Inscriptions.* Baltimore: Johns Hopkins University Press, 1991.

Kloppenborg, John S. "The Theodotos Synagogue Inscription and the Problem of First-Century Synagogue Buildings." Pages 236–82 in *Jesus and Archaeology.* Edited by James H. Charlesworth. Grand Rapids: Eerdmans, 2006.

Kloppenborg, John S., and Richard S. Ascough. *Greco-Roman Associations: Texts, Translations, and Commentary.* Vol. 1, *Attica, Central Greece, Macedonia, Thrace.* BZNW 181. Berlin: de Gruyter, 2011.

Kloppenborg, John S., and Stephen G. Wilson. *Voluntary Associations in the Graeco-Roman World.* London: Routledge, 1996.

Koch, Dietrich-Alex. "The God-Fearers between Facts and Fiction: Two Theosebeis-Inscriptions from Aphrodisias and Their Bearing for the New Testament." *ST* 60 (2006): 62–90.

Koester, Craig R. "Roman Slave Trade and the Critique of Babylon in Revelation 18." *CBQ* 70 (2008): 766–86.

Kraemer, Ross S. "Jewish Tuna and Christian Fish: Identifying Religious Affiliation in Epigraphic Sources." *HTR* 84 (1991): 141–62.

Lampe, Peter. *From Paul to Valentinus: Christians at Rome in the First Two Centuries.* Minneapolis: Fortress, 2003.

Levick, Barbara. "Greek and Latin Epigraphy in Anatolia: Progress and Problems." Pages 371–76 in *Acta of the Fifth International Congress of Greek and Latin Epigraphy Cambridge 1967.* Oxford: Basil Blackwell, 1971.

Longenecker, Bruce W. "Exposing the Economic Middle: A Revised Economy Scale of the Study of Early Urban Christianity." *JSNT* 31 (2009): 243–78.

———. *Remember the Poor: Paul, Poverty and the Greco-Roman World.* Grand Rapids: Eerdmans, 2010.

MacMullen, Ramsay. "The Epigraphic Habit in the Roman Empire." *AJP* 103 (1982): 233–46.

Madigan, Kevin, and Carolyn Osiek. *Ordained Women in the Early Church.* Baltimore: Johns Hopkins University Press, 2005.

McHugh, Michael P. "Inscriptions." Pages 463–65 in *Encyclopedia of Early Christianity.* Edited by Everett Ferguson, Michael P. McHugh, Frederick W. Norris, and David M. Scholer. New York: Garland, 1990.

McLean, Bradley Hudson. *An Introduction to Greek Epigraphy of the Hellenistic and Roman Periods from Alexander the Great Down to the Reign of Constantine.* Ann Arbor: University of Michigan Press, 2002.

Meggitt, Justin J. "The Social Status of Erastus (Rom. 16:23)." *NovT* 38 (1996): 218–23.

Millar, Fergus. "Epigraphy." Pages 80–136 in *Sources for Ancient History.* Edited by Michael Crawford. Cambridge: Cambridge University Press, 1983.

Murphy-O'Connor, Jerome. *St. Paul's Corinth: Texts and Archaeology*. Wilmington, DE: Michael Glazier, 1983.
Price, Jonathan J., and Haggai Misgav. "Jewish Inscriptions and Their Use." Pages 461–83 in *Midrash and Targum, Liturgy, Poetry, Mysticism, Contracts, Inscriptions, Ancient Science and the Languages of Rabbinic Literature*. Part 2 of *The Literature of the Sages*. Edited by Shmuel Safrai, Zeev Safrai, Joshua Schwartz, and Peter J. Tomson. CRINT 2.3b. Assen: Van Gorcum, 2006.
Reynolds, Joyce Maire, and Robert Tannenbaum. *Jews and God-Fearers at Aphrodisias: Greek Inscriptions with Commentary*. Proceedings of the Cambridge Philological Society Supplementary Volume 12. Cambridge: Cambridge Philological Society, 1987.
Riesner, Rainer. *Paul's Early Period: Chronology, Mission Strategy, Theology*. Grand Rapids: Eerdmans, 1998.
Rives, James. "Civic and Religious Life." Pages 118–36 in *Epigraphic Evidence: Ancient History from Inscriptions*. Edited by John Bodel. London: Routledge, 2001.
Rogers, Guy MacLean. *The Sacred Identity of Ephesos: Foundation Myths of a Roman City*. London: Routledge, 1991.
Saller, Richard. "The Family and Society." Pages 95–117 in *Epigraphic Evidence: Ancient History from Inscriptions*. Edited by John Bodel. London: Routledge, 2001.
Slingerland, Dixon. "Acts 18:1–18, the Gallio Inscription, and Absolute Pauline Chronology." *JBL* 110 (1991): 439–49.
Snyder, Graydon F. *Ante Pacem: Archaeological Evidence of Church Life before Constantine*. Macon, GA: Mercer University Press, 1985.
Stanton, Graham N. *Jesus and Gospel*. Cambridge: Cambridge University Press, 2004.
Tabbernee, William. "The Discovery of the Tymion Inscription." Pages 49–74 in *Pepouza and Tymion: The Discovery and Archeological Exploration of a Lost Ancient City and an Imperial Estate*. Edited by William Tabbernee and Peter Lampe. Berlin: de Gruyter, 2008.
———. "Epigraphy." Pages 120–39 in *The Oxford Handbook of Early Christian Studies*. Edited by Susan Ashbrook Harvey and David G. Hunter. Oxford: Oxford University Press, 2008.
———. *Montanist Inscriptions and Testimonia: Epigraphic Sources Illustrating the History of Montanism*. North American Patristic Society Patristic Monograph Series 16. Macon, GA: Mercer University Press, 1997.

Trebilco, Paul R. "The Christian and Jewish Eumeneian Formula." Pages 66–88 in *Negotiating Diaspora: Jewish Strategies in the Roman Empire*. Edited by John M. G. Barclay. LSTS 45. Sheffield: Sheffield Academic, 2004.

Welborn, L. L. *An End to Enmity: Paul and the "Wrongdoer" of Second Corinthians*. Berlin: de Gruyter, 2011.

Weiss, Alexander. "Keine Quästoren in Korinth: Zu Goodrichs (und Theißens) These über das Amt des Erastos (Röm 16.23)." *NTS* 56 (2011): 576–81.

Woodhead, A. G. *The Study of Greek Inscriptions*. 2nd ed. Cambridge: Cambridge University Press, 1981.

Zangenberg, Jürgen K. "Archaeology, Papyri, and Inscriptions." Pages 322–66 in *Early Judaism: A Comprehensive Overview*. Edited by John J. Collins and Daniel C. Harlow. Grand Rapids: Eerdmans, 2012.

Gaia, Polis, and *Ekklēsia* at the Miletus Market Gate: An Eco-critical Reimagination of Revelation 12:16

Brigitte Kahl

1. Reading Texts through Images: The "Visual Turn" in New Testament Studies

Searching ancient epigraphic and literary sources to grasp the sociohistorical contexts of biblical texts is a well-established part of critical methodology in New Testament studies. The work with images, however, and their employment as sources in their own right for contextual and textual clarification has long been entirely neglected. This neglect has multiple reasons, among them the primacy of the verbal over the visual that is deeply ingrained into Western thinking. Judeo-Christian "aniconism"—the firmly established prohibition of the second commandment to depict God in any human or nonhuman representation for cultic purposes (Exod 20:4–5; Deut 5:8–9)—might be another major factor that has contributed to the "visual illiteracy" of historical-critical exegesis as it is commonly practiced.[1] Ancient images are ignored both because of the commonsense assumption that their meaning is plainly before everybody's eyes, and (at a closer look) because of the opaqueness of their visual language with its alien "vocabulary" and "grammar" that we do not know to translate.[2] As a

---

1. See the discussion in Harry O. Maier, *Picturing Paul in Empire* (London: T&T Clark, 2013), 4–5.

2. Based on the work of Paul Zanker, *The Power of Images in the Age of Augustus*, trans. Alan Shapiro (Ann Arbor: University of Michigan Press, 1988), and Tonio Hölscher, *The Language of Images in Roman Art*, trans. Anthony Snodgrass and Annemarie Kunzl-Snodgrass (Cambridge: Cambridge University Press, 2004), in my own approach of "critical reimagination" I treat images in analogy to texts as systems

result, New Testament scholars usually are much better equipped to read texts than to read images. And although images are often added as "illustration," for example, in Bible dictionaries, this mostly happens in a methodologically unreflective way, as if the relation of the visual to the textual and topical was self-evident.

In the past decade something like a "visual turn" has started to profoundly transform New Testament studies.[3] One of its major contributing factors is a growing awareness among ancient and art historians that the transition from Roman Republic to Roman Empire under Augustus was shaped by an innovative, conscious use of images as mass media to communicate the new ideology among the widely illiterate inhabitants of the Roman *oikoumenē*.[4] Paul Zanker's *The Power of Images in the Age of Augustus*[5] has played a key role in this iconographic revival that soon took root in New Testament studies where it partly fused with a new interest in Roman imperial contexts as historical location of New Testament texts—another long neglected topic.[6] Empire-critical approaches from relatively

---

of communication with their own "language" and semiotics, which allows them to function not only as material contexts but also as visual intertexts for sociohistorical and ideological-critical investigation of scriptural texts; see Brigitte Kahl, *Galatians Re-imagined: Reading with the Eyes of the Vanquished*, Paul in Critical Contexts (Minneapolis: Fortress, 2010), 27–29, 250–53.

3. This new interest in "Picturing the New Testament" was signaled in the landmark collection of Annette Weissenrieder, Friederike Wendt, and Petra von Gemünden, eds., *Picturing the New Testament*, WUNT 2/195 (Tübingen: Mohr Siebeck, 2005). An early precursor of visual and spatial studies in New Testament is Halvor Moxnes, "'He Saw That the City Was Full of Idols' (Acts 17:16): Visualizing the World of the First Christians," in *Mighty Minorities? Minorities in Early Christianity—Positions and Strategies*, ed. David Hellholm, Halvor Moxnes, and Turid Karlsen Seim (Oslo: Scandinavian University Press, 1995), 107–31. Furthermore, work with coins to explore contextual settings of texts always necessitated attention to images; see, e.g., Larry Kreitzer, *Striking New Images: Roman Imperial Coinage and the New Testament World* (Sheffield: Sheffield Academic, 1996).

4. See the helpful debate on (il)literacy and the reception of visual imperial propaganda (including architecture, public and sacred space, numismatics) in James R. Harrison, *Paul and the Imperial Authorities at Thessalonica and Rome: A Study in the Conflict of Ideology*, WUNT 273 (Tübingen: Mohr Siebeck, 2011), 19–23.

5. "Rarely has art been pressed into the service of political power so directly as in the Age of Augustus" (Zanker, *Power of Images*, v). "The goal of this book is to examine the complex interrelationship of the establishment of monarchy, the transformation of society, and the creation of a whole new method of visual communication" (ibid., 3).

6. S. R. F. Price's study that was very influential for the empire-critical turn in New

early on developed a strong visual branch.⁷ Although the relationship to Rome is defined variously, ranging from stern critique of empire to compromise or even consent, Roman iconography in many visual approaches at the moment is predominant.⁸

Testament studies did not focus specifically on images, but its subject matter brought the ideological relevance of visuality in the public arena to the foreground—the whole range of visual representations of imperial power through public ritual, architecture, statuary, etc. See *Rituals and Power: The Roman Imperial Cult in Asia Minor* (Cambridge: Cambridge University Press, 1984).

7. Both Zanker's and Price's approach are, e.g., included in the seminal collection of essays in Richard A. Horsley, ed., *Paul and Empire: Religion and Power in Roman Imperial Society* (Harrisburg, PA: Trinity Press International, 1997). It might be worth mentioning that the first of two conferences on the New Testament and Roman Empire convened at Union Theological Seminary New York in 2004 included several key presentations that drew on innovative work with images (Ellen Bradshaw Aitken, John Dominic Crossan, Brigitte Kahl, Davina Lopez, David Sánchez); see the proceedings of the conference in Brigitte Kahl, Davina Lopez, and Hal Taussig, eds., *New Testament and Roman Empire*, USQR 59 (2005): 3–4; for a summary of its visual component, see 181–85. In 2004 also the first strongly image-based study on Paul appeared: John Dominic Crossan and Jonathan L. Reed, *In Search of Paul: How Jesus's Apostle Opposed Rome's Empire with God's Kingdom—A New Vision of Paul's Words and World* (San Francisco: HarperSanFrancisco, 2004).

8. E.g., David L. Balch, *Roman Domestic Art and Early House Churches*, WUNT 228 (Tübingen: Mohr Siebeck, 2008); Rosemary Canavan, *Clothing the Body of Christ at Colossae: A Visual Construction of Identity*, WUNT 2/334 (Tübingen: Mohr Siebeck, 2012); James R. Harrison, "'More Than Conquerors' (Rom 8:37): Paul's Gospel and the Augustan Triumphal Arches of the Greek East and Latin West," in *Buried History: The Journal of the Australian Institute of Archaeology* 47 (2011): 3–20; Kahl, Lopez, and Taussig, *New Testament and Roman Empire*; Kahl, *Galatians Re-imagined*; Kahl, "Krieg, Maskulinität und der imperiale Gottvater: Das Augustusforum und die messianische Re-Imagination von 'Hagar' im Galaterbrief," in *Doing Gender—Doing Religion: Fallstudien zur Intersektionalität im frühen Judentum, Christentum und Islam*, ed. Ute Eisen, Christine Gerber, and Angela Standhartinger, WUNT 302 (Tübingen: Mohr Siebeck, 2013), 273–300; Kahl, "Hagar's Babylonian Captivity: A Roman Re-imagination of Galatians 4:21–31," *Int* 68 (2014): 257–69; Davina C. Lopez, *Apostle to the Conquered: Reimagining Paul's Mission*, Paul in Critical Contexts (Minneapolis: Fortress, 2008); Harry O. Maier, "Barbarians, Scythians and Imperial Iconography in the Epistle to the Colossians," in Weissenrieder, Wendt, and von Gemünden, *Picturing the New Testament*, 385–406; and Maier, *Picturing Paul in Empire*. For a fusion between an empire-critical approach and a postcolonial emphasis on contemporary representations of empire, see David Sánchez, *From Patmos to the Barrio: Subverting Imperial Myths* (Minneapolis: Fortress, 2008); Aliou Cissé Niang, "Seeing and Hearing

Different from Hebrew Bible studies, where especially the Freiburg school around Othmar Keel, Christoph Uehlinger, and Sylvia Schroer has developed a strong tradition of working with ancient Near Eastern imagery, New Testament iconographic study and exegesis are still in their nascent stage, especially with regard to a systematic treatment of methodological and hermeneutical questions.[9] With all caution, one could presently differentiate two major strands of "visual exegesis" in New Testament; both explore the interaction between texts and images in the interpretation of the New Testament, but approach the exegetical task from somewhat dissimilar points of departure.

(1) The scholars mentioned so far combine a double focus on New Testament texts on the one hand and on material culture/*visual images* on the other that are both explored by themselves and in their mutual relationship. "Images" in this context constitute a broad spectrum of visual representations ranging from statuary, monuments, architecture, mosaics, frescoes, and coinage to spatial arrangements, cultic and public performances, and dress. The thickness of this exploration, its hermeneutical presuppositions and underlying methodology (which often remains unstated), can vary considerably in each case, however.

(2) A coherent methodological framework has been and is being developed by Vernon Robbins and his school of sociorhetorical interpretation (SRI), including scholars such as Gregory Bloomquist, Roy Jeal, David DeSilva, and others.[10] Shaped by an emphasis on rhetorical analysis, the *verbal images* that are contained within the text itself in this approach are a primary focus. These "word pictures" internal to the text are explored rhetorically in terms of their meaning-making, including the whole visual inventory that a text uses to produce a strong imprint on the mind and imagination of its readers/hearers. To map the complexity of this overall phenomenon of visual communication, and specifically also its cognitive dimensions, Robbins has coined the term "rhetography."[11]

Jesus Christ Crucified in Galatians 3:1 under Watchful Imperial Eyes," in *Text, Image, and Christians in the Graeco-Roman World: A Festschrift in Honor of David Lee Balch*, ed. Aliou Cissé Niang and Carolyn Osiek, Princeton Theological Monograph Series (Eugene, OR: Pickwick, 2012), 160–82.

9. Maier, *Picturing Paul in Empire*, 17.

10. E.g., Vernon K. Robbins, *Exploring the Texture of Texts* (Harrisburg, PA: Trinity Press International, 1996).

11. Rhetography means not only the rhetorical use of *ekphrasis*, or image-based

Both approaches are complementary and intersect in multiple ways within the framework of a still evolving debate on methods. The concept of rhetography leads naturally from the verbal images inside the text and the mind into the world of visual images and material culture outside the text/mind; reversely, material images in their encounter with text require a literary and rhetorical perspective to understand how they participate in the process of meaning-making. The productivity of such a fusion shows, for example, in the work of Rosemary Canavan, who uses the method of sociorhetorical interpretation to study the verbal images of "putting on and putting off Christ" in Col 3:1-17 in light of imperial clothing and body imagery from the Lycus Valley.[12]

The purposes of our investigation here are not so much to advance the methodological debate, but to show in an exemplary way why the work with iconography in New Testament studies is needed minimally for two reasons. First, images can contribute essential historical-*contextual* information that is vital for textual interpretation but not readily obtainable from written sources. Second, images may provide an indispensable *intertextual* dimension for reading the text critically in its interaction with a given context, in the case of Rev 12:16 the urban environment of Roman-ruled Asia Minor, where the images we choose light up and illuminate aspects of the text that would go (and have gone) otherwise unnoticed. Methodologically, we will proceed in four basic steps of "visual exegesis": (1) A brief introduction and initial exploration of Rev 12:16 will yield a both contextual and interpretational question regarding the role of Gaia in this text; this question will prompt our iconographic investigation. (2)

---

language for persuasion, but also more generally the creation of "a context of communication through statements or signs that conjure visual images in the mind which, in turn, evoke 'familiar' contexts that provide meaning for the reader or hearer" (Vernon K. Robbins, "Rhetography: A New Way of Seeing the Familiar Text," in *Words Well Spoken: George Kennedy's Rhetoric of the New Testament*, ed. Clifton C. Black and Duane F. Watson [Waco, TX: Baylor University Press, 2008], 81). See also Vernon K. Robbins, "Enthymeme and Picture in the *Gospel of Thomas*," in *Thomasine Traditions in Antiquity: The Social and Cultural World of the Gospel of Thomas*, ed. Jon Ma Asgeirsson, April D. DeConick, and Risto Uro (Leiden: Brill, 2006), 175; Roy Jeal, "Blending Two Arts: Rhetorical Words, Rhetorical Pictures and Social Formation in the Letter to Philemon," *Sino-Christian Studies* 5 (2008): 9-38; David A. DeSilva, "Seeing Things John's Way: Rhetography and Conceptual Blending in Revelation 14:6-13," *BBR* 18 (2008): 271-98; and the insightful discussion in Maier, *Picturing Paul in Empire*, 28-31.

12. Canavan, *Clothing the Body of Christ*.

After a few comments on (im)proper "matchmaking" between John's text and the proposed images of Hadrian from the Miletus Market Gate, (3) these images themselves will be briefly introduced, paralleling the initial exploration of the text in step one. (4) The decisive and most comprehensive step to be taken is the final task of meaning-making through the reciprocal (or intertextual) reading of the images in light of the text, and the text in light of the images. The "imperial imagination" regarding Gaia and the conquered nations that is manifested in the two statues of emperor Hadrian will be juxtaposed with John's "apocalyptic counterimagination." As a result, the role of Gaia, polis, and *ekklēsia* in the verbal text-image of Rev 12:16 will be "critically reimagined," compared to standard Roman iconography as well as established Christian interpretation.[13]

2. John's Text (Rev 12:16): Initial Exploration

> Then from his mouth the serpent launched [ἔβαλεν] water like a river after the woman, to sweep her away by the river [αὐτὴν ποταμοφόρητον ποιήσῃ]. And the Earth [ἡ γῆ] helped the woman [ἐβοήθησεν ... τῇ γυναικί], and the Earth opened her mouth and swallowed the river that the dragon had launched from his mouth. Then the dragon was angry with the woman and went away to make war on the rest of her children [σπέρματος], those who keep the commandments of God and have the testimony of Jesus. (Rev 12:15–17, my translation)

In Rev 12:16 an incident is reported that constitutes a somewhat surprising plot element in the big apocalyptic drama John the Seer has unfold before the eyes of the seven embattled Christ communities (*ekklēsiai*) in Asia Minor: Earth/Gaia (or Gē) herself steps up as an active player in support of a woman in distress (who is Ekklēsia) and as an agent of resistance against the imperial power of Rome, a ravaging dragon/serpent who pursues the fugitive woman Ekklēsia. "*And the Earth helped the woman.*" Just a single verse, Rev 12:16 is quite underexplored and has rarely drawn much attention by commentators—even the "Green Letter Bible," which marks all ecologically relevant scriptural passages in green, does not notice it.[14] Common translations such as the New Revised Standard Version (NRSV)

---

13. For the term "critical reimagination," see n. 2 above and Canavan, *Clothing the Body of Christ at Colossae*, 37–39; Maier, *Picturing Paul in Empire*, 20–21.

14. *The Green Bible: New Revised Standard Version* (San Francisco: HarperOne, 2008), 1212.

or the New International Version (NIV) change the Greek pronoun "*her* mouth" into "*its* mouth," thus obliterating both the subject status and the feminine gender of Earth in the text.[15] While this oversight might well reflect the traditionally strained relationship between Christian theology and "pagan" concepts of (mother) nature, it also seems to correspond to a mostly negative classification of Earth in Revelation as location of Satan, curse, and inevitable destruction.[16]

Yet what if Rev 12:16 indeed means what it says, namely, that Earth is a responsive, purposeful, interconnected subject with intrinsic value that both resists and takes care, as the six principles of the Earth Bible project around Norman Habel famously state?[17] In light of current and coming ecological disaster and an urgently needed recovery of the biblical Earth story, the potential implications of Rev 12:16 for an eco-critical reimagination of Earth, city, and church are undoubtedly momentous and require further exploration.

On the literary plane, the narrative grammar of the episode in Rev 12:13–17 is constituted by the classic triangular interplay between a fierce "opponent" and an unexpected yet powerful "helper" who rescues the "heroine" and her mission. The primary agency is with the "big red dragon"

---

15. Interestingly, the King James Version (KJV), Darby, Webster, and the American Standard Version (ASV) keep "*her* mouth."

16. Harry O. Maier notes that John from chapter 6 on "has consistently named the earth as the site of opposition to God and place where God's punishment falls" (*Apocalypse Recalled: The Book of Revelation after Christendom* [Minneapolis: Fortress, 2002], 149). Although in Rev 12 he observes that the "dualism of heaven-earth/sea is interrupted slightly at verse 16, in which the earth comes to the help of the woman," he dismisses this observation in favor of the prevalent negative "association of the dragon with the earth and sea" that is announced in Rev 12:12 and continues in chapter 13. Barbara Rossing has fundamentally challenged this presumed Earth adversity of Revelation by reading the frequent "Woes" over the earth (e.g., in Rev 12:12) not as a curse but a lament in solidarity with Earth ("Alas"), who is suffering under the rule of the imperial "dragon" and longing for liberation; see Barbara Rossing, "For the Healing of the World: Reading *Revelation* Ecologically," in *From Every People and Nation: The Book of Revelation in Intercultural Perspective*, ed. David Rhoads (Minneapolis: Fortress, 2005), 172–73. She interprets the destruction of the earth envisioned by John in analogy of the Egyptian plagues as a wake-up call to repentance and change (Rev 9:20–21); according to Rev 11:18 it is not the earth that is meant to be destroyed, rather the "destroyers of the earth" (Rossing, "For the Healing of the World," 173–76).

17. Norman C. Habel and Vicky Balabanski, eds., *The Earth Story in the New Testament* (Sheffield: Sheffield Academic, 2002), 1–14.

whose seven crowns symbolize universal power and who can sweep stars from heaven with his tail (12:4); in 12:15 he can muster devastating floods to drown a woman he is persecuting. She is the mother of the messianic child he had tried to kill earlier in the chapter in a ghoulish heavenly birth scene where he stood ready to devour the newborn. Yet the child was taken right out of his fangs to the throne of God, and he lost the ensuing battle in heaven (12:4-5, 7-9). As a result, he is thrown down to the earth and sea, where he can act out his wrath, if only for a limited time—a situation that the text laments (12:12).[18] In the next chapter he will bestow his power upon the Roman emperor as the "beast from the sea" (13:2)—it appears as so absolute and incontestable that the "whole earth" (ὅλη ἡ γῆ) subsequently is worshiping (προσεκύνησαν) the beast/dragon (13:3-4).

Nobody but those gifted with heavenly insight like John or the woman can "see" and disclose that in reality the power of the dragon/beast is only temporary and already lost (12:8, 12). The throne of "God" Caesar is not backed up by an all-powerful celestial pantheon under the aegis of Jupiter or Apollon, as it claims. Rather, the one celebrated and worshiped as all-powerful divine emperor is actually the big loser of the cosmic battle, namely, the dragon and "the ancient serpent, who is called the devil and Satan, the deceiver of the whole world" (12:9). This knowledge about the real nature and origin of his power(lessness) is the actual "disclosure" or "revelation" (ἀποκάλυψις) that the dragon/emperor is afraid of and that he tries to suppress: John the Seer is imprisoned on the island of Patmos (1:9), the woman is going to be silenced by water, subsequently "the rest of her children" are targeted as enemies by the dragon's wrath and war-making (12:17). This latter statement contains an important piece of information about the woman. She is not just the (heavenly) queen mother of the Messiah (12:1-5) but also the earthly mother of his followers and siblings, that is, the singular and cohesive body that gives birth to the different *ekklēsiai* John is addressing—she is Ekklēsia herself, Mother Church.[19] She is the source and location of the messianic countervision, counterknowledge and counterworship that threaten the dragon's rule. That is the reason she needs to be eliminated.

The woman is on the run. The wilderness is her destination. She has "a place prepared by God so that there she can be nourished" (12:6, 14). The

---

18. See n. 16 above.

19. David E. Aune calls her "a collective symbol for the totality of the earthly church" (*Revelation 6-16*, WBC 52B [Dallas: Word, 1998], 707).

allusion to the Exodus story of Israel's escape from the infant-murdering grip of Egypt to the divine Manna provisions of the desert are hard to miss, including the safe passage through the waters of the Red Sea that subsequently drowned Pharaoh and his host.[20] Pharaoh-like in his fury, the dragon has to catch the rebellious runaway before she is out of his reach. She receives the "two wings of the great eagle so that she can fly" (12:14)— but strangely this does not imply any heavenly airlift or "rapture" for her as it did for her messianic son.[21] Despite her wings, the church, Ekklēsia, is fully and irrevocably earthbound in Revelation. And then the dragon/serpent strikes.[22] The murderous torrent he releases against the woman from his mouth is going to sweep her away from the face of the earth like a piece of garbage never to be seen again. But in this very moment the most unexpected happens: help comes from below not from above. The Earth opens her mouth to swallow the dragon flood. And she does so with intentionality—"and the Earth helped the woman" (12:16).[23]

Why, for heaven's sake, should the Earth, Gaia or Gē, help the woman? We are talking about something like a biblically based earth-awareness among early Christ followers here, with a strongly anti-imperial thrust that makes Earth an (inter)active respondent to human practices, simultaneously a helper and an opponent. Are we misreading or at least grossly

---

20. See Exod 1:14–6.

21. The term ἁρπάζω used in Rev 12:5 for the heavenly rescue of the messianic child is the same as in 1 Thess 4:17, where it is often interpreted as the "rapture" of the faithful away from earth. This notion has been contested by Rossing, who also strongly insists that earth is not "left behind" in Revelation (169), rather—in a "rapture in reverse"—the new Jerusalem and God eventually come down from heaven to earth in Rev 21–22 (Rossing, "For the Healing of the World," 172).

22. The dragon's alias as "(ancient) serpent" in Rev 12:14–15 refers to Rev 12:9 and constitutes—next to the echoes of Exodus—the second level of scriptural intertextuality operative in Rev 12: The cast of serpent/deceiver, woman, and Earth/Adamah/Gaia clearly points to the creation narrative in Gen 3–4.

23. The role of Earth here is so puzzling to interpreters that its importance is suppressed even where it is recognized. Jürgen Roloff, for example, acknowledges, with reference to Num 16:32 and Exod 1–16, that "the earth intervenes like an acting person, as it were, who comes to the aid of the woman"—yet he dismisses this intervention that "sounds mythological" and attributes it to God, who "stands with the church" (Jürgen Roloff, *The Revelation of John*, trans. John E. Alsup, Continental Commentaries [Minneapolis: Fortress, 1993], 511). This is certainly true but also an overgeneralization that misses the point that God and Earth here obviously collaborate and God relies on Earth's agency.

overinterpreting this little note, driven by legitimate and admittedly pressing twenty-first-century concerns, but hopelessly anachronistic in ancient terms? The text obviously does not give us any explanation for the extraordinary rescue mission of Earth, and we are left with a question that clearly requires an extratextual investigation. Our particular focus for this contextual exploration will be the visual world of urban Asia Minor, where John and his seven churches are at home, with a specific emphasis on Earth imagery.

3. Matchmaking: Is Hadrian's Image at Miletus Compatible with John's Text?

Using visual images to get deeper into the texture of our verbal text images requires some clarification about the criteria guiding such "matchmaking" between text and image. How to find imagery that can adequately inform our reading of Rev 12:16? Obviously there must be a plausible connection between image and text. The historical-critical paradigm would minimally include sufficient evidence that the image(ry) belongs in the closer or wider historical context of the text—geographically and chronologically—and that its subject matter has demonstrable relevance for its reading. Each of these criteria can be open to negotiation. This process of selection and discernment, overall, is a highly complex interdisciplinary endeavor at the intersection of ancient and art history, archaeology, exegesis, and hermeneutics; from the outset it needs careful consideration of objects (textual and visual), origins, locations, and settings as much as it involves a good deal of intuition. Only the actual process of "reading" a specific image and text together, however, and the results it produces (or fails to produce) can ultimately attest to the appropriateness of a specific image choice. At any rate the transformative encounter of text and images in this kind of visual exegesis can profoundly change initial perceptions in both directions and result in a critical reimagination of both text and image.

Topologically and chronologically, the two complementary statues of Emperor Hadrian at the Market Gate of Miletus, dating from around 120 CE, at first sight seem unlikely visual contexts and intertexts of Rev 12:16. Miletus evidently is not one of the seven cities addressed by John in Rev 1–3. And if the book was written during the time of Domitian (81–96), it cannot be interacting yet with images that were probably produced roughly three decades later under Hadrian (117–138).[24] Nonetheless, as we are going to argue, the colossal (though fragmented) twin statues of Hadrian may offer a plausible context as well as intertext for reading Earth and Ekklēsia in Rev 12:16.

(1) Their origin from Miletus, a major harbor city about thirty miles to the south of Ephesus in the Roman province of Asia, locates them in the same geographical and political neighborhood as John's seven cities.[25] More importantly, the island of Patmos as John's location (Rev1:9) is part of "outlying" Milesian territory, which also included the islands of Leros and Lepsia.[26] Some forty miles into the Aegean Sea from Miletus, Patmos was under direct jurisdiction of the city.

(2) From the outset it needs to be stated, however, that historical context and meaningful intertext in terms of images cannot and does not need to be confined to an all-too-narrow topological and chronological framework anyway. In the "language" of imperial images there are communalities that may not only make locations interchangeable on a regional and even transregional scale but also bridge considerable time gaps. A very similar pair of statues depicting Hadrian, for example, was found at the Nympha-

---

24. We will follow the broadest present consensus among art historians and archeologists that the two sculptures (which are missing their heads and arms) represent both Hadrian and date from the early years of his rule, around 120–125 CE (Volker Michael Strocka, *Das Markttor von Milet* [Berlin: de Gruyter, 1981], 29–32; Renate Bol, *Die Marmorskulpturen der Römischen Kaiserzeit aus Milet. Aufstellungskontext und programmatische Aussage. Deutsches Archäologisches Institut, Funde aus Milet* [Berlin: de Gruyter, 2011], 5.2:68–73). Earlier dates, however, are being proposed, either for the time of Hadrian's predecessor Trajan (Martin Maischberger, "Das Nordtor des Südmarktes, sog. Markttor," in *ZeitRäume—Milet in Kaiserzeit und Spätantike*, ed. Ortwin Dally and Martin Maischberger; Berlin: Staatliche Museen, 2009], 116), or already during the time of Domitian (Hans-Ulrich Cain and Michael Pfanner, "Die Agora Milets in der Kaiserzeit und Spätantike," in Dally and Maischberger, *ZeitRäume*, 93). Although this would imply an ideal chronological match with Revelation, it requires further discussion by the experts first.

25. According to Acts 20:15, 17, Paul on his last trip to Jerusalem summons the elders of Ephesus to meet him at close-by Miletus, where obviously a Christian community existed (see also 2 Tim 4:20).

26. Norbert Ehrhardt, *Milet und seine Kolonien: Vergleichende Untersuchung der kultischen und politischen Einrichtungen* (Frankfurt am Main: Lang, 1988), 1:15–17. The political affiliation of Patmos and the rest of the "Milesian Islands" to Miletus dates back at least to Hellenistic times; epigraphic evidence shows that the islands used the same political calendar as Miletus, based on the governing *stephanephoros* (ibid., 15).

eum of Perge in Pamphylia.[27] The Miletus Market Gate itself mirrors the multistoried facades typical of Roman theatres, that is, the characteristic *scenae frons* at the back of the stage; as such it has much in common with the two-storied decorative facade of the Celsus Library in Ephesus (113–117 CE), including its adjacent triple gateway, which dates back to the time of Augustus and resembles the three arches of the Miletus Gate built more than a hundred years later.[28] Because of the "ubiquity" of certain visual elements—a term used by James R. Harrison, though with some caution[29]—one could simply call the Market Gate and its statuary a "typically Roman monument."[30] Despite an endless range of regional and time-sensitive variables, the core elements in the imperial pictorial program that were introduced at the transition from the late Republic to the Augustan Principate remained relatively stable during the first and early second century CE. If the two Miletus images of emperor Hadrian postdate Revelation about three decades, they still are part of a shared symbolic and imaginary universe that links them to the seven cities of Revelation under Domitian.

(3) This finally takes us to the most weighty point in the matchmaking between text and image: content and subject matter. As it turns out, Hadrian's two Miletus statues in a striking way "mirror" the complete set of players involved in Rev 12:16. Their depiction, not surprisingly, is drastically altered, filtered through a radically different political, religious, and social lens that greatly changes their appearance—nonetheless all three of them are there: the emperor (i.e., the "dragon/serpent," according to John), a woman in distress, and the Earth (or rather the cornucopia as her signature attribute). This remarkable (in)congruence, after all, is the decisive reason for mustering these two images as visual intertexts and contexts for reading Rev 12:16. But before we can proceed from matchmaking between text and image to meaning-making, a careful viewing of the Market Gate and its imperial statuary is needed.

---

27. Bol, *Die Marmorskulpturen*, 69.
28. Maischberger, "Das Nordtor des Südmarktes," 110.
29. Harrison, "More Than Conquerors," 4.
30. Irene Blum, "Milet in der römischen Kaiserzeit," in Dally and Maischberger, *ZeitRäume*, 93.

Figure 1. Miletus around 200 CE; model of the city center with Lion Harbor, temple of Apollon Delphinios (upper left end of harbor), processional road flanked by north market (right) and baths of Capito and gymnasium (left), agora with bouleuterion (right) and Nymphaeum (left), and Market Gate (middle) leading to the South Market (arrow). Pergamon Museum, Berlin.

4. Hadrian's Image at the Miletus Market Gate: An Initial Exploration

Miletus was an ancient Ionian city at the western coast of Asia Minor, close to the mouth of the river Meandros and with no less than four harbors that connected it to the Aegean Sea. Once a major political player in the region and with famous names like Anaximander, Thales, Anaximenes, and Hippodamus attached to it, it also became the "mother city" of no less than ninety colonies on the Black Sea and around the Mediterranean.[31] Its power was crushed by Persia in 494 BCE during the Ionian Revolt; the elites were exiled, the general population was sold into slavery, and the city razed to the ground. Part of the Roman province of Asia since 133 BCE, Miletus never regained its former political influence but became an important commercial center for sea trade.[32] The model in figure 1 shows storage build-

---

31. For specifics, see Ehrhardt, *Milet und seine Kolonien*.

32. For an overview see Alan M. Greaves, *Miletos: A History* (New York: Routledge, 2002); Douglas R. Edwards, "Miletus," *OEANA* 4:26–28. For Miletus specifically under Roman supremacy see Gerhard Kleiner, *Das Römische Milet. Bilder aus der Griechischen Stadt in Römischer Zeit* (Stuttgart: Steiner, 1970); Dally and Maischberger, *ZeitRäume*.

ings behind the porticoes adjacent to the upper end of the Lion Harbor and behind them the big square of the North Market. The exceptionally broad road it flanks is standing out in width from the orthogonal Hippodamian street grid structuring the city. It forms the opening part of the large processional way that started from the temple of Apollon Delphinios (also home of the Prytaneum with the sacred hearth of the city) at the Lion Harbor and led from there to the main sanctuary of Apollon at nearby Didyma.[33] The section between harbor and Market Gate was a continuous building site throughout the first and early second centuries: The harbor gate and extensive porticoes were erected, and the Capito baths opposite the North Market and next to the Hellenistic gymnasium were built under emperor Claudius (51–54 CE).[34] Further up and left of the Market Gate, opposite the sizeable bouleuterion with its Altar to Augustus,[35] the ancient city agora was beautified by a technologically and artistically spectacular Nymphaeum under Titus or Domitian;[36] behind a three-storied richly decorated facade it functioned as *castellum dividiculum* (distribution plant) for the brand-new Roman 2.5-km aqueduct that revolutionized the water supply to the city.[37] Within this overall architectural setting the Market Gate was obviously a capstone and crowning highlight; most likely not only a large number of pedestrians in everyday traffic but also the big New Year's procession to Apollon Didymaios would move through.[38]

---

33. Alexander Herda, *Der Apollon-Delphinios-Kult in Milet und die Neujahrsprozession nach Didyma: Ein neuer Kommentar der sog. Molpoi-Satzung* (Mainz: von Zabern, 2006).

34. Vergilius Capito was Roman procurator of the province and the baths are the first evidence of major imperial building projects at Miletus; Blum, "Milet in der römischen Kaiserzeit," 47.

35. The Ara Augusti in front of the Bouleuterion is the earliest known location of imperial cult at Miletus, as the location of the cult of Roma is unknown so far. Only 10 percent of Roman buildings at Miletus, however, have been excavated so far; see Blum, "Milet in der römischen Kaiserzeit," 44–46.

36. An inscription identifies Marcus Ulpius Traianus, the father of the later emperor Trajan, proconsul of the province of Asia under Titus in 79/80 as sponsor, mentioning also that he was commander of the Legio X Fretensis during the Jewish War. For the dating of the Nymphaeum either under Titus or Domitian, see Cain and Pfanner, "Die Agora Milets in der Kaiserzeit und Spätantike," 93.

37. Martin Maischberger, "Das Nymphäum," in Dally and Maischberger, *ZeitRäume*, 97–107.

38. For a detailed description see Strocka, *Das Markttor von Milet*; and Maischberger, "Das Nymphäum," 109–19.

Figure 2. Market Gate of Miletus (ca. 120–125 CE) leading from the agora to the South Market; two-storied ornamental facade with triple-arched gateways and protruding side wings, 17 m in height and 29 m in width. Pergamon Museum, Berlin.

The Miletus Market Gate consists of a large two-storied ornate marble facade with columns, architraves, and two side wings. It rests on a foundation of three stairs and contains three arched gateways (*tripylon*) that lead from the northern part of the city with agora, procession road, and Lion Harbor toward the South Market. This north-south axis is crossed right in front of the gate by the road that links the East Harbor with the West Harbor, where a Roman theater with another most elaborate facade as stage background (*scenae frons*) had been built already under Nero. The Market Gate was excavated 1903–1905 under Theodor Wiegand, transferred to Berlin in 1908, and subsequently restored and rebuilt in the Berlin Pergamon Museum.[39]

The two over-life-sized sculptures were found directly in front of the Market Gate by the excavators, one more to the east and the other to the west, and placed accordingly in the Berlin reconstruction. As their heads

---

39. For the intriguing contemporary debates and disputes around this transfer of no less than 750 tons of marble from Turkey to Germany; see Strocka, *Das Markttor von Milet*, 5–10.

Figure 3. Center arch of the Market Gate with two fragmentary colossal statues of Emperor Hadrian on both sides, one cuirassed and with a kneeling barbarian woman, the other in heroic nudity and with a cornucopia (120–125 CE). Pergamon Museum, Berlin.

are missing, any identification remains hypothetical, but, as already mentioned, most scholars at the moment ascribe them to Hadrian.[40] Their complementary design—Renate Bol classifies them as "Pendantstatuen"—was immediately recognized, although in the earlier Berlin setting of 1930 they were displayed at the upper level of the Market Gate, a placement that Bol proved inadequate.[41] Both statues show a powerful masculine body in matching size and posture, one armored and the other nude, with the short imperial cloak (*paludamentum*) draped over one shoulder.[42] Each statue is stabilized by a tree trunk in the back that functions as support structure,

---

40. See n. 24 above. Originally, upon their excavation, the statues were identified as Marc Aurel and Lucius Verus and dated to the Parthian Wars in the mid-second century CE (162–166); see Bol, *Die Marmorskulpturen*, 69.

41. Ibid., 68–69.

42. According to Caterina Maderna, the *paludamentum* (different from the *Chlamys*) is typical for emperors' statues and signifies specifically the military aspect of their rule (Caterina Maderna, *Iuppiter, Diomedes, und Merkur als Vorbilder für*

and appears behind the inner leg. Attached to this "tree" is, in the figure to the left, a kneeling woman with her hands bound on the back and her head lifted up to the towering military man above her; to the right a cornucopia with overflowing fruit is leaning against it. Both "small shapes" reach approximately to mid-thigh height;[43] they visually correspond to each other as also their respective imperial bodies are complementary.

Figure 4. Cuirassed emperor and kneeling barbarian woman at the Miletus Market Gate. Pergamon Museum, Berlin.

Figure 5. Nude emperor with cornucopia at the Miletus Market Gate. Pergamon Museum, Berlin.

---

römische Bildnisstatuen: Untersuchungen zum römischen statuarischen Idealporträt [Heidelberg: Verlag Archäologie und Geschichte, 1988], 76).

43. The most recent and comprehensive description of the two statues has been given by Bol, *Die Marmorskulpturen*, 68–73. According to Bol, the kneeling woman is 0.85 m in height, compared to 1.33 m for of the imperial torso, who would be more than life-sized with chest and head added (71). It is not only height that matters, however; the woman is also "thinned" to roughly half the width of the emperor.

5. Meaning-Making:
Reading Image through Text and Text through Image

5.1. Imperial Imagination 1: Bound Woman at Her Knees (Fig. 4)

If the almost fatal encounter between dragon and woman in Rev 12 talks about the clash between murderous imperial power and the "weak" messianic force of a newborn and his exposed mother that nonetheless prevail, the Market Gate statuary at Miletus tells a markedly different story. The depiction of emperor/"dragon" and "woman" here is brutally unambiguous. While the woman in Rev 12:14 is escaping with the eagle's wings—images of winged deities like Hermes/Mercury and Nike/Victoria come to mind, or of God carrying Israel "on eagle's wings" (Exod 19:4)—the woman at the Market Gate is pinned to the ground and no longer moving at all.

The woman's hands bound at the back (fig. 6) and her kneeling position signal her defeat. She is a captive without agency, a prisoner of war, and thus a slave of her vanquisher. With her body shrunk to dwarf size in comparison to his, she looks up to him from the side (fig. 4). We cannot say from the faded features of her face whether it expressed anxiety or rage or servility and worship, whether she is appealing to him, mourning, protesting, crying in pain, or conveying pious submission. She definitely tries to communicate with him. Although his chest, arms, and head are missing, we can safely surmise that he is totally oblivious to her. Like a colossus he towers over her, immovably. His massive, heavily armored body radiates the powerful yet relaxed self-confidence of the victor, in stark contrast to the tension and vulnerability in the small figure at his feet. As a concrete human person she is a mere casualty and does not matter. As an iconographic public signifier, however, she is a trophy of war and announces his triumph.

The iconography of the Market Gate was easily readable for its first- to second-century CE viewers in Roman Asia Minor. In the language of images, markers like body size and posture, or spatial relations like small and big, upright and bent, high and low, bound and unbound, are basic "vocabulary" to express power relations and social status; they are instantaneously understood even by the illiterate and uneducated masses. The contrast between "big" people who rule the world and "small" people who have to submit is self-evident.[44]

---

44. It needs to be clarified that especially in ideologically pertinent public Roman

More specifically, the depiction of women who are kneeling or in other ways "down" on the ground was a familiar visual paradigm; in the semiotics of images it denotes the defeat of barbarian nations or tribes who are collectively portrayed as women, that is, subordinate and passive. As military defeat demonstrated a failure of "manliness" on the side of the losers and meant collective enslavement, this could be suitably portrayed as the "feminization" of a whole nation who had become "penetrable" to the victor's military, social, economic, and all too often sexual incursions. This pattern is known from the various emissions of "Capta coins" that show defeated nations like Armenia, Gallia, or Judea as humiliated women underneath a trophy or their triumphant captor, and from a wide range of imperial iconography like the Gemma Augustea, the Prima Porta statue of Augustus, the Great Cameo of France, or the Aphrodisias "Portico of Nations."[45] Many of these depictions give a precise ethnic identification of the vanquished nation-women, no less than about fifty *ethnē* alone at Aphrodisias, for example, including the nation of the *Judaioi*. In contrast, the woman at the Market of Miletus is missing any explicit ethnicity—according to the prevalent scholarly consensus she represents Roman victory and the defeated nations under Rome generically and in their entirety.[46]

Figure 6. Detail of the kneeling barbarian woman with her hands bound at the back. Miletus Market Gate. Pergamon Museum, Berlin.

---

art such binaries are a very common—for easily "readable"—means of conveying "messages" to widely illiterate masses. Maier's critique of employing binary codes in the semiotics of visual exegesis and critical reimagination and thus "to force Roman imperial art into predetermined categories with already fixed outcomes," therefore needs to be discussed in light of the concrete visual evidence (Maier, *Picturing Paul in Empire*, 21).

45. Lopez, *Apostle to the Conquered*; Canavan, *Clothing the Body of Christ at Colossae*; Kahl, "Krieg, Maskulinität und der imperiale Gottvater," and "Hagar's Babylonian Captivity."

46. Bol, *Die Marmorskulpturen*, 72.

Furthermore, Michael Schneider has extensively explored the posture of "kneeling" that in itself became an iconographic marker for the subjugation of inferior Orientals and the victory of the West over the East. While the motif can be traced back to very early stages in the history of ancient victory art, in the pre-Augustan period kneeling enemies first appear on coins of the late Republic. It is not until Augustus, however, and his overall makeover of image production that kneeling as iconographic motif reaches a climax; for example, in one of the largest emissions of the Augustan mint in 19/18 BCE, after the Parthian victory, a kneeling Parthian returns the Roman standards.[47] The very act of kneeling, culturally unacceptable to Greeks and Romans, according to Schneider signals servitude, submission, and the readiness to accept punishment for insurrection; it is therefore often linked to the motive of kneeling barbarians bearing heavy weights on their shoulders.[48] Right opposite the Market Gate of Miletus, at the facade of the Nymphaeum the prototype of this visual pattern was displayed in a prominent position: Atlas, the rebellious Titan, on his knees in his eternal plight of bearing the globe on his shoulders.[49] Interestingly, from the time of the Flavian emperors, we encounter kneeling barbarian figures that are used in this weight-bearing function to serve specifically as support structures for heavy armored marble sculptures that cannot maintain themselves.[50] This strikingly matches Hadrian's statue at the Miletus Market Gate and the structural function of the kneeling woman and the tree trunk to which she is attached. Like the Karyatids, the woman of

---

47. Rolf Michael Schneider, *Bunte Barbaren, Orientalenstatuen aus farbigem Marmor in der römischen Repräsentationskunst* (Worms: Wernersche Verlagsgesellschaft, 1986), 19–31; cf. Zanker, *Power of Images*, 186–88.

48. Schneider, *Bunte Barbaren*, 25–27.

49. Cain and Pfanner, "Die Agora Milets in der Kaiserzeit und Spätantike," 103; cf. Schneider, *Bunte Barbaren*, 47, who points out that according to Greek mythology Atlas was punished to bear the globe for his hubris of participating in the Titan insurgence; his kneeling (*proskynēsis*) signifies both penance and unconditional surrender, expressing the boundless scope of imperial rule and victory.

50. Schneider, *Bunte Barbaren*, 72. As Strocka (*Das Markttor von Milet*, 16) points out, these added barbarian figures ("attributive Barbarenfiguren") of male or female gender, kneeling and with their hands bound on the back, are minimized as a signifier ("bedeutungsvoll verkleinert") and can be placed to the right of left of the armored *imperator*; they became an official topos in the representation of Roman emperors. Starting with Vespasian, Strocka gives no less than thirteen examples, most of which are attributed to Hadrian, however (Strocka, *Das Markttor von Milet*, 51 n. 44).

Karia who according to Vitruvius were transformed into weight-bearing columns to atone for their nation's "sin" (*peccatum*) of insurrection,[51] the woman at Hadrian's feet deserves to bear the burdens of empire.

5.2. Apocalyptic Counterimagination 1: Bound Woman Unbound and Unbent (Figs. 4 and 6)

If the age of Augustus and its successors were as much built on the power of the images as on the power of the legions, John the Seer unleashes the powers of counterimagination to their fullest. "Seeing" is the theological core activity in the book of Revelation that "un-veils" (*apo-kalypto*) reality in new ways. *Apokalypsis* in this sense means the disclosure of the true image of present, past, and future that John sees concealed behind the fake facades of imperial image-production masterminded by the great dragon, the "deceiver of the whole world" (Rev 12:9; 13:14). Arguably, the book of Revelation is the most visual text of the New Testament. Through heavenly guidance, John "sees" (Rev 1:2, 12) and is told to "write in a book" what he sees (1:11, 19). His images are made of words rather than marble that he would not be able to afford, and their dissemination as "audio-text" in private houses during gatherings of the seven *ekklēsiai* is much less conspicuous than the display of imperial statuary in Miletus and elsewhere in urban Asia Minor. Nonetheless they mock, contest, and deconstruct the official imagery with striking precision. Reading Rev 12:16 in the virtual context of the Miletus Market Gate reveals not only a dense intertextuality between the two images and the text but also an iconoclastic irreverence and impertinence embedded into the text that leaves little of the imperial display intact.

The depiction of the emperor as a furious seven-headed, child-devouring monster let loose on earth and sea (12:3–4, 12–13) certainly clashes with an "august" depiction like that of Hadrian. Even worse, his "colossal" strength and superior armor did not help him win the cosmic battle (12:7–9). He also miserably fails in his campaign against a newborn baby (12:4–5) and, finally, against a single woman trying to run (12:13–16). This is a classic trickster story from "below" that subverts and deconstructs the seemingly incontestable imprint of Roman hegemony. The chief target of John's counterimagination all throughout Revelation is imperial ideology

---

51. Vitruvius, *De architectura*, 1, 5; cf. Kahl, "Krieg," 288–89.

with its omnipresent persuasive force: "In amazement the whole earth followed the beast. They worshiped [προσεκύνησαν] the dragon, for he had given his authority to the beast, and they worshiped the beast, saying: 'Who is like the beast, and who can fight [πολεμῆσαι] against it?'" (Rev 13:3–4).

Within the visual context of the Market Gate statuary, two terms in this statement are immediately eye-catching: worshiping (προσεκύνησαν) and war-making (πολεμῆσαι). Nobody on earth can make war against the emperor; everybody therefore worships him, that is, kneels at his feet. The term προσεκύνησαν covers a broad spectrum from making obeisance to worship, with various forms of falling down and showing deference implied, one of them being kneeling or prostration.[52] This fully corresponds to the message of Hadrian's Market Gate sculpture: all the nations have been successfully conquered by Rome, and their people are "kneeling" in front of the emperor as supreme Lord and God. With one exception, though, according to John. Like everybody else the people of the woman in the wilderness are subject to the power of the emperor/dragon to "make war" (ποιῆσαι πόλεμον) against them and gain victory (12:17; 13:7). They are slaughtered and led into captivity, executed or forced into compliance at sword point (13:10). In none of this they are different from the rest of the defeated nations represented by Hadrian's trophy woman—but for one decisive point: they do not kneel before the emperor as God. Unlike everybody else they refuse him worship (προσκυνήσουσιν, 13:8).

Looking through the veil of deception and the facades of official imagery like the one at the Market Gate of Miletus, they "see" that the universal conqueror with everybody kneeling before him is neither the real nor a durable world power. The child that was born and saved, but at the same time is a butchered lamb (Rev 5:6), is destined to "rule [or shepherd] all nations with an iron rod" (12:5). This is why his people, the children of the woman and his siblings, refuse their last allegiance to Cesar and keep the commandments of God instead (12:17). In other words, the woman of Rev 12 is the "queen mother" of Caesar's ultimate pretender, whose counter-kingdom does not derive its power from victory and military might: she embodies the counterformation of defeated nations and barbarian enemy tribes that the dragon has all reason to hunt down. She should be exactly

---

52. See J. M. Nützel, "Proskuneo," *EDNT* 3:419–23. With twenty-four occurrences of the term in Revelation, compared to sixty overall in the New Testament, the question of who can legitimately demand worship/kneeling—God or the emperor—clearly plays a key role for John.

where the woman at the Market Gate is: on her knees, hands bound at the back, forever welded to her role as weight-bearer of the empire, and looking up to him in pious subservience. Yet she is not. That she and her son are still at loose, that the dragon's deadly jaws missed his prey twice is reason for utmost concern to him, while it gives hope to the "rest of her children" in the midst of persecution (12:17).

It also instills "eager longing" or "anxious expectation" (see Rom 8:19) in the third main actor of our episode of Rev 12:13–17: the co-enslaved, co-groaning, and co-laboring Earth.[53]

5.3. Imperial Imagination 2: Cornucopia and Imperial Abundance (Fig. 5)

If John's critical reimagination of the dominant world power of his day might have provoked a sudden realization that Hadrian's statue in the garb of universal power is, in fact, an emperor with no clothes, this is exactly what we get in the second statue to the right of the Miletus Market Gate: a nude emperor. He is, however, far from naked. Hadrian in this depiction wears nothing but the light shoulder mantle (*paludamentum*), signifying supreme military/political power.[54] A mirror image of its left-hand counterpart in size and basic proportions, his muscular body is at full display in all its power and glory, the interplay of his muscles and movements shown in minute precision and impeccable perfection. His nudity, rather than being shameful, clearly signals a superhuman presence. Traditionally employed for semidivine heroes or Hellenistic rulers in the East, nudity or partial nudity from the late Republic on was introduced into honorary Roman statuary as well and during the early years of the empire grew into an iconographic marker of the emperor's divinity.[55] In other words: the "alter ego" of Hadrian the conqueror to the left is God Hadrian to the right of the Market Gate.

Despite its missing arms and head, the sculpted marble figure radiates male beauty and harmonious order, yet at the same time a dynamic and commanding presence.[56] Within the Roman visual paradigm, the message

---

53. The term (συν)ωδίνω = (co)labor occurs (apart from Gal 4:19, 27) only in Rom 8:22 and Rev 12:2; it links Rom 8:18–24 and Rev 12 as arguably two key passages for an ecological rereading of the New Testament.

54. See n. 41 above.

55. Zanker, *Power of Images*, 5–8, 249–50.

56. This impression is a carefully calculated effect of replicating a "canonical"

of beauty and harmony is strongly reinforced by the object attached to the emperor's thigh, corresponding in size and placement to the kneeling woman across the gateway; it is not a human body, however, but a curved cornucopia that sits on the ground. Heaped with grapes, it signals fertility and sustenance as well as overflowing abundance and well-being. The image, in an easily readable form, embodies the blessings of peace, in contrast to its warlike counterpart on the left. Wars destroy the harvest, the land and people who cultivate it—but wars in the Roman mind are also the foundation for peace, prosperity, and perfect order.

This "diptych" sculpture of Emperor Hadrian thus makes a coherent statement in two boldly contrasting sentences. Subjection of the Oikoumene and prosperity for the Oikoumene are two sides of the same coin.[57] As the supreme warrior, the emperor has unlimited power to destroy, deform, and appropriate life as he pleases (fig. 4), yet his superhuman achievement of global victory also translates into godlike capacities to grant universal blessing and fertility for the nations (fig. 5). He holds not only supreme military and political power but also "bio-power." He can take life and give life. If he is God, he is also creator.

While the imperial imagination thus presents the cornucopia and its fertility as organically connected with the superhuman body of the emperor in all its (omni)potent masculinity, it nonetheless evidently belongs "naturally" and "originally," as her signature attribute, to the Earth goddess. It is Gaia who brings forth all the blessings of abundance the

---

prototype of classic Greek art. With his weight shifted to the right leg and the left leg slightly bent in the knee, the foot set back a bit and only lightly touching the ground in an incipient forward movement, the nude Hadrian in fig. 5 features exactly the characteristic "counterposition" (*contrapposto*) that became famous with the Doryphoros (spear-bearer) of the Greek master sculptor Polykleitos (ca. 440 BCE) and, in a slightly later and more dynamic version, Diomedes; see Bol, *Die Marmorskulpturen*, 73. It was copied in numerous variations throughout antiquity and adopted by the classicizing style of the Augustan iconographic program, e.g., in the famous Prima Porta Statue of Augustus; see Zanker, *Power of Images*, 189; and John Pollini, "The Augustus from Prima Porta and the Transformation of the Polykleitan Heroic Ideal: The Rhetoric of Art," in *Polykleitos, the Doryphoros, and Tradition*, ed. Warren G. Moon (Madison: University of Wisconsin Press, 1995), 262–82. For further exploration and critical assessment, see Andrew Stewart, "Notes on the Reception of the Polykleitan Style: Diomedes to Alexander," in Moon, *Polykleitos, the Doryphoros, and Tradition*, 246–61.

57. See Ann Kuttner, who has outlined a very similar visual paradigm for one of the two so-called Boscoreale cups (*Dynasty and Empire in the Age of Augustus: The Case of the Boscoreale Cups* [Berkeley: University of California Press, 1995], 87–88).

cornucopia contains. Yet Mother Earth is conspicuously absent from the Market Gate imagery. How did she get lost—or how did she lose her cornucopia? If we follow the trail of the official images, the immediate answer to this question is disarmingly simple and cheerful. It is Earth herself who has voluntarily offered (and continues to offer) her fruit for the prosperity of the empire. Two panels from the imperial sanctuary at Aphrodisias are paradigmatic for this joyous compliance.

The two images in figures 7 and 8 (p. 136) stand for a whole gallery of similar Earth imagery, which shows the Earth goddess as an extremely "happy camper" under the canopy of Roman rule, surrendering herself graciously, freely, and joyously.[58] And while there is no groaning, no coercion, no suffering on her side, she at the same time appears totally oblivious to the ongoing plight of the enslaved nation-women next to her whose pain in some of the best-known pieces of imperial art is shown in merciless bluntness, not only at Aphrodisias but also, for example, on the Gemma Augustea or the Prima Porta statue.[59] In other words: The official "script" of imperial iconography in the first and early second century CE does not show any disagreement between Earth and empire and thus strictly rules out any possible connection between Gaia and the dissident woman in Rev 12:16.

This seems to bring our investigation to a halt. Far from seeing him as a monstrous "dragon," Earth in the public imagination of the first century CE worships Caesar. The humiliation of the defeated and enslaved nation-women does not bother her, nor has she anything in common with the rebellious Ekklēsia and her cause. There is no reason whatsoever why Earth should have "helped" this woman. Our effort to contextualize Rev 12:16 as resistant Earth statement in the surrounding image world of the first and second century CE has failed. Or do we need to take another and more critical look at these images?

---

58. The twin figures of Earth and Sea in fig. 8 correspond to the mental map of John in Revelation: Earth and Sea (θάλασσα) are under the dragon's sway (Rev 12:12). Both give rise to a beast (Rev 13:1, 11). Furthermore γῆ and θάλασσα are frequently mentioned together, e.g., Rev 5:13; 7:1–3; 10:2, 5, 6; 14:7.

59. The defeated, naked, and half-kneeling nation-woman Armenia under Nero's brutal grip from Aphrodisias is well known, as well as the equally brutalized Britannia under Claudius next to her; see Lopez, *Apostle to the Conquered*, 42–48. Both on the Gemma Augustea and the Prima Porta Statue of Augustus Gaia is shown in a state of happy and adoring (and almost worshipful) subservience to the emperor, in stark contrast to the bound, mourning, kneeling, or otherwise miserable figures of defeated barbarian women (and men) above or underneath her who are forced into compliance.

Figure 7. Gaia, smiling and on the ground, offers Roma (standing) her fruit-filled cornucopia with a small child clinging to it. Figures 7 and 8 both Imperial Sanctuary of Aphrodisias, circa 20–50 CE. Museum of Aphrodisias (Turkey).

Figure 8. Emperor Claudius, shown in heroic nudity as divine epiphany (like the Miletus Hadrian) with a cornucopia handed over to him by a kneeling personification of Earth on the left; to the right a sea tritoness has offered him a ship's steering oar.

5.4. Imperial imagination 3: Retrieving Gaia's Lost Cornucopia at Pergamon

Immediately neighboring the room with the Market Gate, the Pergamon Museum at Berlin displays its signature exhibit and another most remarkable monument: the Great Altar of Pergamon. Built around 170 BCE but still active in the first and second centuries CE, most probably as a prominent setting of emperor worship,[60] it is one of the outstanding pieces of Hellenistic art that have survived into modern times, unsur-

---

60. Holger Schwarzer, "Untersuchungen Zum Hellenistischen Herrscherkult in Pergamon," *IstMitt* 49 (1999): 294–95; Kahl, *Galatians Re-imagined*, 121–25.

passed in beauty and artistic perfection.[61] Its location in one of John's seven cities makes it specifically interesting for our investigation, and if Adela Yarbro Collins is right, John not only knows the altar but also irreverently chastises it as "throne of Satan" in Rev 2:13.[62] In terms of matchmaking between text and images, Pergamon and its Altar to Zeus (and possibly Athena) thus seems a natural context and intertext of Revelation, especially as the topic of "thrones" and universal power/worship claims—legitimate and false ones—are at the core of John's plot.[63] It is very tempting to read the whole mytho-political drama about the dethronement and deceptive re-enthronement of the dragon alias Satan alias beast alias emperor (12:9; 13:2) that John stages in Rev 12–13 as a critical interaction with the visual world of the Great Altar. For our purposes we want to focus exclusively on the story of Gaia and the cornucopia, however. It gets quite a different spin at the "throne of Satan" than the tale of happy subservience we have seen so far.

The most famous part of the Pergamon altar is a monumental combat frieze that surrounds it on the outside, depicting the primeval battle of the Olympic gods against the insurgent giants who try to dethrone them. Law fights against lawlessness, cosmic and social order have to be defended against chaos, and the final victory of the gods under Zeus's leadership means the triumph of civilization over monstrous barbarians, many of whom are persuasively depicted in repulsive beastlike shapes, some of them reminiscent of dragons or serpents. One of the two decisive panels on the east side of the frieze shows Zeus, father of gods and humans, in heroic seminudity in the final round of the battle (fig. 9).

The precise mythological sources for this grandiose combat panorama that is also echoed in the various scenes of a dragon fight in Rev 12 are not easily identifiable; they are both pluriform and ubiquitous all

---

61. For an overall introduction to Pergamon and the Great Altar, see the essays in Helmut Koester, ed., *Pergamon: Citadel of the Gods*, HTS (Harrisburg, PA: Trinity Press International, 1998); Kahl, *Galatians Re-imagined*, 77–127.

62. Adela Yarbro Collins, "Pergamon in Early Christian Literature," in Koester, *Pergamon*, 172.

63. Revelation has no less than forty-seven out of the sixty-two New Testament occurrences of the term θρόνος. The earthly throne of the dragon/Satan/emperor/beast as established in Rev 13:2 has its continuously present counterreality in the heavenly throne of God and the Lamb, where the child is raptured in Rev 12:5 and that finally comes down from heaven in Rev 21 and is located at the center of the new Jerusalem in 22:1, 3.

Figure 9. Zeus (center left) in heroic combat with three attacking giants. The fiercest of them is presumably their monstrous leader Porphyrius (or Typhon) with winding serpent legs (far right). Gigantomachy Frieze of the Pergamon Altar (ca. 170 BCE). Pergamon Museum, Berlin.

throughout the ancient world, including Mesopotamian (Enuma Elish) as well as Ugaritic, Greek, Egyptian, and biblical versions.[64] In all of them, however, "it is clear that the central issue is kingship."[65] At the Pergamon altar, Zeus's victory over the monstrous enemies of gods and humans establishes him as supreme ruler. This construct was easily applicable to emperors and their godlike power as well; for example, both Domitian and Hadrian were celebrated as Zeus Olympios at Ephesus,[66] a claim that is at the heart of John's contestation. To quote Collins again: Revelation "stands the propaganda of the current ruler on its head: Roman imperial power represents the forces of chaos that threatened to dissolve the order intended by the divine ruler of all."[67]

---

64. Collins, "Pergamon in Early Christian Literature," 176–83; David Balch, "'A Woman Clothed with the Sun' and the 'Great Red Dragon' Seeking to 'Devour her Child' in Roman Domestic Art (Rev 12:1, 4)," in Balch, *Roman Domestic Art*, 139–67.
65. Collins, "Pergamon in Early Christian Literature," 177.
66. Ibid., 174–75.
67. Ibid., 184.

Most likely the mythological plot elements underlying the gigantomachy frieze of the Pergamon altar can be traced back to Hesiod's *Theogony* and Apollodorus's *Library*.[68] According to these two, the giants who attack the gods are the children of Gaia, the Earth mother. She brought them forth in an act of rebellion against her primeval partner, the heavenly Father Ouranos, who would not allow their children to see the light of the day, causing Gaia great pain as she had to hold them back in her belly. At Gaia's instigation he is eventually castrated by their son Kronos; from the blood dripping on the ground after the grisly act Gaia becomes pregnant with the giants, who are thus literally the children of a matriarchal rebellion against the heavenly father/tyrant. Their uprising against Mount Olympus and subsequent defeat is beautifully monumentalized at the Great Altar; it establishes not only the mythological archetype of occidental war-making as a primeval act of "creation" against "chaos" but also the classification of Earth as a primordial enemy—a fundamentally hostile force of chaos and barbarism that must be "subdued and ruled" (cf. Gen 1:28). This logic is specifically expressed in the climactic gigantomachy scene directly neighboring the Zeus panel.

The panel in figure 10 is, in a way, the decisive "disclosure" about Gaia and the cornucopia. Buried in the ground up to her chest, the wailing Earth goddess Gē is shown in a fatal encounter with Nike and Athena, the goddesses of victory and civilization above her. She is the only goddess and only female among the roughly fifty male insurgent figures at the bottom of the frieze, which have all been defeated by the deities from above in a brutal large-scale massacre.[69] As goddess she is immortal, yet she has to watch how all her children die. Trying to save her favorite son, Alkyoneus, Gaia offers her cornucopia pleadingly to Athena, the victorious city goddess of Pergamon (and Athens). But Athena cannot have mercy; the iron logic of war-making shelters her from the plight of the losers, as also Hadrian at the Miletus Market Gate cannot take notice of the woman at his feet.

Yet the cornucopia from now onward will be the prime trophy in the battle of civilization against nature, Polis over countryside, metropolis over provinces, empire against foreign (barbarian) lands. Proudly presented by the triumphant emperor as his accomplishment at the entrance

---

68. Hesiod, *Theog.* 132–138, 154–186, 453–506, 616–735, 820–885; Apollodorus, *Library* 1.6.1–2; Nonnos, *Dionysiaca* 12, 29–32.

69. See Kahl, *Galatians Re-imagined*, 92–95, 98–105.

Figure 10. Gaia (note inscription GĒ over her right shoulder) with cornucopia and her favorite son, Alkyoneus, at the bottom; above her winged Nike who crowns city goddess Athena with victory. Athena pushes down Alkyoneus, who has already been bitten by her poisonous snake, while she separates with her left knee the life-saving connection between Gaia and her son. East part of the Giant Battle Frieze at the Pergamon Altar (ca. 170 BCE), flanked by the Zeus panel in figure 9 to the left and the war god Ares/Mars to the right. Pergamon Museum, Berlin.

of the Miletus South Market, it will feed the insatiable greed of Roma (see fig. 7) and of the market whose gate it programmatically adorns—rather than the need of those who fill it.[70] For behind the facade of the official images, the cornucopia will be incessantly replenished by Gaia's and the enslaved woman's labor, through the sweat, blood, and tears of their children. It is the people *and* the land of the vanquished, made taxable to the conqueror through land tax (*tributum solis*), poll tax (*tributum capitis*), and multiple other tributes, which will all magically appear as abundance in the emperor's horn of plenty, as if it were generated there.

---

70. John is obviously strongly critical of the ancient market economy, as passages like Rev 13:17 and 18:11-13 demonstrate; see J. Nelson Kraybill, *Imperial Cult and Commerce in John's Apocalypse* (Sheffield: Sheffield Academic, 1996).

This sheds new light both on the Market Gate statuary and Rev 12:16. The body of the half-buried Pergamene Gaia at the feet of Athena and Victoria (fig. 10) and the "halfling" body of the Miletus woman at the emperor's feet (figs. 4 and 6) embody each other. Both are downsized, downgraded, and downtrodden, reduced to mere booty in the big battle for human and natural resources: exploitable and expendable. The woman on her knees signifies not only the inferior race, culture, religion, class, and gender of the other to be conquered and consumed but also the inferiority and otherness of Earth to be colonized, commodified, and capitalized on. No wonder Rev 12:12 pronounces a lament over the Earth.

5.5. Apocalyptic Counterimagination 2: Gaia's and *Ekklēsia's* Rebellion

In the heartbreaking scene around the Pergamene Gaia and her lost cornucopia we have probably come across one of the defining moments in the history of the Occidental mind-set regarding Earth and empire. John, however, sees things differently. Representing Earth as the archenemy pregnant with chaos and revolt that needs to be "subdued and dominated," for him apocalyptically discloses the rapacious drive that is operative behind the deceptive "veil" of the bucolic Earth imagery at the Miletus Market Gate and elsewhere. The monstrous, the beastly, the serpent-legged and dragon-scaled is not Earth and her sons at the bottom of the cosmic order, but rather the life-devouring war machine of the devilish deceiver who poses as divine Zeus/Caesar. And in an act of prophetic iconoclasm the Great Altar before John's eyes morphs into "Satan's throne."

Reading Rev 12:16 in front of the Miletus Market Gate and at the Pergamon altar has fundamentally changed what we are seeing. Earth, after all, *does* have a reason to "help the woman." The bound and bent woman underneath Hadrian's towering military presence at Miletus and the luscious cornucopia "growing" at the feet of the imperial god are twin images portraying the world as it is meant to be seen from the perspective of Rome, the local elites, and the market. It shows servitude, enforced submission, and ruthless exploitation of both Earth and conquered nations as natural, normative, and necessary for the greater good. The majestic and military representation of imperial power to the left of the Market Gate, as we have seen, is physically supported by the dehumanizing image of a slave woman tied to the "tree" of her servitude (i.e., the trunk-shaped background structure that prevents the colossus from toppling) as if it were her cross—the same "tree" that seems to produce the abundant fruit of the cornucopia "good for food ... and pleasant to the eyes" (Gen 3:6)[71] in the mirror image to the right. What serves as a merely functional element for holding the sculptures upright, however, simultaneously becomes a metaphor of the imagined "orthostatic" order of social, economic, and political life as well.

The story of the woman Ekklēsia who could not be drowned or dragooned, nor bound or bent like the rest of the defeated nations because Earth "helped" her (Rev 12:16), profoundly denaturalizes this image on multiple levels. It appears as a flash of resurrection dynamics that infiltrates the imperial imaginary with the infectious virus of counterimagination, and maybe even a bit of subversive humor. It is not just that the woman firmly tied to her place all of a sudden slips away from the emperor's grip, sending his majestic figure on a less-than-glorious wild goose chase after a prey he seems unable to catch. Even more pathetically, the dreadful dragon/serpent pompously opens his big mouth to release a roaring river that will flush the woman downstream like sewage—yet Earth calmly turns off the oversized imperial water canon by simply opening *her* mouth and swallowing the whole river. Gaia's "mouth" effectively shuts down the dragon's "mouth" that releases not only lethal rivers but also, as the reader must be aware after 12:9, deadly deception. Given the pride Rome put into the ingenuity of its hydraulic engineering as emblematic of Roman city and civilization—its much-admired aqueducts channeling water into "rivers" for a steady supply to households or public baths, to flush out sewage from the city's latrines or gold from the mountains minted into money for the market[72]—the smooth and perplexing victory of Earth over the water-spitting dragon is somewhat humiliating and amusing.

While this overall visual and material context of advanced Roman water technology would be more or less tangible in every one of John's seven cities, it would have been specifically palpable in Miletus, which was situated at the mouth of the river Meandros and surrounded by water

---

71. The intertextuality between the dragon as "ancient serpent" and imperial "deceiver" in Rev 12:9, 16, and the deception of the serpent in Gen 3:6 (that also guides an "imperial" reading of Gen 1:28) cannot be pursued further here; one could argue that the cornucopia at the market gate transforms a need-based perspective on food into a gaze of desire and greed, not unlike the primeval transformation in the garden in Gen 3:6; see Kahl, "Fratricide and Ecocide."

72. Pliny, *Naturalis historia* 33.21 describes the water-based gold mining techniques used, e.g., in Las Medullas in Spain (today a UNESCO World Heritage Site) that were devastating both for the earth and the laborers who had to dig water tunnels into the mountains that made them collapse, often burying the workers with them.

on three sides because of its peninsular location; even more significantly, Miletus was the site of the cutting-edge and much-admired Roman-style Nymphaeum that directly faced the Market Gate, with the baths of Capito further down the processional road. The Nymphaeum, fed by the Roman-built aqueduct, functioned as the main well-house for the city where people came to get their water that the nymphs incessantly poured into a huge basin in front of the facade.[73] Behind the façade was a sophisticated system of water storage, distribution, and sewage disposal—even a sizeable public bathroom to the side.[74] The place was a public park and evoked the idyllic presence of a grove or grotto in the middle of the city, a piece of nature romantically woven into civilization.[75]

It is tempting (though purely speculative) to surmise that John from his watery prison at Patmos looks at the Milesian mother city and "sees" how the beneficial abundance of water provided by Rome—next to the abundance of grain and flocks contained in the cornucopia—turns into a nightmare of destruction. Before his eyes, the peaceful nymphs all of a sudden turn into water-spewing monsters that release a tsunami-like killer wave. This would not necessarily imply an attack on technology and the creaturely pleasures it provides per se—at the end of his book John will draw an urban paradise himself, with the abundance of fruit and water, tree and river organically integrated into the city (Rev 22:1–5), but on fundamentally different terms. Rather one could read Rev 12:16 as a nuclear critique that within an imperial setting the progress of technology does not simply serve the common good of humanity and nature, but is built on violence and (self-)destruction. The burdened figure of Atlas at the top of the Nymphaeum facade, pushed to his knees under the unbearable load imposed on him, recalls those who have to carry the load of Roman progress while they are constantly evoked as its beneficiaries: the vanquished earth and the vanquished nations.[76]

---

73. Nine drains were discovered that channeled water from the storage container behind the facade through the statues of the nymphs (and possibly a few other water-related figures like Poseidon) into the well-basin in front of the facade; Bol, *Die Marmorskulpturen*, 25, 33.

74. For details, see Maischberger, "Das Nymphäum."

75. For the water-generated sound system and other sensory attractions at the Nymphaeum as a "masterpiece of imperial-era hydraulic art and architecture," see Cain and Pfanner, "Die Agora Milets in der Kaiserzeit und Spätantike," 89.

76. See n. 48 above.

Why does Earth just "swallow" the water in Rev 12:16? She could have done something more earth-shattering and spectacular, like unleashing a volcano and spitting fire in return, making the dragon flood go up in a cloud of steam. While Revelation certainly has no scarcity of extremely violent images, this one is remarkably subdued and gentle. And there is clearly some nonnegotiable truth in it. Earth, firmly rooted in the ground (see fig. 10), is a stationary goddess. She does not have wings and cannot run away from what she gets from above. She has to take it in. Again it is tempting to think hypothetically of the concrete Milesian environment where the earthward "disappearance" of water through silting up was a precarious reality—in John's day possibly already the Lion Harbor, one of the main water-bound arteries connecting the markets of the city with global trade, had started to dry up.[77]

At any rate, in John's perception Earth's resistance to the dragon in Rev 12:16 is not only nonviolent and silent but also most powerful and intentional as an act of civil disobedience on behalf of the woman pursued by the dragon. Ekklēsia and Gaia, both birth-givers of life perceived as a threat to the dominant powers, both punished in their children for their nonconformity with established law and order (Rev 12:17), are welded together in a bond of solidarity in Rev 12:16. Earth is the reason Ekklēsia can survive, saving her from the waters of death for a new (interim) life in the wilderness, "baptizing" her as an earthbound creature. Earth indeed morphs from a mere object of abuse and exploitation, or care and "stewardship," into an active subject of caretaking and resistance herself. And as she "helps the woman," Gaia breaks out of the visual consensus that depicts her in happy compliance with the imperial order, regardless of the suffering for human and nonhuman life it produces. Earth is not only responsive to but also gives a powerful reinforcement to social impulses that counteract the logic and law of empire with all it ecocidal, fratricidal, and suicidal implications. Ecojustice and social justice belong inseparably together.

This is not the first time in the Bible that Gaia has "opened her mouth" to counteract the deadly deception of self-serving power and mindless

---

77. Blum, "Milet in der römischen Kaiserzeit," 58; Paul Trebilco points out that because of "the shifting of the course of the Maeander and its silting up, Miletus is now more than five miles from the sea"; see Paul Trebilco, "Asia," in *The Book of Acts in Its Graeco-Roman Setting*, vol. 2. of *The Book of Acts in Its First Century Setting*, ed. David W. J. Gill and Conrad Gempf (Grand Rapids: Eerdmans, 1994), 361 n. 311.

consumption that her adversary the "ancient serpent" introduced in Gen 3:1 and that subsequently made Eden uninhabitable. Already in Gen 4 Gaia/Adamah took the side of the weak and victimized when she "opened her mouth" to take in the blood of Abel and let it cry out in protest against Cain's deceptive denial (Gen 4:9–10)—while she refuses the murderer her strength and makes him a fugitive (4:11–12). In the overall biblical plot this becomes the beginning of the city (Gen 4:17), which will not only bring forth cultural achievements of all kinds (4:21–22) but also and all too soon the unstoppable super-warriors and power figures in the image of Lamech, Nimrod—and Hadrian at the Miletus Market Gate (Gen 4:23–24; 10:8–12).[78] The conflict between Gaia and Polis, Earth and our imperial occidental construct of civilization, profoundly shapes the beginning and end of the biblical Earth story in the books of Genesis and Revelation. John's disclosure (ἀποκάλυψις) aims at a different world that is possible on Earth—another kind of civilization embodied by Mother Ekklēsia and her children, in close connection to Mother Earth. Not accidentally the book of Revelation closes *not* with a vision of rural nostalgia but of sustainable integration of urbanity and ecology—with the tree of life standing in the middle of the city and its leaves and ceaseless harvest of fruit (other than the imperial cornucopia) plenty to heal and nourish the nations. And a river goes out from the throne of God and the Lamb: a river of life, not of death (Rev 22:1–2).

Bibliography

Aune, David Edward. *Revelation 1–5*. WBC 52A. Dallas: Word, 1997.
———. *Revelation 6–16*. WBC 52B. Dallas: Word, 1998.
———. *Revelation 17–22*. WBC 52C. Dallas: Word, 1998.
Balch, David L. "'A Woman Clothed with the Sun' and the 'Great Red Dragon' Seeking to 'Devour her Child' in Roman Domestic Art (Rev 12:1, 4)." Pages 139–67 in *Roman Domestic Art and Early House Churches*. Edited by David Balch. WUNT 228. Tübingen: Mohr Siebeck, 2008.
Balz, Horst, and Gerhard Schneider. *Exegetical Dictionary of the New Testament*. 3 vols. Grand Rapids: Eerdmans, 1990–1993.

---

78. See Kahl, "Fratricide and Ecocide."

Blum, Irene. "Milet in der römischen Kaiserzeit." Pages 43–59 in *ZeitRäume—Milet in Kaiserzeit und Spätantike*. Edited by Ortwin Dally and Martin Maischberger. Berlin: Staatliche Museen, 2009.

Bol, Renate. *Die Marmorskulpturen der Römischen Kaiserzeit aus Milet. Aufstellungskontext und programmatische Aussage. Deutsches Archäologisches Institut, Funde aus Milet, Bd.V, T.2.* Berlin: de Gruyter, 2011.

Cain, Hans Ulrich, and Michael Pfanner. "Die Agora Milets in der Kaiserzeit und Spätantike." Pages 83–95 in *ZeitRäume—Milet in Kaiserzeit und Spätantike*. Edited by Ortwin Dally and Martin Maischberger. Berlin: Staatliche Museen, 2009.

Canavan, Rosemary. *Clothing the Body of Christ at Colossae: A Visual Construction of Identity.* WUNT 2/334. Tübingen: Mohr Siebeck, 2012.

Collins, Adela Yarbro. "Pergamon in Early Christian Literature." Pages 163–84 in *Pergamon: Citadel of the Gods*. Edited by Helmut Koester. Harrisburg, PA: Trinity Press International, 1998.

Crossan, John Dominic, and Jonathan L. Reed, *In Search of Paul: How Jesus's Apostle Opposed Rome's Empire with God's Kingdom—A New Vision of Paul's Words and World*. San Francisco: HarperSanFrancisco, 2004.

Dally, Ortwin, and Martin Maischberger, eds. *ZeitRäume—Milet in Kaiserzeit und Spätantike*. Berlin: Staatliche Museen, 2009.

DeSilva, David A. "Seeing Things John's Way: Rhetography and Conceptual Blending in Revelation 14:6–13." *BBR* 18 (2008): 271–98.

Edwards, Douglas R. "Miletus." *OEANE* 4:26–28.

Ehrhardt, Norbert. *Milet und seine Kolonien: vergleichende Untersuchung der kultischen und politischen Einrichtungen*. 2 vols. Frankfurt am Main: Lang, 1988.

The Green Bible: New Revised Standard Version. San Francisco: HarperOne, 2008.

Greaves, Alan M. *Miletos: A History*. New York: Routledge, 2002.

Günther, Wolfgang. "Zu den Anfängen des Kaiserkults in Milet." *IstMitt* 39 (1989): 173–78.

Habel, Norman C., and Vicky Balabanski, eds. *The Earth Story in the New Testament*. Sheffield: Sheffield Academic, 2002.

Hallet, Christopher. *The Roman Nude: Heroic Portrait Statuary 200 B.C.–A.D. 300*. Oxford: Oxford University Press, 2005.

Harrison, James R. *Paul and the Imperial Authorities at Thessalonica and Rome: A Study in the Conflict of Ideology*. WUNT 273. Tübingen: Mohr Siebeck, 2011.

———. "'More Than Conquerors' (Rom 8:37): Paul's Gospel and the Augustan Triumphal Arches of the Greek East and Latin West." *Buried History: The Journal of the Australian Institute of Archaeology* 47 (2011): 3–20.

Herda, Alexander. *Der Apollon-Delphinios-Kult in Milet und die Neujahrsprozession nach Didyma: Ein neuer Kommentar der sog. Molpoi-Satzung*. Mainz: von Zabern, 2006.

Herrmann, Peter. "Ein Tempel für Caligula in Milet?" *IstMitt* 39 (1989) 191–96.

Hölscher, Tonio. *The Language of Images in Roman Art*. Translated by Anthony Snodgrass and Annemarie Kunzl-Snodgrass. Cambridge: Cambridge University Press, 2004.

Horsley, Richard A., ed. *Paul and Empire: Religion and Power in Roman Imperial Society*. Harrisburg, PA: Trinity Press International, 1997.

Jeal, Roy. "Blending Two Arts: Rhetorical Words, Rhetorical Pictures and Social Formation in the Letter to Philemon." *Sino-Christian Studies* 5 (2008): 9–38.

Jensen, Robin M. "Nudity in Early Christian Art." Pages 296–319 in *Text, Image, and Christians in the Graeco-Roman World: A Festschrift in Honor of David Lee Balch*. Edited by Aliou Cissé Niang and Carolyn Osiek. Princeton Theological Monograph Series. Eugene, OR: Pickwick, 2012.

Kahl, Brigitte. "Fratricide and Ecocide: Rereading Genesis 2–4." Pages 53–70 in *Earth Habitat: Eco-Injustice and the Church's Response*. Edited by Dieter Hessel and Larry Rasmussen. Minneapolis: Fortress, 2001.

———. *Galatians Re-imagined: Reading with the Eyes of the Vanquished*. Paul in Critical Contexts. Minneapolis: Fortress, 2010.

———. "Hagar's Babylonian Captivity: A Roman Re-imagination of Galatians 4:21–31." *Int* 68 (July 2014): 257–69.

———. "Krieg, Maskulinität und der imperiale Gottvater: Das Augustusforum und die messianische Re-Imagination von 'Hagar' im Galaterbrief." Pages 273–300 in *Doing Gender—Doing Religion*. Edited by Ute Eisen, Christine Gerber, and Angela Standhartinger. WUNT 302. Tübingen: Mohr Siebeck, 2013.

Kahl, Brigitte, Davina Lopez, and Hal Taussig, eds. *New Testament and Roman Empire*. USQR 59 (2005).

Kleiner, Gerhard. *Das Römische Milet. Bilder aus der Griechischen Stadt in Römischer Zeit*. Stuttgart: Steiner, 1970.

Koester, Helmut, ed. *Pergamon: Citadel of the Gods*. HTS. Harrisburg, PA: Trinity Press International, 1998.

Kraybill, J. Nelson, *Imperial Cult and Commerce in John's Apocalypse*. Sheffield: Sheffield Academic, 1996.

Kreitzer, Larry J. *Striking New Images: Roman Imperial Coinage and the New Testament World*. Sheffield: Sheffield Academic, 1996.

Kuttner, Ann L. *Dynasty and Empire in the Age of Augustus: The Case of the Boscoreale Cups*. Berkeley: University of California Press, 1995.

Lopez, Davina C. *Apostle to the Conquered: Reimagining Paul's Mission*. Paul in Critical Contexts. Minneapolis: Fortress, 2008.

Maderna, Caterina. *Iuppiter, Diomedes, und Merkur als Vorbilder für römische Bildnisstatuen: Untersuchungen zum römischen statuarischen Idealporträt*. Heidelberg: Verlag Archäologie und Geschichte, 1988.

Maier, Harry O. *Apocalypse Recalled: The Book of Revelation after Christendom*. Minneapolis: Fortress, 2002.

———. "Barbarians, Scythians and Imperial Iconography in the Epistle to the Colossians." Pages 385–406 in *Picturing the New Testament*. Edited by Annette Weissenrieder, Friederike Wendt, and Petra von Gemünden. Tübingen: Mohr Siebeck, 2005.

———. *Picturing Paul in Empire: Imperial Image, Text and Persuasion in Colossians, Ephesians and the Pastoral Epistles*. London: T&T Clark, 2013.

Maischberger, Martin. "Das Nordtor des Südmarktes, sog. Markttor." Pages 109–19 in *ZeitRäume—Milet in Kaiserzeit und Spätantike*. Edited by Ortwin Dally and Martin Maischberger. Berlin: Staatliche Museen, 2009.

———. "Das Nymphäum." Pages 97–107 in *ZeitRäume—Milet in Kaiserzeit und Spätantike*. Edited by Ortwin Dally and Martin Maischberger. Berlin: Staatliche Museen, 2009.

Moxnes, Halvor. "'He Saw That the City Was Full of Idols' (Acts 17:16): Visualizing the World of the First Christians." Pages 107–31 in *Mighty Minorities? Minorities in Early Christianity—Positions and Strategies*. Edited by David Hellholm, Halvor Moxnes, and Turid Karlsen Seim. Oslo: Scandinavian University Press, 1995.

Nawotka, Krzysztof. *Boule and Demos in Miletus and Its Pontic Colonies from Classical Age Until Third Century A.D.* Wroclaw: Zaklad Narodowy im. Ossolińskich, 1999.

Niang, Aliou Cissé. "Seeing and Hearing Jesus Christ Crucified in Galatians 3:1 under Watchful Imperial Eyes." Pages 160–82 in *Text, Image, and*

Christians in the Graeco-Roman World: A Festschrift in Honor of David Lee Balch. Edited by Aliou Cissé Niang and Carolyn Osiek. Princeton Theological Monograph Series. Eugene, OR.: Pickwick, 2012.

Pollini, John. "The Augustus from Prima Porta and the Transformation of the Polykleitan Heroic Ideal: The Rhetoric of Art." Pages 262–82 in *Polykleitos, the Doryphoros, and Tradition.* Edited by Warren G. Moon. Madison: University of Wisconsin Press, 1995.

Price, S. R. F. *Rituals and Power: The Roman Imperial Cult in Asia Minor.* Cambridge: Cambridge University Press, 1984.

Robbins, Vernon K. "Enthymeme and Picture in the *Gospel of Thomas.*" Pages 175–207 in *Thomasine Traditions in Antiquity: The Social and Cultural World of the Gospel of Thomas.* Edited by Jon Ma Asgeirsson, April D. DeConick, and Risto Uro. Leiden: Brill, 2006.

———. *Exploring the Texture of Texts.* Harrisburg, PA: Trinity Press International, 1996.

———. "Rhetography: A New Way of Seeing the Familiar Text." Pages 81–106 in *Words Well Spoken: George Kennedy's Rhetoric of the New Testament.* Edited by C. Clifton Black and Duane F. Watson. Waco, TX: Baylor University Press, 2008.

Roloff, Jürgen. *The Revelation of John.* Translated by John E. Alsup. Continental Commentaries. Minneapolis: Fortress, 1993.

Rossing, Barbara. "For the Healing of the World: Reading *Revelation* Ecologically." Pages 165–82 in *From Every People and Nation: The Book of Revelation in Intercultural Perspective.* Edited by David Rhoads. Minneapolis: Fortress, 2005.

Sánchez, David A. *From Patmos to the Barrio: Subverting Imperial Myths.* Minneapolis: Fortress, 2008.

Schneider, Rolf Michael. *Bunte Barbaren, Orientalenstatuen aus farbigem Marmor in der römischen Repräsentationskunst.* Worms: Wernersche Verlagsgesellschaft, 1986.

Schwarzer, Holger. "Untersuchungen zum Hellenistischen Herrscherkult in Pergamon." *IstMitt* 49 (1999): 249–300.

Stewart, Andrew. *Art, Desire, and the Body in Ancient Greece.* Cambridge: Cambridge University Press, 1997.

———. "Notes on the Reception of the Polykleitan Style: Diomedes to Alexander." Pages 246–61 in *Polykleitos, the Doryphoros, and Tradition.* Edited by Warren G. Moon. Madison: University of Wisconsin Press, 1995.

Strocka, Volker Michael. *Das Markttor von Milet.* Berlin: de Gruyter, 1981.

Trebilco, Paul. "Asia." Pages 291–362 in *The Book of Acts in its Graeco-Roman Setting*. Vol. 2 of *The Book of Acts in Its First Century Setting*. Edited by David W. J. Gill and Conrad Gempf. Grand Rapids: Eerdmans, 1994.

Weissenrieder, Annette, Friederike Wendt, and Petra von Gemünden, eds. *Picturing the New Testament*. WUNT 2/195. Tübingen: Mohr Siebeck, 2005.

Zanker, Paul. *The Power of Images in the Age of Augustus*. Translated by Alan Shapiro. Ann Arbor: University of Michigan Press, 1988.

Coinage and Colonial Identity: Corinthian Numismatics and the Corinthian Correspondence

Bradley J. Bitner

1. Introduction:
The Problems and Potential of "Numismatic Windows"

Three decades ago, Richard Oster admonished scholars to peer into the social world of the New Testament and early Christianity through "numismatic windows."[1] He argued that numismatic evidence, and particularly Roman provincial coinage, was as valuable for New Testament scholars as it was neglected by them.[2] Today, despite certain studies drawing on coins to limited degrees, there remain few systematic attempts to muster the numismatic evidence in the field of New Testament and early Christianity.[3] This is especially true of the provincial coinage, a data set that holds

---

1. Richard Oster, "Numismatic Windows into the Social World of Early Christianity: A Methodological Inquiry," *JBL* 101 (1982): 195–223. The evidence of coins did not come in for scrutiny in Oster's later essay focusing on 1 Corinthians; see Richard E. Oster, "Use, Misuse, and Neglect of Archaeological Evidence in Some Modern Works on 1 Corinthians (1 Cor 7,1–5; 8,10; 11,2–16; 12,14–26)," *ZNW* 83 (1992): 52–73.

2. Oster, "Numismatic Windows," 196–97. More than a decade later, Larry Kreitzer (in a monograph focused on Roman imperial coinage) could still point to the relative lack of engagement in NT scholarship with provincial coinage: Larry J. Kreitzer, *Striking New Images: Roman Imperial Coinage and the New Testament World*, JSNTSup 134 (Sheffield: Sheffield Academic, 1996), 27–28. The same lament is sounded by Marius Reiser, "Numismatik und Neues Testament," *Bib* 81 (2000): 457–88. See also Larry J. Kreitzer, "Coinage: Greco-Roman," in *Dictionary of New Testament Background*, ed. Craig A. Evans and Stanley E. Porter (Downers Grove, IL: InterVarsity Press, 2000), 220–22 (222): "The study of numismatics may be likened to a new continent waiting to be explored as far as New Testament studies is concerned."

3. Many New Testament works draw on coins in a very limited fashion; the trickle

great potential for the "city-by-city"[4] approach to polis and *ekklēsia* cultivated by the present volume and the Society of Biblical Literature consultation from which it has emerged. The aim of this essay is to draw on the Julio-Claudian colonial coinage of Roman Corinth to illustrate possibilities and problems with regard to the use of provincial numismatics in New Testament exegesis and social history. This will involve three major steps. First, a selective survey of the uses to which Corinthian scholars have put numismatic evidence will highlight trajectories to date as well as methodological and thematic lacunae. Second, important methodological issues related to the study of the civic coinage of a colony such as Corinth will be raised. Third, a series of case studies will serve to exemplify the potential the colonial coinage offers for sharpening our understanding of various aspects of Corinthian identity. A final brief reflection will summarize the

---

of sustained integrative work may be tracked among the entries in the "*Numismatica, coins*" subsection (under *Archaeologia*) of the annual *Elenchus of Biblica*. Notable works since 1980 include Oster, "Numismatic Windows," which provides extensive bibliography of older works dealing with coins and of some more recent studies connecting coins to the New Testament. Kreitzer, *Striking New Images*, 222–32, appends an annotated list of works integrating numismatics and New Testament and Second Temple Jewish studies. Steven J. Friesen, *Twice Neokoros: Ephesus, Asia, and the Cult of the Flavian Imperial Family* (Leiden: Brill, 1993); and Christoph vom Brocke, *Thessaloniki: Stadt des Kassander und Gemeinde des Paulus*, WUNT 2/125 (Tübingen: Mohr Siebeck, 2001) balance the use of imperial, *koinon*, and civic coinages in relation to specific New Testament locales. Reiser, "Numismatik und Neues Testament," offers an overview relevant especially to the Second Temple period and the Gospels, including denominational equivalents and tables illustrating relative buying power. Peter Lewis and Ron Bolden, *The Pocket Guide to Saint Paul: Coins Encountered by the Apostle on His Travels* (Kent Town, South Australia: Wakefield, 2002) is a thorough albeit popular work that, despite the questionable assumption in its subtitle and its debatable Pauline chronology, offers a helpful starting point for local or regional numismatic work by New Testament scholars. Both Oster and Reiser call for numismatics to become a more integral part of training for students of the New Testament and for the compilation of a "numismatic Wettstein." It seems doubtful, however, whether the first impulse could (or should?) be realized within the curricula of most departments of theology or religion. And it is unclear what shape the latter suggestion would take or what its ultimate value would be. See Stefan Alkier, " 'Geld' im Neuen Testament–Der Beitrag der Numismatik zu einer Enzyklopädie des Frühen Christentums," *Zeichen aus Text und Stein: Studien auf dem Weg zu einer Archäologie des Neuen Testament*, ed. Stefan Alkier and Jürgen Zangenberg, TANZ 42 (Tübingen: Francke, 2003), 308–55.

4. A phrase coined by Edwin A. Judge; see "The Social Identity of the First Christians: A Question of Method in Religious History," *JRH* 11 (1980): 201–12.

numismatic prospects for a better understanding of polis (or *colonia*) and *ekklēsia* in the Julio-Claudian era, with special reference to the Corinthian letters of the apostle Paul.[5]

In preparation, it is helpful to consider critically how our conceptualization of ancient coins relates to our use of them as evidence and to our view of their value for New Testament and early Christian studies. Oster proposed that we think of coins as "numismatic windows." As a conceptual metaphor shaping our engagement with coins, this is not without difficulties. One problem with the image of a window is that it suggests a direct and unimpeded view of, for example, the first-century "social world." This is hardly the case. Coins are made from alloyed metal and are opaque. We see the crafted images and legends on their surfaces, but do not literally see through them. In fact, the iconic forms we behold on coin surfaces are often quite difficult to interpret decisively with regard to their ancient meanings. Consideration of this basic challenge should caution us as we approach the constructed images found on the coins.[6]

Yet, we may grant Oster his metaphor and note that there were, in fact, ancient windows made from glass; even these, however, were not always transparent. Glass was produced and employed in first-century cities—in Roman Corinth, at least from the time of Augustus—but was usually semi-opaque or opaque. Such glass windows were found primarily in public baths or elite domestic spaces.[7] Thus the window metaphor, especially

---

5. I note that the methodological categories and emphases I focus on also have relevance, with certain modifications, for early Christian texts related to Corinth such as 1 Clement.

6. To be sure, Oster was aware of this fact. But, as we will see below, careful demonstration is needed when making claims about a visual lingua franca when we juxtapose stylized iconography and New Testament texts. For valuable work in this area, see the essay of Brigitte Kahl in this volume. On "visual language" in Roman art generally, see Paul Zanker, *The Power of Images in the Age of Augustus* (Ann Arbor: University of Michigan Press, 1988); and, more recently, Tonio Hölscher, *The Language of Images in Roman Art* (Cambridge: Cambridge University Press, 2004), and the foreword by Jaś Elsner. For an accessible, cautionary introduction to reading numismatic iconography, see Patrick J. Casey, *Understanding Ancient Coins: An Introduction for Archaeologists and Historians* (London: Batsford, 1986), especially chap. 2, "The Iconography of Coinage." See also Volker Heuchert, "The Chronological Development of Roman Provincial Coin Iconography," in *Coinage and Identity in the Roman Provinces*, ed. Christopher J. Howgego, Volker Heuchert, and Andrew M. Burnett (Oxford: Oxford University Press, 2005), 29–56.

7. For glass manufacture and objects in Roman Corinth, including window

when set in an early Roman context, directs us to problems relevant to our use of the numismatic evidence. If looking at a coin is in any sense like gazing through a window, then we should imagine an ancient and not a modern window. That is to say, coins provide a translucent, stylized, and mediated view of ancient life. For instance, the types and legends of the Corinthian coinage were chosen by the colonial elite, presumably for good reasons, and were executed by engravers and artisans in the local *officinae* (workshops) of the colonial mint.[8] In addition, depending on a coin's denomination, it was handled primarily by people of certain socioeconomic levels.[9] For these reasons, if New Testament scholars insist on regarding coins as "numismatic windows," we should at least acknowledge that they are *ancient* windows indeed, and will almost always provide us with a refracted and restricted view of our objects of inquiry.

Another problem with the concept of "numismatic window" is that it foregrounds the *iconographic* value of coins at the expense of other important and relevant features.[10] It is understandable that our attention is drawn

---

panes, see Gladys R. Davidson, *The Minor Objects*, vol. 12 of *Corinth* (Princeton: The American School of Classical Studies at Athens, 1952), 76–121, 143–45. For Roman glassworking and window panes from the Augustan period, see Stuart J. Fleming, *Roman Glass: Reflections on Cultural Change* (Philadelphia: University of Pennsylvania Museum of Archaeology and Anthropology, 1999), 28–30.

8. Michel Amandry (*Le monnayage des duovirs corinthiens*, BCHSupp 15 (Athens: École française d'Athènes, 1988], 89) suggests the existence of at least two *officinae* that struck coins during several (but not all) of the Julio-Claudian issues. *Officinae* are "subdivisions of the same mint—not separate establishments in different localities," whose purpose, according to MacDowall, was "to divide the work at the mint between a number of responsible divisions of manageable proportions, and to exercise a degree of administrative control over the coins produced by different divisions. See David W. MacDowall, "The Organisation of the Julio-Claudian Mint at Rome," in *Scripta Nummaria Romana, Essays Presented to Humphrey Sutherland*, ed. R. A. G. Carson and Colin M. Kraay (London: Spink and Son, 1978), 32–46, at 33–34. I thank Dr. MacDowall for sharing with me a facsimile of his subsequent, unpublished paper, "The Mint Organisation of Early Imperial Corinth."

9. Even those who rightly urge us to widen our field of vision to include the socioeconomic "nothings" in our study of Pauline communities and texts recognize the potential of numismatics. See, e.g., Justin J. Meggitt, *Paul, Poverty and Survival* (Edinburgh: T&T Clark, 1998), 30 n. 112, who correctly associates coins with various subgenres of inscriptions that allow us glimpses of ancient "popular culture."

10. Oster, "Numismatic Windows," rightly highlighted the importance of numismatic iconography as part of a Greco-Roman "visual language" but largely ignored

powerfully to the evocative images displayed on the obverse ("heads") and reverse ("tails") of an ancient coin. But as we will see below, grasping the import of these designs and applying their meanings to the interpretation of New Testament and early Christian texts and communities can be quite difficult. Furthermore, a sole focus on numismatic iconography obscures our view of the features of material production, patterns of circulation, and performative contexts related to the coinage as handled by real people. But actually, these less obvious material and social aspects may offer us insights—in ways that complement the visual attributes of coins—into the economic settings in which early Christian texts were produced and received. With the evident potential and challenging problems of employing numismatic evidence in mind, we will now survey the uses to which scholars of Roman Corinth and the Corinthian correspondence have put the coins.

2. Coins, Corinth, and the Corinthian Correspondence

2.1. Roman Corinth's Colonial Coinage

Only relatively recently have New Testament scholars begun to draw on the colonial coinage of Roman Corinth in their investigations of *colonia*, *ekklēsia*, and Paul's Corinthian correspondence. One important reason for this is the progression of the history of Roman Corinthian numismatics generally. That history bears summarizing briefly.[11]

Roman Corinthian numismatic scholarship related to the Julio-Claudian period divides itself into two phases on either side of Michel Amandry's watershed study *Le monnayage des duovirs corinthiens*, published in 1988.[12] In the century of relevant publications preceding Amandry,[13]

---

other pertinent aspects of coins such as metrology and circulation patterns. The same applies to Kreitzer's monograph.

11. See appendix for a select bibliography of important works related to Roman Corinthian numismatics.

12. Amandry, *Le monnayage*. For a chronological bibliography of this and other short titles related to Corinthian numismatics, see appendix.

13. Fellow numismatist John Kroll is among those who have remarked that the importance of Amandry's work "can hardly be overstated." See John H. Kroll, "Coinage as an Index of Romanization," in *The Romanization of Athens: Proceedings of an International Conference Held at Lincoln, Nebraska (April 1996)*, ed. Michael C. Hoff and Susan I. Rotroff, Oxbow Monograph 94 (Oxford: Oxbow, 1997), 135–50 (135).

initial finds and analyses of the early Roman coinage were placed primarily in the service of Pausanian archaeology[14] or political history.[15] Subsequent to Amandry's comprehensive analysis of the chronology, iconographic typology, die links, and other features of the duoviral coinage—and especially since the inclusion of his results in the monumental first volume of *Roman Provincial Coinage* (1992, hereafter *RPC* 1)[16]—historians, archaeologists, and scholars of early Christianity have begun to engage with the coins not only at the level of political history but also with regard to colonial economics, cult, and identity.[17] We may trace three such trajectories in research on 1 Corinthians by attending in turn to the studies of Andrew Clarke, Jorunn Økland, and Robert Dutch.[18]

---

14. Friedrich Imhoof-Blumer and Percy Gardner, *Ancient Coins Illustrating Lost Masterpieces of Greek Art: A Numismatic Commentary on Pausanias* (Chicago: Argonaut, 1964) preceded the inauguration (in 1896) of excavations by the American School of Classical Studies at Corinth.

15. E.g., Harry Bertram Earle Fox, "The Duoviri of Corinth," *Journal International d'Archéologie Numismatique* 2 (1899): 89–116; Fox, "Colonia Laus Iulia Corinthus," *Journal International d'Archéologie Numismatique* 6 (1903): 5–16, pl. 1; Anita Bagdikian, "The Civic Officials of Roman Corinth" (MA thesis, University of Vermont, 1953).

16. Andrew M. Burnett, Michel Amandry, and Pere Pau Ripollès, eds., *From the Death of Caesar to the Death of Vitellius (44 BC–AD 69)*, part 1, *Introduction and Catalogue*, part 2, *Indexes and Plates*, vol. 1 of *Roman Provincial Coinage* (London: British Museum; Paris: Bibliothèque nationale de France, 1992).

17. The several studies by Mary E. H. Walbank (from 1989–2010, see appendix) are important extensions and applications of the work of Amandry.

18. Both Andrew D. Clarke, *Secular and Christian Leadership in Corinth: A Socio-Historical and Exegetical Study of 1 Corinthians 1–6*, AGJU 18 (Leiden: Brill, 1993), and Jorunn Økland, *Women in Their Place: Paul and the Corinthian Discourse of Gender and Sanctuary Space*, JSNTSup 269 (London: T&T Clark, 2004) made use of Amandry's 1988 study (*Le monnayage*). Neither Økland nor Robert S. Dutch, *The Educated Elite in 1 Corinthians: Education and Community Conflict in Graeco-Roman Context*, JSNTSup 271 (London: T&T Clark, 2005) refers to *RPC* 1, with Dutch making no mention of Amandry at all and relying instead on Katharine M. Edwards, *The Coins 1896–1929*, vol. 6 of *Corinth* (Athens: American School of Classical Studies at Athens; Cambridge, MA: Harvard University Press, 1933). These observations merely illustrate the challenges New Testament scholars often face in being aware of or accessing the most up-to-date resources relevant to their purposes from neighboring subdisciplines such as numismatics.

2.2. Clarke, Coins, and Colonial Authority

One of the earliest studies in which the Corinthian duoviral coinage contributed to the social-historical framework of New Testament interpretation was Andrew Clarke's *Secular and Christian Leadership in Corinth* (1993).[19] Looking primarily to the coins for the sake of onomastics (named figures) and prosopography (social status and interrelations), Clarke reconstructed a political sociology of magisterial wealth and honor in the colony in order to contrast it with the ecclesial ethics of "leadership" found in 1 Cor 1–6. Clarke's handling of the coins was careful and traditional; he used their evidence in conjunction with literary and epigraphical data[20] in order to evoke more specific, personal, elite Corinthian figures as a foil for his exegesis.[21] One wonders, however, if the coins might have yet more to offer in service of Clarke's stated goal of reconstructing Corinthian "leadership profiles and practices,"[22] especially if considered in light of patterns of magistracy holding in the larger region by elites such as C. Iulius Polyaenus[23] (treated further below) or in view of the colonial structures of authority surrounding type selection and the minting of coins.[24]

2.3. Økland, Coins, Colonial Women, and Cultic Spaces

A second example of the use of Corinthian coins for the interpretation of 1 Corinthians is Jorunn Økland's *Women in Their Place: Paul and the Corinthian Discourse of Gender and Sanctuary Space* (2004). Økland employed the coins for their iconographical evidence related to cultic

---

19. Clarke, *Secular and Christian Leadership*, 12 n. 13, 12–15, 135–57 (appendix A). The coins, for Clarke, provide a "frame" in a literal as well as a methodological sense, as they figure explicitly only at the beginning and end of his study.

20. E.g., ibid., 15.

21. A more recent, focused use of the numismatic evidence for prosopography and exegesis is found in L. L. Welborn, *An End to Enmity: Paul and the "Wrongdoer" of 2 Corinthians* (Berlin: de Gruyter, 2011), 290, 301–8, where he makes full use of Edwards, *Coins*; Amandry, *Le monnayage*; and *RPC* 1.

22. Clarke, *Secular and Christian Leadership*, 23–39, 129.

23. Duovir of 57/58 or 58/59. See Amandry, *Le monnayage*, 24–26; *RPC* 1:1201–2; Clarke, *Secular and Christian Leadership*, 148 (appendix A, no. 97).

24. Aspects of which are treated by Amandry, *Le monnayage*, 80–99. See further Peter Weiss, "The Cities and Their Money," in Howgego, Heuchert, and Burnett, *Coinage and Identity*, 57–68.

practices and ritual spaces,[25] focusing somewhat less on prosopography and political history.[26] She drew on coins depicting images and temples related to Aphrodite/Venus, Isis, Serapis, and Asklepios in order to help ground her reconstructions of performative contexts and ritually ordered spaces in which women may have featured in Corinth and the Pauline *ekklēsia*.[27] Appropriately, coins formed one (limited) strand of evidence in the interpretive tapestry she wove. Yet one senses the potential for a deeper reflection, particularly given the challenges of interpreting numismatic iconography. For example, Økland's discussion of the well-known Corinthian issue of the Tiberian era depicting a *Gens Iulia* temple at Corinth (on which, see further below) lacks critical engagement with the fact that the coins point, not necessarily to a physical structure in first-century Corinth, but perhaps to "an event or number of events" they were meant to evoke.[28] This relates to a well-known methodological problem concerning numismatic architectural representations, one about which not all New Testament scholars may be aware.[29]

---

25. Økland, *Women in Their Place*, 93–94, 97–99, 102–7, 249–52, 255. Prior studies drawing on Corinthian coins in a similar, but more limited, manner include Khiok-Khng Yeo, *Rhetorical Interaction in 1 Corinthians 8 and 10: A Formal Analysis with Preliminary Suggestions for a Chinese, Cross-Cultural Hermeneutic*, BibInt 9 (Leiden: Brill, 1995), 104–9; and John Fotopoulos, *Food Offered to Idols in Roman Corinth: A Socio-rhetorical Reconsideration of 1 Corinthians 8:1–11:1*, WUNT 2/151 (Tübingen: Mohr Siebeck, 2003), 29, 135.

26. Økland's short section in *Women in Their Place*, appendix 1 (249–50), listing women connected to the Julio-Claudian house depicted on the Corinthian coinage is more in line with the traditional prosopographical use of numismatic evidence.

27. Økland rightly draws on coins from Kenchreai (ibid., 99–100) for her interpretation of Corinthian cultic practices.

28. See ibid., 102–3 with Mary E. H. Walbank, "Image and Cult: The Coinage of Roman Corinth," in *Corinth in Context: Comparative Studies on Religion and Society*, ed. Steven J. Friesen, Daniel N. Schowalter, and James C. Walters (Leiden: Brill, 2010), 156–62.

29. See Andrew Burnett, "Buildings and Monuments on Roman Coins," in *Roman Coins and Public Life under the Empire: E. Togo Salmon Papers II*, ed. George M. Paul and Michael Ierardi (Ann Arbor: University of Michigan Press, 1999), 137–64; and Christopher Howgego, "Coinage and Identity in the Roman Provinces," in Howgego, Heuchert, and Burnett, *Coinage and Identity*, 1–17, esp. 4–5. Both essays offer important qualifications to the classic treatment of Martin Price and Bluma L. Trell, *Coins and Their Cities: Architecture on the Ancient Coins of Greece, Rome, and Palestine* (London: Vecchi, 1977).

2.4. Dutch, Coins, and Colonial *Paideia*

A third and final instance of Corinthian numismatics and the exegesis of 1 Corinthians is Robert Dutch's *The Educated Elite in 1 Corinthians*.[30] Although he draws exclusively on the earlier work of Katharine Edwards rather than on Amandry's study, Dutch displays a sensitivity to the complexities involved in using the numismatic evidence for discerning the character of Corinthian colonial "identity," particularly with regard to practices and settings of *paideia*. Dutch rightly notes that many of the duoviral coins juxtapose Latin legends with reverse iconography that recalls the older Greek Corinthian tradition. He argues that this implies an important "Greek" aspect that must serve to qualify claims regarding Corinth's first-century "Roman" identity. Another notable feature of Dutch's engagement with the coin evidence is his mention of "coin-like bronzes" known as *tesserae*, possibly issued in connection with local games and festivals.[31] The main focus of Dutch's employment of the coins is his use of issues with Greek athletic iconography to construct an exegetical framework of *paideia* in Paul's Corinth (including nearby Isthmia) and to aid specifically in the interpretation of the running and boxing imagery in 1 Cor 9:24–27.[32] Strengths include his reflection on coins and cultural identity, his appeal to the poorly understood "token" (*tesserae*) issues, and his combination of the coins with epigraphic and other archaeological evidence to evoke a context for interpretation.[33] One wishes, however, that Dutch might have lingered further over matters such as who approved the design and production of these issues (and why), at which moments and in which contexts these coins may have been introduced into circulation, and by whom they may have been handled.

---

30. Dutch, *Educated Elite*, 50–51, 225–29.
31. Ibid., 50–51.
32. Ibid., 225–30.
33. E.g., the connections he draws between coins, Broneer's Type XXII lamps, and the Room C mosaic from the South Stoa are provocative: ibid., 228–29. For similar work, drawing in detail on the coins and related sets of evidence regarding the question of Corinthian "identity," see now Cavan W. Concannon, *"When You Were Gentiles": Specters of Ethnicity in Roman Corinth and Paul's Corinthian Correspondence* (New Haven: Yale University Press, 2014), 61, 121–22.

2.5. Summary: Numismatic Lacunae in New Testament Corinthian Studies

In summary, each of these scholars is to be commended for interacting with the numismatic evidence in an attempt to arrive at new or nuanced contexts of interpretation for 1 Corinthians. As we can see, however, such attempts demonstrate some of the considerable difficulties in doing so carefully and productively. More specifically, we begin to notice certain methodological and thematic *lacunae* emerging in relation to the use of Corinthian numismatics in New Testament scholarship. Several observations along these lines are in order.

In the first instance, it is important to note that none of the three studies analyzed thus far refers to *RPC* 1, the standard provincial numismatic reference work for the Julio-Claudian period.[34] Additionally, none draws in any way on the metrological features (i.e., coin fabric, weight, die-links) of the Corinthian coinage so carefully analyzed by Amandry. Most probably, this is due to a lack of appreciation for how such seemingly mundane features of the coins might be relevant to the historical and exegetical questions these scholars are addressing. Similarly, although Økland briefly examines the coin evidence related to her reconstruction of civic-ritual spaces, neither she nor others consider the evidence, available in Amandry and *RPC* 1, for circulation patterns, performative contexts (i.e., spaces where and occasions when coins were issued or used), or the implications of such facts for the social location of those who used the coinage. Dutch offers a notable exception in referring to the *tesserae* and festivals, but does not pursue the possible connections between issuing authorities (i.e., *duoviri*) and audiences in his reflections on Corinthian colonial "identity." Finally, although Økland and Dutch refer extensively to Corinthian numismatic iconography as they assemble contexts for exegesis, neither evinces a sustained effort to acknowledge and avoid the methodological pitfalls associated with the use of coin types and iconography.

Taken together, the methodological and thematic shortcomings in no way detract from the work that has been done. They serve instead to highlight areas for further reflection and investigation. In order for future studies of early Christianity and Corinth to make progress in the effective

---

34. *RPC* 1 would have appeared too late for Clarke in *Secular and Christian Leadership*, but its omission by Økland, *Women in Their Place*, and Dutch, *Educated Elite*, is less easy to explain. Of the works alluded to in the notes above, only Welborn, *An End to Enmity*, and Concannon, *When You Were Gentiles*, refer to *RPC* 1.

use of numismatics, it is necessary to offer a clear, summary treatment of several methodological aspects in the following section and then to proceed to a series of case studies illustrating potential lines of research for coinage and colonial identity in relation to *colonia*, *ekklēsia*, and the Corinthian correspondence.

3. Figuring Corinthian Colonial Coinage: Methodological Considerations

Allowing the Corinthian coins to figure in our understanding of the public life of the Julio-Claudian colony, its earliest Christian assembly, and its Pauline epistles requires a considered and contextual approach to the evidence. Four methodological considerations relevant to our handling of the Corinthian coinage also direct us to a more careful engagement generally on the part of New Testament scholars with local and regional numismatic evidence. First, such coinage must be understood as Roman provincial coinage. Second, attention must be given to the civic context of mints and the implications of metrology. In addition, civic coinages, especially in the case of Corinth, must be set within the larger colonial territory and regional economy. Finally, careful consideration must be given to the interpretation of numismatic iconography and its import for our understanding of civic ideology.

3.1. Roman Provincial Coinage

Bronze coins minted by cities outside Rome used to be known in scholarship as "Greek Imperials," a term that was for various reasons misleading[35] and that fell out of favor in the 1970s and 1980s.[36] With the publication of *RPC* 1 in 1992, the new designation "Roman provincial coinage" became the indelible state of the art.[37] The difference between the two characterizations is more than semantic; each encodes distinct analytical categories and

---

35. The term's demise was presaged in an important essay by Tom B. Jones, "A Numismatic Riddle: The So-Called Greek Imperials," *Proceedings of the American Philosophical Society* 107 (1963): 308–47.

36. See the transitional title of a work as important and late as Christopher J. Howgego, *Greek Imperial Countermarks: Studies in the Provincial Coinage of the Roman Empire* (London: Royal Numismatic Society, 1985).

37. See now Michel Amandry, "The Coinage of the Roman Provinces through

an attendant shift in historical perspective related to chronology, geography, and ideology.

First, the chronological frame has shifted. By calling coinage such as the duoviral issues of Julio-Claudian Corinth "Roman," attention is drawn first to the era during which the Roman imperium embraced the cities of the Greek East. We are thereby reminded that these coins, though produced outside of the city of Rome, were nonetheless minted in a period when cities held the legal right to mint at the pleasure of the Roman authorities. It is therefore necessary to interpret first-century coinage in the Mediterranean world with reference to Roman power and presence, even when the legends on the coins may be in languages other than Latin and when their images refer, apparently, to "un-Roman" deities, figures, or symbols.

Additionally, however, these latter realities remind us of a geographical stance. That is, while "Roman," this coinage is also "provincial." There was no official program issuing from Rome that dictated the choice of inscriptions or icons by civic magistrates for the local coinages.[38] A viewpoint suited to these coins is one with both feet planted firmly in the minting cities of the provinces, one that looks attentively to regional economic patterns, and that takes note of the political winds blowing from Rome.[39] Roman provincial coinage comprises civic coinages that supplied "pocket change" for local and regional economies[40] and, in doing so, employed a visual language familiar to audiences close to home.

Hadrian," in *The Oxford Handbook of Greek and Roman Coinage*, ed. William E. Metcalf (Oxford: Oxford University Press, 2012), 391–404.

38. Evidence gathered for our period by Andrew Burnett, "The Augustan Revolution Seen from the Mints of the Provinces," *JRS* 101 (2011): 1–30.

39. The editors of *RPC* 1 note in the preface: "the contemporary change of emphasis from 'Greek Imperial' to 'Roman Provincial' prompts the choice of the Roman province as the basic unit.... a new arrangement [of the data by province] may perhaps underline the shift over the last few years in the way these coinages are regarded. Instead of seeing the provincial coinage as the dying gasps of the coinage of the Greek world there is now a tendency to appreciate its vitality as the city coinage of the Roman provinces" (xv).

40. Christopher J. Howgego, "After the Colt Has Bolted: A Review of Amandry on Roman Corinth," *NumC* 149 (1989): 199–208, notes, at 199–200, the relatively small output of the Corinthian mint in our era in terms of overall Roman value (i.e., approximately 500,000 denarii over 110 years, or the rough equivalent of four to five months' worth of pay for a Roman legion in over a century of sporadic minting). Cf.

Finally, the connection between civic coinages and ideology has been clearly established. At least since the earlier work of Ken Harl,[41] it has become necessary to link the civic coinages with the construction of civic identities. Coin legends and reverse types were most often employed for this purpose, increasingly so as our period progressed.[42] Recently, Christina Katsari and Stephen Mitchell have undertaken a broad statistical analysis of civic coinage from colonies in the Greek East with an eye toward marking trends of civic "political ideology."[43] They argue that, "since ... local magistrates were responsible for the types, the language and the weight standards of the local coinages, their choices certainly reflected their awareness of the priorities of the central state as well as their local pride and civic patriotism."[44]

In sum, for reasons of chronology, geography, and political ideology, colonial coinage produced by cities such as Corinth is now conceptualized as *Roman provincial coinage*. This important shift in viewpoint—and its entailments—must be kept in mind by New Testament scholars

---

RPC 1:16-17. An overview of coins and exchange in civic contexts may be found in Michael Crawford, "Money and Exchange in the Roman World," *JRS* 60 (1970): 40-48.

41. Kenneth W. Harl, *Civic Coins and Civic Politics in the Roman East, AD 180-275* (Berkeley: University of California Press, 1987); Harl, *Coinage in the Roman Economy, 300 BC to AD 700* (Baltimore: Johns Hopkins University Press, 1996).

42. Burnett, "Augustan Revolution," 24-29. Cf. the earlier, impressionistic sketch of Alfred R. Bellinger, "Greek Mints under the Roman Empire," in *Essays in Roman Coinage Presented to Harold Mattingly*, ed. R. A. G. Carson and C. H. V. Sutherland (London: Oxford University Press, 1956; repr., Darmstadt: Scientia, 1979), 137-48 (142-44).

43. Christina Katsari and Stephen Mitchell, "The Roman Colonies of Greece and Asia Minor: Questions of State and Civic Identity," *Athanaeum* 96 (2008): 219-47. The authors are aware of debates concerning the nature of "identity" in the Greco-Roman world, and contrast "political ideology" with "cultural identity"; the former, they rightly claim, is more accessible through the numismatic evidence.

44. Ibid., 220. See George Williamson, "Aspects of Identity," in Howgego, Heuchert, and Burnett, *Coinage and Identity in the Roman Provinces*, 19-27. For a discussion of this in relation to New Testament texts and settings, see Mark A. Chancey, *Greco-Roman Culture and the Galilee of Jesus*, SNTSMS 134 (Cambridge: Cambridge University Press, 2005), 166-92 (chap. 6, "The Coinage of Galilee"); Marcus Sigismund, "Small Change? Coins and Weights as a Mirror of Ethnic, Religious, and Political Identity in First and Second Century C.E. Tiberias," in *Religion, Ethnicity, and Identity in Ancient Galilee: A Region in Transition*, ed. Harold W. Attridge, Dale B. Martin, and Jürgen Zangenburg, WUNT 210 (Tübingen: Mohr Siebeck, 2007), 315-36.

who attempt to correlate the civic coinages with early Christian texts and communities.

3.2. Mints and Metrology

Consideration of the civic context of coin production and use in the Roman provinces also requires us to take into account the processes of minting and the metrological features observable in the numismatic evidence. This involves reflecting on local minting authorities, mint organization, and features of coin fabric in relation to the minting process. Furthermore, placing these aspects in civic context reminds us that coins, though an important set of evidence, can rarely stand alone for our purposes. Rather, they must be integrated with other texts and materials in the interests of a robust contextualization of polis and *ekklēsia*.

To begin with, it is important to remember with respect to the duoviral coinage that not only does the money give us evidence for the men; the men gave us the money. Coinage issued in Roman Corinth was issued on authority; this fact helps us to interpret it with reference to colonial politics and named figures. There is certainly more we would like to know about the chain of imperial, provincial, and civic authority in relation to civic coinages such as that of Roman Corinth.[45] But we do know that any city issuing coinage only did so with Roman permission.[46] Moreover, the "signatures" of the *duoviri* on their issues not only imply their authorization generally[47] but also suggest that—perhaps in cooperation with the decurional council—they approved coin designs, were aware of denominational features, and were involved in the timing of the release of coin into the local economy. They may also have financed many of the issues themselves, viewing the coinage as a medium of both personal and colonial advertising.[48] The mag-

---

45. Burnett, "Augustan Revolution," 7: "We have no direct evidence for how the system worked. Inferences have to be drawn from the surviving coins themselves."

46. See *RPC* 1:1–5.

47. The relatively small number of coins issued, in addition to the sporadic minting, accounts for the absence of a separate colonial magistracy overseeing the coinage. See Howgego, *Greek Imperial Countermarks*, 85.

48. Amandry, *Le monnayage*, 9–10, places the accent on the *duoviri* in our period, but see Howgego, "Colt," 200. The evidence of die-links and "alternating" signatures pointed to by MacDowall (summarized below) offers another way to connect *duoviri* as "supervisors" of the minting process.

COINAGE AND COLONIAL IDENTITY 165

istrates and "money men"[49] who authorized the minting of coinage relied on the craftsmen and apparatuses of production associated with the mints that actually generated the bronze coins.

A second aspect of coin production deserving mention, therefore, is the mint organization at Corinth. External or direct evidence for the physical structures involved in minting at Roman Corinth is almost wholly lacking.[50] Based on evidence from Roman Athens and elsewhere, it is possible that minting may have taken place within a civic building near the forum, but this cannot be proved in the case of Corinth.[51] Traces of bronze-working in the Corinthian forum area have been discovered,[52] but since minting was only ever sporadic, even during the well-represented Julio-Claudian period, the absence of secure archaeological evidence for civic mints such as that at Corinth should not necessarily surprise us. Inferences from the coins themselves are therefore the best approach to describing the organization of the colonial minting process. Evidence for die-links and for the alternation of named *duoviri* demonstrates that during the Tiberian era, and perhaps at other times, the Corinthian mint operated with two, coordinated *officinae* (workshops).[53] We may imagine

---

49. Corinthian magistrates were drawn from a fairly small pool of elites, many of whom had family histories intertwined with Roman business interests in the region. See Antony J. S. Spawforth, "Roman Corinth: The Formation of a Colonial Elite," in *Roman Onomastics in the Greek East: Social and Political Aspects*, ed. A. D. Rizakis (Athens: Research Center for Greek and Roman Antiquity, 1996), 167–82; Benjamin W. Millis, "The Local Magistrates and Elite of Roman Corinth," in *Corinth in Contrast*, ed. Steven J. Friesen, Sarah A. James, and Daniel N. Schowalter (Leiden: Brill, 2014), 38–53. I thank Dr. Millis for discussing his essay with me.

50. Christopher Howgego, *Ancient History from Coins* (London: Routledge, 1995), 26–30. Cf. Andrew Burnett, "The Invisibility of Roman Imperial Mints," in *I luoghi della moneta: Le sedi delle zecche dall'antichità all'età moderna: atti del convegno internazionale, 22-23 ottobre 1999, Milano*, ed. R. La Guardia (Milan: Comune di Milano, 2001), 41–48. Prof. Amandry kindly drew my attention to the latter essay.

51. Burnett, "Invisibility," 45: "Mints could be located anywhere, and were not grand structures with dedicated functions. It was as easy for a city to set up its mint in some suitable building, as it was for a forger to set up a mint in his own house or back yard."

52. Carol C. Mattusch, "Corinthian Metalworking: The Forum Area," *Hesperia* 46 (1977): 380–89.

53. Amandry, *Le monnayage*, 69, 89. Amandry refers to, and modifies, the unpublished essay by David W. MacDowall, "The Mint Organisation of Early Imperial Corinth." I thank Dr. MacDowall for sharing with me a facsimile of his paper. Both

that connected to these *officinae*, there were duoviral agents who functioned as mint masters, die engravers, and other craftsmen and laborers.[54] That minting required workshops under the ultimate authority of colonial magistrates, but involving many other figures, helps us to see the coinage as an official product of the colony, a product with ideological, as well as economic, currency.

In addition, the colonial process of coin production necessitates a focus on the physical fabric of the coins handled by the mints and the metrological features attested by various issues and denominations. At Corinth, the flans (prefabricated blank metal discs) from which the bronze coinage was struck were distinguished in the pre-Augustan era by their beveled shape and central punch; the same attributes are visible in other contemporary coinages in the Peloponnese. A range of denominations, from the tiny *sextans* (10–11 mm; 1.76–1.97 g) to the standard *ass(arion)* (18–21 mm; 6.43–9.22 g), appear from the earliest issues, with extensive countermarking added to clarify denominational value.[55] With the Augustan era and its attendant monetary standardization, the smallest denominations (*sextans*, *quadrans*) disappear and the flans become squared or slightly rounded. As Amandry has demonstrated, these features of the coin fabric and the

---

Amandry and MacDowall detail the evidence for shared obverse dies among issues struck with the names of alternating *duoviri*. This evidence suggests, in certain Julio-Claudian eras, the operation of two workshops, possibly each under the oversight of one *duovir*; these regrouped at day's end to assess production, errors, and to secure dies against unauthorized usage.

54. On the model of the Roman mint: MacDowall, "Julio-Claudian Mint," 32–34, 42–44; Howgego, *Ancient History from Coins*, 26. By analogy with the *lex Ursonnensis* 62, the Corinthian constitution will have provided for various assistants (*apparitores*) to the *duoviri*; see Michael C. Crawford, ed., *Roman Statutes I*, Bulletin for the Institute of Classical Studies Supplements 64 (London: Institute for Classical Studies, 1996), no. 25.

55. Howgego, *Greek Imperial Countermarks*, ix, defines countermarks as "stamps applied to coins by means of engraved punches ... [that] may tell us who was using a particular coin, where it was, or at what value it was circulating when it was countermarked.... Thus one may begin to discern how coins were supplied to certain users, in what directions coins moved, and how they changed in value." Evidence and analysis of Corinthian countermarked coins: David W. MacDowall, "Countermarks of Early Imperial Corinth," *NumC* (1962): 113–23, and pl. 9; Howgego, *Greek Imperial Countermarks*, x, 4, 6; Amandry, *Le monnayage*, 35, 82–89, 258; *RPC* 1:250. For denominational values, see *RPC* 1:245–57: 4 *asssaria* = 1 *sestertius*; 16 *assaria* (or 4 *sestertii*) = 1 *denarius*.

evolution of techniques are explicable with reference to surrounding civic coinages and have implications for colonial "economic identity."[56] Notwithstanding, as Kroll has insisted, the "weight standards, denominational structure, and Latin nomenclature" for the trend-setting, *as*-based coinage found at Corinth was "explicitly modeled on that of Rome" and is thus one crucial index of "Romanization" among communities in Greece during the Julio-Claudian period.[57]

Overall, then, we must bear in mind that coins were physical objects produced by actors working within specific political-economic and Roman colonial structures. These realities demand that, whenever possible, we seek to set our interpretations of coinage within a properly reconstructed context of minting organized by Corinthian elites and in relation to other sets of evidence and the colonial "unitary living reality" they attest.[58]

3.3. Territory and Economy

Corinth, as a Roman colony, had a physically and ritually bounded civic center ("forum area") such as one frequently sees reconstructed in New Testament publications. But a focus on Corinth's monumental center may tend to eclipse the fact that the colony was part of a larger *territorium*—including neighboring Isthmia and Kenchreai—and of a yet greater regional setting in the province of Achaia. These geographical realities require attention to regional economic and political dynamics, various consumer "audiences" within and beyond these regional zones, circulation patterns, and plausible performative contexts for the Corinthian coinage.

First, Corinth's political geography obliges us to think in terms of concentric circles in which its coinage was employed. Nestled at the base of the Acrocorinth, the urban cluster of the early Roman colony—which grew and expanded over the course of the first century especially—formed an epicenter of economic activity that rippled outward through its official territory on the isthmus and beyond. Temples, shops, and markets in the Corinthian civic center were certainly a compact zone of economic exchange. But we may not isolate these from the ports of Kenchreai and

---

56. Amandry, *Le monnayage*, 80–82.
57. Kroll, "Coinage as an Index of Romanization," 139–41. For additional indices, see Anthony J. S. Spawforth, *Greece and the Augustan Cultural Revolution* (Cambridge: Cambridge University Press, 2012) 52–54.
58. Weiss, "Cities," 58.

Lechaion, the festival site of Isthmia, or, further afield, commerce at locales such as Sicyon, Argos, Nemea, or even Athens. All these sites, and others, were linked to Corinth by the political geography of *territorium* and province and are therefore relevant when we consider the uses and meanings of the colonial coinage.[59]

Second, these geographical circles serve to remind us of consumer "audiences" who interacted with the duoviral coinage within and beyond Corinth and Achaia. At the most basic level, we should think in terms of the varieties of "colonial," "provincial," and "imperial" audiences (which might overlap) who may have utilized coins for exchange or taken note of their iconography. These consumer audiences, to varying degrees, were predictable to those who designed and authorized the inscriptions and iconography of the Corinthian coinage. They were thus interlocutors in the identity discourse[60] stimulated by the coins in their purses.

Third, a consideration of the audiences interacting with the Corinthian coinage highlights the importance of tracing patterns of monetary circulation. Coinage moves, and the archaeology of Greece allows us glimpses of how the coins of Roman Corinth made their way into the wider world.[61] A recent publication from nearby Nemea, site of the Nemean Games (under Argive control), epitomizes this circulation. In total, examples of seventeen out of the twenty-four Corinthian duoviral issues studied by Amandry were found in the Nemean excavation (along with three Corinthian *tesserae*).[62] Investigations at Kenchreai, Isthmia, Argos, Olympia, and Athens grant a similar view of the wide circulation enjoyed by the Corinthian coinage.[63] This circulation pattern, when joined with the concentric circles of audience-consumers suggested above, drives home the point that

---

59. For an interpretation of the harbor towns of Kenchreai and Lechaion as *emporia* in the Corinthia, see David K. Pettegrew, "The Diolkos and the Emporion: How a Land Bridge Framed the Commercial Economy of Roman Corinth," in Friesen, James, and Schowalter, *Corinth in Contrast*, 126–42.

60. On Roman provincial identity discourse in Corinth (focusing on ethnic and cultural identity), material evidence, and relevant literature, see Concannon, *When You Were Gentiles*, 16–19 and passim.

61. Amandry, *Le monnayage*, 94–99.

62. Robert C. Knapp and John D. MacIsaac, *The Coins*, vol. 3 of *Excavations at Nemea* (Berkeley: University of California Press, 2005), 116–20.

63. See notes in Amandry, *Le monnayage*, 94–99, as well as subsequent publications from each of these sites.

Corinth's coins played a role in a complex economic network and contributed to the dynamic political discourse of identity occurring in the region.

Finally, these considerations of spaces, audiences, and the movement of coinage suggest certain performative contexts in which Corinthian duoviral issues figured. By "performative context," we refer to situations in which the coinage was distributed, employed, or emphasized in some manner. Whereas above the accent was on the figures handling the coins, here the emphasis is on the settings in which the coins especially featured. We do not have direct evidence for how new coinage was injected into the colonial economy. But by analogy with epigraphically attested scenarios, we may envision a few plausible situations. Volume 8.3 of *Corinth*, text 306, describes an official announcement and distribution centered on the *bema/rostra* in the Corinthian forum.[64] Similarly, text 153 records a banquet given, with the possibility of a donative distributed, by L. Castricius Regulus.[65] In addition, Regulus is honored in this inscription for his magistracies in relation to the local Isthmian and Caesarian Games.

These games and the markets attached to them provide further suggestive scenarios for the introduction of coinage into the economy; they are performative contexts with extensive opportunities for exchange.[66]

---

64. John Harvey Kent, *The Inscriptions, 1926–1950*, vol. 8, part 3 of *Corinth* (Princeton: The American School of Classical Studies, 1966), ll. 3–6: ἐπεὶ οὖν καὶ ἐν τούτῳ φιλοτείμως | ὁ Πρεῖ[σκ]ος ἀναστρέφεται ὥστε ὑπὲρ τῆς τειμῆς | τοῦ προδηλουμένου τόπου δοῦναι τοῖς πο[λ]ίταις | ἑκάστῳ δηνάριον ἕν. This is a distribution of Roman *imperial* coinage (a *denarius*) rather than a colonial coin. For P. Licinius Priscus Iuventianus, see RPC I COR 378.

65. Line 12: "[—]to peregit epulumq(ue) [omnibus co]lonis dedit." Regulus was almost certainly the *duovir quinquennalis* (chief magistrate in the quinquennial census year) of 21/22 CE or possibly the mid-50s. See Amandry, *Le monnayage*, 59, 165–68; pl. 18; RPC 1:1149–50; RPC I COR 146. Cf. Bruce W. Winter, *After Paul Left Corinth: The Influence of Secular Ethics and Social Change* (Grand Rapids: Eerdmans, 2001), 5, 94.

66. See Knapp and MacIsaac, *Coins*, 46–47, "Thus use of bronze coinage in commerce at the festival—purchasing sacrifices, souvenirs, staples for sustenance, and snacks from vendors—was perhaps much freer than in a town: sanctuaries had no coinage to protect. While there is much evidence of governments controlling currency in a town, there is no evidence for such control at sanctuary festivals administered by towns. Thus, even though Argos might be thought to control currencies at Nemea, or Elis at Olympia, given the total lack of evidence for this at any site, we can cautiously maintain that currency was exchanged in more a 'free market' fashion than in towns." See Luuk de Ligt, *Fairs and Markets in the Roman Empire: Economic and Social Aspects*

Another set of inscriptions, which would have applied to Roman Corinth, in adapted form, suggest further occasions on which coinage may have entered the local economy. Both the *lex Ursonensis*[67] and the *lex Irnitana*,[68] colonial charters of the same template as Corinth would have had,[69] include chapters regulating the payment of magisterial assistants or *apparitores* (*lex Urs.* 62–63; *lex Irn.* 73), the letting of public contracts and payment of contractors (*lex Urs.* 69, 72, 80; *lex Irn.* J, 63–70), and limits on gifts by magisterial candidates (*lex Urs.* 132; *lex Irn.* 77).[70] Taken together, the scenarios envisaged here provide ample opportunity for the movement of Corinthian coinage into and through local and regional spaces and occasions.

In summary, the features of political geography and economy that framed the spaces and exchanges of early Roman Corinth require us to attend to the colony's position within its *territorium*, the province of Achaia, and the larger region. This position prompts us to think in terms of concentric circles with regard both to the audiences who interacted with the colonial coinage and the circulation patterns of those coins.[71] Finally, these interactions and the identity discourse toward which the coinage contributed took place within a variety of performative contexts. Consideration of these features may open up new interpretive possibilities involving the duoviral coinage and Paul's Corinthian correspondence.

3.4. Iconography and Ideology

Coin images were long viewed as photographic representations but are now understood to speak in a more subtle and sophisticated visual language. Mary Walbank has proposed that digital photography offers a more apt analogy, since with such technology one "can alter the original so convincingly

---

of *Periodic Trade in a Pre-Industrial Society* (Amsterdam: Gieben, 1993); Harl, *Coinage in the Roman Economy*, 254–62.

67. Crawford, *Roman Statutes*, no. 25.

68. Julián González and Michael C. Crawford, "The Lex Irnitana," *JRS* 76 (1986): 147–243.

69. See Bradley J. Bitner, *Paul's Political Strategy in 1 Corinthians 1–4: Constitution and Covenant*, SNTSMS 163 (Cambridge: Cambridge University Press, 2015).

70. This is not to suggest that payment was necessarily made in local currency in these instances. In fact, some of the amounts involved probably necessitated payment in imperial coinage.

71. See Heuchert, "Chronological Development," 40–44.

to suit a particular need."[72] Imperial portraits, local mythological figures, and civic buildings were liable to stylistic alteration in the design process. With such crafted portrayals, colonial elites at Corinth attempted to accomplish a variety of ideological ends as they provided pocket change for the local and regional audiences alluded to above.[73] Coming to terms with this visual numismatic language presents a challenge for the student of polis and *ekklēsia*.[74] To meet this challenge we must consider the dynamics of choice in designing obverse and reverse images, the correlation of Corinthian coin types in view of other Greek and Roman coinages, and the relation of the colonial coin types to archaeological and historical "reality."

To begin with, two complementary perspectives on the design of obverse and reverse types point to the web of connections between iconography and political ideology. First, Katsari and Mitchell analyzed a large and representative data set including Corinthian duoviral coinage found in *RPC* 1, dividing obverse and reverse types into the two thematic categories of "state/imperial" and "local/civic."[75] The authors recognize the dynamics of choice exercised by local magistrates and emphasize the awareness of these elites regarding both imperial and local sensibilities. Magistrates were strategic in their deployment of types that addressed these ideological priorities while also advancing their own political and cultural aspirations. Second, on the basis of her familiarity with the Corinthian coinage, Walbank draws out several important observations rooted in the dynamics of type selection attributable to colonial elites. She proposes thinking in terms of two categories: "popular types which

---

72. Walbank, "Image and Cult," 195.

73. Barbara Levick, "Messages on the Roman Coinage: Types and inscriptions," in Paul and Ierardi, *Roman Coins and Public Life*, 41–60, points to the dynamic interrelation, at the imperial level, of minting authority, minting process, and audience(s).

74. Walbank, "Image and Cult," 195: "Using coins as a primary source is not straightforward. The problem for us is in viewing the coin images as the Corinthians would have done.... Coins were intended only for local consumption: the city usually coined when there was a need for small change or to commemorate an important occasion, such as the reopening of the mint or the arrival of the emperor. Other important events may be totally unknown to us, and we may not understand an image that was very familiar to the Corinthians."

75. Katsari and Mitchell, "Roman Colonies," method and categories: 228–33; analysis and conclusions: 233–47. See Harikleia Papageorgiadou-Bani, *The Numismatic Iconography of the Roman Colonies in Greece: Local Spirit and the Expression of Imperial Policy*, Meletemata 39 (Paris: de Boccard, 2004).

signify a common identity" and the more "personal" choices of the elite. Images falling into either category (or both, given that they are not mutually exclusive) may have served various public and personal functions, from the commemoration of a building dedication, to the promotion of colonial cult in the interests of provincial rivalry, to the more idiosyncratic attention given to a magistrate's favorite cult.[76] Both approaches outlined here demonstrate that the choice of coin images was fundamentally ideological and that the correlation of obverse and reverse types with broader patterns of imperial and provincial coinages is critical in tracing the way Corinth "established its own individual character within the spectrum of different civic constitutions."[77]

Existing analyses, then, of this kind of correlation are important for discerning how and why the Corinthian coin types track variously with imperial types, with iconography found on other contemporary Greek provincial coinages, and even with images on older Greek coins predating the Roman foundation of the colony in 44 BCE. In the transitional period from the late Republic to the Augustan hegemony, the Corinthian coin types show a predilection for "local" types on both the obverse and reverse.[78] From 27/26 BCE (Amandry issue VIII) the head of Augustus begins to appear on the obverses of *asses*, while the lower denominations (*semis*, *quadrans*) continue to highlight local and regional types. Subsequently, obverse images of the emperor or the imperial family dominate while local types continue to feature on the reverse.[79] In addition to the analysis of Amandry, the recent studies of Katsari and Mitchell and of Walbank argue that these patterns give us important information about colonial trends of political ideology. In particular, the evidence points to colonial elites who were alert to the regional economy and local mythologies as they established the early Roman colony in its Peloponnesian

---

76. Walbank, "Image and Cult," 196.

77. Katsari and Mitchell, "Roman Colonies," 241.

78. Types found on *asses* and *semis* among Amandry issues I–VII (ca. 44–30 BCE): Pegasos and the Peirene fountain, Bellerophon and the chimaera, Poseidon/Neptune, and other Isthmian imagery (e.g., dolphin, trident, wreath), Aphrodite. Explicable exceptions include the laureate head of Julius Caesar on the obverse of issue I (see further below) and the bare head of Antony on the obverse of issue V (an example of the so-called Antonian fleet coinage; see *RPC* 1:264–66).

79. But Katsari and Mitchell, "Roman Colonies," 238, note that Corinth especially poses an occasional exception to "state" imagery on the obverse in the early imperial period, choosing instead to assert its civic identity with "local" types on the obverse.

setting. Later, colonial elites interwove displays of loyalty to the Julio-Claudian house with important local cult and events in a way that befitted the status of Corinth as the *caput provinciae*. We point now briefly to three observations regarding types on the colonial coinage that illustrate these imperial, regional, and local ideological vectors. First, Amandry's issue XIII (4/5 CE), which features visages of no fewer than five members of the Augustan circle,[80] epitomizes just how sensitive the money men of Corinth could be to imperial political ideology (see fig. 1).

Figure 1. Portraiture of the imperial circle in the Augustan era at Corinth. A. *Obv.* Head of Augustus: *rev.* Laureate head of Julius Caesar, 10–4 BCE (Amandry Xb; *RPC* 1:1134). B. *Obv.* Head of Augustus: *rev.* Facing heads of Gaius and Lucius, 2/1 BCE (Amandry XIa; *RPC* 1:1136). C. *Obv.* Head of Agrippa Postumus: *rev.* Duoviral names in pine wreath, 4/5 CE (Amandry XIIId; *RPC* 1:1141). D. *Obv.* Head of Drusus Minor: *rev.* Duoviral names in pine wreath, 4/5 CE (Amandry XIIIg; *RPC* 1:1143). E. *Obv.* Head of Tiberius: *rev.* Duoviral names in pine wreath, 4/5 CE (Amandry XIIIb; *RPC* 1:1140). A, C–E: Lanz Auktion 105, 2001 nos. 335, 353, 357, 348. B: Naville Numismatics auction 8, 2014, no. 120.

---

80. Augustus, Tiberius, Agrippa, Drusus, and Germanicus feature on the obverses of this issue; see Amandry, *Le monnayage*, 43–55; pl. 12–16; *RPC* 1:1139–43. See the high concentration of early Julio-Claudian imperial sculpture found at Corinth in structures such as the Julian Basilica: e.g., E. H. Swift, "A Group of Roman Imperial Portraits at Corinth I–II: Augustus, Tiberius, Gaius and Lucius," *AJA* 25 (1921): 142–59, 248–65, 337–63. *RPC* 1:250 also notes that nos. 1124, 1149–50, 1153–56, 1159–61, 1178–79, also reflect types deriving "from Roman official [i.e., imperial] coinage."

Second, the coins marking Nero's celebrated visit to Greece and dramatic announcement of provincial freedom at Corinth (see fig. 2) evince the Corinthian magistrates' attempts to position themselves competitively among other Achaian cities such as Patras and Sicyon and their coinages.[81]

Figure 2. ADVENTVS AVGVSTI types in the Peloponnese. A. Corinth: *Obv.* Radiate head of Nero: *rev.* Galley with four rowers with imperial standard (Amandry XXIIf; *RPC* 1:1204) 66/67 CE. B. Patras: *Obv.* Laureate head of Nero: *rev.* Galley (*RPC* 1:1271) reign of Nero. A: Lanz Auktion 105, 2001 no. 470. B: Monnaies d'Antan auction 8, 2010, no. 742.

Third, images related to the Pegasos myth (a type present from the first colonial coin minted at Corinth) feature prominently in the coinage, inter alia, on the smaller denominations of Amandry issue III. For example, on Series d (a *sextans*) the stylized Ϙ (the old Corinthian *koppa*) appears between the legs of Pegasos flying left; it is a reverse that very nearly approaches the style and entire effect found on *staters* from Greek Corinth (see fig. 3). Even more remarkably, both the obverse and reverse match those of an *obol* from Greek Corinth, the only major differences being the coin fabric (bronze versus silver) and the Latin inscription on the Roman *sextans*.[82] In this particular case, the craftsmen assigned to

---

81. In the iconography of these coins we see a combination of imperial and provincial dynamics. For issue XXII, see Amandry, *Le monnayage,* 19–22, 215–21, pl. 38–39; *RPC* 1:1203–6. For other regional coins related to the ADVENTVS AVGVSTI, see especially *RPC* 1:1238–44 (Sicyon; Greek legends; these are the only coins issued by Sicyon in the imperial period); *RPC* 1:1257–81 (Patras; Latin legends).

82. The Ϙ (koppa) also appears with a Nikē on the obverse of Series b (a *semis*), with the chimaera on the reverse; see Amandry, *Le monnayage,* 34, 126–28, pl. 4; *RPC* 1:1119, 1121. Further types related to Pegasos: *RPC* 1:1116, 1117, 1127–28, 1181, 1201; and on the *tesserae*: ibid., 247–48, pl. 48. Ibid., 30, points to similar types on the reverse of staters of Greek Corinth; Ϙ was the well-known abbreviation for Greek Corinth.

designing the types of the early Roman coins were clearly drawing from the images on extant Greek coins available to them. Both the iconography and epigraphy of these early issues effectively evokes the political identity of Old (Greek) Corinth, establishing solidarity between the new Roman colony and the older city in a way that would appeal to local (and regional) audiences.[83] These cursory examples show just how self-conscious and multidirectional were the dynamics of political ideology and iconography on the colonial coinage.

The third issue arising from the interrelation of image and ideology is the question of fit between coin types and reality. As alluded to earlier, digital photography—with its manipulation of images—is a better way to think of the types on coins in relation to historical figures and physical structures. Simply put, one cannot assume that an image on a coin always provides evidence for "the way it was." A well-known example from the Corinthian duoviral coinage illustrates this point for us. Walbank has demonstrated that the Tiberian coins (Amandry issue XVI)[84] with the hexastyle temple bearing the inscription GENT IVLI on the architrave (see fig. 4) have been used imprecisely as evidence.

Figure 3. Corinthian ♀ on coinage of Greek and Roman Corinth. *Obv.* Pegasos with ♀ between hooves: *rev.* Helmeted head of Athena, Corinthian silver *stater* (BCD Corinth 110) 345–307 BCE. A: Naville Numismatics auction 8, 2014, no. 48.

Based on a close examination of the type features (including the critical observation that the architrave inscription on some of these coins was "reworked" in modern times), literary testimony, and archaeological evidence for temple structures in Corinth, Walbank concludes,

> The image of the *gens Iulia* temple commemorated an event or a number of events rather than the building itself. This is one of the problems in interpreting representations of buildings. It is not always clear whether the die engraver is depicting the actual monument—providing a photograph

---

83. See Angela Ziskowski, "The Bellerophon Myth in Early Corinthian History and Art," *Hesperia* 83 (2014): 81–102, esp. 99–100.

84. Amandry, *Le monnayage*, 55–69, 168–76, pl. 19–23; *RPC* 1:1151–71.

Figure 4. The *gens Iulia* temple. *Obv.* Laureate head of Tiberius: *rev.* Hexastyle temple with GENT IVLI on the architrave, Corinthian *as* 32/33 CE (Amandry XVI; *RPC* 1:1158). Lanz Auktion 114, 2003, no. 259.

as it were—or whether he is recording an event or anniversary that is connected with the monument.[85]

This bears consideration as an important example of the complexity of interpreting iconography and ideology in our reconstruction of colonial or civic identity and its application to the study of early Christianity.

To conclude this section, we note that the images on coins are important witnesses to the ideological dynamics of ancient cities and are thus worthy of careful consideration. In particular, care must be taken to interpret the obverse and reverse iconography of provincial coinage in relation to the context and interests of the magistrates and mint workers who designed the types, in connection with other coin types (imperial and regional), and with regard to other evidence (archaeological, literary) that may nuance our understanding of coin images as stylized, "digital photographs."

4. Case Studies from the Julio-Claudian Corinthian Coinage

We turn now to the application of these methodological principles to the three studies of the Corinthian correspondence mentioned earlier. Each study drew on the numismatic evidence to evoke a fresh context for exegesis. Here we will sketch potential avenues for further research along the lines initiated by Clarke, Økland, and Dutch with particular reference to the duoviral coinage of Roman Corinth.

4.1. Authority and Political Ideology

To extend Clarke's analysis of Roman Corinthian "leadership profiles and practices" relevant to *colonia* and *ekklēsia* we may draw on several features of the duoviral coinage. These include the ways that authority and political

---

85. Walbank, "Image and Cult," 156–59. See Burnett, "Buildings and Monuments"; Howgego, "Coinage and Identity," 4–5.

ideology manifest themselves in the numismatic evidence as a function of colonial structures surrounding type selection and minting as well as in patterns of magistracy holding in the region by elite "leaders." Analysis of such features offers a more detailed framework for reconstructing the role of colonial authority and ideology as it may have impinged on the colonial "underlays" of conflict within the Pauline assembly.[86]

Apart from the fact that coin production was, by legal and political necessity, under magisterial oversight, there are other traces of colonial structures of authority visible in the coinage: inscriptions occasionally bear witness to the approval of the council of decurions, a variety of countermarks witness to official recommissioning or revaluing of coins, patterns of type selection (both inclusion and exclusion) attest magisterial decisions as to the evolving shape of colonial identity and ideology, and named magistrates who sign the coinage provide us with profiles of "secular (i.e., colonial) leadership" in Roman Corinth and the region.

First, there are a few coins that bear the authoritative mark D D (*decreto decurionum*, i.e., struck by decree of the decurional council).[87] Although all coins minted in Roman Corinth will have had the tacit approval of the decurions, these instances in which that approval becomes visually explicit remind us of the involvement of the colonial elite ("leaders") in the design and production of Corinth's money. Two examples may illustrate this phenomenon. *Tesserae* of Amandry's second group are inscribed D D below Melikertes riding a dolphin[88] (fig. 5) and an *as* issued in the reign of Galba by L. Caninius Agrippa is countermarked with DDCO (*decreto decurionum corinthiorum?*) on the obverse (which bears the crowned head of Tyche-Roma).[89] In both cases the link between the authority of

---

86. See Bruce W. Winter, "The Underlays of Conflict and Compromise in 1 Corinthians," in *Paul and the Corinthians: Studies on a Community in Conflict. Essays in Honour of Margaret Thrall*, ed. Trevor I. Burke and J. Keith Elliott (Leiden: Brill, 2003), 139–55.

87. See Amandry, *Le monnayage*, 8–10, at 9: "La situation est donc différente selon les colonies et la presence (ou l'absence) de la mention D D ne semble pas obéir à une règle très stricte."

88. Amandry, *Le monnayage*, 10, 248, pl. 48. Amandry dates these D D *tesserae* to the second century primarily on the basis of stylistic resemblance of the pine in the background to other coinage post-Hadrian. But see Edwards, *Coins*, 9, who dates them to the first century; cf. Howgego, "Colt," 200.

89. Issue XXIV8 1 Ib10; Amandry, *Le monnayage*, 75–76, 230, pl. 43; Howgego, *Greek Imperial Countermarks*, no. 589.

Figure 5. Corinthian *tessera* with Melikertes on dolphin, pine tree behind, D D below (Amandry anonymous series 2 D10?). Lanz Auktion 105, 2001, no. 525.

colonial elites, the types chosen to advertise Corinth's colonial identity, and the sanction of everyday currency and small change is clarified.

Second, there is a wide range of countermarks on the coinage throughout the Julio-Claudian period.[90] At the very least, this activity demonstrates consistent involvement of Corinthian magistrates over time in clarifying denominational value and/or returning coinage into circulation at various points. What it also suggests is an economic and political attentiveness on the part of the Corinthian "leaders" to colonial finances and larger regional denominational standards and availability of coin.[91] The very first duoviral issue displays extensive countermarking and also provides a bridge to our third point emphasizing colonial authority structures and the selection of types (see fig. 6 below).

Third, then, we see the political ideology of Corinth's colonial magistrates emerging in the types they select (or decline to employ). This is strikingly evident in the case of the very first *as* from Roman Corinth (issue I). Unsurprisingly, Julius Caesar, who reconstituted Corinth as a Roman colony, appears on the obverse along with the fullest example of the colonial ethnic (LAVS IVLI CORINT). Here we see the decision on the part of Roman Corinth's first money men to honor their patron-founder and his house (even after his assassination) and to display their prestigious colonial status. But quite unexpected, at first glance, is the Pegasos type on the reverse of this first issue. One might have expected instead the *aratrum*, or ritual plow, guided by the veiled *deductor*, or colonial commissioner, or some other similar iconography associated with colonial foundation. These colonial foundation types are proudly displayed on other contemporary coinages in Greece (see fig. 6). Nevertheless, it would appear that the Corinthian *duoviri* chose instead to take up a more familiar local reverse image with a regionally respected pedigree, with the result that, from its very first issue, the Corinthian coinage effectively integrated

---

90. See n. 55.

91. Amandry, *Le monnayage*, 32, rightly emphasizes that the significance of some of these countermarks escapes us.

the Roman (obverse) and Greek (reverse) aspects of its identity in a way that would be acceptable to the concentric audiences and users of the provincial coinage of the new Roman colony.

Figure 6. Corinth issue I among regional colonial "foundation issues." A. Corinth (*RPC* 1:1116): *Obv.* Head of Julius Caesar, colonial ethnic in field to left, open hand countermark: *rev.* Bellerophon riding Pegasos, *as* 44/43 BCE. B. Patras (*RPC* 1 1253): *Obv.* Radiate head of Divus Augustus: *rev.* Togate man with measuring rod (?) and *vexillum* behind oxen and plow, *as* 14–37 CE. C. Dyme (*RPC* 1:1283): *Obv.* Diademed head of Julius Caesar: *rev.* Plow, As 40 BCE. D. Philippi (*RPC* 1:1646) *Obv.* Head of Antony: Veiled man with measuring rod (?) behind oxen and plow, *as* 40 BCE. A: Dr. Busso Peus Nachfolger Auktion 369, 2001, no. 1026. B: Naville Numismatics auction 8, 2014, no. 123. C: LHS Numismatik Auktion 96, 2006, no. 491. D: Dr. Busso Peus Nachfolger Auktion 398, 2009, no. 643.

Additionally, we glimpse by means of the coins an important reality concerning magistracy holding by elites in Corinth and the Peloponnese. One example of this comes from the coins of C. Iulius Polyaenus (57/58 or 58/59 CE).[92] At Corinth Polyaenus signed as *duovir* issue XXI. This was inscribed (as usual) in Latin and featured Nero on the obverse and on the reverse Bellerophon with Pegasos (a myth located at the Peirene fountain,

---

92. C. Iulius Polyaenus (*RPC* I COR 350) is known only by the numismatic evidence; but see Allen B. West, *Latin Inscriptions 1896–1926*, vol. 8, part 2 of *Corinth* (Cambridge, MA: The American School of Classical Studies, 1931), no. 15; and Kent, *Inscriptions*, no. 180. See also no. 165 for an apparently distinct, contemporaneous *duovir* with the same cognomen (restored tentatively as Tiberius Polyaenus). *RPC* I COR 351 records a C. Iulius Polyaenus during the time of Hadrian (137 CE). See *LGPN III.A*, 367 s.v. Πολυαίνος.

restored in the Roman Corinthian forum).⁹³ A variant of the same issue moves beyond the urban center of Corinth toward Isthmia, again with Nero on the obverse but this time with a victor's wreath of parsley encircling ISTHMIA on the reverse. In the same period, Polyaenus also signed, as δυάνδρος, the only known imperial issue from nearby Sicyon (*rev.* ΕΠΙ Γ ΙΟΥ ΠΟΛΥΑΙΝΟΥ, CI). These coins also featured Nero on the obverse (associating him with Zeus Eleutherios) and on the reverse a figure on horseback (arguably an equestrian victor at the Isthmian Games).⁹⁴

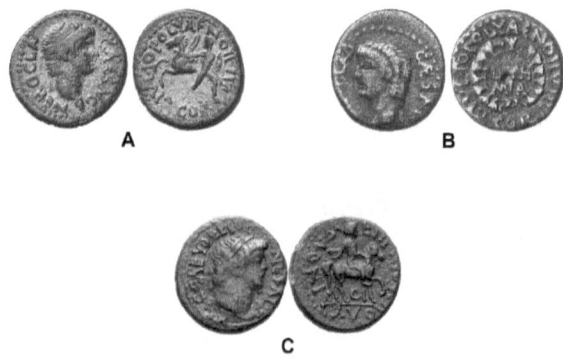

Figure 7. A: Corinth (*RPC* 1:1201): *Obv.* Head of Nero: *rev.* Bellerophon leading Pegasos, *as* 57/58 or 58/59 CE. B: Corinth (*RPC* 1:1202): *Obv.* Head of Nero: *rev.* ISTHMIA encircled by parsley wreath, *as* 57/58 or 58/59 CE. C: Sicyon (*RPC* 1:1238): *Obv.* Laureate head of Nero: *rev.* Equestrian figure, *as* reign of Nero. A, B: Lanz Auktion 105, 2001, nos. 459, 466. C: Auction 268, 2011, no. 79.

Polyaenus himself probably hailed from Sicyon. As a native Greek, and one of four known Corinthian *duoviri* with the *nomina* C. Iulii, Polyaenus represented a class of provincial elites who, especially from the time of Claudius onward, "used the colony as a showcase for their provincial ambitions."⁹⁵ Recently, Jean-Sébastien Balzat and Benjamin Millis

---

93. For the restoration and significance of the fountain in early Roman Corinth, see Betsey A. Robinson, *Histories of Peirene: A Corinthian Fountain in Three Millennia* (Athens: The American School of Classical Studies, 2011), chap. 7.
94. *RPC* 1:258.
95. Jean-Sébastien Balzat and Benjamin W. Millis, "M. Antonius Aristocrates: Provincial Involvement with Roman Power in the Late 1st Century B.C.," *Hesperia* 82 (2013): 651–72 (666).

have shown how such elites, associated with Corinth and other cities in the region, embody a magisterial paradigm for civic "leadership" in mid-first-century Corinth, precisely the sort of paradigm to which Clarke wants to appeal as a colonial foil for the very different kind of ecclesial "leadership" espoused by Paul in the Corinthian correspondence.[96] It is a pattern that connects wealthy diaspora Romans and well-born Greek provincial elites with the practices of oratory, benefaction/patronage, local cults, the gymnasium, and the underwriting of games such as those at Isthmia.[97] Further, Polyaenus and those like him who held magistracies in Corinth and elsewhere in the Peloponnese exhibit the characteristics of "a broad Romanity of cultural outlook" that fits within contemporary debates concerning a colonial profile that is "fluid, with an emphasis on multiple identities, code-switching and 'shuttling' between Greek and Roman."[98] Taken in the political terms most accessible to us via the coinage, this is nonetheless an identity shaped in response to "the acculturating exposure to Roman administrative structures routinely experienced by provincials taking part in local government as civic magistrates and officials."[99] Type selection and the oversight of minting fall squarely within such structures. Which is all to say, a colonial coin such as that signed by Polyaenus provides an entrée (if not quite a window) into a much larger provincial world and network of evidence that both anchors in Corinth and suggests a more detailed texture for the kind of magisterial pattern of *politeia* sketched by Clarke. Use of the coins

---

96. Clarke (*Secular and Christian Leadership*, 21) wants to move from named Corinthian magistrates and the "administrative structures for leadership" toward "the dynamics of those leaders and how they exerted influence." But in moving from the local evidence he cites in chap. 2 ("Evidence of Secular Leaders in Corinth") to the paradigm he constructs in chap. 3 ("Profile and Practices of Secular Leaders in Corinth"), Clarke drifts away from local and regional documentary evidence. Coins like that of Polyaenus, when linked to evidence for similar Greek provincials active in and around Corinth (such as M. Antonius Aristocrates), offer a way to build a more localized and fine-grained pattern.

97. Balzat and Millis, "M. Antonius Aristocrates," passim, fill out this pattern with rich detail based on the epigraphic and numismatic "dossier" of the provincial elite named in the title of their essay. The authors name Polyaenus, 666, as another who fits the profile they reconstruct.

98. Spawforth, *Greece and the Augustan Cultural Revolution*, 55–58 (56).

99. Ibid.; Balzat and Millis, "M. Antonius Aristocrates," 665–68.

in these and related ways may further advance the exegetical efforts of Pauline scholars.

Thus, if only in outline, we see that traces of colonial structures of authority borne by coin inscriptions, by countermarks, and evident in type selection help us to construct more detailed contexts for exegesis relevant to 1 and 2 Corinthians. So too does the patient teasing out of the local and regional profiles of magistrates who as colonial "leaders" and provincial elites signed the Corinthian coinage.

4.2. Cults, Architecture, and Political Ideology

When we turn to consider Økland's use of the coins, we again see additional potential in the numismatic evidence. This is true especially in the use of temple images found on the coins and other ways in which the numismatically attested women and cults might be linked to Corinthian people, places, and political ideology.

We have already dealt above with the tendency among scholars (not only Økland) to incautiously handle the architectural depictions such as the GENT IVLI temple on issue XVI of the Corinthian coinage. Not only does Walbank urge us to avoid identifying the hexastyle temple on these coins with any historical structure at Corinth,[100] but she also encourages us to think in terms of the commemoration of a larger building project (or series of projects). This numismatically generated insight should lead us to consider, for the Julio-Claudian period, the possible links between cultic architecture depicted on the coins and commemorative, public events such as accession announcements, building programs, architectural dedications, and their significance for the sometimes ambiguous gendering of sanctuary spaces and rituals of the kind analyzed by Økland.[101] One productive way to do this would be to consider the relations among people, spaces, and practices suggested by the complex variation of obverse images (radiate Augustus, laureate Tiberius, Liva/Salus, Livia/Pietas) that are paired with the *gens Iulia* temple reverse on

---

100. Contra Økland, *Women in Their Place*, 102: "Based on coins, a temple of the *Gens Iulia* is also known to have existed in Roman Corinth."

101. Ibid., 92, notes, "Places may be gendered according to the gender of the people who have access to or dominate the place, or according to notions of the actions taking place there, or according to the mythological and/or cosmological universe that is drawn upon in the discourse of the space."

this prolific run of Tiberian coins. Attention to this variation in light of colonial and provincial currents, both political and cultural, may allow us to set the gendering of Corinthian spaces more firmly within an evolving building program and an unfolding political ideology.

Another promising avenue would be to further Økland's analysis of imperial women by thinking about patterns that emerge when those women are associated with both the reverse images of the coins on which they feature (on the obverse) and the profiles of the magistrates who signed those same coins.[102] To mention only two examples in this vein, one might analyze the interrelations among the coins on which Livia or Octavia appear with the cults and structures attested by the reverse images, the named magistrates who chose to place their likenesses on the coins, and the spaces in which portrait sculpture with their visages featured.[103] The results of such analysis would likely yield a layer of political ideology connecting Corinth to Rome, the Augustan house, and its cosmic claims that could be productively overlaid on, inter alia, Økland's examination of 1 Cor 11:1–16 within the frame of a "ritual gathering in the form of a cosmic hierarchy."[104]

In summary, the kind of analysis engaged in by Økland would only be enhanced by a methodological caution regarding the complexities of architectural depictions on coins and a more detailed study of Corinthian women associated on the coins with various structures, cults, and magistrates.

4.3. Games and Political Ideology

In turning last to the use of the coins for *paideia* and political ideology, we may reflect on ways to deepen the kind of study conducted by Dutch. The reasons motivating the use of Isthmian and other "Greek" iconography on the coinage, circulation patterns related to Greek games, and the possible links between the *tesserae* and agonistic settings of *paideia* deserve further

---

102. Ibid., 249–51, goes no further than cataloging the women who appear on the obverse.

103. As Økland begins to do, ibid., 103–11, 249–51. See also above (§3.4).

104. Ibid., 170. Økland emphasizes the importance of putting "women in the correct place in the cosmological hierarchy [precisely] when it comes to ritual" because sociopolitical gender systems both influence and are potentially (de)legitimized by ritual discourses of the type Paul engages in when writing to the Corinthian *ekklēsia* in 1 Cor 11–14 and elsewhere.

consideration in the interest of the exegesis of 1 Cor 9:24–27 and other texts within the Corinthian epistles.

For example, although Dutch (building on Walbank) notes the employment of Greek deities and mythologies—including Isthmian iconography—on the colonial coinage, the inference he draws is only partially correct. He rightly links these images to a Corinthian desire to focus on the colony's "Greek past," but he errs in thinking this necessarily entails that "the Corinthians placed less emphasis on their contact with Rome."[105] More important, Dutch misses the opportunity to examine in more detail the patterns linking the Isthmian Games with the Greek numismatic iconography and Greek-language inscriptions from Julio-Claudian Corinth. This could be done by weaving together the threads that bind the magistrates in both sets of evidence (numismatic and epigraphical) with the regional gymnasia and the Isthmian Games.[106]

Furthermore, as we have seen above, Corinthian coins circulated in a pattern that embraced the other agonistic and civic centers of *paideia* in the region.[107] Also, as Dutch was aware, there are anonymous bronzes and *tesserae* bearing images associated with *paideia* and particularly with the Isthmian Games.[108] In each of these instances it would be productive to explore the possible performative contexts where these coins may have been introduced into circulation or handled by "consumers" in relation to these settings of *paideia*.[109]

To sum up, there is ample room to extend, with help from the coins, the investigation of *paideia* in and around Roman Corinth as a framework

---

105. Dutch, *Educated Elite*, 51. For the dynamics of emphasizing Greek pasts within provincial and imperial political and cultural discourses, see now Spawforth, *Greece and the Augustan Cultural Revolution*; and Concannon, *When You Were Gentiles*.

106. For overtures in this direction, see Timothy A. Brookins, *Corinthian Wisdom, Stoic Philosophy, and the Ancient Economy* (Cambridge: Cambridge University Press, 2014), 134–47; and Adam White, *Where Is the Wise Man? Graeco-Roman Education as a Background to the Divisions in 1 Corinthians 1–4* (London: T&T Clark, 2015).

107. See above (section 3.3).

108. For key literature on the Caesarian and Isthmian Games, see Balzat and Millis, "M. Antonius Aristocrates," 663–64 and 663 n. 62.

109. Dutch, *Educated Elite*, 50, is aware that Edwards thought it possible to argue for such links to performative contexts, but he draws only the obvious conclusion that her work "shows that Roman Corinth had clear links with its Greek past, which continued into the present with its athletic games."

for exegesis of Paul's Corinthian correspondence and other early Christian literature such as 1 Clement.

5. CONCLUSION: PROSPECTS FOR ROMAN PROVINCIAL COINAGE, COLONIA, AND EKKLĒSIA

In conclusion, we have attempted to outline the problems and potential that the Roman provincial coinage presents for scholarship on 1 and 2 Corinthians and early Christian studies related to Corinth. We began by noting that Oster's "numismatic windows" metaphor for the use of coins may be misleading in its methodological implications. Next, we surveyed three examples of New Testament studies in the Corinthian correspondence that each drew productively on the colonial numismatic evidence. But we saw too that each was subject to certain methodological shortcomings. This led us to enumerate a series of issues relating to the use of coins as evidence, issues we urged must be kept in mind by scholars who want to handle the coins carefully and draw on the wealth of information they present in constructing contexts of interpretation that are rooted in Corinth and the region and that respect the features of the coins as evidence. Finally, we returned to the studies of Clarke, Økland, and Dutch with a more specific methodology informed by advances in Roman provincial numismatics and sketched all too briefly questions and investigative trajectories that promise to advance our understanding of Julio-Claudian Corinth at the intersection of *colonia* and *ekklēsia*.[110]

APPENDIX: SELECT CHRONOLOGICAL BIBLIOGRAPHY
FOR ROMAN CORINTHIAN NUMISMATICS

Imhoof-Blumer, Friedrich, and Percy Gardner. *Ancient Coins Illustrating Lost Masterpieces of Greek Art: A Numismatic Commentary on Pausanias*. Chicago: Argonaut, 1964. Expanded and enlarged from Imhoof-Blumer and Gardner. "Numismatic Commentary on Pausanias, I."

---

110. I am grateful to Dr. Ken Sheedy, director of the Australian Centre for Ancient Numismatic Studies (ACANS), associated with the department of Ancient History at Macquarie University, for his guidance during my tenure as a junior fellow in numismatics during 2011 and to Prof. Michel Amandry, whose kind advice at an early stage of my research reoriented my approach. All shortcomings and numismatic lacunae that remain are certainly my own.

JHS 6 (1885): 50–101; Imhoof-Blumer and Gardner. "Numismatic Commentary on Pausanias, II." *JHS* 7 (1886): 57–113; and Imhoof-Blumer and Gardner. "Numismatic Commentary on Pausanias, III." *JHS* 8 (1887): 6–63.

Fox, Harry Bertram Earle. "The Duoviri of Corinth." *Journal International d'Archéologie Numismatique* 2 (1899): 89–116.

Fox, Harry Bertram Earle. "Colonia Laus Iulia Corinthus." *Journal International d'Archéologie Numismatique* 6 (1903): 5–16, pl. 1.

Bellinger, Alfred R. *Catalogue of the Coins Found at Corinth, 1925*. Athens: The American School of Classical Studies at Athens; New Haven: Yale University Press, 1930.

Edwards, Katharine M. *The Coins 1896–1929*. Vol. 6 of *Corinth*. Athens: The American School of Classical Studies at Athens; Cambridge, MA: Harvard University Press, 1933.

Bagdikian, Anita. "The Civic Officials of Roman Corinth." MA thesis, University of Vermont, 1953.

MacDowall, David W. "Countermarks of Early Imperial Corinth." *NumC* 122 (1962): 113–23.

Amandry, Michel. *Le monnayage des duovirs corinthiens*. BCHSupp 15. Paris: Diffusion de Boccard, 1988.

Howgego, Christopher J. "After the Colt Has Bolted: A Review of Amandry on Roman Corinth." *NumC* 149 (1989): 199–208.

Walbank, Mary E. H. "Pausanias, Octavia and Temple E at Corinth." *ABSA* 84 (1989): 361–94.

Walbank, Mary E. H. "Marsyas at Corinth." *American Journal of Numismatics*. NS 1 (1989): 79–87.

Engels, Donald W. *Roman Corinth: An Alternative Model for the Classical City*. Chicago: University of Chicago Press, 1990.

Walbank, Mary E. H. "Evidence for the Imperial Cult in Julio-Claudian Corinth." Pages 201–14 in *Subject and Ruler: The Cult of the Ruling Power in Classical Antiquity*. Edited by Duncan Fishwick and Alastair Small. Journal of Roman Archaeology Supplementary Series 17. Ann Arbor: Journal of Roman Archaeology, 1996.

Walbank, Mary E. H. "The Foundation and Planning of Early Roman Corinth." *JRA* 10 (1997): 95–130.

Walbank, Mary E. H. "What's in a Name? Corinth under the Flavians." *ZPE* 139 (2002): 251–64.

Walbank, Mary E. H. "Aspects of Corinthian Coinage in the Late 1st and Early 2nd Centuries A.C." Pages 337–49 in *The Centenary, 1896–1996*.

Vol. 20 of *Corinth*. Princeton: The American School of Classical Studies at Athens, 2003.

Gebhard, Elizabeth. "Rites for Melikertes-Palaimon in the Early Roman Corinthia." Pages 165–203 in *Urban Religion in Roman Corinth: Interdisciplinary Approaches*. Edited by Daniel N. Schowalter and Steven J. Friesen. HTS 53. Cambridge, MA: Harvard University Press, 2005), 165–203.

Walbank, Mary E. H. "Image and Cult: The Coinage of Roman Corinth." Pages 151–97 in *Corinth in Context: Comparative Studies on Religion and Society*. Edited by Steven J. Friesen, Daniel N. Schowalter, and James C. Walters. Leiden: Brill, 2010.

Hesperia: The Journal of the American School of Classical Studies at Athens (various; 1932–).

Corinth coin database (Kress Coin Project). http://ascsa.net/research?q=collection:Corinth.

The Polis and the Poor: Reconstructing Social Relations from Different Genres of Evidence

L. L. Welborn

1. The Problem

Whoever goes in search of the poor in the polis must confront the problem of the silence of the sources.[1] There are few portraits of the poor in Greco-Roman literature, and these occur, for the most part, in fictitious genres—satire, mime, the fictional letter, and the novel (e.g., Martial 10.5; P.Oxy. 413; P.Vars. 2; Alciphron, *Letters of Parasites* 24; Apuleius, *Metam.* 1.6–7).[2] Historians and orators write of the urban mob.[3] Doubtless many of those who composed this multitude suffered scarcity, hunger, and destitution,[4] but the poor are not identified in this literature as a distinct

---

1. C. R. Whittaker, "The Poor in the City of Rome," in *Land, City and Trade in the Roman Empire* (Aldershot: Variorum, 1993), 1–25; Neville Morley, "The Poor in the City of Rome," in *Poverty in the Roman World*, ed. Margaret Atkins and Robin Osborne (Cambridge: Cambridge University Press, 2006), 21–39, esp. 31–32.

2. See the discussion in Fergus Millar, "The World of the *Golden Ass*," *JRS* 71 (1981): 63–75, esp. 63, 65, 71.

3. P. A. Brunt, "The Roman Mob," in *Studies in Ancient Society*, ed. M. I. Finley (London: Routledge and Kegan Paul, 1974), 74–102; Fergus Millar, *The Crowd in Rome in the Late Republic* (Ann Arbor: University of Michigan Press, 2002).

4. Zvi Yavetz, "The Living Conditions of the Plebs in Republican Rome," *Latomus* 17 (1958): 500–17; Brunt, "Roman Mob," 84–92; Barbara Kühnert, *Die Plebs Urbana der späten römischen Republik: Ihre ökomomische Situation und soziale Struktur* (Berlin: Akademie, 1991); Cam Grey and Anneliese Parkin, "Controlling the Urban Mob," *Phoenix* 57 (2003): 284–99; Morley, "The Poor in the City of Rome," 33–36; William V. Harris, "Poverty and Destitution in the Roman Empire," in *Rome's Imperial Economy* (Oxford: Oxford University Press, 2011), 27–56.

group within the populace.⁵ Moreover, the sources reflect an elite bias.⁶ Hence, it is precarious to infer social reality from such representations.⁷ The vast majority of surviving inscriptions from the cities of the Greco-Roman world celebrate the benefactions of the elite,⁸ or commemorate the lives of freedmen.⁹ The free poor and most slaves failed to leave any significant mark in the public record.¹⁰ One might hope that archaeology would supply what is lacking in the literary and documentary sources, through excavations of mass graves¹¹ or caches of infant corpses (presumed to be victims of infanticide),¹² and through analysis of skeletons.¹³ But mass burials and

---

5. Marcus Prell, *Sozialökonomische Untersuchungen zur Armut in antiken Rom von den Gracchen bis Kaiser Diokletian* (Stuttgart: Steiner, 1997), ch. 3; see also Robin Osborne, "Roman Poverty in Context," in *Poverty in the Roman World*, ed. Margaret Atkins and Robin Osborne (Cambridge: Cambridge University Press, 2006), 2-3.

6. Brunt, "Roman Mob," 96-99; Osborne, "Roman Poverty in Context," 14-15; Greg Woolf, "Writing Poverty in Rome," in Atkins and Osborne, *Poverty in the Roman World*, 83-99. The problem of dependence on elite sources is clearly identified by Justin Meggitt, *Paul, Poverty and Survival* (Edinburgh: T&T Clark, 1998), 12.

7. Osborne, "Roman Poverty in Context," 17; Woolf, "Writing Poverty in Rome," 86, 92-93, 99.

8. Arjan Zuiderhoek, *The Politics of Munificence in the Roman Empire: Citizens, Elites and Benefactors in Asia Minor* (Cambridge: Cambridge University Press, 2009).

9. Ramsay MacMullen, "The Epigraphic Habit in the Roman Empire," *AJP* 103 (1982): 233-46; Andrik Abramenko, *Die munizipale Mittelschicht im kaiserlichen Italien: Zu einem neuen Verständnis von Sevirat und Augustalität* (Frankfurt: Lang, 1993).

10. Nicholas Purcell, "The City of Rome and the *plebs urbana* in the Late Republic," in *The Last Age of the Roman Republic, 146-43 B.C.*, vol. 9 of *Cambridge Ancient History*, ed. J. A. Crook, Andrew Lintott, and Elizabeth Rawson (Cambridge: Cambridge University Press, 1994), 644-88, esp. 656-57; Whittaker, "The Poor in the City of Rome," 4; Morley, "The Poor in the City of Rome," 31-32.

11. E.g., like that found outside the Esquiline gate at Rome, filled with 24,000 corpses sometime in the late Republic; see Rodolfo Lanciani, *Ancient Rome in the Light of Recent Archaeological Discoveries* (London: Macmillan, 1888), 64-67, discussed by Keith Hopkins, *Death and Renewal: Sociological Studies in Roman History* (Cambridge: Cambridge University Press, 1983), 2:207-10. See also John Bodel, *Graveyards and Groves: A Study of the Lex Lucerina*, American Journal of Ancient History 11 (Cambridge, MA: Harvard University Press, 1994), 40-47.

12. William V. Harris, "Child Exposure in the Roman Empire," *JRS* 84 (1994): 1-22, esp. 7, 13.

13. E.g., Sarah Bisel, "Human Bones at Herculaneum," *Rivista di Studi Pompeiani* 1 (1987): 123-29; Giuseppe Maggi, "Lo scavo dell' area suburban meridionale di Ercolano," *Rivista di Studi Pompeiani* 9 (1998): 167-72; Sherry C. Cox, "Health in

collections of infant corpses are rare finds,[14] even if they provide reliable proxy evidence of intense poverty.[15] And skeletal remains from burial grounds must not be assumed to be representative of the populace.[16] For the most part, archaeologists have focused on the public centers, with their temples, basilica, and stoas, and on the great houses of the elite, leaving the urban slums unexcavated.[17]

Given the silence of the sources, the historian's task must be, first, to identify the lacunae, the gaps and breaks in the discourse of poverty,[18] and then to develop methodologies appropriate to the diverse genres of evidence,[19] in order to make the existence and experience of the poor in the polis more audible. This essay will exemplify the application of such methodologies to a variety of sources, probing the limits of legitimate inference. In each case, we shall discover that reliable information about the lives of the poor emerges from heightened awareness of the conventions of genre and the biases of authors. To anticipate: the glimpses of the impoverished afforded by satirists such as Martial can be evaluated, once one has recognized that the poetic discourse of poverty served various purposes—professional, ethical, polemical.[20] Further, characterizations of the *plebs* as "sordid" and "violent" by historians and orators permit

---

Hellenistic and Roman Times: The Case Studies of Paphos, Cyprus and Corinth," in *Health in Antiquity*, ed. Helen King (New York: Routledge, 2005), 59–82.

14. Bodel, *Graveyards and Groves*, 81–83, 114 n. 194.

15. Hopkins, *Death and Renewal*, 208–9; Harris, "Poverty and Destitution," 50.

16. Keith Hopkins, "Graveyard for Historians," in *La Mort, Les Morts et L'Au-Delà dans Le Monde Romain*, ed. François Hinard (Caen: Centre de Publications, 1987), 113–26; Ian Morris, *Death Ritual and Social Structure in Classical Antiquity* (Cambridge: Cambridge University Press, 1992), 41–42, 101; Harris, "Poverty and Destitution," 48–50.

17. Ramsay MacMullen, *Roman Social Relations 50 B.C. to A.D. 284* (New Haven: Yale University Press, 1974), 93; Andrew Wallace-Hadrill, "Houses and Households: Sampling Pompeii and Herculaneum," in *Marriage, Divorce and Children in Ancient Rome*, ed. Beryl Rawson (Oxford: Oxford University Press, 1991), 198; Susan Alcock, *Graecia Capta: The Landscapes of Roman Greece* (Cambridge: Cambridge University Press, 1993), 96; Meggitt, *Paul, Poverty and Survival*, 35–36, 62.

18. Similarly, Morley, "The Poor in the City of Rome," 31–32.

19. See Meggitt, *Paul, Poverty and Survival*, 18–19.

20. Edward Charles Witke, "Juvenal III. Eclogue for the Urban Poor," *Hermes* 90 (1962): 244–48; Duncan Cloud, "The Client-Patron Relationship: Emblem and Reality in Juvenal's First Book," in *Patronage in Ancient Society*, ed. Andrew Wallace-Hadrill (London: Routledge, 1990), 205–18; Woolf, "Writing Poverty in Rome," 83–99.

inferences about the privations and grievances of the poor, once one has become conscious of the elite perspective that shaped such vocabulary and the political purposes to which it was put—that is, to arouse fear of upheaval and to discredit rivals.[21] We shall discover that violence plays a special role in making the conditions of the poor audible;[22] the historians' accounts of tumults and riots (e.g., Tacitus, *Ann.* 12.43; 14.42-45; Suetonius, *Claud.* 18.2)[23] tend to confirm the dictum of Martin Luther King: "Riots are the language of the unheard."[24] Though the majority of inscriptions advertise the munificence of the elite, a handful speak of the poor, for example, as the subjects of a decree on municipal expenditure[25] or as the agents of a suppressed revolt;[26] such inscriptions merit special consideration. Archaeology does not tell us all that we might wish to know, but we should not fail to attend to what it does provide: for example, tenuous evidence of slave markets (IEph 7.1.3025)[27] and glimpses of the conditions of life in *insulae*.[28] Analysis of skeletal remains may yield reliable results in rare instances where the remains appear to be demographically representative[29] or where studies are genuinely comparative.[30]

Yet even when the historian succeeds in identifying the gaps in the sources in which the poor must have existed, the results are hardly sat-

---

21. Whittaker, "The Poor in the City of Rome," 2-7; Robert Morstein-Marx, *Mass Oratory and Political Power in the Late Roman Republic* (Cambridge: Cambridge University Press, 2004), 13-23; Morley, "The Poor in the City of Rome," 25-27.

22. Osborne, "Roman Poverty in Context," 8; Morley, "The Poor in the City of Rome," 25-27; Meggitt, *Paul, Poverty and Survival*, 20-22.

23. See G. E. M. de Ste. Croix, *The Class Struggle in the Ancient Greek World* (Ithaca, NY: Cornell University Press, 1981), 372.

24. Martin Luther King, "The Other America," a speech delivered at Stanford University in 1967.

25. *SEG* 51.1573; IEph 1a 18c *ll*. 13-18.

26. *SIG* 2.684.

27. Ferdinand J. de Waele, "The Roman Market North of the Temple at Corinth," *AJA* 34 (1930): 432-54, esp. 453-54.

28. Andrew Wallace-Hadrill, "*Domus* and *Insulae* in Rome: Families and Housefuls," in *Early Christian Families in Context: An Interdisciplinary Dialogue*, ed. Carolyn Osiek and David Balch (Grand Rapids: Eerdmans, 2003), 3-18.

29. Bisel, "Human Bones at Herculaneum," 123-29; Luigi Capasso, *I Fuggischi di Ercolano. Paleobiologia delle vittime dell'eruzione vesuviana* (Rome: L'Erma di Bretschneider, 2001); Andrew Wallace-Hadrill, *Herculaneum, Past and Present* (London: Frances Lincoln, 2011), 128-30.

30. Cox, "Health in Hellenistic and Roman Times," 59-82.

isfactory, for the lacunae in discourse are not incidental, not merely the consequence of aversion from an unpleasant reality, but constructions (whether conscious or unconscious) that legitimize the social hierarchy by rendering the poor innocuous, ridiculous, and repulsive.[31] Hence, we must endeavor to identify sources produced by the nonelite, sources that reflect the experiences and voice the concerns of the poor, such as the fables of Phaedrus, a slave of Thracian origin, which satirize slaveowners and the politically powerful;[32] the *Life of Aesop*, a genuine folk book that subjects the claims of the educated elite to vulgar and witty criticism;[33] the *Philogelos*, a joke book that offers glimpses of the vulnerability, exclusion, and shame experienced by the poor;[34] fragments of the popular mime, which take as their subject matter the coarse reality of everyday life among the urban lower classes;[35] and the writings of the New Testament, which make explicit reference to persons of low social status: beggars, the uneducated, the lowborn, slaves, the "have-nots" (e.g., Luke 16:20–21; 1 Cor 1:26–28; 7:20–21; 11:17–34). A sample of these nonelite sources, which seldom figure in discussions of poverty in the Greco-Roman world by classicists,[36] will conclude our investigation.

---

31. Similarly, Whittaker, "The Poor in the City of Rome," 2; Morley, "The Poor in the City of Rome," 26–27; Woolf, "Writing Poverty in Rome," 98–99.

32. B. E. Perry, *Fables: Babrius and Phaedrus* (Cambridge, MA: Harvard University Press, 1965); see further Keith Bradley, *Slaves and Masters in the Roman Empire* (Oxford: Oxford University Press, 1987), 150–53; John Henderson, *Telling Tales on Caesar: Roman Stories from Phaedrus* (Oxford: Oxford University Press, 2001).

33. B. E. Perry, *Aesopica* (New York: Arno Press, 1980), 35–130; Lloyd W. Daly, *Aesop without Morals* (New York: Thomas Yoseloff, 1961); Keith Hopkins, "Novel Evidence for Roman Slavery," *Past and Present* 138 (1993): 3–27.

34. Andreas Thierfelder, *Philogelos der Lachfreund, von Hierokles und Philagrios* (Munich: Heimeran, 1968); Barry Baldwin, *The Philogelos or Laughter-Lover* (Amsterdam: Gieben, 1983).

35. Jeffrey Rusten and I. C. Cunningham, eds. and trans., *Characters. Herodas: Mimes. Sophron and Other Mime Fragments*, LCL (Cambridge, MA: Harvard University Press, 2002); Helmut Wiemken, *Der griechische Mimus: Dokumente zur Geschichte des antiken Volkstheaters* (Bremen: Schüemann, 1972); Marius Bonaria, ed., *Mimorum Romanorum Fragmenta* (Geneva: Instituto di Filologia Classica, 1955).

36. None of the above-mentioned sources are cited or discussed in the following works on poverty in the Roman world: Prell, *Armut im antiken Rom*; Morley, "The Poor in the City of Rome"; Woolf, "Writing Poverty in Rome"; Harris, "Poverty and Destitution"; a partial exception is de Ste. Croix, *Class Struggle*. Among scholars of the New Testament, the most important exception is Meggitt, *Paul, Poverty and Survival*.

2. Definitions

Before turning to the sources and the evidence, we must address two preliminary questions—one of definition, the other of differentiation. Who were the poor in the polis? And what portion of the populace did they represent? It has long been recognized that any attempt to define the poor on the basis of usage of Greek and Latin terms is frustrated by the indiscriminate and moralistic character of the vocabulary employed by elite authors when speaking of poverty.[37] When Cicero, for example, distinguishes between *assidui* and *proletarii* (Cicero, *Rep.* 2.40), or contrasts the "respectable" with the "sordid" *plebs* (Cicero, *Cat.* 4.14–17; see also *Mur.* 1; *Dom.* 89),[38] he is not offering objective descriptions of social groups, but is attempting to discredit the followers of Catiline, Clodius, and the like.[39] Similarly, when Tacitus contrasts "the part of the populace who were virtuous and attached to the great houses" with the "dirty *plebs* accustomed to the circus and the theater,"[40] he is naming a symptom of the decadence of the Principate, not providing an account of subsets of the urban population.[41] The Greek terms πένης and πτωχός appear to offer greater specificity: as Moses Finley observed, it is generally the case that "*penia* meant the hard compulsion to toil, whereas the pauper, the man who was altogether without resources, was customarily called a *ptochos*, a beggar, not a *penes*."[42] Thus in Aristophanes's *Plutus*, the goddess Penia resists the suggestion that she is the sister of Ptocheia: "The life of a πτωχός [beggar], whom you describe, consists in having nothing, that of the πένης [poor man] in living sparsely and sticking to the work, with nothing in surplus but not lacking in necessities" (Aristophanes, *Plut.* 552–554). Yet the distinction between πένης and πτωχός is not consistently maintained: for example, Menander in his *Dyskolus* has a character named Gorgias describe himself as a

---

37. See esp. the "Lexicon of Snobbery" (appendix B) in MacMullen, *Roman Social Relations*, 138–41; see also Whittaker, "The Poor in the City of Rome," 2–7.

38. See Zvi Yavetz, "Plebs sordida," *Athenaeum* 43 (1965): 295–311.

39. See the discussion in Brunt, "Roman Mob," 97–98; Prell, *Armut in antiken Rom*, 58–63; Morstein-Marx, *Mass Oratory and Political Power*, 13–23.

40. Tacitus, *Hist.* 1.4: "Pars populi integra et magnis dominus adnexa ... plebs sordida et corco ac theatris sueta."

41. See the comments of Whittaker, "The Poor in the City of Rome," 6; Prell, *Armut in antiken Rom*, 58–63.

42. M. I. Finley, *The Ancient Economy* (Berkeley: University of California Press, 1973), 41; followed by Osborne, "Roman Poverty in Context," 11.

πτωχός, even though he owns land (Menander, *Dysk.* 284–86).[43] Because usage is flexible and subjective, one must take care in drawing conclusions about the level of poverty associated with the terms πτωχός and πένης.[44] Even more problematic is the Latin term *pauper*, which does not denote an absolute, but a relative state of lack, and only means "pauper" in the modern sense in combination with other terms such as *egens*, *inops*, and *mendicus*.[45]

Historians have long recognized that political and legal status supplied the categories of identity in the cities of the Greco-Roman world, rather than social class: that is, the basic social divisions were between citizen and noncitizen, free and slave, rather than between levels of wealth and poverty.[46] Consequently, the poor emerge as a distinct social group in the ancient sources only gradually, as a result of the erosion of the distinction between citizens and other urban residents, and after considerable struggle, such as the violence that accompanied the introduction of the free grain dole at Rome by Clodius.[47] Even the distinction between *honestiores* and *humiliores*, which was formalized in the reign of Hadrian,[48] is of little assistance in defining the poor, since it distinguishes between those who actively participated in Roman imperial rule (senators, equestrians, and decurions, plus army veterans) and pretty much everyone else, including merchants, shopkeepers, artisans, unskilled laborers, and the unemployed.[49]

In sum, neither ancient vocabulary nor legal categories provide a useful definition of the poor as a socioeconomic group. For the purposes of this study, therefore, we adopt the modern definition proposed by Peter Garnsey and Greg Woolf: "The poor are those living at or near subsistence level, whose prime concern is to obtain the minimum of food, shelter, and

---

43. For further examples of the relative use of πτωχός, see Alexis in Athenaeus, *Deipn.* 54e, and Demosthenes, *In Midiam* 211.

44. Prell, *Armut in antiken Rom*, 47–49; Osborne, "Roman Poverty in Context," 11; Harris, "Poverty and Destitution," 31.

45. Prell, *Armut in antiken Rom*, 49; Harris, "Poverty and Destitution," 31.

46. Finley, *Ancient Economy*, 45–49.

47. Ibid., 170–71; Brunt, "Roman Mob," 92–101.

48. Peter Garnsey, *Social Status and Legal Privilege in the Roman Empire* (Oxford: Oxford University Press, 1970), ch. 11.

49. Prell, *Armut in antiken Rom*, 63–64; Osborne, "Roman Poverty in Context," 10–11.

clothing necessary to sustain life, whose lives are dominated by the struggle for physical survival."[50]

As a final preliminary, we ask whether it is possible to determine what percentage of the population the poor represented, and whether it is useful to differentiate within the poor as a group. Earlier, historians were inclined to a binary view of the Roman economy: accordingly, a minute fraction of the population, composed of the three highest orders (*ordines*) of senators, knights, and municipal decurions, perhaps as few as 1 percent, owned and controlled the available resources, while the remaining 99 percent had only what was required for subsistence, enduring lives of hard work and occasional deprivation.[51] In effect, there was no "middle class" intervening between the imperial elite and the masses of the poor, except for some rich freedmen.[52] But more than forty years ago, H. W. Pleket pointed out that this dichotomous view of Roman society reflects and perpetuates the perspective of the elite, who tended to portray the rest of the population as a "gray uniform mass," in contrast to the "honorable" people.[53] Recently Walter Scheidel has developed a more complex analysis of Roman society by quantifying the different census classes across the empire.[54] Drawing on

---

50. Peter Garnsey and Greg Woolf, "Patronage of the Poor in the Roman World," in *Patronage in Ancient Society*, ed. Andrew Wallace-Hadrill (London: Routledge, 1990), 153; cf. Meggitt, *Paul, Poverty and Survival*, 5; Harris, "Poverty and Destitution," 30.

51. E.g., Geza Alföldy, *Römische Sozialgeschichte*, 3rd ed. (Stuttgart: Steiner, 1984), 125; ET: *The Social History of Rome* (London: Croom Helm, 1985), 127; Alföldy, *Die römische Gesellschaft: Ausgewählte Beiträge* (Stuttgart: Steiner, 1986), 52–53, 55; Hans Kloft, *Die Wirtschaft der griechisch-römische Welt* (Darmstadt: Wissenschaftliche Buchgesellschaft, 1992), 203; Meggitt, *Paul, Poverty and Survival*, 13, following Alföldy.

52. Alföldy, *Die römische Gesellschaft*, 52–53; P. A. Brunt, *Italian Manpower 225 B.C.–A.D. 14* (Oxford: Oxford University Press, 1987), 383; J. P. Toner, *Rethinking Roman History* (Cambridge: Cambridge University Press, 2002), 50–51. Andrik Abramenko (*Die munizipale Mittelschicht*, 58–82) attempts to identify *seviri* and *augustales* as a "municipal middle class." Harris (*Rome's Imperial Economy*, 15–25) distinguishes three classes: the rich who exploited the work of others; householders who owned the means of production, but also engaged in work; hired and slave laborers.

53. H. W. Pleket, "Sociale stratificatie en sociale mobiliteit in de romeinse keizertijd," *Tijdschrift voor Geschiedenis* 84 (1971): 237.

54. Walter Scheidel and Steven J. Friesen, "The Size of the Economy and the Distribution of Income in the Roman Empire," *JRS* 99 (2009): 61–91; Walter Scheidel,

archaeological surveys of housing in Syria,[55] and property records and tax assessments from Egypt,[56] Scheidel concludes that a large percentage of all assets were concentrated in the top 3 to 5 percent of the total population,[57] while a segment somewhere between 6 and 12 percent enjoyed "middling" incomes.[58] Scheidel acknowledges that the size of the "poor" population is more difficult to pin down, but allows that "the majority of the population *could* have lived at a very low level of subsistence."[59] In this calculation, the size of the population is the crucial factor: the more people, the more poor.[60]

Two distinctions within the population of the poor have proved useful to historians: the first, between conjunctural and structural poverty; the second, between poverty and destitution.[61] "Conjunctural poverty" describes the condition into which some might fall as a result of misfortune; "structural poverty" designates the product of an economic system

---

"Approaching the Roman Economy," in *The Cambridge Companion to the Roman Economy*, ed. Walter Scheidel (Cambridge: Cambridge University Press, 2012), 1–24.

55. Luuk de Ligt, "Demand, Supply, Distribution: The Roman Peasantry between Town and Countryside: Rural Monetization and Peasant demand," *Münstersche Beiträge zur antiken Handelsgeschichte* 9 (1990): 24–56.

56. Alan K. Bowman, "Landholding in the Hermopolite Nome in the Fourth Century AD," *JRS* 75 (1985): 137 63; Roger S. Bagnall, "Landholding in Late Roman Egypt: The Distribution of Wealth," *JRS* 82 (1992): 128–49.

57. Scheidel and Friesen, "Distribution of Income," 83. Cf. Willem M. Jongman, "A Golden Age: Death, Money Supply and Social Cuccession in the Roman Empire," in *Credito e moneta nel mondo romano. Atti degli Incontri capresi di storia dell' economia antica (Capri 12–14 ottobre 2000)*, ed. Elio LoCascio (Bari: Edipuglia, 2003), 181–96; Jongman, "The Early Roman Empire: Consumption," in *The Cambridge Economic History of the Greco-Roman World*, ed. Walter Scheidel, Ian Morris, and Richard Saller (Cambridge: Cambridge University Press, 2007), 592–618; Keith Hopkins, "The Political Economy of the Roman Empire," in *The Dynamics of Ancient Empires*, ed. Ian Morris and Walter Scheidel (New York: Oxford University Press, 2009), 178–204.

58. Scheidel and Friesen, "Distribution of Income," 84–85.

59. Walter Scheidel, "Stratification, Deprivation and Quality of Life," in Atkins and Osborne, *Poverty in the Roman World*, 40–59, here 54.

60. In consequence of the Malthusian principle; see Scheidel, "Stratification," 54. See further Bruce W. Frier, "More Is Worse: Some Observations on the Population of the Roman Empire," in *Debating Roman Demography*, ed. Walter Scheidel (Leiden: Brill, 2001), 139–59.

61. Morley, "The Poor in the City of Rome," 28–29; Harris, "Poverty and Destitution," 28–33.

that renders some impoverished from birth to death.[62] Of course, it must be recognized that this distinction is not meaningful in all cases, and that the application of these terms to particular circumstances is disputed. The poverty of widows, orphans, and the disabled might be described as both the result of misfortune and the neglect of society.[63] Historians debate whether the results of bad harvests should be counted as "conjunctural," given the frequency of such failures in the Mediterranean.[64] The usefulness of the distinction between conjunctural and structural poverty for the present study will be to focus attention on the structural, that is, the systemic factors that made it difficult, and in some cases impossible, to obtain the necessities of life.[65]

The distinction between poverty and destitution is also useful, even if it is difficult to maintain,[66] because it focuses attention on the conditions (e.g., sickness) that routinely pushed the inhabitants of the cities below the level of subsistence,[67] and on the categories of persons (e.g., widows) who were most vulnerable.[68] In exploring this distinction, historians have been led to consider how long it would have been possible to survive by living hand to mouth, through begging, prostitution, and theft.[69] More importantly, historians have found occasion to reevaluate assumptions about the endemic level of destitution in the empire, where no serious counter-

---

62. For these generally accepted definitions, see Osborne, "Roman Poverty in Context," 1; Morley, "The Poor in the City of Rome," 28. For discussion of the various categories of persons, see Anneliese R. Parkin, "Poverty in the Early Roman Empire: Ancient and Modern Conceptions and Constructs" (PhD diss., University of Cambridge, 2001).

63. Osborne, "Roman Poverty in Context," 5–6; Morley, "The Poor in the City of Rome," 28–29.

64. Harris, "Poverty and Destitution," 33.

65. Similarly, ibid., 28–33. See, e.g., Prell, *Armut in antiken Rom*, 190, who calculates that a day laborer could have supported a three-person family only if he were fortunate enough to find work an improbable 260 days a year.

66. Purcell, "City of Rome," 656–57; Morley, "The Poor in the City of Rome," 29.

67. Grey and Parkin, "Controlling the Urban Mob," 287; Osborne, "Roman Poverty in Context," 5–6.

68. Roger S. Bagnall and Bruce W. Frier, *The Demography of Roman Egypt* (Cambridge: Cambridge University Press, 1994), 73, 125; Jens-Uwe Krause, *Witwen und Waisen im römischen Reich II: Wirtschaftliche und Gesellschaftliche Stellung von Witwen* (Stuttgart: Steiner, 1994).

69. Whittaker, "The Poor in the City of Rome," 4; Morley, "The Poor in the City of Rome," 31.

measures lessened the impact of poverty, and where no institutions were developed to protect poor noncitizens from hunger and starvation.[70] The distribution of grain by city magistrates in times of crisis was limited to citizens.[71] The scheme of family allowances, known as the *alimenta*, initiated by Nerva and Trajan, was limited to a group of Italian towns for the most part, though it survived for about a century.[72] The poorest in Roman society rarely enjoyed the benefits of patronage, because they had nothing to offer patrons in return.[73] The evidence of pagan almsgiving to beggars and the disabled,[74] such as it is, does not suggest that these gifts provided a significant palliation of the horrors of destitution.[75]

In sum, the economy of the Roman Empire may have been more complex than earlier generations of scholars assumed, so that there was, in fact, a substantial "middle" class; yet the gap between the rich and the poor was enormous. "The concentration of resources at the top led to deprivation and impoverishment of the general population."[76] We must reckon with the possibility that historians "have generally tended to underestimate the direness and horror of Roman destitution."[77]

---

70. Harris, "Poverty and Destitution," 33, 39–43.

71. As documented by Peter Garnsey, *Famine and Food Supply in the Graeco-Roman World: Responses to Risk and Crisis* (Cambridge: Cambridge University Press, 1988). See further Greg Woolf, "World Systems Analysis and the Roman Empire," *JRA* 3 (1990): 213–14.

72. Richard Duncan-Jones, *The Economy of the Roman Empire: Quantitative Studies* (Cambridge: Cambridge University Press, 1982), 288–319. See also Paul Veyne, "Le table des Ligures Baebiani et l'institution alimentaire de Trajan," *MEFR* 70 (1958): 177–241, esp. 223–41. More recently, Greg Woolf, "Food, Poverty and Patronage: The Significance of the Epigraphy of the Roman Alimentary Schemes in Early Imperial Italy," *Papers of the British School at Rome* 58 (1990): 197–228.

73. Koenraad Verboven, *The Economy of Friends: Economic Aspects of* Amicitia *and Patronage in the Late Republic* (Brussels: Latomus, 2002), 113.

74. E.g., Seneca the Elder, *Controv.* 1.1.14, 10.4.20; Seneca the Younger, *Clem.* 2.6.3.

75. Anneliese Parkin, "'You Do Him No Service': An Exploration of Pagan Almsgiving," in Atkins and Osborne, *Poverty in the Roman World*, 60–82; Harris, "Poverty and Destitution," 52.

76. Scheidel, "Stratification," 40.

77. Harris, "Poverty and Destitution," 33.

3. Fictitious Genres

Now, at last, we may turn to analysis of a representative selection of sources from different genres, in search of evidence of the experience of the poor. We begin with the fictitious genres, and specifically with the poetry of Martial, who is the imperial author most often quoted in discussions of poverty at Rome.[78] In two epigrams, Martial seeks to blacken his rivals— one in love, the other in art—by portraying them as wretched beggars. In the first, Martial pictures a certain Mamurianus as entirely destitute, with "no hearth, no fireplace, no bed," dressed in a "stained and patched loin cloth," whose "only food is the smell of a greasy kitchen" (Martial, *Ep.* 1.92.5–9). The most abject feature of the portrait associates Mamurianus with the dogs: "you lie on your belly with the dog to drink filthy water" (Martial, *Ep.* 1.92.10).[79] In the second epigram, Martial pronounces a curse on a poet who has "abused with his wicked verse those whom he should respect":

> Let him wander through the city, an exile from bridge and hill [resorts of beggars]
> and last among the hoarse-throated beggars
> let him pray for the crusts of rotten bread thrown to the dogs.
> To him may December be long and winter wet,
> and the shutting of the arcade [the beggars' refuge] prolong his miserable chill.
> Let him call those blest and acclaim those fortunate
> who are carried on the litter of Orcus [the pauper's bier].
> But when the threads of his last hour have been spun,
> and his tardy day has come, let him feel the wrangling of dogs,
> and flap away noxious birds with waving rags. (Martial, *Ep.* 10.5.3–12)[80]

---

78. E.g., Ludwig Friedländer, *Roman Life and Manners under the Early Empire* (New York: Barnes & Noble, 1968), 1:144–46; Prell, *Armut in antiken Rom*, 69–71, 125; Meggitt, *Paul, Poverty and Survival*, 24, 63, 64, 71; Woolf, "Writing Poverty in Rome," 94–97; Harris, "Poverty and Destitution," 39.

79. On the association of the poor with dogs, see Alexander Scobie, "Slums, Sanitation and Mortality in the Roman World," *Klio* 68 (1986): 399–433.

80. The translation slightly modifies Walter C. A. Ker, trans., *Martial. Epigrams*, 2 vols., LCL (Cambridge, MA: Harvard University Press, 1978), 2:157.

In this savage portrait, the dogs and birds are ready to eat the anonymous poet-as-pauper even before he has expired.

What should we make of Martial's poetic images of poverty? Has Martial provided us with realistic glimpses of the privations of life and the horrors of death among the beggars of Rome? We may concede that these epigrams are invective: Martial's aim is not to describe social reality, but to attack and demean his rivals.[81] Yet we may ask whether the invective would be effective if it did not evoke the specter of what Martial's readers had actually seen in the streets and under the bridges.[82] Critics have discovered the literary models of the epigrams cited above—namely, the poems of Catullus and Ovid's *Ibis*;[83] thus, the real-life referents of Martial's images are, to some extent, secondhand. Yet, as Woolf observes: Martial "goes further [than his models] in painting a vivid picture of the physical squalor of poverty."[84] Finally, we should not forget that Martial was a man of equestrian rank.[85] Martial's epigrams betray no sympathy for the poor; on the contrary, his invective portraits have the effect of dehumanizing paupers as those who live and die as dogs.[86] Martial assumes that readers with money will find beggars repulsive, and exploits their sense of moral superiority. Nevertheless, Martial's portraits of the privations of life in the open may be as realistic as they are graphic: even into late antiquity, Rome remained notable for the number of destitute living "informally in the crevices of towering buildings, sleeping rough in the *tabernae* or huddled in the vaults beneath the seating of theaters, circuses and amphitheaters."[87]

---

81. Woolf, "Writing Poverty in Rome," 94–95.

82. E. E. Best, "Martial's Readers in the Roman World," *CJ* 64 (1969): 208–12.

83. The most likely models of Martial, *Ep.* 1.92, are Catullus poems 15 and 21, according to Woolf, "Writing Poverty in Rome," 95. For Ovid's curse poem *Ibis* as the model of Martial, *Ep.* 10.5, see Ker, *Epigrams*, 157 n. 8.

84. Woolf, "Writing Poverty in Rome," 95.

85. J. P. Sullivan, *Martial: The Unexpected Classic* (Cambridge: Cambridge University Press, 1991), 119; Alex Hardie, *Statius and the Silvae: Poets, Patrons and Epideixis in the Greco-Roman World* (Liverpool: Francis Cairns, 1983), 51, 54–56.

86. Woolf, "Writing Poverty in Rome," 95.

87. Nicholas Purcell, "Rome and Its Development under Augustus and His Successors," in *The Augustan Empire, 43 B.C.–A.D. 69*, vol. 10 of *Cambridge Ancient History* (Cambridge: Cambridge University Press, 1996), 784, citing Ammianus Marcellinus, *Res Gestae* 14.6.25. See also the scenes of beggars at Rome in Appian, *Bell. civ.* 2.120; Juvenal, *Sat.* 5.8.

Next we move out of Rome to a city in the provinces, while remaining within the fictitious genres. Alciphron's fictitious epistles draw on comedy and satire to portray low-class character types—fishermen, farmers, parasites, and prostitutes.[88] In one of Alciphron's *Letters of Parasites*, he speaks of the glaring contrast between the rich and the poor at Corinth: "I did not go further into Corinth," one parasite explains to another, "having learned in a short time the sordidness of the rich there and the misery [ἀθλιότης] of the poor" (Alciphron, *Letters of Parasites* 24 [3.60.1]).[89] The Greek word ἀθλιότης describes wretchedness and degradation, the suffering to which poverty gives rise.[90] Alciphron's parasite proceeds to relate a scene of starvation-level poverty that he witnessed in one of the suburbs of Corinth:

> At midday, after most people had bathed, I saw some talkative and clever young men creeping about, not near the residences but near the Craneium, and especially where the women who sell bread and fruit are accustomed to do their business. There the young men would stoop to the ground, and one would pick up lupine pods, another would examine the nutshells to make sure that none of the edible part was left anywhere and had escaped notice, while another would scrape with his fingernails the pomegranate rinds ... to see whether he could extract any of the seeds anywhere, while others would actually gather up and devour the pieces that fell from the loaves of bread—pieces that had already been trodden under many feet. (Alciphron, *Letters of Parasites* 24 [3.60.2])[91]

Alciphron's parasite reflects bitterly: "Such is the gateway to the Peloponnesus, the city that lies between two seas, a city charming indeed to look upon and taking in luxuries abundantly on both sides, but possessing inhabitants who are ungracious and entirely without love" (Alciphron, *Letters of Parasites* 24 [3.60.3]).[92] The parasite concludes with an ironic epilogue to the myth of Aphrodite's blessing of Corinth: "If perhaps to the

---

88. Little is known about Alciphron. On the basis of his similarity to Lucian, a date in the second or third century CE has been suggested. See Francis H. Fobes, introduction to *The Letters of Alciphron*, trans. A. R. Benner, LCL (Cambridge, MA: Harvard University Press, 1962), 3–18.
89. In Benner, *Letters of Alciphron*, 208–9.
90. LSJ 32, s.v. ἀθλιότης.
91. The translation modifies Benner, *Letters of Alciphron*, 208, 210.
92. The translation modifies ibid., 210.

women Aphrodite is consecrated as guardian of the city, to the men only Famine" (Alciphron, *Letters of Parasites* 24 [3.60.3]).[93]

How seriously should we take Alciphron's portrait of poverty at Corinth, where poor women survived by prostitution and poor men by picking through garbage heaps? Is Alciphron's account of less worth because it is couched in a fictitious epistle, or of greater value because it builds on an existing reputation? The apostle Paul attests that some in the assembly of Christ believers at Corinth had fallen below subsistence level and had consequently succumbed to illnesses (1 Cor 11:22, 30). Plutarch puts Corinth at the head of a list of cities in Roman Greece where the rapacity of money lenders produced a crippling burden of debt (Plutarch, *Mor.* 830D–831A). Apuleius repeatedly emphasizes the covetousness of the rich at Corinth, who were willing to make money by any means, however sordid and violent (Apuleius, *Metam.* 10.18–33, esp. 10.19, 10.23, 10.25–27, 10.28, 10.33).[94] It should not be surprising that an extraordinary concentration of wealth at the top of Corinthian society left a substantial portion of the population impoverished. The population of Roman Corinth increased dramatically in the century and a half that followed the foundation of the colony.[95] The increase in population must have put a strain on resources beyond the capacity of Corinth's limited agricultural *territorium*.[96] The urban poor had no direct access to the means of agricultural production, no source of food other than the market, theft, or charity. In Corinth, as in Rome, urbanization and poverty must have gone hand in hand.[97] Thus the scene of starvation-level poverty depicted by Alciphron has plausibility.

---

93. The translation modifies ibid., 210.

94. See the discussion in H. J. Mason, "Lucius at Corinth," *Phoenix* 25 (1971): 160–65.

95. The population of Roman Corinth expanded from ca. 3,000 original colonists sent out in 44 BCE to approximately 80,000 by the middle of the first century CE. For these estimates, see Donald Engels, *Roman Corinth* (Chicago: University of Chicago Press, 1990), 22, 28, 33, 66, 79–84.

96. The *territorium* of Corinth was approximately 825 km^2, but only about 207 km^2 were capable of supporting agriculture. Hence, Engels (*Roman Corinth*, 28) calculates "that the number of persons living in the city of Corinth who were directly supported by agricultural production probably never exceeded 10,000." See more recently David Gilman Romano, "Urban and Rural Planning in Roman Corinth," in *Urban Religion in Roman Corinth*, ed. Daniel N. Schowalter and Steven Friesen (Cambridge, MA: Harvard University Press, 2005), 25–60.

97. See Purcell, "City of Rome," 647; Morley, "The Poor in the City of Rome," 37.

Among the fictitious genres, we turn last to a novel. In the *Metamorphoses*, or *Golden Ass*,[98] Apuleius places in the mouth of the hero of the tale a description of a scene in a baker's mill:

> Good gods! What sort of little men were there: some had their skin bruised all over black and blue, some had their backs striped with lashes, and were only covered rather than clothed with torn rags, some had their private parts hidden only by a narrow cloth, all wore such ragged shreds that you could see through them all their naked bodies, some were marked and burned in the forehead with hot irons, some had their hair half shaved, some had shackles on their legs, ugly and evil looking, some could hardly see, their eyes and faces were so black and smeared with smoke, their eyelids all cankered with the darkness of that reeking place, half blind and sprinkled black and white with dirty flour, like boxers who fight together covered with sand. (Apuleius, *Asinus Aureus* 9.12)[99]

Such a passage forms the basis of the judgment of Fergus Millar that Apuleius "expresses a rare and distinctive level of sympathy with the lives of the poor."[100]

Reflecting on the foregoing collection of passages, we find ourselves asking why the most detailed and graphic portraits of the poor in Greco-Roman literature should be found in fictitious genres, so that sober historians regard these accounts as realistic, and even infer sympathetic motives in the authors. The surest clue to an answer appears in Apuleius's novel: Lucius is able to see and hear things that are normally withheld from a man of his status, because he is concealed beneath the hide of an ass.[101] Similarly, Martial glimpses the lives of beggars from a dog's-eye perspective,[102] and Alciphron spies starving men in the persona of a parasite. Fiction permits an upper-class author such as Martial or Apuleius

---

98. On the question of the genre of the *Golden Ass*, variously categorized as a novel, a comic romance, an aretalogy, a philosophical or religious allegory, or a fictionalized autobiography, see John J. Winkler, *Auctor and Actor: A Narratological Reading of Apuleius's* Golden Ass (Berkeley: University of California Press, 1985), 2–8.

99. The translation modifies S. Gaselee, trans., *Apuleius. The Golden Ass*, LCL (Cambridge, MA: Harvard University Press, 1977), 419, 421.

100. Millar, "The World of the *Golden Ass*," 63–75, here 65.

101. See the penetrating analysis of the narrator's identity under the rubrics "The ass I was" and "the Lucius I was" by Winkler, *Auctor and Actor*, 149–53.

102. Woolf, "Writing Poverty in Rome," 95.

to transfer his consciousness temporarily to a degraded body,[103] and to transiently experience the privations of the poor. That the resulting discoveries should appear realistic to ancient and modern readers[104] reflects the operation of the principle that even fiction may be characterized by verisimilitude.[105]

4. HISTORIANS AND ORATORS

Measured by the standards of realism and sympathy, the orators and historians would seem to have little to offer to our search for the poor in the polis, since they are, in varying degrees, avowed ideological combatants in political struggles. Yet behind the politicized accounts of Cicero and Sallust we may be able to reconstruct the social realities of inequality and exploitation that gave rise to party conflicts. Indeed, the same elite authors who routinely impugn the motives of the *plebs* and its leaders nonetheless acknowledge that a broad material and conceptual divergence between popular and aristocratic programs ran through the fabric of public affairs, like a seam in a piece of iron (e.g., Sallust, *Bell jug.* 41.5; *Hist.* 1.6–13; Cicero, *Rep.* 1.31; *Sest.* 96–97; Caesar, *Bell. civ.* 1.35; Pseudo-Sallust, *Ep.* 2.5.1).

Sallust allows that at first the whole *plebs* was on the side of Catiline against the Senate, then tries to explain the solidarity of the common people as a symptom of moral decline:

> In general, the whole *plebs* approved of Catiline's designs out of a desire for new things. In this it seemed to act according to its custom. For always in a city those who have no resources envy the good men, extol the evil, hate what is old and established, and long for something new,

---

103. See esp. Apuleius, *Asinus Aureus* 3.26: "But I, though a perfect ass and a beast now in place of Lucius, nevertheless retained my human consciousness."

104. Note the puzzlement of Augustine whether the *Golden Ass* should be described as fiction or history: "Just as Apuleius said happened to himself in the book he entitled *Golden Ass*—whether he told what really happened or just made it up" (*Civ.* 18.18). On the mining of Martial's epigrams for the *Realien* of social history by modern historians, see Woolf, "Writing Poverty in Rome," 94.

105. G. W. Bowersock, *Fiction as History: Nero to Julian* (Berkeley: University of California Press, 1997), 1–28.

and from discontent with their own situation they desire everything to be changed. (Sallust, *Cat.* 37.1–3)[106]

Although Sallust represents the *plebs*' adherence to Catiline as a "disease" (*morbus* and *tabes*) (Sallust, *Cat.* 36.5),[107] he does not conceal the fact that the condition which drove most people to act was one of "destitution" (*egentas*) (*Cat.* 36.4). Analyzing the various situations that drew the commons to Catiline's side, Sallust observes that some "had squandered their inheritance in riotous living," and others "had been forced to leave home by disgrace or crime" (*Cat.* 37.5).[108] "Young men who had maintained a wretched existence by manual labor in the country were tempted by private and public doles to come into the city" (*Cat.* 37.7).[109] Sallust summarizes: "Therefore it is not surprising that men who were destitute, of bad character, of unlimited hope, should respect their country as little as they did themselves" (*Cat.* 37.8).[110] Behind Sallust's persistent moralizing, it is not difficult to reconstruct the social realities that nurtured the upheaval of 63 BCE: debt, homelessness, and unemployment. The concentration of property in fewer hands and the use of slave labor on large estates led to widespread impoverishment in the countryside and drove the surplus population into the city, where the majority lived at subsistence level.[111]

In two of Cicero's orations (*Pro Sestio* and *De domo suo*) he provides information about the composition of the groups that formed around Publius Clodius, promoter of the interests of the urban *plebs*. Cicero describes the members of the Clodian bands as "domestic robbers," "assassins let loose out of the jails," "raw gladiators," and "runaway slaves" (Cicero, *Sest.* 1, 53, 78, 81, 85; *Dom.* 5, 6, 7, 53, 54). According to Cicero, they sought to achieve their political aims through violence—"stones and swords and

---

106. The translation modifies J. C. Rolfe, *Sallust. The War with Catiline. The War with Jugurtha*, LCL (Cambridge, MA: Harvard University Press, 1985), 63.

107. See D. S. Levene, "Sallust's Catiline and Cato the Censor," *CQ* 50 (2000): 170–91.

108. "Alii per dedecora patrimoniis amissis, postremo omnes, quos flagitium aut facinus domo expulerat."

109. "Iuventus, quae in agris manuum mercede inopiam toleraverat, privatis atque publicis largitionibus excita urbanum."

110. "Quo minus mirandum est homines egentis, malis moribus, maxuma spe, rei publicae iuxta ac sibi consuluisse."

111. See Brunt, "Roman Mob," 96; Morley, "The Poor in the City of Rome," 27, 36–37.

firebrands" (*Sest.* 2, 53, 78).[112] Cicero's rhetorical purpose is abundantly clear: to criminalize the political activity of those sections of the urban *plebs* controlled by his enemy Clodius. Given the force of Cicero's oratory, it is remarkable that he is unable to execute his portrait of the Clodians as robbers and assassins consistently. At a number of points, the social realities obtrude: the followers of Clodius are "laborers" (*operae*), "hired workers" (*conducti, mercennarii*), and "shopkeepers" (*tabernarii*) (*Sest.* 57, 65, 106, 126; *Dom.* 13); as a group, the Clodians constitute "an assembly of laborers" (*contio operarum*) (*Sest.* 127). Moreover, Cicero acknowledges that the Clodians were "men desperate through want" (*homines egestate*) (*Sest.* 2, 85), and that their leaders acted "at a time when the price of grain was high, under pretence of espousing the cause of the poor and ignorant" (*Dom.* 13).[113] No doubt many Clodians were freedmen, slaves, and gladiators.[114] Nor is there any reason to doubt that violence marked the movement led by Clodius. As Finley observed: "the ancient sources are unanimous in their view of the grain dole [introduced by Clodius] as a form of poor relief won by the *plebs* after considerable struggle."[115] In sum, Cicero's orations aim to discredit his political opponent by criminalizing the poverty of his followers: the Clodians are "a multitude collected of slaves, of hirelings, of criminals, of beggars" (*Dom.* 89). Yet the destitution, wretchedness, and starvation of the urban poor are ineradicable features of Cicero's portrait, imperfectly repressed by Cicero's rhetoric.

Poverty is a persistent theme in the *Controversiae* of Seneca the Elder, a collection of practice speeches on legal issues, written for the education of the author's sons.[116] That poverty has such a prominent place in these rhetorical exercises is probably a reflection of the anxieties about impov-

---

112. *Dom.* 89: "bloodshed, conflagration, and plunder."

113. See the conclusion of Brunt, "Roman Mob," 100: "in the heyday of Clodius' ascendancy ... hunger seems to have been the chief motive force."

114. But it is difficult to square Cicero's reference to "assassins freed from jail" (*Sest.* 78) with Roman law, in which imprisonment was not a penalty; as Brunt ("Roman Mob," 98) suggests, "if Clodius freed prisoners, they may have been men seized for debt."

115. Finley, *Ancient Economy*, 170–71.

116. On the life of Seneca the Elder, see Janet A. Fairweather, *Seneca the Elder* (Cambridge: Cambridge University Press, 1981). On the *controversiae*, see Stanley F. Bonner, *Roman Declamation in the Late Republic and Early Empire* (Liverpool: University Press of Liverpool Press, 1949). On poverty as a theme in the *controversiae*, see Woolf, "Writing Poverty in Rome," 88–92.

erishment that haunted even men of Seneca's class.[117] The discussion of poverty also played a role in the socialization of wealthy Roman men.[118] Yet, granting these motivations and functions, there is a vividness and poignancy about the descriptions of poverty in the *Controversiae* that is arresting: speaker after speaker evokes the pangs of hunger, the burdens of disability, the humiliation of begging (e.g., Seneca the Elder, *Controv.* 1.1; 10.4). Are these features of Seneca's declamations merely the epiphenomena of the genre, products of the orators' argumentative ingenuity and rhetorical virtuosity?[119] Or does something of the actual experience of the poor reside in these stock exempla, and if so, in what manner?

We take as our test case a controversy about a man who has made a living by crippling and mutilating exposed children, and then sending them out to beg (*Controv.* 10.4).[120] A description of what the cruel beggar-master has done is placed in the mouth of Cassius Severus[121] near the beginning of the exercise:

> Here roam the blind, leaning on sticks, here others carry around stumps of arms. This child has had the joints of his feet torn, his ankles wrenched; this one has had his legs crushed. Another's thighs he has smashed. … Finding a different savagery for each, this bone-breaker cuts off the arms of one, slices the sinews of another; one he twists, another he castrates. In yet another he stunts the shoulder-blades, beating them into an ugly hump, looking for a laugh for his cruelty. Come on, bring out your troop half-alive, shaking, feeble, blind, crippled, starving; show us your prisoners. I want to get to know that cave of yours, that factory in human misery, that stripping-place for children. (Seneca, *Controv.* 10.4.2)[122]

Other orators embellish this sinister portrait, imagining the beggar-master sitting before his day book as the children return from the districts

---

117. Woolf, "Writing Poverty in Rome," 90–91.
118. Ibid., 89.
119. On the uses and conventions of these rhetorical exercises, see Robert A. Kaster, "Controlling Reason: Declamation in Rhetorical Education at Rome," in *Education in Greek and Roman Antiquity*, ed. Yun Lee Too (Leiden: Brill, 2001), 317–37.
120. See the discussion of this text by Parkin, "An Exploration," 71–73, focused on the question of whether pity for beggars motivated pagan almsgiving.
121. See the vivid picture of this Augustan orator in Seneca, *Controv.* 3 pref.
122. The translation is that of Michael Winterbottom, trans., *Seneca the Elder. Declamation, Volume II: Controversies, Books 7–10*, LCL (Cambridge, MA: Harvard University Press, 1974), 423.

to which they have been assigned, devising further mutilation for further profit: "This one doesn't get alms easily; let him have something more pulled off" (*Controv.* 10.4.7).

Is this picture of crippled children employed as beggars purely fantastic, a scenario contrived to encourage students in the rhetorical schools to sharpen their skills in the making of pathetic appeals? Much contributes to the appearance of artificiality. The elder Seneca informs his sons that this *controversia* was "renowned" (*celebris*) among the Greeks (*Controv.* 10.4.18), and proceeds to quote many striking epigrams of Greek rhetoricians. Moreover, the action of which the defendant is culpable seems doubtful, since no special law on "harming the state" is known to have existed in Greece or Rome.[123] The repeated appeals to the judges to "pity" the mutilated children (*Controv.* 10.4.1, 2, 4, 6, 9, 10, 19, 20) belong to the rhetorical exercise as well, since teachers of rhetoric regarded the appeal to pity as the weightiest of the pathetic proofs.[124] This is not to deny that certain types of beggars—the old, the disabled, and especially children—elicited pity and received alms.[125] But Seneca the Younger reveals that most people, including those who wished to be thought pitiful, "fling their alms insultingly, and scorn those whom they help, and shrink from contact with them" (Seneca, *Clem.* 2.6.2).[126] Finally, *controversiae* were extreme by design, posing the most difficult cases to test the declaimers' ingenuity.[127] The competitive dynamic of the genre encouraged displays of virtuosity, rather than statements of fact.[128] But before we conclude that the case of the crippled children is entirely fictitious, "a horror story invented to spur

---

123. Seneca, *Controv.* 10.4 pref.: "An action may lie for harming the state." See Bonner, *Roman Declamation*, 97–98.

124. Quintilian, *Inst.* 6.1.23: "but the appeal which will carry the most weight is the appeal to pity, which not merely forces the judge to change his view, but even to betray his emotions by tears." See Josef Martin, *Antike Rhetorik: Technik und Methode* (Munich: Beck, 1974), 162: "Die Hauptrolle bei der Verwendung des πάθος spielt der ἔλεος, οἶκτος, die *commiseration*."

125. Parkin, "An Exploration," 73–74, who concedes that her conclusion that almsgiving was common and normal "rests on common sense rather than on a mass of primary evidence."

126. The translation is that of John W. Basore, *Seneca. Moral Essays, Vol. 1*, LCL (Cambridge, MA: Harvard University Press, 1994), 441.

127. Woolf, "Writing Poverty in Rome," 89.

128. Well illustrated by Seneca's adjudication between arguments and epigrams as to which are the most powerful and striking in *Controv.* 10.4.18–25.

a good argument,"¹²⁹ we should recall that the jurist Paulus censured persons who displayed poor children in public places to arouse pity (Paulus, *Digest* 25.3.4), and that John Chrysostom claimed that some poor parents blinded their children to make beggars of them (John Chrysostom, *Homiliae in Epistulam I ad Corinthios* 21.5, PG 61:176).

Ironically, we come closer to the actual experiences of poor children in the speeches in support of the beggar-master! The basic argument of the other side is that the man who crippled the children did them less harm than the parents who exposed them (Seneca, *Controv.* 10.4.10, 12, 15, 16). As a corollary, several speakers observe that since exposed children (like slaves) are no part of the state, there can be no legal action on their behalf (*Controv.* 10.4.11, 12, 13, 14). Behind these arguments looms the cruel specter of the routine exposure of weak and disabled infants.¹³⁰ Seneca awards the prize for the most eloquent declamation on either side to Labienus, who spoke in favor of the man who crippled exposed children as follows:

> To think that people have time to care what a beggar among beggars gets up to! Distinguished men use their wealth to combat nature: they own troops of castrated youths, they cut their darlings, to fit them to submit to their lusts over a longer period…. No one rushes to the aid of *these* pampered and pretty cripples. It occurs to you to worry who is taking from lonely places children who would die if they were left there; you don't worry that the rich employ workhouses full of free-born men to cultivate their own lonely places, that they trick the naïveté of unfortunate youths, and throw into the gladiatorial school all the best looking, the most fit for combat. It occurs to you to pity *these* persons for not having limbs; why not pity *those* for having them? (*Controv.* 10.4.17–18)

Beyond the case of the crippled beggars, which may be artifice, we glimpse the reality of poor youths who were routinely exploited for sexual pleasure and entertainment, actions that were not illegal, not even controversial.¹³¹

---

129. Parkin, "An Exploration," 71.

130. *Controv.* 10.4.16: "Many fathers are in the habit of exposing offspring who are no good. Some right from birth are damaged in some part of their bodies, weak and hopeless."

131. See the similar argument in Seneca, *Controv.* 10.4.11: "'Yet he is acting cruelly' [you might say]. So is a trainer who forces young men to run on the sword—but

In sum, the *controversia* of the crippled beggars might be dismissed as an exercise in ventriloquism: the voices of the poor are impersonated by speakers trained in the rhetorical schools. Yet, in the declamations, the children remain stubbornly silent. The orators repeatedly remark on this silence (Seneca, *Controv.* 10.4.6, 8, 22, 24) and coax the children to speak: "Come, wretches, today for the first time ask something for yourselves!" (*Controv.* 10.4.6). Seneca tells us that beggar children were in the habit of "presenting themselves as evil omens at marriages, as gloomy signs at public sacrifices; particularly on holidays, days traditionally dedicated to cheerfulness, these flocks of half-dead creatures intrude" (*Controv.* 10.4.8)—hoping that they would be paid to go away. The child beggars persist—the silent cause of the declaimers' speeches, the real beyond the orators' gestures. Seneca adds that when such beggars show up at a sacrifice or on a holy day, "Someone, maybe, bears to the gods an offering received from you" (*Controv.* 10.4.8), a surmise that anticipates Walter Benjamin's dictum about the one place where the lives of the poor are not forgotten: the mind of God.[132]

Tacitus's well-known description of the lowest classes in the city of Rome as "addicted to the circus and the theater" (Tacitus, *Hist.* 1.4) tells us little about the culture of the Roman *plebs*, since it belongs to a laconic sketch of corruption under Nero. Considerably more may be learned from Tacitus's account of a spontaneous protest of the *plebs* of Rome against the mass execution of the slaves of Pedanius Secundus in 61 CE (Tacitus, *Ann.* 14.42–45). Pedanius, the urban prefect, was murdered by one of his own slaves, either in a dispute over the price of his emancipation, or in a lovers' quarrel. In accordance with the ancient custom, all of the domestic slaves who had been resident under Pedanius's roof (four hundred in all) were to be executed for not preventing the murder. Tacitus relates that "the *plebs* rapidly assembled, bent on protecting so many innocent lives, brought matters to the point of sedition, and the senate house was besieged" (*Ann.* 14.42).[133] Nero suppressed the riot of the *plebs* by lining the whole length of the road along which the condemned were marched to their death with

---

he isn't convicted of harming the state; so is a brothel-keeper who forces unwilling girls into the sexual act—yet *he* does not harm the state."

132. Walter Benjamin, *Illuminations*, ed. Hannah Arendt (Glasgow: Fontana/Collins, 1979), 170.

133. The translation is that of John Jackson, *Tacitus. The Annals, Books XIII–XVI*, LCL (Cambridge, MA: Harvard University Press, 1981), 175.

detachments of soldiers (*Ann*.14.45). Tacitus devotes most of his account of this episode to the speech of the jurist Gaius Cassius urging that the slaves should be put to death so that men of rank may sleep soundly, adding that the motley crew of slaves from many nations that now fill Roman households "can only be coerced by terror" (*Ann*. 14.43–44). Whatever Tacitus's own opinion of the protest of the *plebs* might have been, his account provides a glimpse of something of which only sporadic glimmerings are to be found in ancient literature: class consciousness among the poor.[134]

We conclude our survey of the orators and historians with Dio Chrysostom. Late in his career Dio composed a discourse known as the *Euboean*,[135] in which he discusses whether it is possible for the poor (οἵ πένητες) "to live in a decent manner and in accordance with nature [τὸ ζῆν εὐσχημόνως καὶ κατὰ φύσιν]" or whether they are "at a disadvantage in comparison with the rich on account of their poverty [διὰ τὴν πενίαν]" (Dio Chrysostom, *Or.* 7.81).[136] The first part of the discourse examines the lives of the rural poor—farmers, hunters, and shepherds (*Or.* 7.1–103).[137] In the second part, Dio considers "the life and occupations of poor men who live in the capital or some other city" (*Or.* 7.104–152). Dio begins with an account of the greater difficulties that the urban poor have to contend with.

> For the poor of this type suitable work may perhaps be hard to find in the cities, and will need to be supplemented by outside resources when they have to pay house-rent and buy everything they get, not merely clothes, household belongings, and food, but even the wood to supply the daily need for fire, ... and when they are compelled to pay money for everything but water, since everything is kept under lock and key, and nothing is exposed to the public except, of course, the many expensive things for sale. It will perhaps seem hard for people to subsist under such conditions who have no other possession than their own bodies, espe-

---

134. De Ste. Croix, *Class Struggle*, 372.

135. C. P. Jones, *The Roman World of Dio Chrysostom* (Cambridge, MA: Harvard University Press, 1978), 121, suggests that the Euboean, like the discourses *On Kingship*, was delivered before Trajan in Rome.

136. See also the summary in 7.125: "but we set out to discuss poverty and to show that its case is not hopeless, as the majority think, who hold that it is an evil which should be avoided, but that it affords many opportunities of making a living that are neither unseemly nor injurious to men who are willing to work with their hands."

137. Dio claims that his account of the rural poor is based upon his own experiences among them.

cially as we do not advise them to take any kind of work that offers or all kinds indiscriminately from which it is possible to make money. (*Or.* 7.105–106)[138]

The difficulties faced by the urban poor are so great that Dio muses that it might be best to remove the poor from the cities and resettle them in the countryside: "So perhaps we shall be forced in our discussion to banish the respectable poor [οἱ κομψοὶ πένητες] from the cities in order to make our cities really 'well-inhabited,' as Homer calls them, where only the prosperous dwell, and we shall not allow any free laborer, it seems, within the walls. But what shall we do with all these poor people? Shall we disperse them in settlements in the country?" (*Or.* 7.107). Naturally, Dio concedes that this is only a theoretical remedy, a possibility in the ideal state he is constructing "in discourse [τῷ λόγῳ]" (*Or.* 7.107).[139]

Since the poor cannot be removed from the cities in practice, Dio contents himself with enumerating the occupations that the poor must avoid if they are to be accounted "respectable." All occupations must be avoided that engender turpitude in the soul and contribute to the luxury of the cities: dyeing, perfumery, hair dressing, cosmetics, acting, especially in the mimes, dancing, auctioneering, and above all, brothel-keeping (*Or.* 7.109–138). Dio's account of the evils of brothel keepers (πορνοβοσκοί) is especially vivid: "They must not take hapless women or children, captured in war or else purchased with money, and expose them for shameful ends in dirty booths which are flaunted before the eyes in every part of the city" (*Or.* 7.133).[140] Dio's concern for poor women and girls who have been forced into prostitution carries him beyond his artificial exercise in the advantages or disadvantages of poverty: "It is our duty, therefore, to give some heed to this and under no condition to bear this mistreatment of outcast and enslaved creatures with calmness and indifference, because

---

138. The translation slightly modifies J. W. Cohoon, *Dio Chrysostom I: Discourses I–IX*, LCL (Cambridge, MA: Harvard University Press, 1971), 345. See John Day, "The Value of Dio Chrysostom's Euboean Discourse for the Economic Historian," in *Studies in Roman Economic and Social History*, ed. Paul Robinson Coleman-Norton (Princeton: Princeton University Press, 1951), 209–35.

139. See also 7.130, where Plato's *Republic* is referenced as a predecessor.

140. See, in general, Rebecca Fleming, "*Quae Corpore Quaestum Facit*: The Sexual Economy of Female Prostitution in the Roman Empire," *JRS* 89 (1999): 38–61.

all humanity has been held in honor and in equal honor by God" (*Or.* 7.138).[141]

Some final reflections are in order on what we have learned about the lives of the poor from the historians and orators, and how we have learned it. Despite the obvious intentions of these authors to pathologize, criminalize, and idealize poverty, it is astonishing how much we have learned about the hunger, homelessness, and joblessness of the poor, and about the exposure, exploitation, and abuse of poor children. The obtrusive presence of the poor in texts that seem determined to repress them tempts us to embrace the hypothesis of a "political unconscious" in which the poor are the Real that resists symbolization.[142] However that may be, it is simplistic to dismiss scholars who "trawl through the writings of Cicero, Seneca, Dio Chrysostom and Plutarch" in search of social history.[143] Such a blinkered judgment overestimates the ideological prowess of the elite and undervalues the resistance of the poor as the subjects of discourse.

More productive is the methodological question: How have we extracted information about the lives of the poor from the texts of elite authors? First, we have resisted the tendency of some older scholarship to take the representations of poverty by upper-class authors as "illustrations" of the social world, as "vignettes" of urban experience.[144] Between literary representation and social reality two filters interpose themselves: the conventions of genre and the biases of authors.[145] By remaining conscious of the dynamics and perspectives at work in the production of this textualized poverty, we have been able to distinguish with some precision between the world constructed for political, rhetorical, or moralistic purposes and the actual experiences of the poor. The resulting picture is less

---

141. See P. A. Brunt, "Aspects of the Social Thought of Dio Chrysostom and of the Stoics," *Proceedings of the Cambridge Philological Society* 19 (1973): 9-34.

142. Fredric Jameson, *The Political Unconscious: Narrative as a Socially Symbolic Act* (Ithaca, NY: Cornell University Press, 1981). Walter Benjamin goes further in his "Theses on the Philosophy of History," in *Illuminations*, 262: "Not man or men but the struggling, oppressed class itself is the depository of historical knowledge."

143. Meggitt, *Paul, Poverty and Survival*, 12.

144. See Ray Laurence, "Writing the Roman Metropolis," in *Roman Urbanism: Beyond the Consumer City*, ed. Helen Parkins (London: Routledge, 1997), 1-20; Woolf, "Writing Poverty in Rome," 83-99, esp. 84-88.

145. The best general discussion of the sociology of this literature is that of Elain Fantham, *Roman Literary Culture: From Cicero to Apuleius* (Baltimore: Johns Hopkins University Press, 1996).

detailed and vivid than that found in the school of social realism but more solid than we had any right to expect.

5. Inscriptions

As noted above, the inscriptions of the Greco-Roman world make little mention of the poor. A rare exception is an edict of Paulus Fabius Persicus, proconsul of Asia (44 CE), in which he instructs the city of Ephesus to stop wasting money by employing free men and to replace them with slaves: "Likewise all those free men who do the jobs of public slaves and burden the community with an excessive expense must be dismissed and replaced in their jobs by public slaves."[146] This decree reveals that the wage rates of the free poor were limited by competition with the costs of maintaining slaves.[147] The lives of laborers, especially unskilled laborers, must have been precarious, since whatever employment they found would have been short term.[148] Indeed, Susan Treggiari judges that "many of them [the humbler *mercennarii*] did work too dangerous for slaves.[149]

A second noteworthy inscription preserves an imperial *epistula* responding to complaints about abuses perpetrated by money changers at Pergamum.[150] The author of the epistle is probably Hadrian, writing in connection with one of his tours of Asia in 123-124 CE or 129-131 CE.[151]

---

146. IEph 1a 18c *ll.* 13–18; translation by David C. Braund, *Augustus to Nero: A Sourcebook in Roman History 31 BC–AD 68* (London: Croom Helm, 1985), 214. See further Friedrich Karl Dörner, *Der Erlass des Statthalters von Asia, Paullus Fabius Persicus* (Greifswald: Adler, 1935); Harris, "Poverty and Destitution," 46.

147. Finley, *Ancient Economy*, 79–81. See further Peter Garnsey, "Non-slave Labour in the Roman World," in *Non-slave Labour in the Greco-Roman World*, ed. Peter Garnsey (Cambridge: The Cambridge Philological Society, 1980), 34–47.

148. Brunt, "Roman Mob," 87–90; de Ste. Croix, *Class Struggle*, 192–93. Cf. H. W. Pleket, "Labour and Unemployment in the Roman Empire," in *Soziale Randgruppen und Aussenseiter in Altertum*, ed. Ingomar Weiler (Graz: Leykam, 1988), 267–76.

149. Susan M. Treggiari, "Urban Labour in Rome: *Mercennarii* and *tabernarii*," in Garnsey, *Non-slave Labour*, 48–64, here 51–52, adding that they had no compensation for injury, appealing to the discussion in John Cook, *Law and Life of Rome* (Ithaca, NY: Cornell University Press, 1967), 198–200.

150. The text used here is *OGI* 2.484. See the discussion in David Magie, *Roman Rule in Asia Minor* (Princeton: Princeton University Press, 1950), 624–25; Raymond Bogaert, *Banques et banquiers dans les cites greques* (Leiden: Brill, 1968), 231–34.

151. *OGI* 2.484 n. 1; Magie, *Roman Rule in Asia Minor*, 612–15; A. D. Macro, "Imperial Provisions for Pergamum: *OGIS* 484," *GRBS* 17 (1976): 173–74.

The groups who have petitioned the emperor against the money changers are described in the rescript as ἐργασταί, κάπηλοι, and ὀψαριοπῶλαι.[152] As Wilhelm Dittenberger observes, the identities of the latter groups are clear enough: they are "peddlers" and "fish-mongers."[153] But who are the ἐργασταί? A. D. Macro translates "tradesmen."[154] In a city like Pergamum, tradesman might run the gamut from small holders whose products required little capital and who could operate from a booth on the pavement to notable *negotiatores* who did business on a large scale.[155] In view of the fact that the ἐργασταί are grouped with peddlers and fish sellers, "all of whom are accustomed to dealing in small change," as the emperor observes,[156] it seems best to regard the ἐργασταί as craftsmen in small shops, members of that class Cicero described as "artisans, shopkeepers, and all that filth of the cities."[157] The rescript makes clear that the money changers have not only overcharged in the exchange of *asses* for *denarii*[158] but in some cases have also taken over the entire businesses of the tradesmen when they happened to fall into debt.[159] The emperor's letter, predictably paternalistic in tone, shows some concern for the injustices done to the artisans, shopkeepers, and fishmongers, and seeks to correct abuses,[160] but ultimately confirms the monopoly that the exchange dealers held under contract (συναλλγή) from the city.[161]

It might be supposed that epitaphs would provide a rich resource for the lives of the poor, not only because tombstones survive in such vast numbers,[162] but also because, as Richard Lattimore observes, "they cut through the strata of society from top to bottom."[163] Among the epitaphs

---

152. *OGI* 2.484, ll. 8, 9, 21, 23, 30, 39.
153. *OGI* 2.484 n. 13.
154. Macro, "Imperial Provisions," 171–73.
155. *OGI* 2.484 n. 13. See in general Treggiari, "Urban Labour in Rome," 55.
156. *OGI* 2.484, l. 9.
157. Cicero, *Pro Flacco* 18. See Yavetz, "Plebs sordida," 295–311.
158. *OGI* 2.484, ll. 8–24; commentary of Macro, "Imperial Provisions," 174–76.
159. *OGI* 2.484, ll. 41–57.
160. *OGI* 2.484, ll. 7, 13, 24–40.
161. *OGI* 2.484, ll. 8, 23, with the conclusions of Macro, "Imperial Provisions," 169, 174, 176, 179.
162. Morris, *Death Ritual*, 156–73, who counts more than 180,000 epitaphs from the Western Roman Empire alone.
163. Richard Lattimore, *Themes in Greek and Latin Epitaphs* (Urbana: University of Illinois Press, 1962), 16.

Lattimore surveys are those of merchants, artisans, bakers, nurses, sailors, gladiators, actors, procurers, and prostitutes.[164] Obviously, many poor persons would have been too destitute to pay for a tombstone. Yet Richard Saller and Brent Shaw, who have made the most thorough investigation of Latin epitaphs from the first century BCE to the third century CE, conclude that "while not all Romans were commemorated after death, memorial stones were within the means of modest men."[165]

Unfortunately, the tombstones of these modest persons tell us much less than we might wish.[166] This is largely because the genre of the epitaph was governed by certain conventions,[167] chief among which was the principle *de mortuis nil nisi bonum dicendum est*.[168] So when epithets appear they emphasize the piety, devotion, affection, and obedience of the deceased.[169] Lattimore speaks of a "politeness which, in the epitaphs, extends even to the lowest classes."[170] A recent study of epitaphs set up for foundlings (θρεπτοί) by their adoptive parents and masters praise the deceased person as "most valued" and "beloved" (τειμώτατος, φίλτατος), "unforgettable" and "strongly missed" (ἀειμνήτος, ποθεινότητος), "most frank" and "faithful" (ἁπλούστατος, πιστός), "sweetest" (γλυκύτατος), and so on.[171]

---

164. Ibid., 16–17. See, more recently, Sandra R. Joshel, *Work, Identity, and Legal Status at Rome: A Study of the Occupational Inscriptions* (Norman: University of Oklahoma Press, 1992).

165. Richard Saller and Brent D. Shaw, "Tombstones and Roman Family Relations in the Principate: Civilians, Soldiers and Slaves," *JRS* 74 (1984): 124–56, here 128. But contrast the conclusions of Werner Eck, "Aussagefähigkeit epigraphischer Statistik und die Bestattung von Sklaven im kaiserlichen Rom," in *Alte Geschichte und Wissenschaftsgeschichte*, ed. Peter Kneissl (Darmstadt: Wissenschaftliche Buchgesellschaft, 1988), 130–39.

166. MacMullen, *Roman Social Relations*, 93: "Tombstones offer no help [in the search for the free poor]. None tells us that the deceased was penniless."

167. See, in general, MacMullen, "Epigraphic Habit," 233–34; Elizabeth A. Meyer, "Explaining the Epigraphic Habit in the Roman Empire," *JRS* 80 (1990): 74–96.

168. Lattimore, *Greek and Latin Epitaphs*, 299.

169. Ibid.

170. Ibid., 283.

171. Marijana Ricl, "Legal and Social Status of *threptoi* and Related Categories in Narrative and Documentary Sources," in *From Hellenism to Islam: Cultural and Linguistic Change in the Roman Near East*, ed. Hannah Cotton (Cambridge: Cambridge University Press, 2009), 93–114, esp. 105–6.

If the epitaphs tell us little about the poor as individuals, Saller and Shaw are nevertheless convinced that patterns emerge from their investigation that shed light on the urban poor in general. First, among the lower orders in the city of Rome, 66 percent of commemorations before 300 CE are between husbands and wives, but only 22 percent among the imperial elite. Saller and Shaw explain this difference as a function of inheritance: the rich were commemorated by the children to whom their property was transmitted; where there was less property to transmit at death, the spouse was the normal dedicator.[172] Second, Shaw sees a pattern of "descending" commemoration of children by parents among the urban poor, whereas "ascending" commemoration of parents by children predominates among the rich. Shaw suggests: "A peculiar type of social life was forged by them [the urban lower classes] in the milieu of the Roman town and city that was taken to be *their* practice and was, moreover, apparently hypostatized as an ideal of behavior [among Christians] in the centuries after A.D. 300."[173]

Graffiti provide access to the experiences and relationships of ordinary people in urban contexts.[174] The cities of the Vesuvian region are the most important source of graffiti, supplying 10,916 texts, mostly in Latin, but some in Greek, cut, painted, and traced in charcoal.[175] While it is not always possible to discern the social level of the men and women who formulated these messages, grammatical mistakes are indicative in some cases. How many of the anonymous authors of insults, imprecations, protests, prayers, boasts, and laments were day laborers, or unemployed, or homeless?[176] Two graffiti from Pompeii may be sampled that mention the poor explicitly. First, a declaration written up on a wall by a frustrated Pompeian merchant: "I detest poor people. If anyone wants something for free, he's a fool. Let him pay cash and he'll get it" ("abomino pauperos. Quisquis quid gratis rogat, fatuus est; aes det et accipiat rem," *CIL* 4.9839). Second, an electoral notice: "Modestus for aedile. The laborers and the poor elect him."[177]

---

172. Saller and Shaw, "Tombstones and Roman Family Relations," 138.
173. Brent D. Shaw, "Latin Funerary Epigraphy and Family Life in the Later Roman Empire," *Historia* 33 (1984): 457–97, here 474.
174. See the important new study by Peter Keegan, *Graffiti in Antiquity* (London: Routledge, 2014).
175. Ibid., 6.
176. Ibid., 185.
177. *CIL* 4.9932: "Modestum aedilem. proletari et pauperos facite." See also a

6. Archaeology

Archaeology has begun to cast light on the living conditions of the urban poor through excavations of *insulae* at Rome, Ostia, and Herculaneum[178] and of quarters behind and above workshops in Ostia and Corinth.[179] Andrew Wallace-Hadrill has suggested that, in neighborhoods such as the Termini Quarter of Rome and Herculaneum's Insula Orientalis II, the apartment buildings and the dense blocks of associated shops and flats belonged to the owners of the nearby *domus* and were valuable sources of rental income.[180] The upper floors of apartment buildings were subdivided into small units of wooden *cellae*,[181] often precariously built.[182] The day-to-day experiences of the tenants in these blocks will have varied greatly from place to place,[183] and will have depended, in large measure, on the dispositions and proclivities of the landlords.[184] Cicero, whose tenements on the Aventine and in the Argiletum were bringing him an income of eighty thousand *sestertii* in 44 BCE (the equivalent of the pay of 160 legionaries

---

notice written on a wall above a bench in the forum where the poor sat through the day: "The beggars demand his election," in Matteo Della Corte, *Case ed Abitanti di Pompei* (Rome: L'Erma, 1956), 151.

178. Amedeo Maiuri, *Ercolano: I nuovi scavi (1927–1958)* (Rome: Instituto Poligrafico dello Strato, 1958), 1:113–43; James E. Packer, *The Insulae of Imperial Ostia* (Rome: American Academy in Rome, 1971); Wallace-Hadrill, "*Domus* and *Insulae* in Rome," 3–18; Andrew Wallace-Hadrill, *"Low Life" in Herculaneum, Past and Present* (London: Frances Lincoln, 2011), 257–85.

179. James E. Packer, "Housing and Population in Imperial Ostia and Rome," *JRS* 57 (1967): 80–95; Charles K. Williams and O. H. Zervos, "Corinth, 1985: East of the Theater," *Hesperia* 55 (1986): 129–75; Williams and Zervos, "Corinth, 1987: South of Temple E and East of the Theater," *Hesperia* 57 (1988): 95–146.

180. Wallace-Hadrill, "*Domus* and *Insulae* in Rome," 10–14; Wallace-Hadrill, *Herculaneum*, 260. On this point, see already Peter Garnsey, "Urban Property Investment," in *Studies in Roman Property*, ed. M. I. Finley (Cambridge: Cambridge University Press, 1976), 123–36.

181. Scobie, "Slums, Sanitation, and Mortality," 406.

182. Yavetz, "Living Conditions," 500–517, here 509 and 511. See further O. F. Robinson, *Ancient Rome: City Planning and Administration* (London: Routledge, 1994), 34–38.

183. See the conclusion of Wallace-Hadrill (*Herculaneum*, 285) regarding Insula Orientalis II at Herculaneum: "the Insula Orientalis II proves to be full of objects, many of which suggest a level well above poverty (marble busts, gemstones, and good quality bronze-ware), while its sewers point to a varied and healthy diet."

184. Yavetz, "Living Conditions," 509–11; Brunt, "Roman Mob," 85–87.

for a year) (Cicero, *Att.* 12.32.2; 15.17.1), reported to his friend Atticus that two of his tenements had fallen down, and that cracks were showing in others (Cicero, *Att.* 14.9.1). Obviously, a crucial variable in the daily lives of the poor in the *insulae* was population density. Ramsay MacMullen judges that densities approached two hundred per acre in the lower-class districts of Rome and Ostia, significantly higher than the range found in modern slums.[185] Even in the overcrowded *insulae*, rents were often high,[186] repeatedly giving rise to violent protests.[187] Peter Brunt summarizes the conditions of the housing of the poor at Rome: "ill-lit, ill-ventilated and unwarmed; facilities for cooking were inadequate; water had to be fetched from the public fountains ... ; further, the tenements were not connected with the public sewers. We may fairly suppose that most of the inhabitants of Rome lived in appalling slums."[188]

Of course, the poorest at Rome and elsewhere simply lacked the money for rent.[189] Many built shanties "similar to the improvised shacks in slums which skirt the capitals of many developing countries."[190] Archaeologists have found evidence of the use of *subscalaria* (spaces under the stairs of apartment buildings) at Ostia.[191] Others lodged in cellars and vaults,[192] or sheltered beneath bridges and aqueducts.[193] Doubtless many slept rough in the open.[194]

---

185. MacMullen, *Roman Social Relations*, 62–63, 168n16, drawing on evidence gathered by Julius Beloch, *Die Bevölkerung der griechisch-römischen Welt* (Leipzig: Duncker & Humbot, 1886), 410, as updated by Pierre Lavedan and Jeanne Hugueney, *Histoire de l'urbanisme: Antiquite* (Paris: Laurens, 1966), 350–56.

186. Bruce W. Frier, "The Rental Market in Early Imperial Rome," *JRS* 67 (1977): 27–37.

187. Caesar, *Bell. civ.* 3.20–21; Appian, *Bell. Civ.* 2.48; Dio Cassius, *Historiae Romanae* 41.37–38; 42.29–33.

188. Brunt, "Roman Mob," 85–86.

189. Frier, "Rental Market," 30.

190. Scobie, "Slums, Sanitation and Mortality," 402, drawing on archaeological information and the evidence of the *Digest*.

191. G. Hermansen, "The Population of Imperial Rome: The Regionaries," *Historia* 27 (1978): 129–68, here 167.

192. Scobie, "Slums, Sanitation and Mortality," 403.

193. O. F. Robinson, "The Water Supply of Rome," *Studia et Documenta Historiae et Iuris* 46 (1980): 44–86, here 72.

194. See the observation of Gregory of Nyssa (*De pauper. amand.* 1, PG 46:457) on homeless beggars: "The open air is their dwelling, their lodgings are the porticoes

Sadly, archaeology has also brought to light evidence of the dehumanizing end that awaited many of the urban poor. Excavations in the late nineteenth century outside the Esquiline Gate at Rome uncovered a number of burial pits, in many of which, according to the excavator Rodolfo Lanciani, the contents had been "reduced to a uniform mass of black, viscid, pestilent, unctuous matter,"[195] a mixture of human and animal corpses. Scholiasts to Horace (*Sat.* 1.8) and the grammarian Festus (s.v. *puticuli*) explain that the corpses of the poor and cheap slaves were dumped and left to rot in these pits.[196] These collective burials date to some time in the late Republic.[197] John Bodel has argued plausibly that mass crematoria replaced mass inhumation in the first century CE.[198]

Analysis of skeletal remains from Herculaneum provides rare glimpses into the lives of some poor residents of this Campanian city who sought refuge in the vaults by the seashore on the day when Vesuvius erupted. The 139 skeletons studied by Sarah Bisel seem to represent a cross-section of the population, of different ages and social standings.[199] Wallace-Hadrill offers a helpful summary of the findings: "a high proportion of the skeletons showed signs of stressful hard work: excessive development of limited muscle groups and injuries, both breakages and conditions like arthrosis and hernias. Many of the young too were overworked."[200] Skeleton Erc27 may serve as an example: a forty-six-year-old man showing conspicuous signs of overwork, thin bones suggesting poor nutrition, overdeveloped upper body muscles, and a spine with seven thoracic vertebrae fused by disease.[201]

---

and street corners and the less frequented parts of the marketplace"; cited in MacMullen, *Roman Social Relations*, 87.

195. Lanciani, *Ancient Rome*, 65.
196. Cited and discussed by Hopkins, *Death and Renewal*, 208n7.
197. Lanciani, *Ancient Rome*, 65.
198. Bodel, *Graveyards and Groves*, 40–47, 81–83, 114 n. 194, appealing to Martial, *Ep.* 8.75; Lucan, *Bellum civile* 8.736–738.
199. Bisel, "Human Bones at Herculaneum," 123–29; Sarah Bisel and Jane Bisel, "Health and Nutrition at Herculaneum: An Examination of Human Skeletal Remains," in *The Natural History of Pompeii*, ed. Wilhelmina Jashemski and Fredreick G. Meyer (Cambridge: Cambridge University Press, 2002), 451–75.
200. Wallace-Hadrill, *Herculaneum*, 130.
201. Bisel and Bisel, "Health and Nutrition at Herculaneum," 470; Wallace-Hadrill, *Herculaneum*, 130.

Figure 1. Bronze statuette caricaturing a hunchbacked beggar. Alexandrian work of the second to first century BCE. Berlin Museum.

Finally, artifacts: while virtually all of the objects recovered by archaeology derive from levels well above poverty, one catefory merits our attention: so-called genre sculpture. Numerous statues survive depicting lower-class types—the old fisherman, the gardener, the cook.[202] These characters are represented with brutal, exaggerated naturalism. A relevant example is a bronze statuette of a hunchbacked beggar, an Alexandrian work of the first century BCE.[203]

What should we make of this caricature of poverty? Is the image, as Paul Veyne asserts, "nothing but a spectacle for the diversion of indifferent aesthetes…, an occasion for smiles"?[204] Such humor may be repugnant to

---

202. Hans Peter Laubscher, *Fischer und Landleute: Studien zur hellenistischer Genreplastik* (Mainz: von Zabern, 1982).

203. Pictured in Giovanni Becatti, *The Art of Greece and Rome* (Englewood Cliffs, NJ: Prentice Hall, 1975), 272, fig. 258.

204. Paul Veyne, "The Roman Empire," in *From Pagan Rome to Byzantium*, vol. 1 of *A History of Private Life*, ed. Paul Veyne (Cambridge, MA: Harvard University Press, 1987), 135–36.

our modern sensibilities. But ancient rhetorical theorists make clear that humor in the Greco-Roman world was grounded in contemplation of the base and defective.[205] Quintilian summarizes a long tradition: "Laughter is never far from derision. Laughter has its basis in some kind or other of deformity or ugliness" (Quintilian, *Inst.* 6.3.8).

For the wealthy, representations of poverty and deformity were welcome reminders of how good it was to be a fully human part of society. In sum, the statue of the hunchbacked beggar is an expression of aesthetic disdain—a beggar as viewed through the eyes of the upper class. But, like every caricature, it preserves the object it exaggerates.

7. Nonelite Writers

We conclude our survey with a selection of sources from different genres, whose common denominator is that they are the products of authors who represent the subelite class. To be sure, the category "subelite" is problematic in several respects. In some cases, such as that of the *Philogelos*, the identities of the authors are unknown.[206] Phaedrus may have begun life as a slave in Thracia, but he received a good education somewhere, probably in Italy, and became a freedman of Augustus.[207] The apostle Paul made himself the advocate of the poor and lowborn, but his epistles reflect an educational level that is relatively high,[208] providing evidence of social

---

205. Aristotle, *Poet.* 1449a30: "the laughable is a species of the base or ugly"; similarly, Cicero, *De or.* 2.236. See, in general, Mary Grant, *The Ancient Rhetorical Theories of the Laughable* (Madison: University of Wisconsin Press, 1924), esp. 19; Robert Garland, *The Eye of the Beholder: Deformity and Disability in the Greco-Roman World* (Ithaca, NY: Cornell University Press, 1995), esp. 73–86.

206. The *Philogelos* is ascribed to an otherwise unidentifiable Hierocles; see Barry Baldwin, "The Philogelos: An Ancient Jokebook," in *Roman and Byzantine Papers* (Amsterdam: Gieben, 1989), 624–37, here 625–26. On the authorship of the *Life of Aesop*, see Daly, *Aesop without Morals*, 22: "Internal evidence makes it likely that the *Life* was written by a Greek-speaking Egyptian, in Egypt, probably in the first century after Christ." The author of the "Charition" mime (P.Oxy. 413) is unknown; see Wiemken, *Der griechische Mimus*, 48–50.

207. On the little that is known of Phaedrus's life, see Perry, *Babrius and Phaedrus*, lxxiii–lxxxii; Alessandro Schiesaro, "Phaedrus (4)," *OCD* 1119. Edward Champlin ("Phaedrus the Fabulous," *JRS* 95 [2005]: 97–123) argues that Phaedrus was a Roman aristocrat masquerading as a man of the people.

208. Abraham J. Malherbe, "Social Level and Literary Culture," in *Social Aspects of Early Christianity* (Philadelphia: Fortress, 1983), 29–59; Ronald F. Hock, "Paul and

origins well above the bottom. Lucian's claim to have been a stonecutter earlier in his life (Lucian, *Somn.* 3) is probably a *topos*; his polished and witty essays reveal a good education. Perhaps it is better to describe these authors as those who have taken the side of the poor and oppressed against the rich and powerful, whatever their social status, and who have sought to create a discourse for those who were previously of no account, doomed to the anonymity of work and reproduction.

In the tradition of Aesop, Phaedrus (15 BCE–50 CE) employs animal fables to say what could not safely be said otherwise about relations between the weak and the powerful. Phaedrus explains why the fable was invented: "The slave, being liable to punishment for any offence, since he dared not say outright what he wished to say, projected his personal sentiments into fables and eluded censure under the guise of jesting with made up stories" (Phaedrus, *Fab. Aes.* 3. Prologue 34–37). In a number of fables, Phaedrus emphasizes the capacity of the powerful to inflict harm on the weak: thus, "The Wolf and the Lamb" was composed "to fit those persons who invent false charges by which to oppress the innocent" (*Fab. Aes.* 1.1.13–14); "The Eagle and the Crow" teaches that "no one is sufficiently fortified against the powerful" (*Fab. Aes.* 2.6.1). In other fables, servants talk back to their masters: the ass asks the shepherd, who fears that his beast of burden will be seized by marauding soldiers, "What difference does it make to me whose slave I am, so long as I carry only one pack at a time?" (*Fab. Aes.* 1.15.9–10). This retort is the more remarkable, since Phaedrus knows well that "it is sacrilege for a man of low birth to murmur in public" (*Fab. Aes.* 3. Epilogue 34). In yet another fable, workers unexpectedly receive back the expropriated fruit of their labors: the wise wasp renders judgment for the bees and against the drones: "It is plainly evident who can't have made and who did make the combs; wherefore, I restore the fruit of their labors to the bees" (*Fab. Aes.* 3.13.14–15).

The hero of the *Life of Aesop* is an ugly, deformed slave who is beaten and tormented, but who triumphs over mistreatment with astonishing cleverness.[209] The opening lines of the *Life* emphasize Aesop's ugliness and deformity: "revolting to look at, putrid and worthless, potbellied, mis-

---

Greco-Roman Education," in *Paul in the Greco-Roman World*, ed. J. Paul Sampley (Harrisburg, PA: Trinity Press International, 2003), 198–227.

209. On the history of the text and its tradition, see B. E. Perry, *Studies in the Text History of the Life and Fables of Aesop* (Haverford, PA: American Philological Association, 1936), esp. 24–26; Heinrich Zeitz, "Der Aesoproman und seine Geschichte:

shapen of head, snub-nosed, swarthy, stunted, bandy-legged, short-armed, squint-eyed, liver-lipped—a portentous monstrosity" (*Vit. Aesop.* 1 [MS G]). At the beginning of the *Life*, Aesop is mute, and hence the target of abuse by his fellow slaves, who assume he is powerless to retaliate (*Vit. Aesop.* 2). As a reward for Aesop's kindness to a priestess of Isis who has strayed from the highway and become lost, Aesop is granted the power of speech and the ability to conceive and elaborate fables (*Vit. Aesop.* 4–7). The thesis of the *Life of Aesop*, to the extent that a folk book of this kind may be said to have a "thesis," is that true wisdom resides outside the academies of the elite, and that even a deformed slave, who suffers every possible disadvantage, can triumph over the guardians of Hellenic culture by exercise of his native wit and common sense.[210]

Nevertheless, Aesop's gifts remain unrecognized by the majority of those whom Aesop meets. Only a few are able to look beyond Aesop's grotesque appearance and grasp his astonishing cleverness. The motif of contrasting responses to Aesop is a constant feature of the *Life*, and must have belonged to the inherited tradition. On the way to the slave market in Ephesus, Aesop's fellow slaves judge him to be the "worst fool" they have ever seen, because he chooses to carry the heaviest load, a basket of bread. Only one of the slaves suspects the truth: "He's no fool; he's starved and wants to get his hands on the bread so he can eat more than the rest" (*Vit. Aesop.* 18 [MS G]). Similarly, in the lengthy section of the *Life* devoted to Aesop's service to Xanthus, the proud philosopher and most of his graduate students regard Aesop as "a repulsive piece of human garbage" (*Vit. Aesop.* 27, 31, 69). Speaking for the majority, one of the students advises the professor: "If you pay attention to him, he'll soon drive you mad. Like body, like mind. This abusive and malicious slave isn't worth a penny" (*Vit. Aesop.* 55). Only one of the scholars invited to Xanthus's banquet shows himself to be a true philosopher by answering the question that Aesop, serving as doorman, poses to each of the guests in a manner which demonstrates that he comprehends Aesop's coarse wit (*Vit. Aesop.* 77b [MS W]).

Irony is the resolution of the contrast between the transformation in Aesop wrought by the goddess and the perception that persists among the majority of those whom Aesop encounters. A cunning irony, generally

---

Eine Untersuchung im Anschluss an die neugefundenen Papyri," *Aegyptus* 16 (1936): 225–56.

210. Daly, *Aesop without Morals*, 20–21; Winkler, *Auctor and Actor*, 282.

masked as obtuseness, characterizes most of Aesop's relationships.[211] The irony seems especially heavy-handed in the section of the *Life* devoted to Aesop's service to Xanthus. Looking for a pretext to give Aesop a beating, Xanthus sets Aesop a series of onerous tasks (*Vit. Aesop.* 38–64). Aesop's repeated failure to fulfill the tasks as expected demonstrates, ironically, not the slave's incompetence, but rather the master's ignorance of how to give orders.[212] The irony in Aesop's relationship with Xanthus often takes the form of a reversal of the "professor joke" known from the *Philogelos* (e.g., *Philogelos* 43). By taking Xanthus's words in a strictly literal sense, Aesop demonstrates that the philosopher does not know what he is saying: for example, ordered to prepare "lentil" for Xanthus's guests, Aesop bakes a single bean (*Vit. Aesop.* 41). The repetition of this dull ruse may be tedious for modern readers, but one must reckon with the reality that such irony, disguised as obtuseness, provided the only art of resistance, and occasional revenge, for those who routinely suffered mistreatment.

The extensive correspondence of the apostle Paul with the assembly of Christ believers at Corinth provides valuable evidence of the lives of the poor in this Roman provincial capital.[213] In 1 Cor 1:26–28, Paul reminds his readers of their social condition, in order to illustrate the paradoxical character of the divine purpose:

> For consider your calling, brothers and sisters, that not many of you were learned by worldly standards, not many were powerful, not many were nobly born; but God chose the foolish of the world to humiliate the learned, and God chose the weak of the world to humiliate the strong, and God chose the lowborn of the world and the despised, things that are nothing, to nullify the things that are, so that no human being might boast in the presence of God.

Paul's studied use of litotes in this passage (οὐ πολλοί for ὀλίγοι) reveals that a few, if only a few, possessed the advantages that distinguished members

---

211. E.g., the self-deprecating humor employed in Aesop's advice to the slave dealer in *Vit. Aesop.* 15, and the laconic reply to the policeman in *Vit. Aesop.* 65.

212. Stated explicitly as the goal of Aesop's actions in *Vit. Aesop.* 38.

213. On Paul's Corinthian correspondence in general, see L. L. Welborn, "The Corinthian Correspondence," in *All Things to All Cultures: Paul among Jews, Greeks, and Romans*, ed. Mark Harding and Alanna Nobbs (Grand Rapids: Eerdmans, 2013), 205–42.

THE POLIS AND THE POOR 227

of the upper class: education, wealth, and birth.[214] But Paul's statement leaves no doubt that the majority of Christ believers at Corinth were poor, perhaps very poor.[215] Indeed, Paul employs hyperbole to dramatize the disdain in which the mostly impoverished Christians at Corinth were held by the elite. Paul's use of the neuter plural (τὰ μωρά κτλ.) to designate persons in 1:27-28 not only emphasizes the abstract qualities of those who have been chosen by God but also signals the denigration of this class of subjects by objectification: in the eyes of the educated and the powerful, the Christians are "foolish *things*, weak *things*, etc."[216] Paul adds that the poor Corinthian Christians are "despised" (ἐξουθενημένα), employing the participle of a verb that consistently suggests disdain and derision elsewhere in Paul (Rom 14:3, 10; 1 Cor 6:4; 16:11; 2 Cor 10:10; Gal 4:14; 1 Thess 5:20). Finally, there is Paul's choice of the highly unusual expression τὰ μὴ ὄντα as the climactic description of the insignificance of the Christ believers: the expression has philosophical connotations (Plato, *Phaedr.* 234E; *Theaet.* 176C; Epictetus, *Diatr.* 3.9.14; 4.8.25), in addition to its sociological reference (Philo, *Virt.* 173-74),[217] so that it does not suffice to translate "the nobodies"; rather, Paul means to say that, in the eyes of the cultured elite, the poor Christians at Corinth simply do not exist at all.[218]

In 1 Cor 4:9-13, Paul describes himself and his colleagues in graphic and vulgar terms which make it clear that the apostles belonged to a socially inferior group.

> We are fools [μωροί], ... we are weak [ἀσθενεῖς], ... we are dishonored [ἄτιμοι]; we are hungry and thirsty [πεινῶμεν καὶ διψῶμεν], we are naked [γυμνιτεύομεν], we are beaten [κολαφιζόμεθα], we are homeless [ἀστατοῦμεν], and we labor, working with our own hands; we are

---

214. On the litotes in 1 Cor. 1:26 and its implications, see Edwin A. Judge, *The Social Pattern of the Christian Groups in the First Century* (London: Tyndale Press, 1960), 59; Gerd Theissen, *The Social Setting of Pauline Christianity: Essays on Corinth* (Philadelphia: Fortress, 1983), 70, 72.
215. Theissen, *Social Setting*, 71-73.
216. Johannes Weiss, *Der erste Korintherbrief* (Göttingen: Vandenhoeck & Ruprecht, 1910), 36.
217. Theissen, *Social Setting*, 71; Andreas Lindemann, *Der erste Korintherbrief* (Tübingen: Mohr Siebeck, 2000), 50: "τὰ μὴ ὄντα bezeichnet das 'Nicht-Seiende' und enthält insofern die schärfste Form sozialer Diskriminierung."
218. Weiss, *Der erste Korintherbrief*, 37.

reviled, ... harassed, ... slandered; we have become like the refuse [περικαθάρματα] of the world, the scum [περίψημα] of all things, to this very day.

Each of the terms in Paul's self-description has a history of usage in relation to the poor, both in perception and reality.[219] Lucian describes the poor as perpetually hungry, hovering just above the starvation line (Lucian, *Saturn.* 19, 31, 38). Even artisans often went hungry, despite having worked day and night (Lucian, *Gallus* 1; *Cataplus* 20; *Saturn.* 20). As a handworker (1 Cor 4:12; 1 Thess 2:9), Paul would frequently have suffered hunger (see 2 Cor 11:27; Phil 4:12). Not surprisingly, Epictetus associates poverty and nakedness: "And how is it possible for a man who has nothing, who is naked [γυμνόν], without home and hearth, in squalor, ... to live serenely?" (Epictetus, *Diatr.* 3.22.45; see also Rev 3:17). Beatings were part of the experience of the poor in the Roman world, where the law did little to constrain the hubris of the rich and the powerful (Sallust, *Hist.* 1.44; Valerius Maximus, *Facta et Dicta Memorabilia* 9.2.1; Seneca, *De ira* 3.18.1; Plutarch, *Cic.* 49.2);[220] thus a poor man might be thrashed for making an impertinent joke (Gellius, *Noct. att.* 10.3.5). As we have learned, homelessness was the condition of many of the poor in the cities of the Roman Empire.[221] The verb Paul chooses to describe his condition, ἀστατέω, is a frequentative that expresses incessant movement: it means "to be unsettled," "to be without a permanent residence";[222] it depicts the life of a vagabond, who is constantly moving from place to place.[223] As the climax of his account of his experience, Paul echoes the judgment of the world upon the apostles of Christ, employing the worst terms of abuse in the Greek language: "We have become like the refuse [περικαθάρματα] of the world, the scum [περίψημα] of all things." In popular usage, the terms κάθαρμα and περίψημα express the contempt of the rich for the poor (Demosthenes, *Or.* 21.185, 198; Philo, *Virt.* 174; Josephus, *B.J.* 4.241;

---

219. For the poor as "weak" (ἀσθενεῖς), see Plato, *Resp.* 364A; Philo, *Somn.* 155. For the poor as "dishonored" (ἄτιμοι), see Plato, *Resp.* 364A; Prov 22:22 (LXX). See Theissen, *Social Setting*, 72–73.

220. See the section on "cruelty," in T. P. Wiseman, *Catullus and His World* (Cambridge: Cambridge University Press, 1985), 5–10.

221. MacMullen, *Roman Social Relations*, 92–93.

222. BDAG 145, s.v. ἀστατέω.

223. Weiss, *Der erste Korintherbrief*, 111.

Lucian, *Hermot.* 81; Pollux, *Onomasticon* 3.66; 5.163) and for those, such as vagabonds and parasites,[224] who lived at the margins of society.

In several passages in 1 Corinthians Paul makes clear that slaves belonged to the assembly of those "in Christ" at Corinth. Twice Paul reminds his readers: "You were bought with a price" (1 Cor 6:20; 7:22), evoking the experience of the large Roman slave market at Corinth.[225] In 1 Cor 7:21, Paul acknowledges, "You were called as a slave," then advises: "Do not worry about it. But if you can indeed become free, make use [of freedom] instead."[226] In 1 Cor 7:22 Paul explains, "for the person who is a slave at the time when he or she was called in the Lord is a freed-person of the Lord," making use of the technical Greek term for a freed-person, ἀπελεύθερος.[227] Paul's point is that distinctions of status are null and void of meaning for those who are "in Christ."

In 1 Cor 11:17–34 Paul deals with the problem of divisions that appeared when the Christ believers gathered to eat their communal meal, the "Lord's Supper." Paul speaks of some who are "hungry" and others who are "satiated." Because several elements of the descriptive core of Paul's evaluation of the Corinthians' conduct in 1 Cor 11:21 are ambiguous, various reconstructions of what happened at the meal are possible.[228] Perhaps some (the rich) began to eat before others (slaves and the poor) had arrived.[229] Or perhaps the rich feasted sumptuously while the poor looked

---

224. For vagabonds as "scum," see Philo, *Vit. Mos.* 1.30; on parasites, see Lucian, *Pisc.* 34; *Merc. cond.* 24.

225. Laura Salah Nasrallah, "'You Were Bought with a Price': Freedpersons and Things in 1 Corinthians," in *Corinth in Context: Studies in Inequality*, ed. Steven J. Friesen (Leiden: Brill, 2014), 54–73.

226. Translating the brachylogy μᾶλλον χρῆσαι in an adversative sense, with J. Albert Harrill, *The Manumission of Slaves in Early Christianity* (Tübingen: Mohr Siebeck, 1995), 76–121.

227. Nasrallah, "You Were Bought with a Price," 55.

228. Theissen, *Social Setting*, 145–74; Bruce W. Winter, "The Lord's Supper at Corinth: An Alternative Reconstruction," *RTR* 37 (1978): 73–82; Hans-Josef Klauck, *Herrenmahl und hellenistischer Kult: Eine religionsgeschichtliche Untersuchung zum ersten Korintherbrief* (Münster: Aschendorff, 1982), 285–332; Peter Lampe, "Das korinthische Herrenmahl im Schnittpunkt hellenistischer Mahlpraxis und paulinischer Theologia Crucis (1 Kor 11,17–34)," *ZNW* 82 (1991): 183–213.

229. Günther Bornkamm, "Herrenmahl und Kirche bei Paulus," in *Studien zu Antike und Christentum: Gesammelte Aufsätze II* (Munich: Kaiser, 1959), 138–76, here 142; Theissen, *Social Setting*, 151; Lampe, "Das korinthische Herrenmahl," 198.

on!²³⁰ Perhaps the Lord's Supper at Corinth was a kind of "potluck" to which individual Christ believers contributed according to their means.²³¹ A better-grounded reconstruction suggests that a single patron supplied the meal for the group that met in his or her house, apportioning food to the guests as the patron saw fit.²³² In any case, Paul is concerned that the unequal distribution of food and drink has resulted in the "humiliation" of "the have-nots" (οἱ μὴ ἔχοντες) (1 Cor 11:22).²³³ Paul's description of the "hunger" of those who "have not" suggests that some in the Christian community were living below the subsistence level. Indeed, Paul states that "many have become weak and sick, and some have even died," on account of the failure of the Corinthians to discern the needs of members of the body of Christ (1 Cor 11:29–30). Paul advises the Corinthians to "wait for one another" (1 Cor 11:33) and to share. The Lord's Supper was not meant to be a private supper (ἴδιον δεῖπνον), but a communal meal.

In 2 Cor 8, Paul appeals to the Corinthians to make a contribution to a collection for the poor among the saints in Jerusalem.²³⁴ Paul invokes the memory of Jesus as the archetype of the action he is asking the Corinthians to take: "For you know the grace of our Lord Jesus Christ, that on account of you he became poor [ἐπτώχευσεν], although he was rich, in order that by means of his poverty [πτωχεία] you might become rich" (2 Cor 8:9).²³⁵ Paul then spells out a rudimentary theory of economic relations between Christ believers, articulated around the ideal of "equality" (ἰσότης): "At the present time, your abundance should alleviate their lack, in order that their abundance may also be for your lack, so that there may

---

230. Winter, "Lord's Supper," 73–77.

231. Bornkamm, "Herrenmahl und Kirche bei Paulus," 143–44; Theissen, *Social Setting*, 148; Lampe, "Das korinthische Herrenmahl," 198–200.

232. Thomas Schmeller, *Hierarchie und Egalität: Eine sozialgeschichtliche Untersuchung paulinischer Gemeinden und griechisch-römischer Vereine* (Stuttgart: Katholisches Bibelwerk, 1995), esp. 60, 71.

233. See Wayne A. Meeks, *The First Urban Christians: The Social World of the Apostle Paul* (New Haven: Yale University Press, 1983), 68: "the phrase is to be taken absolutely, 'the have-nots,' that is, the poor."

234. See the commentary by Hans Dieter Betz, *2 Corinthians 8 and 9: Two Administrative Letters of the Apostle Paul* (Philadelphia: Fortress, 1985).

235. As Betz (ibid., 62) observes, the notion that Jesus was impoverished and lived in circumstances of beggary (πτωχεία) is without parallel in the New Testament.

be equality" (2 Cor 8:14).²³⁶ Paul buttresses this radical principle with a quotation of Exod 16:18: "The one who has much should not have more, and the one who has little should not have less" (2 Cor 8:15).²³⁷

We conclude with Lucian of Samosata, whose essays and dialogues often reveal sympathy with the poor, and who gives voice to their complaints and protests.²³⁸ In the satire *Necyomantia*, Lucian describes the descent of Menippus to the underworld and his return as the prophet of a paradoxical truth: that "the life of the common sort is best" (Lucian, *Nec.* 21).²³⁹ What Lucian's Menippus sees in the underworld is a reversal of the status and values of society.²⁴⁰ Before the throne of Minos, people of wealth and power are arraigned for their evil deeds, prosecuted by the most implacable of witnesses—their own shadows (*Nec.* 11)! The worst malefactors are found to be "those puffed up with wealth and power." Minos feels a special indignation at their "ephemeral imposture and arrogance": "So they were stripped of their short-lived splendor—I mean their wealth, birth, and power—and stood there naked, with hanging heads, reviewing, point by point, their happy life among us as if it had been a dream" (*Nec.* 12). Menippus relates that an assembly of the dead was convoked, and a motion was passed to punish the rich who in life had plundered, oppressed, and humiliated the poor: after their deaths, the bodies of the rich are to be tortured like other malefactors, but their souls are to be sent back to live in donkeys for 250,000 years, in which they will be subjected to the poor (*Nec.* 20).

---

236. See L. L. Welborn, "'That There May Be Equality': The Contexts and Consequences of a Pauline Ideal," *NTS* 59 (2013): 73–90.

237. On the subtle alterations that Paul makes to the text of Exod 16:18 (LXX) in order to emphasize that equality is to be achieved through redistributive action between persons of different resources, see Welborn, "That There May Be Equality," 87–88.

238. E.g., in *Saturnalia*, *Cataplus*, and *Gallus*. See Barry Baldwin, *Studies in Lucian* (Toronto: Hakkert, 1973), 112; R. Bracht Branham, *Unruly Eloquence: Lucian and the Comedy of Traditions* (Cambridge, MA: Harvard University Press, 1989).

239. See R. Bracht Branham, "The Wisdom of Lucian's Tiresias," *JHS* 109 (1989): 154–68.

240. Branham, *Unruly Eloquence*, 23.

8. Conclusions

Most of the sources consulted above speak of the privation, exploitation, and wretchedness experienced by the poor in the cities of the Roman Empire.[241] Elite authors treat the poor about whom they write with a mixture of contempt, pity, and paternalistic concern. But in the writings of the subelite we encounter something more: courage, cunning, humor, imagination—spiritual resources that call into question the monopoly of the elite on material things. It may be argued that in the letters of Paul we witness the emergence of an ethic with the potential to transform relations between the rich and the poor.[242] If the Corinthians had followed Paul's advice to "wait for one another" before beginning the communal meal, the result would have been a routine redistribution of resources that might qualify as a "structural strategy for offsetting poverty."[243] In 2 Cor 8, Paul goes much further, attempting to mediate a relationship between Christians of different social classes, the goal of which was to achieve "equality" through redistributive action.

Bibliography

Abramenko, Andrik. *Die munizipale Mittelschicht im kaiserlichen Italien: Zu einem neuen Verständnis von Sevirat und Augustalität*. Frankfurt: Lang, 1993.

Alcock, Susan. *Graecia Capta: The Landscapes of Roman Greece*. Cambridge: Cambridge University Press, 1993.

Alföldy, Geza. *Die römische Gesellschaft: Ausgewählte Beiträge*. Stuttgart: Steiner, 1986.

———. *Römische Sozialgeschichte*. 3rd ed. Stuttgart: Steiner, 1984; ET: *The Social History of Rome*. London: Croom Helm, 1985.

---

241. Morley ("The Poor in the City of Rome," 33–36) organizes his summary of the experience of poverty under three headings: vulnerability, exclusion, and shame.

242. Edwin Judge, "Cultural Conformity and Innovation in Paul," *TynBul* 35 (1985): 3–24; reprinted in Judge, *Social Distinctives of the Christians in the First Century*, ed. David M. Scholer (Peabody, MA: Hendrickson, 2008), 157–74, esp. 159.

243. Something that Bruce W. Longenecker claims was "out of reach of the sub-elite" of the Greco-Roman world, in *Remember the Poor: Paul, Poverty, and the Greco-Roman World* (Grand Rapids: Eerdmans, 2010), 107.

Bagnall, Roger S. "Landholding in Late Roman Egypt: The Distribution of Wealth." *JRS* 82 (1992): 128–49.
Bagnall, Roger S., and Bruce W. Frier. *The Demography of Roman Egypt.* Cambridge: Cambridge University Press, 1994.
Baldwin, Barry. "The Philogelos: An Ancient Jokebook." Pages 624–37 in *Roman and Byzantine Papers.* Amsterdam: Gieben, 1989.
———. *The Philogelos or Laughter-Lover.* Amsterdam: Gieben, 1983.
———. *Studies in Lucian.* Toronto: Hakkert, 1973.
Basore, John W., trans. *Seneca: Moral Essays.* Vol. 1. LCL. Cambridge, MA: Harvard University Press, 1994.
Becatti, Giovanni. *The Art of Greece and Rome.* Englewood Cliffs, NJ: Prentice Hall, 1975.
Beloch, Julius. *Die Bevölkerung der griechisch-römischen Welt.* Leipzig: Duncker & Humbot, 1886.
Benjamin, Walter. *Illuminations.* Edited by Hannah Arendt. Glasgow: Fontana/Collins, 1979.
Benner, A. R., trans. *The Letters of Alciphron.* LCL. Cambridge, MA: Harvard University Press, 1962.
Best, E. E. "Martial's Readers in the Roman World." *CJ* 64 (1969): 208–12.
Betz, Hans Dieter. *2 Corinthians 8 and 9: Two Administrative Letters of the Apostle Paul.* Philadelphia: Fortress, 1985.
Bisel, Sarah. "Human Bones at Herculaneum." *Rivista di Studi Pompeiani* 1 (1987): 123–29.
Bisel, Sarah, and Jane Bisel. "Health and Nutrition at Herculaneum: An Examination of Human Skeletal Remains." Pages 451–75 in *The Natural History of Pompeii.* Edited by Wilhelmina Jashemski and Fredreick G. Meyer. Cambridge: Cambridge University Press, 2002.
Bodel, John. *Graveyards and Groves: A Study of the Lex Lucerina.* American Journal of Ancient History 11. Cambridge, MA: Harvard University Press, 1994.
Bogaert, Raymond. *Banques et banquiers dans les cites greques.* Leiden: Brill, 1968.
Bonaria, Marius, ed. *Mimorum Romanorum Fragmenta.* Geneva: Instituto di Filologia Classica, 1955.
Bonner, Stanley F. *Roman Declamation in the Late Republic and Early Empire.* Liverpool: University Press of Liverpool Press, 1949.
Bornkamm, Günther. "Herrenmahl und Kirche bei Paulus." Pages 138–76 in *Studien zu Antike und Christentum: Gesammelte Aufsätze II.* Munich: Kaiser, 1959.

Bowersock, G. W. *Fiction as History: Nero to Julian.* Berkeley: University of California Press, 1997.

Bowman, Alan K. "Landholding in the Hermopolite Nome in the Fourth Century AD." *JRS* 75 (1985): 137–63.

Bradley, Keith. *Slaves and Masters in the Roman Empire.* Oxford: Oxford University Press, 1987.

Branham, R. Bracht. *Unruly Eloquence: Lucian and the Comedy of Traditions.* Cambridge, MA: Harvard University Press, 1989.

———. "The Wisdom of Lucian's Tiresias." *JHS* 109 (1989): 154–68.

Braund, David C. *Augustus to Nero: A Sourcebook in Roman History 31 BC–AD 68.* London: Croom Helm, 1985.

Brunt, P. A. "Aspects of the Social Thought of Dio Chrysostom and of the Stoics." *Proceedings of the Cambridge Philological Society* 19 (1973): 9–34.

———. *Italian Manpower 225 B.C.–A.D. 14.* Oxford: Oxford University Press, 1987.

———. "The Roman Mob." Pages 74–102 in *Studies in Ancient Society.* Edited M. I. Finley. London: Routledge and Kegan Paul, 1974.

Capasso, Luigi. *I Fuggischi di Ercolano. Paleobiologia delle vittime dell'eruzione vesuviana.* Rome: L'Erma di Bretschneider, 2001.

Cloud, Duncan. "The Client-Patron Relationship: Emblem and Reality in Juvenal's First Book." Pages 205–18 in *Patronage in Ancient Society.* Edited by Andrew Wallace-Hadrill. London: Routledge, 1990.

Cohoon, J. W., trans. *Dio Chrysostom I: Discourses I–IX.* LCL. Cambridge, MA: Harvard University Press, 1971.

Cook, John. *Law and Life of Rome.* Ithaca, NY: Cornell University Press, 1967.

Corte, Matteo Della. *Case ed Abitanti di Pompei.* Rome: L'Erma, 1956.

Cox, Sherry C. "Health in Hellenistic and Roman Times: The Case Studies of Paphos, Cyprus and Corinth." Pages 59–82 in *Health in Antiquity.* Edited by Helen King. New York: Routledge, 2005.

Croix, G. E. M. de Ste. *The Class Struggle in the Ancient Greek World.* Ithaca: Cornell University Press, 1981.

Rusten, Jeffrey, and I. C. Cunningham, eds. and trans. *Characters. Herodas: Mimes. Sophron and Other Mime Fragments.* LCL. Cambridge, MA: Harvard University Press, 2002.

Daly, Lloyd W., ed. and trans. *Aesop without Morals.* New York: Thomas Yoseloff, 1961.

Day, John. "The Value of Dio Chrysostom's Euboean Discourse for the Economic Historian." Pages 209–35 in *Studies in Roman Economic and Social History*. Edited by Paul Robinson Coleman-Norton. Princeton: Princeton University Press, 1951.

Dörner, Friedrich Karl. *Der Erlass des Statthalters von Asia, Paullus Fabius Persicus*. Greifswald: Adler, 1935.

Duncan-Jones, Richard. *The Economy of the Roman Empire: Quantitative Studies*. Cambridge: Cambridge University Press, 1982.

Eck, Werner. "Aussagefähigkeit epigraphischer Statistik und die Bestattung von Sklaven im kaiserlichen Rom." Pages 130–39 in *Alte Geschichte und Wissenschaftsgeschichte*. Edited by Peter Kneissl. Darmstadt: Wissenschaftliche Buchgesellschaft, 1988.

Engels, Donald. *Roman Corinth*. Chicago: University of Chicago Press, 1990.

Fairweather, Janet A. *Seneca the Elder*. Cambridge: Cambridge University Press, 1981.

Fantham, Elain. *Roman Literary Culture: From Cicero to Apuleius*. Baltimore: Johns Hopkins University Press, 1996.

Finley, M. I. *The Ancient Economy*. Berkeley: University of California Press, 1973.

Fleming, Rebecca. "*Quae Corpore Quaestum Facit*: The Sexual Economy of Female Prostitution in the Roman Empire." *JRS* 89 (1999): 38–61.

Fobes, Francis H. Introduction to *The Letters of Alciphron*. Translated by A. R. Benner. Cambridge, MA: Harvard University Press, 1962.

Friedländer, Ludwig. *Roman Life and Manners under the Early Empire*. Vol. 1. New York: Barnes & Noble, 1968.

Frier, Bruce W. "More Is Worse: Some Observations on the Population of the Roman Empire." Pages 139–59 in *Debating Roman Demography*. Edited by Walter Scheidel. Leiden: Brill, 2001.

———. "The Rental Market in Early Imperial Rome." *JRS* 67 (1977): 27–37.

Garland, Robert. *The Eye of the Beholder: Deformity and Disability in the Greco-Roman World*. Ithaca, NY: Cornell University Press, 1995.

Garnsey, Peter. *Famine and Food Supply in the Graeco-Roman World: Responses to Risk and Crisis*. Cambridge: Cambridge University Press, 1988.

———. "Non-slave Labour in the Roman World." Pages 34–47 in *Non-slave Labour in the Greco-Roman World*. Edited by Peter Garnsey. Cambridge: Cambridge Philological Society, 1980.

———. *Social Status and Legal Privilege in the Roman Empire*. Oxford: Oxford University Press, 1970.

———. "Urban Property Investment." Pages 123–36 in *Studies in Roman Property*. Edited by M. I. Finley. Cambridge: Cambridge University Press, 1976.

Garnsey, Peter, and Greg Woolf. "Patronage of the Poor in the Roman World." Pages 153–70 in *Patronage in Ancient Society*. Edited by Andrew Wallace-Hadrill. London: Routledge, 1990.

Gaselee, S., trans. *Apuleius. The Golden Ass*. LCL. Cambridge, MA: Harvard University Press, 1977.

Champlin, Edward. "Phaedrus the Fabulous." *JRS* 95 (2005): 97–123.

Grant, Mary. *The Ancient Rhetorical Theories of the Laughable*. Madison: University of Wisconsin Press, 1924.

Grey, Cam, and Anneliese Parkin. "Controlling the Urban Mob." *Phoenix* 57 (2003): 284–99.

Hardie, Alex. *Statius and the Silvae: Poets, Patrons and Epideixis in the Greco-Roman World*. Liverpool: Francis Cairns, 1983.

Harrill, J. Albert. *The Manumission of Slaves in Early Christianity*. Tübingen: Mohr Siebeck, 1995.

Harris, William V. "Child Exposure in the Roman Empire." *JRS* 84 (1994): 1–22.

———. "Poverty and Destitution in the Roman Empire." Pages 27–56 in *Rome's Imperial Economy*. Oxford: Oxford University Press, 2011.

Henderson, John. *Telling Tales on Caesar: Roman Stories from Phaedrus*. Oxford: Oxford University Press, 2001.

Hermansen, G. "The Population of Imperial Rome: The Regionaries." *Historia* 27 (1978): 129–68.

Hock, Ronald F. "Paul and Greco-Roman Education." Pages 198–227 in *Paul in the Greco-Roman World*. Edited by J. Paul Sampley. Harrisburg, PA: Trinity Press International, 2003.

Hopkins, Keith. *Death and Renewal: Sociological Studies in Roman History*. Vol. 2. Cambridge: Cambridge University Press, 1983.

———. "Graveyard for Historians." Pages 113–26 in *La Mort, Les Morts et L'Au-Delà dans Le Monde Romain*. Edited by François Hinard. Caen: Centre de Publications, 1987.

———. "Novel Evidence for Roman Slavery." *Past and Present* 138 (1993): 3–27.

———. "The Political Economy of the Roman Empire." Pages 178–204 in

The Dynamics of Ancient Empires. Edited by Ian Morris and Walter Scheidel. New York: Oxford University Press, 2009.
Jackson, John, trans. Tacitus. *The Annals, Books XIII–XVI*. LCL. Cambridge, MA: Harvard University Press, 1981.
Jameson, Fredric. *The Political Unconscious: Narrative as a Socially Symbolic Act*. Ithaca, NY: Cornell University Press, 1981.
Jones, Christopher P. *The Roman World of Dio Chrysostom*. Cambridge, MA: Harvard University Press, 1978.
Jongman, Willem M. "The Early Roman Empire: Consumption." Pages 592–618 in *The Cambridge Economic History of the Greco-Roman World*. Edited by Walter Scheidel, Ian Morris, and Richard Saller. Cambridge: Cambridge University Press, 2007.
———. "A Golden Age: Death, Money Supply and Social Cuccession in the Roman Empire." Pages 181–96 in *Credito e moneta nel mondo romano: Atti degli Incontri capresi di storia dell' economia antica (Capri 12–14 ottobre 2000)*. Edited by Elio LoCascio. Bari: Edipuglia, 2003.
Joshel, Sandra R. *Work, Identity, and Legal Status at Rome: A Study of the Occupational Inscriptions*. Norman: University of Oklahoma Press, 1992.
Judge, Edwin A. *The Social Pattern of the Christian Groups in the First Century*. London: Tyndale Press, 1960.
———. "Cultural Conformity and Innovation in Paul," *TynBul* 35 (1985): 3–24. Reprinted as pages 157–74 in *Social Distinctives of the Christians in the First Century*. Edited by David M. Scholer. Peabody, MA: Hendrickson, 2008.
Kaster, Robert A. "Controlling Reason: Declamation in Rhetorical Education at Rome." Pages 317–37 in *Education in Greek and Roman Antiquity*. Edited by Yun Lee Too. Leiden: Brill, 2001.
Keegan, Peter. *Graffiti in Antiquity*. London: Routledge, 2014.
Ker, Walter C. A. *Martial. Epigrams*. 2 vols. LCL. Cambridge, MA: Harvard University Press, 1978.
Klauck, Hans-Josef. *Herrenmahl und hellenistischer Kult: Eine religionsgeschichtliche Untersuchung zum ersten Korintherbrief*. Münster: Aschendorff, 1982.
Kloft, Hans. *Die Wirtschaft der griechisch-römische Welt*. Darmstadt: Wissenschaftliche Buchgesellschaft, 1992.
Krause, Jens-Uwe. *Witwen und Waisen im römischen Reich II: Wirtschaftliche und Gesellschaftliche Stellung von Witwen*. Stuttgart: Steiner, 1994.

Kühnert, Barbara. *Die Plebs Urbana der späten römischen Republik: Ihre ökomomische Situation und soziale Struktur.* Berlin: Akademie, 1991.

Lampe, Peter. "Das korinthische Herrenmahl im Schnittpunkt hellenistischer Mahlpraxis und paulinischer Theologia Crucis (1 Kor 11,17–34)." *ZNW* 82 (1991): 183–213.

Lanciani, Rodolfo. *Ancient Rome in the Light of Recent Archaeological Discoveries.* London: Macmillan, 1888.

Lattimore, Richard. *Themes in Greek and Latin Epitaphs.* Urbana: University of Illinois Press, 1962.

Laubscher, Hans Peter. *Fischer und Landleute: Studien zur hellenistischer Genreplastik.* Mainz: von Zabern, 1982.

Laurence, Ray. "Writing the Roman Metropolis." Pages 1–20 in *Roman Urbanism: Beyond the Consumer City.* Edited by Helen Parkins. London: Routledge, 1997.

Lavedan, Pierre, and Jeanne Hugueney. *Histoire de l'urbanisme: Antiquite.* Paris: Laurens, 1966.

Ligt, Luuk de. "Demand, Supply, Distribution: The Roman Peasantry between Town and Countryside: Rural Monetization and Peasant Demand." *Münstersche Beiträge zur antiken Handelsgeschichte* 9 (1990): 24–56.

Lindemann, Andreas. *Der erste Korintherbrief.* Tübingen: Mohr Siebeck, 2000.

Longenecker, Bruce W. *Remember the Poor: Paul, Poverty, and the Greco-Roman World.* Grand Rapids: Eerdmans, 2010.

MacMullen, Ramsay. "The Epigraphic Habit in the Roman Empire." *AJP* 103 (1982): 233–46.

———. *Roman Social Relations 50 B.C. to A.D. 284.* New Haven: Yale University Press, 1974.

Macro, A. D. "Imperial Provisions for Pergamum: OGIS 484." *GRBS* 17 (1976): 169–79.

Maggi, Giuseppe. "Lo scavo dell' area suburban meridionale di Ercolano." *Rivista di Studi Pompeiani* 9 (1998): 167–72.

Magie, David. *Roman Rule in Asia Minor.* Princeton: Princeton University Press, 1950.

Maiuri, Amedeo. *Ercolano: I nuovi scavi (1927–1958).* Rome: Instituto Poligrafico dello Strato, 1958.

Malherbe, Abraham J. "Social Level and Literary Culture." Pages 29–59 in *Social Aspects of Early Christianity.* Philadelphia: Fortress, 1983.

Mason, H. J. "Lucius at Corinth." *Phoenix* 25 (1971): 160–65.

Martin, Josef. *Antike Rhetorik: Technik und Methode*. Munich: Beck, 1974.
Meggitt, Justin. *Paul, Poverty and Survival*. Edinburgh: T&T Clark, 1998.
Meeks, Wayne A. *The First Urban Christians: The Social World of the Apostle Paul*. New Haven: Yale University Press, 1983.
Meyer, Elizabeth A. "Explaining the Epigraphic Habit in the Roman Empire." *JRS* 80 (1990): 74–96.
Millar, Fergus. *The Crowd in Rome in the Late Republic*. Ann Arbor: University of Michigan Press, 2002.
———. "The World of the *Golden Ass*." *JRS* 71 (1981): 63–75.
Morris, Ian. *Death Ritual and Social Structure in Classical Antiquity*. Cambridge: Cambridge University Press, 1992.
Morley, Neville. "The Poor in the City of Rome." Pages 21–39 in *Poverty in the Roman World*. Edited by Margaret Atkins and Robin Osborne. Cambridge: Cambridge University Press, 2006.
Morstein-Marx, Robert. *Mass Oratory and Political Power in the Late Roman Republic*. Cambridge: Cambridge University Press, 2004.
Nasrallah, Laura Salah. "'You Were Bought with a Price': Freedpersons and Things in 1 Corinthians." Pages 54–73 in *Corinth in Context: Studies in Inequality*. Edited by Steven J. Friesen. Leiden: Brill, 2014.
Osborne, Robin. "Roman Poverty in Context." Pages 1–20 in *Poverty in the Roman World*. Edited by Margaret Atkins and Robin Osborne. Cambridge: Cambridge University Press, 2006.
Packer, James E. "Housing and Population in Imperial Ostia and Rome." *JRS* 57 (1967): 80–95.
———. *The Insulae of Imperial Ostia*. Rome: American Academy in Rome, 1971.
Parkin, Anneliese R. "Poverty in the Early Roman Empire: Ancient and Modern Conceptions and Constructs." PhD diss. University of Cambridge, 2001.
———. "'You Do Him No Service': An Exploration of Pagan Almsgiving." Pages 60–82 in *Poverty in the Roman World*. Edited by Margaret Atkins and Robin Osborne. Cambridge: Cambridge University Press, 2006.
Perry, B. E. *Aesopica*. New York: Arno Press, 1980.
———, trans. *Fables: Babrius and Phaedrus*. LCL. Cambridge, MA: Harvard University Press, 1965.
———. *Studies in the Text History of the Life and Fables of Aesop*. Haverford, PA: American Philological Association, 1936.
Pleket, H. W. "Labour and Unemployment in the Roman Empire." Pages

267–76 in *Soziale Randgruppen und Aussenseiter in Altertum.* Edited by Ingomar Weiler. Graz: Leykam, 1988.

———. "Sociale stratificatie en sociale mobiliteit in de romeinse keizertijd." *Tijdschrift voor Geschiedenis* 84 (1971): 215–51.

Prell, Marcus. *Sozialökonomische Untersuchungen zur Armut in antiken Rom von den Gracchen bis Kaiser Diokletian.* Stuttgart: Steiner, 1997.

Purcell, Nicholas. "The City of Rome and the *plebs urbana* in the Late Republic." Pages 644–88 in *The Last Age of the Roman Republic, 146–43 B.C.* Vol. 9 of *Cambridge Ancient History.* Edited by J. A. Crook, Andrew Lintott, and Elizabeth Rawson. Cambridge: Cambridge University Press, 1994.

———. "Rome and Its Development under Augustus and His Successors." Pages 782–811 in *The Augustan Empire, 43 B.C.–A.D. 69.* Vol. 10 of *Cambridge Ancient History.* Edited by Alan K Bowman, Edward Champlin, and Andrew Lintott. Cambridge: Cambridge University Press, 1996.

Ricl, Marijana. "Legal and Social Status of *Threptoi* and Related Categories in Narrative and Documentary Sources." Pages 93–114 in *From Hellenism to Islam: Cultural and Linguistic Change in the Roman Near East.* Edited by Hannah Cotton. Cambridge: Cambridge University Press, 2009.

Robinson, O. F. *Ancient Rome: City Planning and Administration.* London: Routledge, 1994.

———. "The Water Supply of Rome." *Studia et Documenta Historiae et Iuris* 46 (1980): 44–86.

Rolfe, J. C. *Sallust. The War with Catiline. The War with Jugurtha.* LCL. Cambridge, MA: Harvard University Press, 1985.

Romano, David Gilman. "Urban and Rural Planning in Roman Corinth." Pages 25–59 in *Urban Religion in Roman Corinth.* HTS. Edited by Daniel N. Schowalter and Steven Friesen. Cambridge, MA: Harvard University Press, 2005.

Saller, Richard, and Brent D. Shaw. "Tombstones and Roman Family Relations in the Principate: Civilians, Soldiers and Slaves." *JRS* 74 (1984): 124–56.

Scheidel, Walter. "Approaching the Roman Economy." Pages 1–24 in *The Cambridge Companion to the Roman Economy.* Edited by Walter Scheidel. Cambridge: Cambridge University Press, 2012.

———. "Stratification, Deprivation and Quality of Life." Pages 40–59 in

Poverty in the Roman World. Edited by Margaret Atkins and Robin Osborne. Cambridge: Cambridge University Press, 2006.

Scheidel, Walter, and Steven J. Friesen. "The Size of the Economy and the Distribution of Income in the Roman Empire." *JRS* 99 (2009): 61–91.

Schiesaro, Alessandro. "Phaedrus (4)." *OCD* 1119.

Schmeller, Thomas. *Hierarchie und Egalität: Eine sozialgeschichtliche Untersuchung paulinischer Gemeinden und griechisch-römischer Vereine.* Stuttgart: Katholisches Bibelwerk, 1995.

Scobie, Alexander. "Slums, Sanitation and Mortality in the Roman World." *Klio* 68 (1986): 399–433.

Shaw, Brent D. "Latin Funerary Epigraphy and Family Life in the Later Roman Empire." *Historia* 33 (1984): 457–97.

Sullivan, J. P. *Martial: The Unexpected Classic.* Cambridge: Cambridge University Press, 1991.

Theissen, Gerd. *The Social Setting of Pauline Christianity: Essays on Corinth.* Philadelphia: Fortress, 1983.

Thierfelder, Andreas. *Philogelos der Lachfreund, von Hierokles und Philagrios.* Munich: Heimeran, 1968.

Toner, J. P. *Rethinking Roman History.* Cambridge: Cambridge University Press, 2002.

Treggiari, Susan M. "Urban Labour in Rome: *Mercennarii* and *tabernarii.*" Pages 48–64 in *Non-slave Labour in the Greco-Roman World.* Edited by Peter Garnsey. Cambridge: Cambridge Philological Society, 1980.

Verboven, Koenraad. *The Economy of Friends: Economic Aspects of* Amicitia *and Patronage in the Late Republic.* Brussels: Latomus, 2002.

Veyne, Paul. "The Roman Empire." Pages 5–234 in *From Pagan Rome to Byzantium.* Vol. 1 of *A History of Private Life.* Edited by Paul Veyne. Cambridge, MA: Harvard University Press, 1987.

———. "Le table des Ligures Baebiani et l'institution alimentaire de Trajan." *MEFR* 70 (1958): 177–241.

Waele, Ferdinand J. de. "The Roman Market North of the Temple at Corinth." *AJA* 34 (1930): 432–54.

Wallace-Hadrill, Andrew. "*Domus* and *Insulae* in Rome: Families and Housefuls." Pages 3–18 in *Early Christian Families in Context: An Interdisciplinary Dialogue.* Edited by Carolyn Osiek and David Balch. Grand Rapids: Eerdmans, 2003.

———. *Herculaneum, Past and Present.* London: Frances Lincoln, 2011.

———. "Houses and Households: Sampling Pompeii and Herculaneum." Pages 191–227 in *Marriage, Divorce and Children in Ancient Rome*. Edited by Beryl Rawson. Oxford: Oxford University Press, 1991.

———. *"Low Life" in Herculaneum, Past and Present*. London: Frances Lincoln, 2011.

Welborn, L. L. "The Corinthian Correspondence." Pages 205–42 in *All Things to All Cultures: Paul among Jews, Greeks, and Romans*. Edited by Mark Harding and Alanna Nobbs. Grand Rapids: Eerdmans, 2013.

———. " 'That There May Be Equality': The Contexts and Consequences of a Pauline Ideal." *NTS* 59 (2013): 73–90.

Weiss, Johannes. *Der erste Korintherbrief*. KEK 5. Göttingen: Vandenhoeck & Ruprecht, 1910.

Whittaker, C. R. "The Poor in the City of Rome." Pages 1–25 in *Land, City and Trade in the Roman Empire*. Aldershot: Variorum, 1993.

Wiemken, Helmut. *Der griechische Mimus: Dokumente zur Geschichte des antiken Volkstheaters*. Bremen: Schüemann, 1972.

Winkler, John J. *Auctor and Actor: A Narratological Reading of Apuleius's Golden Ass*. Berkeley: University of California Press, 1985.

Winter, Bruce W. "The Lord's Supper at Corinth: An Alternative Reconstruction." *RTR* 37 (1978): 73–82.

Winterbottom, Michael, trans. *Seneca the Elder. Declamation, Volume II: Controversies, Books 7–10*. LCL. Cambridge, MA: Harvard University Press, 1974.

Wiseman, T. P. *Catullus and His World*. Cambridge: Cambridge University Press, 1985.

Witke, Edward Charles. "Juvenal III. Eclogue for the Urban Poor." *Hermes* 90 (1962): 244–48.

Woolf, Greg. "Food, Poverty and Patronage: The Significance of the Epigraphy of the Roman Alimentary Schemes in Early Imperial Italy." *Papers of the British School at Rome* 58 (1990): 197–228.

———. "World Systems Analysis and the Roman Empire." *JRA* 3 (1990): 213–14.

———. "Writing Poverty in Rome". Pages 83–99 in *Poverty in the Roman World*. Edited by Margaret Atkins and Robin Osborne. Cambridge: Cambridge University Press, 2006.

Yavetz, Zvi. "The Living Conditions of the Plebs in Republican Rome," *Latomus* 17 (1958): 500–517.

———. "Plebs sordida." *Athenaeum* 43 (1965): 295–311.

Zeitz, Heinrich. "Der Aesoproman und seine Geschichte: eine Untersuchung im Anschluss an die neugefundenen Papyri." *Aegyptus* 16 (1936): 225–56.
Zuiderhoek, Arjan. *The Politics of Munificence in the Roman Empire: Citizens, Elites and Benefactors in Asia Minor.* Cambridge: Cambridge University Press, 2009.

Methodological Considerations in Using Epigraphic Evidence to Determine the Socioeconomic Context of the Early Christians

Julien M. Ogereau

Ainsi l'épigraphie apporte à l'histoire ancienne une fraîcheur toujours renouvelée; elle lutte contre la sècheresse des discussions sans fin sur des textes malaxés depuis quatre siècles. Elle tranche de vieilles controverses. Elle est l'eau de Jouvence de nos études. Elle maintient toujours grand ouvert le domaine de la découverte et de sa joie. Un perpétuel apport vivifie l'histoire de l'antiquité dans ses parties les plus variées.[1]

1. Introduction: The Enduring Significance of Inscriptions

The study of the humble beginnings and expansion of early Christianity as an urban phenomenon poses a singular problem to students of the New Testament and early Christianity, namely, that of the dearth of primary evidence. While a few literary sources from the first and second centuries CE have miraculously endured the passing of time, archaeological evidence is almost nonexistent. Christian epigraphic sources in particular are frustratingly scarce, sometimes difficult to access, and consequently have often been neglected.[2] The technical skills required to decipher, transcribe,

---

1. Louis Robert, "L'épigraphie," in *L'histoire et ses méthodes*, ed. C. Samaran (Paris: Gallimard, 1961), 462–63; repr. in *Opera Minora Selecta* 5 (Amsterdam: Hakkert, 1989).

2. Important volumes on Christian inscriptions from Asia Minor are William M. Ramsay, *The Cities and Bishoprics of Phrygia: Being an Essay of the Local History of Phrygia from the Earliest Times to the Turkish Conquest*, vol. 1, parts 1 and 2 (Oxford: Clarendon, 1895–1897); Henri Grégoire, *Recueil des inscriptions grecques-chrétiennes d'Asie Mineure*, vol. 1 (Amsterdam: Hakkert, 1968); Gary J. Johnson, *Early-Christian Epitaphs from Anatolia* (Atlanta: Scholars Press, 1995); William Tabbernee, *Mon-*

and analyze inscriptions in general can also often act as a strong deterrent for the uninitiated, who may not be able to appreciate their historical value and interpret their significance. Understandably, many New Testament and early Christianity scholars probably find themselves ill-equipped, and may even be reluctant, to delve into this sort of material, which many, ancient historians included, have been tempted to view as the epigraphists' private turf.

New Testament and early Christianity scholars aspiring to study ancient inscriptions should nonetheless take some comfort in the fact that, in recent years, epigraphists, as well as epigraphically inclined scholars of early Christianity, have striven to make inscriptions more accessible to the novice through the publication of epigraphic corpora, annotated bibliographies,[3] as well as introductory manuals and sourcebooks.[4] This noteworthy development is in itself an admission of the enduring significance of epigraphic sources. As a renowned historian once noted: "Anyone who wants to acquaint himself with the religious life of the empire, whatever literary sources he may also find useful, must really begin and end with inscriptions."[5] This observation could be applied more generally: the ancient world, in its various historical and sociocultural manifestations, simply cannot be fully and adequately understood without the help of

---

tanist Inscriptions and Testimonia: Epigraphic Sources Illustrating the History of Montanism (Macon, GA: Mercer University Press, 1997). Readers should also be aware of the database of Christian inscriptions from Greece and Asia Minor being currently developed by the Exzellenzcluster Topoi B-5-3 research group at Berlin. See Cilliers Breytenbach et al., eds., "Inscriptiones Christianae Graecae (ICG): Eine Datenbank der frühchristlichen Inschriften Kleinasiens und Griechenlands," http://www.epigraph.topoi.org.

3. The *Guide de l'épigraphiste* needs no introduction, the latest (fourth) edition being François Bérard et al., *Guide de l'épigraphiste: Bibliographie choisie des épigraphies antiques et médiévales*, 4th ed. (Paris: Presses de l'École normale supérieure, 2010).

4. A good place to start is with Robert, "L'épigraphie"; John Bodel, ed., *Epigraphic Evidence: Ancient History from Inscriptions* (London: Routledge, 2001); Bradley H. McLean, *An Introduction to Greek Epigraphy of the Hellenistic and Roman Periods from Alexander the Great down to the Reign of Constantine (323 B.C.–A.D. 337)* (Ann Arbor: University of Michigan Press, 2002); Alison E. Cooley, *The Cambridge Manual of Latin Epigraphy* (Cambridge: Cambridge University Press, 2012). For sourcebooks specifically tailored for Early Christian studies, see the series *NewDocs*.

5. Ramsay MacMullen, *Christianizing the Roman Empire (A.D. 100–400)* (New Haven: Yale University Press, 1984), 102.

epigraphic material, which New Testament and early Christianity scholars would be wise not to ignore.

While nonspecialists may still have some reservation in venturing into such a technical field as epigraphy, it is encouraging to note that epigraphists themselves have become more open to outsiders exploring the possibilities of their discipline. In the conclusion of his closing address to the Thirteenth International Congress of Greek and Roman Epigraphy in 2007, Angelos Chaniotis, for instance, confessed that he preferred "the scholar who uses inscriptions imperfectly to the scholar who does not use them at all."[6] Chaniotis's position somewhat contrasts with that of two masters of epigraphy: Louis Robert, who thought it hazardous both to overlook inscriptions and to use them poorly; and A. Geoffrey Woodhead, who deemed epigraphy to be "a subject in which it is unwise merely to dabble."[7] Yet even Robert warned against exaggerating the *technique* required to work with inscriptions, suggesting that "la part de la 'technique' n'est pas si grande en ces disciplines; chacun peut s'en rendre maître sans tant d'efforts."[8] What is important to have is "du bon sens et de la critique comme en toute étude historique," as well as some "curiosité qui entraîne à des lectures très étendues."[9] I readily count myself in Chaniotis's first category of scholars, among those who use inscriptions imperfectly, and do not claim to be an expert. Yet I have long been convinced of the usefulness of inscriptions for the study of early Christianity and consider that the benefits of employing them far outweigh any of the technical inconveniencies and difficulties one may encounter.

Given the number of introductory resources already available, it would be superfluous herein to lay out a basic methodology on how to engage in epigraphy. Rather, the aim of this chapter shall merely be to illustrate further, if it needed to be, the invaluable insight epigraphic documents provide on civic and religious aspects of the early Christians' urban

---

6. Angelos Chaniotis, "Listening to Stones: Orality and Emotions in Ancient Inscriptions," in *Epigraphy and the Historical Sciences*, ed. John Davies and John Wilkes (Oxford: Oxford University Press, 2012), 320. Cf. John Bodel, "Epigraphy and the Ancient Historian," in *Epigraphic Evidence: Ancient History from Inscriptions*, ed. John Bodel (London: Routledge, 2001), 1.

7. Robert, "L'épigraphie," 472; A. Geoffrey Woodhead, *The Study of Greek Inscriptions*, 2nd ed. (Cambridge: Cambridge University Press, 1981), viii.

8. Robert, "L'épigraphie," 472.

9. Ibid.

environment. This will be achieved through a quick overview of relevant secondary sources and a case study, which will be accompanied with succinct methodological remarks as may be required. Focus shall especially be placed on the socioeconomic dimension of the early Christians' context, which in recent years has increasingly attracted the attention of scholars of early Christianity.[10] However, despite the growing recognition of the importance of socioeconomic issues in the life of the first Christians, New Testament and early Christianity scholars have yet to delve more seriously into epigraphic material (most likely for the reasons explained above).

The current situation is regrettable but not irremediable. New Testament and early Christianity scholars should in fact be encouraged by the wealth of resources published by epigraphists and ancient historians over the last century.[11] For example, although now dated, the six-volume collection of papyrological and epigraphic texts edited by Tenney Frank, *An Economic Survey of Ancient Rome*, still provides a good entry point into the economic history of the Greco-Roman world and is an indispensable companion to the (untranslated) sourcebooks edited by H. W. Pleket and Raymond Bogaert (TextMin 31 and 47).[12] The latter's work on the financial institutions of ancient Greece and Asia Minor itself remains a vital contribution to our knowledge of ancient banking.[13] Bernhard Laum's two

---

10. See, for instance, Bruce W. Longenecker and Kelly D. Liebengood, eds., *Engaging Economics: New Testament Scenarios and Early Christian Reception* (Grand Rapids: Eerdmans, 2009). The initiation by John T. Fitzgerald et al. of the SBL consultation on Early Christianity and the Ancient Economy is a welcome development and a clear indication of a more focused interest in the topic.

11. The following review does not aim to be exhaustive, but merely to point to a few helpful resources. Readers looking for a more comprehensive review and bibliography of the most significant studies on the ancient economy are advised to consult Walter Scheidel, Ian Morris, and Richard Saller, eds., *The Cambridge Economic History of the Greco-Roman World* (Cambridge: Cambridge University Press, 2007); and Walter Scheidel, ed., *The Cambridge Companion to the Roman Economy* (Cambridge: Cambridge University Press, 2012).

12. Tenney Frank, ed., *An Economic Survey of Ancient Rome*, 6 vols. (Paterson, NJ: Pageant, 1959); H. W. Pleket, ed., *Texts on the Economic History of the Greek World*, Epigraphica 1 (Leiden: Brill, 1964); Raymond Bogaert, ed., *Texts on Bankers, Banking and Credit in the Greek World*, Epigraphica 3 (Leiden: Brill, 1976).

13. Raymond Bogaert, *Banques et banquiers dans les cités grecques* (Leyde: Sijthoff, 1968). For his work on Roman Egypt more specifically, see Bogaert, *Trapezitica Aegyptiaca: Recueil de recherches sur la banque en Égypte gréco-romaine* (Florence: Gonnelli, 1994). For the Latin West, Andreau's work remains unsurpassed. See for instance Jean

tomes on ancient foundations (*Stiftungen*), as well as Léopold Migeotte's volumes on public loans and voluntary collections (*epidoseis*), are also essential resources to understand more accurately the economic institutions of ancient Greek cities.[14] As for professional associations specifically, Jean-Pierre Waltzing's four-volume survey still provides one of the best introductions to a massive corpus of inscriptions,[15] although it has been recently complemented by studies by Onno M. van Nijf,[16] Carola Zimmermann,[17] Monique Dondin-Payre and Nicolas Tran,[18] Jinyu Liu,[19] and, to some extent, by John S. Kloppenborg and Richard S. Ascough's collection of Greco-Roman associations.[20] The reader will of course find other useful resources, but few will prove as helpful as the above-mentioned in guiding the novice through an abundance of (mostly translated) epigraphic material.[21]

Andreau, *La vie financière dans le monde romain: Les métiers de manieurs d'argent (IVe siècle av. J.-C.–IIIe siècle ap. J.-C)* (Rome: École Française de Rome, 1987).

14. Bernhard Laum, *Stiftungen in der griechischen und römischen Antike: Ein Beitrag zur antiken Kulturgeschichte*, 2 vols. (Leipzig: Scientia, 1964); Léopold Migeotte, *L'emprunt public dans les cités grecques: Recueil des documents et analyse critique* (Paris: Les Belles Lettres, 1984); Migeotte, *Les souscriptions publiques dans les cités grecques* (Geneva: Droz, 1992). See also his latest volume *Les finances des cités grecques* (Paris: Les Belles Lettres, 2014).

15. Jean-Pierre Waltzing, *Étude historique sur les corporations professionnelles chez les Romains: Depuis les origines jusqu'à la chute de l'Empire d'Occident*, 4 vols. (Louvain: Peeters, 1895–1900; repr., Hildesheim: Olms, 1970).

16. Onno M. van Nijf, *The Civic World of Professional Associations in the Roman East* (Amsterdam: Gieben, 1997).

17. Carola Zimmermann, *Handwerkervereine im griechischen Osten des Imperium Romanum* (Mainz: Römisch-germanisches Zentralmuseum, 2002).

18. Nicolas Tran, *Les membres des associations romaines: Le rang social des* collegiati *en Italie et en Gaule sous le haut empire* (Rome: École Française de Rome, 2006); Monique Dondin-Payre and Nicolas Tran, eds., *Collegia: Le phénomène associatif dans l'Occident romain* (Bordeaux: Ausonius, 2012).

19. Jinyu Liu, *Collegia Centonariorum: The Guilds of Textile Dealers in the Roman West* (Leiden: Brill, 2009).

20. Kloppenborg and Ascough's primary interest is not the professional character of Greco-Roman associations. See John S. Kloppenborg and Richard S. Ascough, eds., *Attica, Central Greece, Macedonia, Thrace*, vol. 1 of *Greco-Roman Associations: Texts, Translations, and Commentary*, BZNW 181 (Berlin: de Gruyter, 2011). See also Richard S. Ascough, *Paul's Macedonian Associations: The Social Context of Philippians and 1 Thessalonians*, WUNT 2/161 (Tübingen: Mohr Siebeck, 2003).

21. Other valuable contributions that use inscriptions include Beate Dignas,

The rest of this essay shall proceed as follows. It will offer a succinct overview of the range and quality of the epigraphic evidence currently available and discuss how we may approach it. The significance of such material in ascertaining the socioeconomic environment of the first Christians shall then be highlighted by focusing on Nero's revised customs law of Asia, the *lex portorii Asiae*.

2. Inscriptions and the Ancient Economy: A General Overview and Methodological Discussion

The insight on the ancient economy that can be derived from epigraphic material, and especially from inscribed temple accounts or *instrumentum domesticum* such as ostraca,[22] is by no means negligible and now generally well accepted.[23] One might recall that it was Michael Ivanovitch Rostovtzeff who, in the late nineteenth century, was the first to make full use of epigraphic and archaeological evidence in his *Die Geschichte der Staatspacht in der romischen Kaiserzeit bis Diokletian* (1899),[24] and in his four-volume economic history of the Hellenistic and Roman world (1926, 1941).[25] While Rostovtzeff's views about the rationality and capitalistic

---

Economy of the Sacred in Hellenistic and Roman Asia Minor (Oxford: Oxford University Press, 2002); Stephen Mitchell and Constantina Katsari, eds., *Patterns in the Economy of Roman Asia Minor* (Swansea: Classical Press of Wales, 2005).

22. See, for instance, Jean Bousquet, ed., *Les comptes du quatrième et du troisième siècle*, vol. 2 of *Corpus des inscriptions de Delphes* (Paris: de Boccard, 1989); Giuseppe Pucci, "Inscribed *instrumentum* and the Ancient Economy," in *Epigraphic Evidence: Ancient History from Inscriptions*, ed. John Bodel (London: Routledge, 2001), 137–52; Véronique Chankowski, *Athènes et Délos à l'époque classique: Recherches sur l'administration du sanctuaire d'Apollon délien* (Athènes: École française d'Athènes, 2008); William V. Harris, ed., *The Inscribed Economy: Production and Distribution in the Roman Empire in the Light of* instrumentum domesticum (Ann Arbor: University of Michigan Press, 1993). For additional references, see the relevant sections in Bérard et al., *Guide de l'épigraphiste*, 194–204, 259–65.

23. See, most recently, the contributions by Alain Bresson and Giovanni Salmeri, "Greek Epigraphy and Ancient Economics" and "Epigraphy and the Economy of the Roman Empire" in Davies and Wilkes, *Epigraphy and the Historical Sciences*, 223–67.

24. The German translation of the original Russian text appeared in 1902: Michael Ivanovitch Rostovtzeff, *Geschichte der Staatspacht in der römischen Kaiserzeit bis Diokletian* (Leipzig: Dieterich, 1902).

25. Michael Ivanovitch Rostovtzeff, *The Social and Economic History of the Roman Empire*, 2 vols. (Oxford: Clarendon, 1926); Rostovtzeff, *The Social and Economic His-*

outlook of the ancient economy attracted much criticism and revived the Bücher-Meyer controversy between primitivists and modernists,[26] the legitimacy of his use of epigraphic material was never really contested, not even by scholars such as Moses I. Finley, one of the most influential proponents of the primitivistic view in the twentieth century.[27] In fact, Finley's own study of Athenian boundary stones (*horoi*) would later help further establish epigraphy as a major contributor to the study of the ancient economy (along with some of the resources already mentioned in the introduction).[28]

While past and present debates about the nature and structure of the ancient economy remain unsettled, it has now become clear to the great majority of ancient historians that inscriptions constitute a vital piece of the puzzle, one that illuminates peripheral "places which, due to the preponderance of the centre of power, lurk in the dark in our sources."[29] This

---

tory of the Hellenistic World, 2 vols. (Oxford: Clarendon, 1941). Cf. Arnaldo Momigliano, "M. I. Rostovtzeff," *Cambridge Journal* 7 (1954): 334–46; and Giovanni Salmeri, "Epigraphy and the Economy of the Roman Empire," in Davies and Wilkes, *Epigraphy and the Historical Sciences*, 249–51.

26. The controversy takes its name from the two nineteenth-century German scholars, Karl Bücher and Eduard Meyer, who shared opposing views vis-à-vis the development and sophistication of the ancient economy. Primitivists (also known as Finleyans) generally emphasize the archaic nature of the ancient economy, while modernists minimize the structural *altérité* between ancient and modern economies. One should note that the distinctions between these two opposing viewpoints often tend to be schematic, caricatural, and even pejorative. For helpful introductory discussions and suggestions on future research directions beyond this controversy, see Alain Bresson, *L'économie de la Grèce des cités (fin VIe–Ier siècle a.C.)* (Paris: Colin, 2008), 1:7–36; Peter F. Bang, *The Roman Bazaar: A Comparative Study of Trade and Markets in a Tributary Empire* (Cambridge: Cambridge University Press, 2008), 17–60; Jean Andreau, *L'économie du monde romain* (Paris: Ellipses, 2010), 13–26; Scheidel, Morris, and Saller, *Cambridge Economic History*, 1–12.

27. See the classic study of Moses I. Finley, *The Ancient Economy* (Berkeley: University of California Press, 1973).

28. Moses I. Finley, *Studies in Land and Credit in Ancient Athens, 500–200 B.C.: The Horos-Inscriptions* (New Brunswick, NJ: Rutgers University Press, 1952). Earlier noteworthy contributions that made use of epigraphic evidence were by Peter Landvogt and Helen J. Loane. Peter Landvogt, *Epigraphische Untersuchungen über den ΟΙΚΟΝΟΜΟΣ: Ein Beitrag zum hellenistischen Beamtenwesen* (Strassburg: Schauberg, 1908); Helen J. Loane, *Industry and Commerce of the City of Rome (50 B.C.–200 A.D.)* (Baltimore: Johns Hopkins University Press, 1938).

29. H. W. Pleket, "Economic History of the Ancient World and Epigraphy: Some

recognition invites a few nuanced comments on the quality and nature of epigraphic material, however. Anyone wanting to delve into inscriptions must take into account the fact that the preservation of ancient documents is a random and discriminatory process, one that is entirely dependent on the accidents of time as well as on the evolution of ancient epigraphic habits (for example, the amount of Latin inscriptions decreases significantly from the third century CE for no immediately apparent reason).[30] Only too rarely are exceptional documents such as the *Monumentum Ephesenum*, Nero's revised customs law of Asia (*lex portorii Asiae*), recovered from the rubble of ancient cities.[31] For the most part, our primary sources remain a fragmentary and disparate arrangement of materials from various geographical origins and historical periods, which tends to impose upon modern eyes a rather truncated and lopsided vision of the past.

This state of affairs naturally poses a number of problems to epigraphists and ancient historians seeking to draw a synthetic picture of the ancient economy in Hellenistic and Roman times. Inevitably it confines their interpretive reconstruction to approximate and piecemeal descriptions of the ancient reality. In a way, their reconstructive work is akin to that of a conservationist restoring a badly damaged mosaic. The final product invariably remains incomplete, with many gaps in between the patches of mosaic, and can only represent a pale copy of the original. The lacunose state of the primary sources also constantly confronts historians with the temptation of filling the remaining gaps with their own imaginative interpretation and, in the case of inscriptions, with their own textual restorations. The ultimate risk is of course to produce what Ernst Badian once called "a history of square brackets"[32] that would slightly, if not entirely, distort the ancient evidence.[33] Or as Robert would put it: "Le danger est sans doute de leur [i.e., inscriptions] demander plus qu'elles ne

---

Introductory Remarks," in *Akten des VI. Internationalen Kongresses für Griechische und Lateinische Epigraphik, München, 1972* (Munich: Beck, 1973), 255.

30. See Ramsay MacMullen, "The Epigraphic Habit in the Roman Empire," *AJP* 103 (1982): 233–46; Elizabeth A. Meyer, "Explaining the Epigraphic Habit in the Roman Empire: Evidence of Epitaphs," *JRS* 80 (1990): 74–98.

31. In the case of the *Monumentum Ephesenum*, the stone had been reused face down as an ambo plate in the Church of St. John in Selçuk, which explains its survival.

32. The square brackets make reference to the brackets encompassing textual lacunae according to the Leiden editorial convention.

33. Ernst Badian, "History from 'Square Brackets,'" *ZPE* 79 (1989): 59–70.

peuvent donner et de trop systématiser."³⁴ Historians must therefore learn to exercise prudence and self-restraint, harbor "un mélange de hardiesse et de circonspection" in the face of the paucity of the primary evidence, and not go too far in their restoration or interpretation.³⁵ This is a fundamental methodological point to bear in mind as one approaches epigraphic material: each stone is but a tiny, tainted window through which we peer at a shadowy distant past.

For this reason, epigraphy will never substitute itself for the other historical disciplines, as indeed "la pierre ne nous apporte pas un cours d'histoire suivi fait pour la postérité."³⁶ Rather, it should be seen as complementing more traditional and literary-based studies of the ancient world, on whose *histoire sociale* epigraphy offers precious insight.³⁷ Ideally, inscriptions should thus always be confronted to, compared with, and interpreted alongside other primary evidence, such as literary, papyrological, numismatic, and archaeological sources. As Pleket once rightly observed, "epigraphy will have a good deal to say on problems of economic history, though always in combination with and on the *basis* of what the literature conveys to us about the structure of ancient society, its values and attitudes."³⁸ Even more important still is to examine a stone (as far as is possible) in the light of the local dossier of inscriptions to which it belongs, that is, in its sociohistorical, archaeological, and geographical context. As Robert again wisely advised: "L'inscription doit être mise à la fois dans la série des inscriptions du même lieu, de la même époque et du même sujet."³⁹

These limitations having been acknowledged, inscriptions remain an indispensable primary source of historical knowledge and, in the absence of preserved public archives, have (paradoxically) taken on the role of the ancient archives themselves (though they were never intended to fulfill that role).⁴⁰ Of course, this does not mean that epigraphic materials

---

34. Robert, "L'épigraphie," 466.
35. Ibid., 472.
36. Ibid., 463.
37. Ibid., 466–72.
38. Pleket, "Economic History," 255, emphasis original.
39. Robert, "L'épigraphie," 473.
40. Pleket, "Economic History," 255. Cf. Alain Bresson, "Greek Epigraphy and Ancient Economics," in Davies and Wilkes, *Epigraphy and the Historical Sciences*, 223–25. For a dissenting opinion, see Salmeri, "Epigraphy," 252. See also Robert, "L'épigraphie," 458–59. Very few private archives have survived. For a magisterial study

provide us with all the statistical data historians long for, which makes quantitative analyses particularly difficult though not impossible,[41] but at least they allow us to conduct qualitative surveys on a reasonably significant scale. In most cases, such studies will require a considerable investment of time and energy to cull and collect all the necessary data, which is often scattered across a multitude of epigraphic volumes, before it can be processed and analyzed. But for those armed with patience and perseverance, the dividends can be quite substantial and the results groundbreaking. Sandra R. Joshel and Nicolas Tran's meticulous investigations of hundreds of epitaphs from Rome and Italy perfectly illustrate this point, for they have helped historians better understand the importance of professional occupations for the social status, ambitions, mobility, and self-identity of the free, freed, and servile Roman "working classes" about whom aristocratic literary sources are mostly silent.[42]

While the relevance of such survey for the study of early Christianity may not be immediately apparent, it must be kept in mind that whatever contributes to a more accurate appreciation of the sociohistorical context of the early Christians represents a significant advance. Guy Labarre and Marie-Thérèse Le Dinahet's examination of inscriptions relating to the textile industry in Asia Minor is another case in point. It revealed an unsuspected socioeconomic stratification and hierarchy among textile workers based on the quality of the material one worked with and/or produced,[43] a hierarchical stratification that has since then been documented in greater

---

of L. Caecilius Jucundus's financial dossier, an *argentarius* from Pompeii, see Jean Andreau, *Les affaires de Monsieur Jucundus* (Rome: École Française de Rome, 1974).

41. Seminal studies (partly based on epigraphic evidence) remain those by Duncan-Jones. Richard Duncan-Jones, *The Economy of the Roman Empire: Quantitative Studies*, 2nd ed. (Cambridge: Cambridge University Press, 1982); Duncan-Jones, *Structure and Scale in the Roman Economy* (Cambridge: Cambridge University Press, 1990). More recently, see Alan Bowman and Andrew Wilson, eds., *Quantifying the Roman Economy: Methods and Problems* (Oxford: Oxford University Press, 2009).

42. Sandra R. Joshel, *Work, Identity, and Legal Status at Rome: A Study of the Occupational Inscriptions* (Norman: University of Oklahoma Press, 1992); Tran, *Les membres des associations*.

43. Guy Labarre and Marie-Thérèse Le Dinahet, "Les métiers du textile en Asie Mineure de l'époque hellénistique à l'époque impériale," in *Aspects de l'artisanat du textile dans le monde méditerranéen (Égypte, Grèce, monde romain)*, Collection de l'institut d'archéologie et d'histoire de l'antiquité, Université Lumière-Lyon 2 (Paris: de Boccard, 1996), 64–67.

details in Tran's survey of the *artisans* and *commerçants* of the Latin West.[44] Labarre and Le Dinahet's study thus confirmed the existence in the eastern part of the Roman Empire of what Paul Veyne had identified as the *plebs media*,[45] and somewhat anticipated Nijf's discovery in Asian inscriptions of craftsmen and traders among the local elites, a phenomenon also clearly observed in the western regions.[46] Though often overlooked by New Testament and early Christianity scholars, such studies could potentially help resolve the ongoing debate about the social composition of the first Christians, and help elaborate a more sophisticated social modeling of Roman society than the simplistic bipolarity once proposed by Justin J. Meggitt.[47] In other words, even if one may still be reluctant to immerse oneself in epigraphic sources, there is much insight to be gained from cross-disciplinary interaction with epigraphists and from regularly consulting the literature they produce.[48]

These generalities having been noted, we may now proceed to examine a particular inscription in detail and briefly explore how it might shed

---

44. Tran, *Les membres des associations*; Nicolas Tran, Dominus tabernae: *Le statut de travail des artisans et des commerçants de l'Occident romain (Ier siècle av. J.-C.-IIIe siècle ap. J.-C.)* (Rome: École Française de Rome, 2013), 2-5.

45. Paul Veyne, "La 'plèbe moyenne' sous le Haut-Empire romain," *Annales* 55, no. 6 (2000): 1169-99; cf. Emanuel Mayer, *The Ancient Middle Classes: Urban Life and Aesthetics in the Roman Empire* (Cambridge: Harvard University Press, 2012).

46. Nijf, *Civic World*, 21-22, 42; Tran, *Les membres des associations*.

47. Justin J. Meggitt, *Paul, Poverty and Survival* (Edinburgh: T&T Clark, 1998). Meggitt's thesis prompted a number of critical responses and studies. See Dale B. Martin, "Review Essay: Justin J. Meggitt, *Paul, Poverty and Survival*," *JSNT* 24 (2001): 51-64; Gerd Theissen, "The Social Structure of Pauline Communities: Some Critical Remarks on J. J. Meggitt, *Paul, Poverty and Survival*," *JSNT* 24 (2001): 65-84; Theissen, "Social Conflicts in the Corinthian Community: Further Remarks on J. J. Meggitt, *Paul, Poverty and Survival*," *JSNT* 25 (2003): 371-91; Steven J. Friesen, "Poverty in Pauline Studies: Beyond the So-called New Consensus," *JSNT* 26, no. 3 (2004): 323-61; John M. G. Barclay, "Poverty in Pauline Studies: A Response to Steven Friesen," *JSNT* 26 (2004): 363-66; Bruce W. Longenecker, "Exposing the Economic Middle: A Revised Economy Scale for the Study of Early Urban Christianity," *JSNT* 31 (2009): 243-78.

48. Among highly recommended journals and reviews are (in alphabetical order) the *American Journal of Philology*, *L'Année épigraphique*, the *Annual of the British School at Athens*, the *Bulletin de correspondance hellénique*, *Chiron*, *Epigraphica Anatolica*, *Hesperia*, the *Journal of Hellenic Studies*, the *Bulletin épigraphique* in the *Revue des études grecques*, *Supplementum Epigraphicum Graecum*, *Tyche*, and *Zeitschrift für Papyrologie und Epigraphik*.

light on the socioeconomic context of the early Christians. Focusing on one example, rather than conducting a broad and superficial survey of a wider corpus, should enable us to illustrate more precisely how inscriptions might be employed in studies of early Christianity.

3. The *lex portorii Asiae* and the Socioeconomic Context of Early Christianity in the Roman Province of Asia

As briefly mentioned, one of the most exciting epigraphic discoveries in recent years has been the unearthing of the *Monumentum Ephesenum*, a large marble slab containing the details of the *lex portorii Asiae* (the customs tax law of Asia), which was found in the Church of St. John in Selçuk (Ephesus) in 1976, only a year after the publication of Siegfried J. de Laet's magisterial study of *portoria*.[49] Initially deciphered and published by Helmut Engelmann and Dieter Knibbe in a special edition of *Epigraphica Anatolica*,[50] the inscription has since then received considerable attention from epigraphists and Roman historians, and has recently been reedited and amply commented on in a critical edition in the Oxford Studies in Ancient Documents series.[51] This is no doubt due to the significance of its text, which enlightens us on the geographical, social, and administrative structure of the Roman province of Asia under the Julio-Claudians. To date, it represents "the most substantial and significant of a corpus of surviving documents ... that offer information both about imperial and local customs dues and their development in the Late Republic and Empire, and about the relations between the *publicani* who exacted the taxes and Roman officials and the *Aerarium Saturni* [the state treasury at Rome]."[52] Self-evidently, this makes it a vital document for our understanding of the social world of the first Christian communities of western Asia Minor.

---

49. Siegfried J. de Laet, *Portorium: Étude sur l'organisation douanière chez les Romains, surtout à l'époque du Haut-Empire* (New York: Arno, 1975).

50. Helmut Engelmann and Dieter Knibbe, "Das Zollgesetz der Provinz Asia: Eine neue Inschrift aus Ephesos," *Epigraphica Anatolica* 14 (1989): 1–206.

51. M. Cottier et al., eds., *The Customs Law of Asia* (Oxford: Oxford University Press, 2008). For a bibliography of earlier studies of the inscriptions, see ibid., 19. Photographs of the slab may be viewed online at "The Customs Law of Asia (Oxford Studies in Ancient Documents, 2008)—Plates," http://www.csad.ox.ac.uk/lex-portorii/.

52. Cottier et al., *Customs*, 2.

The *lex* indeed gives remarkable insight into the development of fiscal and administrative policies during the late Republican and early Roman imperial eras, that is, between 75 BCE and 62 CE, during which the amendments (ll. 72-154) to the original *lex* (ll. 7-72), which may have been drafted as early as 120s BCE,[53] were appended by various consuls and three Neronian curators. Thus it provides evidence for Nero's taxation reforms in the face of popular discontentment toward the *societates publicanorum*, the equestrian tax-farming companies in charge of collecting indirect taxes on behalf of the state. It brings to light the administrative organization of the provincial taxation system, about which literary sources are parsimonious, revealing that such "system relied on a dense network of customs officials spread over a relatively wide geographical area."[54] It also confirms the importance of Ephesus, a strategic locus of Christian missionary activity in the 50s CE, as the administrative and economic center of the Roman province of Asia.

To be more specific, the *lex* gives ample details of Rome's legal dispositions to curb tax evasion and fight contraband (ll. 15-16, 20-22, 53-55), and to prevent the *publicani*'s abuses of power and corruption (ll. 47, 50-57).[55] It establishes the legal tax rate for most commercial goods at 2.5 percent (ll. 10-11), which was much less than at the most eastern frontier (25 percent).[56] However, rates were slightly higher for murex (5 percent; l. 20), a rare and luxurious commodity, and capped at five *denarii* per head for slaves (then 2.5 *denarii* from 17 BCE onward; ll. 12, 98), many of whom were imported from Asia Minor (and regions further east) and transited through its main harbors.[57] It enforces the registration of imported and exported commercial merchandise with customs officials, determines penalties for tax evasion, and sets rules for tax exemption on materials, personal belongings, or equipment to be used for private, public, or military purposes (ll. 10-15, 20-28, 40-66, 74-78, 88-98, 128-33). It prohibits *publicani* from demanding multiple customs dues and from holding up

---

53. Ibid., 8-10.

54. Onno van Nijf, "The Social World of Tax Farmers and their Personnel," in Cottier et al., *Customs*, 287.

55. See de Laet, *Portorium*, 437-46.

56. Richard Duncan-Jones, "Roman Customs Dues: A Comparative View," *Latomus* 65 (2006): 4.

57. William V. Harris, "Towards a Study of the Slave Trade," in *Rome's Imperial Economy: Twelve Essays* (Oxford: Oxford University Press, 2011), 70, 78-81.

ore cargo destined for Rome (ll. 16–18, 78–80). It regulates the location, maximum dimension, and signage of customs offices (ll. 29–38, 50–58, 120–21), where inscribed tariffs such as that discovered in Palmyra (*IGRR* 3.1056) were likely displayed.[58] It lays out the legal procedures for the attribution and administration of tax-farming leases, including the schedule for down payments, and the appointment of the lease *magistri* (ll. 99–112, 124–27, 133–46). It finally concludes with (fragmentary) regulations on the conduct of legal suits by Roman citizens and, possibly, *peregrini*, against *publicani* (ll. 147–53).[59]

As one can easily appreciate, the *lex portorii Asiae* is of crucial importance for our understanding of the Roman imperial and provincial administration under the Julio-Claudians. It reinforces the generally accepted view that the Roman Empire was rather well organized and carefully managed, with Rome, as the seat of legislative and executive power, being able to devise and implement regionally integrated legal and fiscal policies (which varied from emperor to emperor).[60] While this need not mean that Rome conceived and scrupulously executed a central economic policy, *une politique économique*, as modern states do[61]—Rome did have a "rudimentary and empirical" monetary policy[62]—it suggests that it was

---

58. See especially J. Teixidor, "Le tarif de Palmyre: 1. Un commentaire de la version palmyrénienne," *AuOr* 1 (1983): 235–52; John F. Matthews, "The Tax Law of Palmyra: Evidence for Economic History in a City of the Roman East," *JRS* 74 (1984): 157–80.

59. The damage to the stone is quite significant, with most of the bottom section missing. Stephen Mitchell has estimated that about a quarter of the remainder of the text may have been lost (approximately forty letters from each of the first twenty-four lines). Cottier et al., *Customs*, 18.

60. Dominic Rathbone, "Nero's Reforms of *Vectigalia* and the Inscription of the *Lex Portorii Asiae*," in Cottier et al., *Customs*, 251.

61. For a more exhaustive treatment of this question, see Andreau, *L'économie*, 201–216; Gloria Vivenza, "Roman Economic Thought," in Scheidel, *Cambridge Companion to the Roman Economy*, 25–44. Bowman and Wilson also refute the idea of a deliberate and planned economic policy and prefer to explain the Roman economy in terms of "an array of integrated economic institutions or patterns of behaviour." Bowman and Wilson, *Quantifying*, 21.

62. Elio Lo Cascio, "The Early Roman Empire: The State and the Economy," in Scheidel, Morris, and Saller, *Cambridge Economic History*, 629. Cf. A. H. M. Jones, "Inflation under the Roman Empire," in *The Roman Economy: Studies in Ancient Economic and Administrative History*, ed. P. A. Brunt (Oxford: Basil Blackwell, 1974), 187–227; Matthew Ponting, "Roman Silver Coinage: Mints, Metallurgy, and Production,"

interested in providing a basic legal and economic framework for its subjects to pursue commercial activities in a relatively peaceful and prosperous environment.[63]

More precisely, the *lex* is a telling testimony to the "Roman concern for the smooth working of the system of taxation through the employment of *publicani*, whose obligations—the take-up of their contracts, provisions of sureties, and the timing of payments—are carefully regulated, and for the integrity of military arrangements—for the free passage of war materials, soldiers, and their equipment."[64] At the same time, Rome's restrictive measures against the *publicani* plainly demonstrates its concern for popular complaints, as well as its determination to fight corruption, maintain the rule of law, and preserve the rights of both citizens and *peregrini* (see ll. 115–16). For as Nijf aptly explains, the corruption of the *publicani* was rife, indeed proverbial (see Tacitus, *Ann.* 13.50–51; *Dial.* 39.4.12):

> The creativity of the tax farmers [in exacting dues] was probably infinite, and the more audacious among them must have been able to amass considerable personal fortunes. I suspect that the corrupt tax collector is rather representative of how the system worked in practice. Peculation may well have outstripped *peculium* as a source of income and power of the *uilici* and *uicarii* involved in tax collection. But even when they were not personally corrupt, the fact that the tax farmers worked on commission can only have increased their zeal to tax whatever they could lay their hands on, thus raising state revenue. This may well have dampened official willingness to investigate anything but the worst excesses too deeply.[65]

The purpose of the *lex* was precisely to curb such abuses and to restore a sense of "justice" in imperial taxation. Thus it served a wider political

---

269–80, and Bruce Hitchner, "Coinage and Metal Supply," 281–86, both in Bowman and Wilson, *Quantifying the Roman Economy*. With regard to Ephesus specifically, see for instance Lyn Kidson, "Early Elements of the Corporate Form: Depersonalization of Business in Ancient Rome," *JNAA* 23 (2013): 27–36.

63. See Andreau, *L'économie*, 206–10; William V. Harris, "Roman Governments and Commerce, 300 BC–AD 300," in *Mercanti e politica nel mondo antico*, ed. Carlo Zaccagnini (Rome: L'Erma di Bretschneider, 2003), 275–309.

64. Cottier et al., *Customs*, 2.

65. Nijf, "Social World," 296–97. Cf. P. A. Brunt, "Publicans in the Principate," in *Roman Imperial Themes* (Oxford: Clarendon, 1990), 383; Bang, *Roman Bazaar*, 202–38.

agenda and propaganda purpose.⁶⁶ This demonstrates that, despite endemic corruption and maladministration,⁶⁷ Rome did try to maintain a certain administrative control of territories subjected to its *imperium*,⁶⁸ and that Nero aspired to be perceived as a benevolent ruler (following the view that "emperors were meant to spend generously and tax sparingly").⁶⁹ Inscriptions erected in honor of customs officials, and dedications by tax farmers to the emperor, also illustrate that *publicani* were in search of social recognition and legitimacy, and that the state perceived them to be vital elements for its financial prosperity.⁷⁰ The earliest clauses of the *lex* (i.e., prior to the Augustan revisions of 17 BCE) in fact reveal that Rome had identified and taken advantage of "the most lucrative source of tolls," the Bosporus (whose southern side was initially included in the province of Asia; see ll. 13–14, 22–25). In a sense, these clauses present the annexation of the Attalid Kingdom, which spanned from the Bosporus to Bithynia, as "a highly intrusive act of economic imperialism"⁷¹—the economic incentive is particularly evident in Cicero's speech in support of C. Pompeius's Asian campaign against Mithridates (*Leg. man.* 2.4–6; 5.11; 6.14–19).

Stephen Mitchell's remark raises some intriguing questions as to the nature of the Roman economy and taxation system, especially vis-à-vis its evolution from the Republican era to the imperial era and its relation to Roman imperialism. To what extent might have economic interests fueled imperialistic aspirations, foreign markets and tribute (in the form of war booty and taxation revenues) functioning as an incentive for military expansion? To what extent might have Rome's prosperity been an indirect consequence of military ambitions? In other words, were Rome's

---

66. Rathbone, "Nero's Reforms," 260–67, 275–78.

67. See for instance P. A. Brunt, "Charges of Provincial Maladministration under the Early Principate," in *Roman Imperial Themes*, 53–95.

68. Much has been written on the subject. For a good introductory summary, see John Richardson, "The Administration of the Empire," in *The Last Age of the Roman Republic, 146–43 B.C.*, vol. 9 of, *Cambridge Ancient History*, ed. J. A. Crook, Andrew Lintott, and Elizabeth Rawson (Cambridge: Cambridge University Press, 1994), 564–98. For a helpful bibliographic review, see Nathalie Barrandon and François Kirbihler, eds., *Administrer les provinces de la République romaine: Actes du colloque de l'université de Nancy II 4–5 juin 2009* (Rennes: Presses Universitaires de Rennes, 2010), 9–20.

69. Rathbone, "Nero's Reforms," 276.

70. Nijf, "Social World," 301–305; Rathbone, "Nero's Reforms," 267.

71. Stephen Mitchell, "Geography, Politics, and Imperialism in the Asian Customs Law," in Cottier et al., *Customs*, 201.

conquests purely motivated by military and political agendas? Or were they driven by economic interests as well? Unsurprisingly, Rostovtzeff thought the latter played a major role in Roman imperialism. Victories in the Punic wars, he surmised, greatly enriched the peasant state that was Rome and allowed the emergence of a well-to-do bourgeoisie that cultivated capitalistic interests, and that would later support the state's imperialistic expansion throughout the Mediterranean.[72] Badian objected, finding this interpretation too anachronistic, while Frank rejected mercantilism as the driving force of Roman imperialism.[73]

To be fair to Rostovtzeff, it is hard to deny that Roman imperialism was without any economic consequences.[74] In the late Republican era, one could certainly make the case that foreign tribute greatly contributed to Rome's enrichment (and paid for its expensive wars),[75] at least up until the beginning of the Principate, from which time wealth started to be redistributed to the provinces (mainly in the form of civic benefactions and the construction of public infrastructure).[76] As Rome expanded, the burden of taxation was also progressively shifted away from Roman citizens and Italians and placed on subdued provincial subjects, exemption from taxes being one of the greatest privileges an emperor could bestow. This new policy effectively benefited the imperial elites, which leased the farming of indirect taxes, as well as the provincial elites, to whom Caesar had granted the right to collect local direct taxes.[77] At the same time, the advent of the

---

72. Michael Ivanovitch Rostovtzeff, "The Role of Economic Motivation," in *Imperialism in the Roman Republic*, ed. Erich S. Gruen (New York: Holt, Rinehart and Winston, 1970), 85–90.

73. Ernst Badian, "The Lack of Economic Motivation," in Gruen, *Imperialism*, 91–94; Tenney Frank, *Roman Imperialism* (New York: Macmillan, 1914), 277–97.

74. See especially William V. Harris, "On War and Greed in the Second Century B.C.," *AHR* 76 (1971): 1371–85. Cf. Pleket, "Economic History," 248–51.

75. See for instance Toni Ñaco del Hoyo, "The Republican 'War Economy' Strikes Back: A 'Minimalist' Approach," in *Administrer les provinces de la République romaine: Actes du colloque de l'université de Nancy II 4–5 juin 2009*, ed. Nathalie Barrandon and François Kirbihler (Rennes: Presses Universitaires de Rennes, 2010), 171–80.

76. A. H. M. Jones, "Ancient Empires and the Economy: Rome," in Brunt, *Roman Economy*, 114–39. For a recent examination of civic munificence in the Greek East, see Arjan Zuiderhoek, *The Politics of Munificence in the Roman Empire: Citizens, Elites, and Benefactors in Asia Minor* (Cambridge: Cambridge University Press, 2009).

77. Ernst Badian, *Publicans and Sinners: Private Enterprise in the Service of the Roman Republic* (Oxford: Basil Blackwell, 1972), 26–47; Claude Nicolet, *Tributum: Recherches sur la fiscalité directe sous la république romaine* (Bonn: Habelt, 1976);

pax Romana would profit the Roman and Italian merchants and financiers present throughout the Mediterranean since the third to second centuries BCE, and especially in the Aegean islands and Asia Minor.[78] By building roads, bridges, or water points, which facilitated transportation and communication, by practically eradicating piracy, and by establishing garrisons along the major trade routes, the Roman army also played an important role, albeit an indirect one, in the prosperity of the empire, and facilitated commercial exchanges between its various provinces and with distant eastern regions such as Arabia or even India.[79] Meanwhile, the direct taxation (in coins) of conquered provinces stimulated interregional trade and monetary circulation.[80] It is therefore not unreasonable to conclude that, not unlike modern empires, a confluence of political and economic interests gave rise to this "intrusive economic imperialism of the Roman state."[81]

More often than not, it is in fact quite difficult to distinguish politics from socioeconomics. As Jean Andreau has remarked, the two remain intertwined: Rome's "vie économique dépendait de l'existence de l'Empire

---

Brunt, "Publicans," 354–57, 388–93; Claude Nicolet, *Censeurs et publicains: Économie et fiscalité dans la Rome antique* (Paris: Fayard, 2000), 297–319.

78. See especially Hatzfeld's epigraphic survey, and its revision by Müller and Hasenohr. Jean Hatzfeld, "Les Italiens résidant à Délos mentionnés dans les inscriptions de l'île," *BCH* 36 (1912): 5–218; Hatzfeld, *Les trafiquants italiens dans l'Orient hellénique* (New York: Arno, 1975); Christel Müller and Claire Hasenohr, eds., *Les Italiens dans le monde grec: IIe siècle av. J.-C.-Ier siècle ap. J.-C.: Circulation, activités, intégration: Actes de la table ronde, École normale supérieure Paris 14–16 mai 1998*, BCH-Supp 41 (Athens: École française d'Athènes, 2002). Cf. Harris, "War and Greed," 1383.

79. See Steven E. Sidebotham, *Roman Economic Policy in the Erythra Thalassa 30 B.C.-A.D. 217* (Leiden: Brill, 1986); Dick Whittaker, "Le commerce romain avec l'Inde et la prise de décision économique," *Topoi* 10 (2000): 267–88. See also the contributions by I. Haynes ("Britain's First Information Revolution: The Roman Army and the Transformation of Economic Life"), L. Wierschowski ("Das römische Heer und die ökonomische Entwicklung Germaniens in den ersten Jahrzehnten des 1. Jahrhunderts"), and P. Morizot ("Impact de l'armée romaine sur l'économie de l'Afrique") in *The Roman Army and the Economy*, ed. Paul Erdkamp (Amsterdam: Gieben, 2002), 111–26, 264–92, 345–74.

80. Keith Hopkins, "Taxes and Trade in the Roman Empire (200 B.C.-A.D. 400)," *JRS* 70 (1980): 101–25. Cf. Barbara Levick, "The Roman Economy: Trade in Asia Minor and the Niche Market," *GR* 51 (2004): 186–88.

81. Cottier et al., *Customs*, 3. Cf. Harris, "War and Greed," 1385. See also the instructive discussion in Harris, "Governments and Commerce."

... elle était liée à l'existence même de l'Empire comme domination unique contrôlant l'ensemble de la Méditerranée."[82] Unsurprisingly, the symbiosis between politics and economics, and the duplicity between imperial and private interests, are in evidence in the *lex* itself, which makes reference to a certain P. Vedius Pollio, a close equestrian friend of Augustus who served as his procurator in Asia (even though he did not have *imperium*), and the only named individual in the whole inscription (apart from the consuls responsible for the various amendments). Initially sent to Ephesus after the battle of Actium around 31–30 BCE to implement a διάταξις (i.e., a *constituo*), and thus to put an end to the fraudulent sales of priesthoods at the Artemis sanctuary and to organize the quinquennial games in honor of Augustus,[83] Pollio effectively acted as the "*quasi*-governor of Asia" on behalf of Augustus.[84]

Interestingly, it is not with regard to his official administrative functions that he receives a mention in the *lex*, but with regard to the grant of a partial immunity (ἀτέλια) of customs dues for imports and exports of up to 10,000 *denarii* (ll. 96–97), which he was awarded by senatorial decree (συγκλήτου δόγματι). Unfortunately, the *lex* clarifies neither the nature nor the purpose (i.e., whether it was for public or private use) of the goods that Pollio might have been importing and exporting in and out of Asia. Given that he owned wine estates in Campania, Chios, and Cos, one is tempted to think that these shipments contained some of the refined wine he produced and exported throughout the Mediterranean.[85] Pollio

---

82. Andreau, *L'économie*, 246.

83. K. M. T. Atkinson, "The 'Constitutio' of Vedius Pollio at Ephesus," *RIDA* 9 (1962): 261–89; Peter Scherrer, "Augustus, die Mission des Vedius Pollio und die Artemis Ephesia," *JÖAI* 60 (1990): 87–101.

84. Cottier et al., *Customs*, 142. Cf. Paulus de Rohden and Hermann Dessau, "213. P. Vedius Pollio," in *Prosopographia Imperii Romani* 3:390–91; J. Keil, "8. P. Vedius Pollio," PW 8A:568–70; Ségolène Demougin, "73. P. Vedius Pollio," in *Prosopographie des chevaliers romains julio-claudiens (43 av. J.-C.–70 ap. J.-C.)* (Rome: École Française de Rome, 1992), 83–84; Ronald Syme, "Who Was Vedius Pollio?" *JRS* 51 (1961): 23–30; Atkinson, "Vedius." His influence in the province remained visible for decades, and many of his direct and indirect descendants became Asiarchs, *archiereis*, and even senators in the second–third century CE. See François Kirbihler, "P. Vedius Rufus, père de P. Vedius Pollio," *ZPE* 160 (2007): 261–71; Kirbihler, "Vivre à Rome pour les Flavii Vedii: L'installation d'une famille provinciale dans la capitale," in *Habiter en ville au temps de Vespasien*, ed. Marie-José Kardos (Nancy: ADRA, 2011), 117–38.

85. Amphora bearing the stamp "PVEPOL" have recently been discovered at

may have indeed used his official position and connection with Augustus, whose cult he helped organize in Asia and beyond,[86] to secure an advantageous tax rate for his trading activities. This apparent conflict of interest, as moderns might view it, thus further illustrates the blurred line between public and private interests, between official function and private enterprise, which was characteristic of Roman economic imperialism.

But to return to matters of greater relevance to New Testament and early Christianity scholars, the *lex* offers some interesting, though indirect, insight into the way an Ephesian audience might have understood Paul's evangelistic message and the moral exhortations contained in the letter to which it was supposedly destined (assuming, for the sake of experiment, that the letter was written to the first Ephesian Christians).[87] In light of the *lex*, the admonition to lie and steal no longer in Eph 4:25 and 4:28 takes on a new resonance and might have been an unpleasant reminder to Christian traders seeking to evade *portoria* (or to Christian *publicani* accustomed to exact more than they should). Likewise, the imperative to refrain from filthy and foolish language (λόγος σαπρός, αἰσχρότης, μωρολογία, εὐτραπελία) in 4:29 and 5:4 may have been aimed at the popular sport of calling *publicani* names.[88] The reference to the seal (see σφραγίζω) of the Holy Spirit in Eph 1:13 and 4:30 (cf. 2 Cor 1:22) also takes on a new significance in light of the σφραγίς identifying slaves mentioned in the *lex*

Masada, at Caesarea, and in Herod the Great's fortified complex in southern Judea. See Gérald Finkielsztejn, "P. Vedius Pollio, producteur de vin à Chios et Cos et fournisseur d'Hérode le Grand," in *Grecs, Juifs, Polonais: À la recherche des racines de la civilisation européenne: Actes du colloque organisé à Paris par l'Académie Polonaise des Sciences le 14 novembre 2003* (Paris: Académie Polonaise des Sciences, 2006), 123–39. Cf. Kirbihler, "Vedius," 263–65.

86. See Atkinson, "Vedius"; Scherrer, "Vedius."

87. The reference ἐν Ἐφέσῳ in Eph 1:1 is missing in the oldest and most significant manuscripts (e.g., P[46] ℵ* B), and it is likely that the letter was never written to the first Ephesian Christians. The authorship is of course much disputed as well. See Philipp Vielhauer, *Geschichte der urchristlichen Literatur: Einleitung in das Neue Testament, die Apokryphen und die Apostolischen Väter* (Berlin: de Gruyter, 1975), 204–212; Helmut Koester, *History and Literature of Early Christianity*, vol. 2 of *Introduction to the New Testament*, 2nd ed. (Berlin: de Gruyter, 2000), 271–75; Paul R. Trebilco, *The Early Christians in Ephesus from Paul to Ignatius* (Cambridge: Eerdmans, 2007), 89–94.

88. See Nijf, "Social World," 281–82. For a more detailed discussion of this Ephesian passage, see Jeremy F. Hultin, *The Ethics of Obscene Speech in Early Christianity and Its Environment* (Leiden: Brill, 2008), 173–213.

(most likely a neck collar, rather than a brand or tattoo; l. 119).[89] The term is likely to have focused the audience's attention on the visible aspect of such immaterial spiritual reality, thereby implying somewhat that those who have been sealed by the Spirit ought to be clearly recognizable by their morally upright life.

In addition, the *lex* helps clarify the socioeconomic context that might have informed Luke's account of the social disturbances at Ephesus and of Paul's farewell speech at Miletus in Acts 19–20.[90] Paul's detachment from materialistic concerns and his exemplary attitude with financial matters strikingly contrast with the avarice of the local silversmiths and the corruption of the *publicani* and Artemesion priests. Contrary to some of his contemporaries, Paul is presented as morally irreproachable and innocent of any wrongdoing in his ministry (Acts 20:26), as having coveted no one's silver or gold (20:33), but as having provided for his own needs by his own means (20:34).[91] Paul's leadership style, whereby he put the needs of others first and sought to alleviate the plight of the weak and suffering (20:35; cf. Phil 2:3–8), could not have differed more from the self-serving and self-gratifying behavior of the civic and religious local authorities. By thus emulating Christ's dictum that it is better to give than to receive (20:35), Paul's leadership is effectively depicted as a powerful alternative to the dominant culture of idolatry and materialism in Ephesus, and "as embodying and passing on the model of Christian discipleship and leadership taught and lived by Jesus."[92]

Finally, the *lex* plainly illustrates that Rome was concerned with maintaining the effective and unrestrained circulation of people and resources throughout the provinces, and that it recognized the importance of Ephesus as a strategic commercial hub, the largest *emporium* in Asia according to Strabo (*Geogr.* 12.8.15, 14.1.24).[93] It further suggests that the rapid

---

89. See Christoph Schäfer, "Zur Cφραγίc von Sklaven in der lex portorii provinciae Asiae," *ZPE* 86 (1991): 193–98.

90. For a detailed treatment of the significance of this speech vis-à-vis Paul's leadership ethos and lifestyle, see in particular Steve Walton, *Leadership and Lifestyle: The Portrait of Paul in the Miletus Speech and 1 Thessalonians*, SNTSMS 108 (Cambridge: Cambridge University Press, 2000).

91. See ibid., 89–91.

92. Ibid., 134–35; see also 183–84.

93. See Hatzfeld, *Les trafiquants italiens*, 101–4; Levick, "Roman Economy." On the importance of its harbor, see for instance Heinrich Zabehlicky, "Preliminary Views of the Ephesian Harbor," in *Ephesos, Metropolis of Asia: An Interdisciplinary Approach*

propagation of Christian missionaries throughout the empire was greatly facilitated by the pacification of the provinces (despite residual pockets of banditry), by a reasonably effective enforcement of the rule of law, by good transport infrastructures,[94] and by existing networks of artisans, traders, and commercial and/or professional associations.[95] The *lex* thus indirectly offers additional explanation for Paul's lengthy stay in the city. As a bustling commercial and religious center (with its Artemesion), Ephesus would have provided him with a reasonably safe and politically stable environment (despite Acts 19:23-40), and with an economically and demographically dynamic context in which to pursue his occupational and missionary activities. The steady flow of travelers visiting the city and/or passing through the province must thus have renewed his audience regularly and effortlessly, which must have contributed to the rapid and effective dissemination of his message among Italian and Roman travelers, who constituted the majority of his missionary support group.[96]

At the same time, Ephesus's easy accessibility by road and sea would have helped Paul stay in contact with disciples and churches he had established or hoped to visit (see 1 Cor 16:19; 2 Cor 1:8; Phlm 22, if indeed it was written from Ephesus), as well as with coworkers and independent missionaries such as Apollos (see 1 Cor 16:12)—Cicero had no difficulty sending and receiving private mail from Ephesus (*Att.* 6.8.4; cf. 5.13.1, 6.8.1). From there, Paul could have organized and supervised evangelistic activities up the Maeander river toward the eastern frontier of the province, as far as Laodicea, Hierapolis, and Colossae in the Lycus Valley, by sending missionary delegates such as Epaphras (see Col 1:7, 4:12-13).[97] Just as

---

to Its Archaeology, Religion, and Culture, ed. Helmut Koester, HTS 41 (Valley Forge, PA: Trinity Press International, 1995), 201-15.

94. See Cilliers Breytenbach, "The Rise and Expansion of Christianity in Asia Minor: First Steps towards a New Harnack," Early Christianity 2 (2011): 549-50.

95. See most recently Richard S. Ascough, "Redescribing the Thessalonians' 'Mission' in Light of Graeco-Roman Associations," NTS 60 (2014): 61-82. See also Dominic Rathbone, "Merchant Networks in the Greek World: The Impact of Rome," in Greek and Roman Networks in the Mediterranean, ed. Irad Malkin, Christy Constantakopoulou, and Katerina Panagopoulou (London: Routledge, 2009), 299-310.

96. See Edwin A. Judge, "The Roman Base of Paul's Mission," in The First Christians in the Roman World: Augustan and New Testament Essays, ed. James R. Harrison (Tübingen: Mohr Siebeck, 2008), 553-67; repr. from TynBul 56 (2005): 103-17. Cf. Breytenbach, "Rise," 550.

97. Cilliers Breytenbach, "Probable Reasons for Paul's Unfruitful Missionary

Corinth, where Paul spent considerable time, Ephesus was undoubtedly a strategic location that would have allowed him to optimize the exposure of his evangelistic message, and thus maximize the success of his mission. Paul, who lacked no strategic thinking when it came to funding his missionary activities,[98] must have immediately recognized the potential of Ephesus and exploited it to the full. As a vibrant city located at the junction between East and West, Ephesus itself represented a wide-open door to the rest of the world (see 1 Cor 16:9).

Bibliography

Andreau, Jean. *Les affaires de Monsieur Jucundus*. Rome: École Française de Rome, 1974.

———. *L'économie du monde romain*. Paris: Ellipses, 2010.

———. *La vie financière dans le monde romain: Les métiers de manieurs d'argent (IVe siècle av. J.-C.–IIIe siècle ap. J.-C)*. Rome: École Française de Rome, 1987.

Ascough, Richard S. *Paul's Macedonian Associations: The Social Context of Philippians and 1 Thessalonians*. WUNT 2/161. Tübingen: Mohr Siebeck, 2003.

———. "Redescribing the Thessalonians' 'Mission' in Light of Graeco-Roman Associations." *NTS* 60 1 (2014): 61–82.

Atkinson, K. M. T. "The 'Constitutio' of Vedius Pollio at Ephesus." *RIDA* 9 (1962): 261–89.

Badian, Ernst. *Publicans and Sinners: Private Enterprise in the Service of the Roman Republic*. Oxford: Basil Blackwell, 1972.

———. "History from 'Square Brackets.'" *ZPE* 79 (1989): 59–70.

Attempts in Asia Minor (A Note on Acts 16:6–7)," in *Die Apostelgeschichte und die hellenistische Geschichtsschreibung*, ed. Eckhard Plümacher, Cilliers Breytenbach, and Jens Schröter (Leiden: Brill, 2004), 163. On Epaphras's role in Paul's "missionary network," see Paul R. Trebilco, "Christians in the Lycus Valley: The View from Ephesus and from Western Asia Minor," 180–211, and Michael Trainor, "Excavating Epaphras of Colossae," 232–46, both in *Colossae in Space and Time: Linking to an Ancient City*, ed. Alan H. Cadwallader and Michael Trainor (Göttingen: Vandenhoeck & Ruprecht, 2011).

98. Julien M. Ogereau, *Paul's Koinonia with the Philippians: A Socio-historical Investigation of a Pauline Economic Partnership*, WUNT 2/377 (Tübingen: Mohr Siebeck, 2014).

Bang, Peter F. *The Roman Bazaar: A Comparative Study of Trade and Markets in a Tributary Empire*. Cambridge: Cambridge University Press, 2008.

Barclay, John M. G. "Poverty in Pauline Studies: A Response to Steven Friesen." *JSNT* 26 (2004): 363–66.

Barrandon, Nathalie, and François Kirbihler. *Administrer les provinces de la République romaine: Actes du colloque de l'université de Nancy II 4–5 juin 2009*. Rennes: Presses Universitaires de Rennes, 2010.

Bérard, François, et al. *Guide de l'épigraphiste: Bibliographie choisie des épigraphies antiques et médiévales*. 4th ed. Paris: Presses de l'École normale supérieure, 2010.

Bodel, John, ed. *Epigraphic Evidence: Ancient History from Inscriptions*. London: Routledge, 2001.

Bogaert, Raymond. *Banques et banquiers dans les cités grecques*. Leyde: Sijthoff, 1968.

———, ed. *Texts on Bankers, Banking and Credit in the Greek World*. Epigraphica 3. Leiden: Brill, 1976.

———. *Trapezitica Aegyptiaca: Recueil de recherches sur la banque en Égypte gréco-romaine*. Florence: Gonnelli, 1994.

Bousquet, Jean, ed. *Les comptes du quatrième et du troisième siècle*. Vol. 2 of *Corpus des inscriptions de Delphes*. Paris: de Boccard, 1989.

Bowman, Alan, and Andrew Wilson, eds. *Quantifying the Roman Economy: Methods and Problems*. Oxford: Oxford University Press, 2009.

Bresson, Alain. *L'économie de la Grèce des cités (fin VIe–Ier siècle a.C.): 1. Les structures et la production*. Paris: Colin, 2008.

Breytenbach, Cilliers. "Probable Reasons for Paul's Unfruitful Missionary Attempts in Asia Minor (A Note on Acts 16:6–7)." Pages 157–69 in *Die Apostelgeschichte und die hellenistische Geschichtsschreibung*. Edited by Eckhard Plümacher, Cilliers Breytenbach, and Jens Schröter. Leiden: Brill, 2004.

———. "The Rise and Expansion of Christianity in Asia Minor: First Steps towards a New Harnack." *Early Christianity* 2 (2011): 547–52.

Breytenbach, Cilliers, et al., eds. "Inscriptiones Christianae Graecae (ICG): Eine Datenbank der frühchristlichen Inschriften Kleinasiens und Griechenlands." http://www.epigraph.topoi.org.

Brunt, P. A. *Roman Imperial Themes*. Oxford: Clarendon, 1990.

Cadwallader, Alan H., and Michael Trainor, eds. *Colossae in Space and Time: Linking to an Ancient City*. Göttingen: Vandenhoeck & Ruprecht, 2011.

Chankowski, Véronique. *Athènes et Délos à l'époque classique: Recherches sur l'administration du sanctuaire d'Apollon délien*. Athens: École française d'Athènes, 2008.

Cooley, Alison E., ed. *Cambridge Manual of Latin Epigraphy*. Cambridge: Cambridge University Press, 2012.

Cottier, M., M. H. Crawford, C. V. Crowther, J. L. Ferrary, B. M. Levick, O. Salomies, and M. Wörrle, eds. *The Customs Law of Asia*. Oxford: Oxford University Press, 2008.

Davies, John, and John Wilkes, eds. *Epigraphy and the Historical Sciences*. Proceedings of the British Academy 177. Oxford: Oxford University Press, 2012.

Deissmann, Adolf. *Light from the Ancient East: The New Testament Illustrated by Recently Discovered Texts of the Graeco-Roman World*. 4th rev. ed. Translated by Lionel R. M. Strachan. New York: Harper & Brothers, 1927.

Demougin, Ségolène. *Prosopographie des chevaliers romains julio-claudiens (43 av. J.-C.–70 ap. J.-C.)*. Rome: École Française de Rome, 1992.

Dignas, Beate. *Economy of the Sacred in Hellenistic and Roman Asia Minor*. Oxford: Oxford University Press, 2002.

Dondin-Payre, Monique, and Nicolas Tran, eds. *Collegia: Le phénomène associatif dans l'Occident romain*. Bordeaux: Ausonius, 2012.

Duncan-Jones, Richard. *The Economy of the Roman Empire: Quantitative Studies*. 2nd ed. Cambridge: Cambridge University Press, 1982.

———. *Structure and Scale in the Roman Economy*. Cambridge: Cambridge University Press, 1990.

———. "Roman Customs Dues: A Comparative View." *Latomus* 65 (2006): 3–16.

Engelmann, Helmut, and Dieter Knibbe. "Das Zollgesetz der Provinz Asia: Eine neue Inschrift aus Ephesos." *Epigraphica Anatolica* 14 (1989): 1–206.

Erdkamp, Paul, ed. *The Roman Army and the Economy*. Amsterdam: Gieben, 2002.

Finkielsztejn, Gérald. "P. Vedius Pollio, producteur de vin à Chios et Cos et fournisseur d'Hérode le Grand." Pages 123–39 in *Grecs, Juifs, Polonais: À la recherche des racines de la civilisation européenne: Actes du colloque organisé à Paris par l'Académie Polonaise des Sciences le 14 novembre 2003*. Paris: Académie Polonaise des Sciences, 2006.

Finley, Moses I. *The Ancient Economy*. Berkeley: University of California Press, 1973.

———. *Studies in Land and Credit in Ancient Athens, 500–200 B.C.: The Horos-Inscriptions*. New Brunswick, NJ: Rutgers University Press, 1952.

Frank, Tenney. *Roman Imperialism*. New York: Macmillan, 1914.

———, ed. *An Economic Survey of Ancient Rome*. 6 vols. Paterson: Pageant, 1959.

Friesen, Steven J. "Poverty in Pauline Studies: Beyond the So-called New Consensus." *JSNT* 26, no. 3 (2004): 323–61.

Gerber, Albrecht. *Deissmann the Philologist*. Berlin: de Gruyter, 2010.

Grégoire, Henri. *Recueil des inscriptions grecques-chrétiennes d'Asie Mineure*. Vol. 1. Amsterdam: Hakkert, 1968.

Gruen, Erich S., ed. *Imperialism in the Roman Republic*. New York: Holt, Rinehart and Winston, 1970.

Harris, William V. "On War and Greed in the Second Century B.C." *AHR* 76 (1971): 1371–85.

———, ed. *The Inscribed Economy: Production and Distribution in the Roman Empire in the Light of instrumentum domesticum*. Ann Arbor: University of Michigan Press, 1993.

———. "Roman Governments and Commerce, 300 BC–AD 300." Pages 275–309 in *Mercanti e politica nel mondo antico*. Edited by Carlo Zaccagnini. Rome: L'Erma di Bretschneider, 2003.

———. *Rome's Imperial Economy: Twelve Essays*. Oxford: Oxford University Press, 2011.

Harrison, James R. *Paul's Language of Grace in Its Graeco-Roman Context*. WUNT 2/172. Tübingen: Mohr Siebeck, 2003.

Hatzfeld, Jean. "Les Italiens résidant à Délos mentionnés dans les inscriptions de l'île." *BCH* 36 (1912): 5–218.

———. *Les trafiquants italiens dans l'Orient hellénique*. New York: Arno, 1975.

Hultin, Jeremy F. *The Ethics of Obscene Speech in Early Christianity and Its Environment*. Leiden: Brill, 2008.

Johnson, Gary J. *Early-Christian Epitaphs from Anatolia*. Atlanta: Scholars Press, 1995.

Jones, A. H. M. *The Roman Economy: Studies in Ancient Economic and Administrative History*. Edited by P. A. Brunt. Oxford: Basil Blackwell, 1974.

Joshel, Sandra R. *Work, Identity, and Legal Status at Rome: A Study of the Occupational Inscriptions*. Norman: University of Oklahoma Press, 1992.

Judge, Edwin A. "The Roman Base of Paul's Mission." Pages 553–67 in *The First Christians in the Roman World: Augustan and New Testament Essays*. Edited by James R. Harrison. Tübingen: Mohr Siebeck, 2008. Repr. from *TynBul* 56 (2005): 103–17.
Keil, J. "8. P. Vedius Pollio." PW 8A:568–70.
Kidson, Lyn. "Early Elements of the Corporate Form: Depersonalization of Business in Ancient Rome." *JNAA* 23 (2013): 27–36.
Kirbihler, François. "P. Vedius Rufus, père de P. Vedius Pollio." *ZPE* 160 (2007): 261–71.
———. "Vivre à Rome pour les Flavii Vedii: L'installation d'une famille provinciale dans la capitale." Pages 117–38 in *Habiter en ville au temps de Vespasien*. Edited by Marie-José Kardos. Nancy: ADRA, 2011.
Kloppenborg, John S., and Richard S. Ascough, eds. *Attica, Central Greece, Macedonia, Thrace*. Vol. 1 of *Greco-Roman Associations: Texts, Translations, and Commentary*. BZNW 181. Berlin: de Gruyter, 2011.
Koester, Helmut. *History and Literature of Early Christianity*. Vol. 2 of *Introduction to the New Testament*. 2nd ed. Berlin: de Gruyter, 2000.
Labarre, Guy, and Marie-Thérèse Le Dinahet. "Les métiers du textile en Asie Mineure de l'époque hellénistique à l'époque impériale." Pages 49–116 in *Aspects de l'artisanat du textile dans le monde méditerranéen (Egypte, Grèce, monde romain)*. Collection de l'institut d'archéologie et d'histoire de l'antiquité, Université Lumière-Lyon 2. Paris: de Boccard, 1996.
Laet, Siegfried J. de. *Portorium: Étude sur l'organisation douanière chez les Romains, surtout à l'époque du Haut-Empire*. New York: Arno, 1975.
Landvogt, Peter. *Epigraphische Untersuchungen über den ΟΙΚΟΝΟΜΟΣ: Ein Beitrag zum hellenistischen Beamtenwesen*. Strassburg: Schauberg, 1908.
Laum, Bernhard. *Stiftungen in der griechischen und römischen Antike: Ein Beitrag zur antiken Kulturgeschichte*. 2 vols. Leipzig: Scientia, 1964.
Levick, Barbara. "The Roman Economy: Trade in Asia Minor and the Niche Market." *GR* 51 (2004): 180–98.
Liu, Jinyu. Collegia Centonariorum: *The Guilds of Textile Dealers in the Roman West*. Leiden: Brill, 2009.
Loane, Helen J. *Industry and Commerce of the City of Rome (50 B.C.–200 A.D.)*. Baltimore: Johns Hopkins University Press, 1938.
Longenecker, Bruce W. "Exposing the Economic Middle: A Revised Economy Scale for the Study of Early Urban Christianity." *JSNT* 31 (2009): 243–78.

Longenecker, Bruce W., and Kelly D. Liebengood, eds. *Engaging Economics: New Testament Scenarios and Early Christian Reception*. Grand Rapids: Eerdmans, 2009.

MacMullen, Ramsay. "The Epigraphic Habit in the Roman Empire." *AJP* 103 (1982): 233–46.

———. *Christianizing the Roman Empire (A.D. 100–400)*. New Haven: Yale University Press, 1984.

Martin, Dale B. "Review Essay: Justin J. Meggitt, *Paul, Poverty and Survival.*" *JSNT* 24 (2001): 51–64.

Matthews, John F. "The Tax Law of Palmyra: Evidence for Economic History in a City of the Roman East." *JRS* 74 (1984): 157–80.

McLean, Bradley H., ed. *An Introduction to Greek Epigraphy of the Hellenistic and Roman Periods from Alexander the Great down to the Reign of Constantine (323 B.C.–A.D. 337)*. Ann Arbor: The University of Michigan Press, 2002.

Meggitt, Justin J. *Paul, Poverty and Survival*. Edinburgh: T&T Clark, 1998.

Meyer, Elizabeth A. "Explaining the Epigraphic Habit in the Roman Empire: Evidence of Epitaphs." *JRS* 80 (1990): 74–98.

Migeotte, Léopold. *L'emprunt public dans les cités grecques: Recueil des documents et analyse critique*. Paris: Les Belles Lettres, 1984.

———. *Les souscriptions publiques dans les cités grecques*. Geneva: Droz, 1992.

———. *Les finances des cités grecques*. Paris: Les Belles Lettres, 2014.

Mitchell, Stephen, and Constantina Katsari, eds. *Patterns in the Economy of Roman Asia Minor*. Swansea: Classical Press of Wales, 2005.

Momigliano, Arnaldo. "M. I. Rostovtzeff." *The Cambridge Journal* 7 (1954): 334–46.

Müller, Christel, and Claire Hasenohr, eds. *Les Italiens dans le monde grec: IIe siècle av. J.-C.–Ier siècle ap. J.-C. Circulation, activités, intégration: Actes de la table ronde, École normale supérieure Paris 14–16 mai 1998*. BCHSupp 41. Athens: École française d'Athènes, 2002.

Nicolet, Claude. *Tributum: Recherches sur la fiscalité directe sous la république romaine*. Bonn: Habelt, 1976.

———. *Censeurs et publicains: Économie et fiscalité dans la Rome antique*. Paris: Fayard, 2000.

Nijf, Onno M. van. *The Civic World of Professional Associations in the Roman East*. Amsterdam: Gieben, 1997.

Ogereau, Julien M. *Paul's Koinonia with the Philippians: A Socio-Historical Investigation of a Pauline Economic Partnership.* WUNT 2/377. Tübingen: Mohr Siebeck, 2014.

Pleket, H. W. "Economic History of the Ancient World and Epigraphy: Some Introductory Remarks." Pages 243–57 in *Akten des VI. Internationalen Kongresses für Griechische und Lateinische Epigraphik, München, 1972.* Munich: Beck, 1973.

———, ed. *Texts on the Economic History of the Greek World.* Epigraphica 1. Leiden: Brill, 1964.

Ramsay, William M. *The Cities and Bishoprics of Phrygia: Being an Essay of the Local History of Phrygia from the Earliest Times to the Turkish Conquest.* Vol. 1. Parts 1 and 2. Oxford: Clarendon, 1895–1897.

Rathbone, Dominic. "Merchant Networks in the Greek World: The Impact of Rome." Pages 299–310 in *Greek and Roman Networks in the Mediterranean.* Edited by Irad Malkin, Christy Constantakopoulou, and Katerina Panagopoulou. London: Routledge, 2009.

Richardson, John. "The Administration of the Empire." Pages 564–98 in *The Last Age of the Roman Republic, 146–43 B.C.* Vol. 9 of *Cambridge Ancient History.* Edited by J. A. Crook, Andrew Lintott, and Elizabeth Rawson. Cambridge: Cambridge University Press, 1994.

Robert, Louis. "L'épigraphie." Pages 453–97 in *L'histoire et ses méthodes.* Edited by C. Samaran. Paris: Gallimard, 1961. Repr., pages 65–109 in vol. 5 of *Opera Minora Selecta.* Amsterdam: Hakkert, 1989.

Rohden, Paulus de, and Hermann Dessau. *Prosopographia Imperii Romani.* Vol. 3. Berlin: Reimer, 1898.

Rostovtzeff, Michael Ivanovitch. *Geschichte der Staatspacht in der römischen Kaiserzeit bis Diokletian.* Leipzig: Dieterich, 1902.

———. *The Social and Economic History of the Hellenistic World.* 2 vols. Oxford: Clarendon, 1941.

———. *The Social and Economic History of the Roman Empire.* 2 vols. Oxford: Clarendon, 1926.

Schäfer, Christoph. "Zur Cφραγίc von Sklaven in der lex portorii provinciae Asiae." *ZPE* 86 (1991): 193–98.

Scheidel, Walter, ed. *The Cambridge Companion to the Roman Economy.* Cambridge: Cambridge University Press, 2012.

Scheidel, Walter, Ian Morris, and Richard Saller, eds. *The Cambridge Economic History of the Greco-Roman World.* Cambridge: Cambridge University Press, 2007.

Scherrer, Peter. "Augustus, die Mission des Vedius Pollio und die Artemis Ephesia." *JÖAI* 60 (1990): 87–101.

Sidebotham, Steven E. *Roman Economic Policy in the Erythra Thalassa 30 B.C.–A.D. 217*. Leiden: Brill, 1986.

Syme, Ronald. "Who Was Vedius Pollio?" *JRS* 51 (1961): 23–30.

Tabbernee, William. *Montanist Inscriptions and Testimonia: Epigraphic Sources Illustrating the History of Montanism*. Macon, GA: Mercer University Press, 1997.

Teixidor, J. "Le tarif de Palmyre: 1. Un commentaire de la version palmyrénienne." *AuOr* 1 (1983): 235–52.

Theissen, Gerd. "Social Conflicts in the Corinthian Community: Further Remarks on J. J. Meggitt, *Paul, Poverty and Survival*." *JSNT* 25 (2003): 371–91.

———. "The Social Structure of Pauline Communities: Some Critical Remarks on J. J. Meggitt, *Paul, Poverty and Survival*." *JSNT* 24 (2001): 65–84.

Tran, Nicolas. *Les membres des associations romaines: Le rang social des collegiati en Italie et en Gaule sous le haut empire*. Rome: École Française de Rome, 2006.

———. *Dominus tabernae: Le statut de travail des artisans et des commerçants de l'Occident romain (Ier siècle av. J.-C.–IIIe siècle ap. J.-C.)*. Rome: École Française de Rome, 2013.

Vielhauer, Philipp. *Geschichte der urchristlichen Literatur: Einleitung in das Neue Testament, die Apokryphen und die Apostolischen Väter*. Berlin: de Gruyter, 1975.

Walton, Steve. *Leadership and Lifestyle: The Portrait of Paul in the Miletus Speech and 1 Thessalonians*. SNTSMS 108. Cambridge: Cambridge University Press, 2000.

Waltzing, Jean-Pierre. *Étude historique sur les corporations professionnelles chez les Romains: Depuis les origines jusqu'à la chute de l'Empire d'Occident*. 4. vols. Louvain: Peeters, 1895–1900. Repr., Hildesheim: Olms, 1970.

Whittaker, Dick. "Le commerce romain avec l'Inde et la prise de décision économique." *Topoi* 10 (2000): 267–88.

Wissowa, G., et al., eds. *Paulys Realencyclopädie der classischen Altertumswissenschaft*. Stuttgart: Metzler, 1894–1978.

Woodhead, A. Geoffrey. *The Study of Greek Inscriptions*. 2nd ed. Cambridge: Cambridge University Press, 1981.

Zimmermann, Carola. *Handwerkervereine im griechischen Osten des Imperium Romanum.* Mainz: Römisch-germanisches Zentralmuseum, 2002.

Zuiderhoek, Arjan. *The Politics of Munificence in the Roman Empire: Citizens, Elites, and Benefactors in Asia Minor.* Cambridge: Cambridge University Press, 2009.

URBAN PORTRAITS OF THE "BARBARIANS" ON THE FRINGES OF THE ROMAN EMPIRE: THE ARCHAEOLOGICAL, NUMISMATIC, EPIGRAPHIC, AND ICONOGRAPHIC EVIDENCE

James R. Harrison

It is ironic that the barbarians, whom the Romans confined to the margins of their empire, were nonetheless depicted prominently in the triumphal iconography of Roman cities and colonies. The Augustan triumphal arches were ubiquitous in the Greek East and Latin West, as were the carefully placed barbarian reliefs on monuments within the sacred spaces of Rome itself.[1] In each case, the propagandist value of the monument—including its reliefs, inscriptions, and placement—was intended to have full ideological impact on city dwellers, who probably had never encountered members of the barbarian tribes except at a distance. The imperial poets also continuously referred to the conquest of the barbarian hordes by the iconic Augustus.[2] Apparently the barbarian tribes, who were marginalized

---

1. See James R. Harrison, "'More Than Conquerors' (Rom 8:37): Paul's Gospel and the Augustan Triumphal Arches of the Greek East and Latin West," *Buried History* 47 (2011): 3–20. This article draws on its discussion of three of the Augustan arches, while adding new inscriptional and sacred space discussion in the presentation below. See also Harrison, "Paul's 'Indebtedness' to the Barbarian (Rom 1:14) in Latin West Perspective," *NovT* 55 (2013): 311–48. For general discussions of Roman attitudes to barbarians, see Yves Albert Dauge, *Le barbare: recherches sur la conception romaine de la barbarie et de la civilisation*, Collection Latomus 176 (Brussels: Latomus, 1981); Iain M. Ferris, *Enemies of Rome: Barbarians through Roman Eyes* (Stroud: Sutton, 2000). For Greek attitudes, see Thomas Harrison, ed., *Greeks and Barbarians* (Edinburgh: Edinburgh University Press, 2011).

2. Horace continually emphasizes Augustus's subjugation of the nations on behalf of Rome (*Carm.* 1.2.50–53; 1.12.33–60; 1.35.25–40; 1.37; 3.3.37–48; 3.5; 3.14; 4.2.33–

by virtue of their inferior culture and speech, had unwittingly become the center of their conquerors' attention.

At the outset, a brief example of this Roman preoccupation with the barbarians in the hallowed sacred spaces of Rome is apposite. The inscriptional eulogies, erected in honor of Roman commanders who had achieved victories over the barbarian hordes at the edges of empire, present triumphal accounts of the conquest of the "barbarian" hordes threatening the far-flung rule of Rome. For example, Aulus Didius, the consul and governor of Moesia in 36 CE, overcame a Gallic invader from the Danube,[3] depositing the barbarian leader's girdle in the temple of Jupiter Capitolinus (?) at Rome. Didius's meticulous concern with the sacred space of Rome in this instance is a potent tribute to the seriousness with which Romans viewed their military victories. Consequently the "glorious legate of Caesar," representing "war-powerful Rome," rendered to Jupiter the appropriate thanks for victory over the barbarian tribes threatening Roman civilization within the Danube boundary. Significantly, the language employed in the inscription also borders on a quasi-providential call to duty in the case of the commander: "Rome, O Aulus, raised you to a seat attended by ten thousand men ... deeds which called a consul to the great command." The inscription celebrates Aulus Didius's achievement over the subjugated barbarians thus:

> Didius begat you, but war-powerful Rome, O Aulus, raised you to a seat attended by ten thousand armed men. You drove out a Gaul who had looked upon the boundaries of the fair-flowing Danube, a scourge of Paeonia, by lighting fire signals and collecting troops. He from whom you sent to Zeus (Jupiter Capitolinus?) the token dedication of a (barbarian's) girdle when you were a glorious legate of Caesar, he loved arms and did with them deeds which called a consul to the great command.[4]

By contrast, those unfortunate individuals who had been exiled by Augustus to the periphery of the Roman Empire felt intensely their own marginalization as they eked out an existence among the marginalized barbarian tribes. This was particularly the case with the poet Ovid, whom

---

36; 4.5.25–36; 4.14; 4.15; *Saec.* 54–60; *Epod.* 9; *Ep.* 2.1.250–257). See also Ovid, *Tr.* 2.225–236; 4.2.1–74; Propertius, *Elegiae* 2.10; 3.4; 4.6.

3. On the anomaly of a Gallic invader from the Danube, see J. H. Oliver, "Epigramma magni momenti: *IG* IX, 1135," *GRBS* 8 (1967): 238–39.

4. For full discussion, see ibid., 237–39.

Augustus had exiled after a (still obscure) misdemeanor against the princeps (*Tr.* 2.121–154, 207–215, 240; 3.6.32).[5] The poet was removed from Rome to Tomis, which was situated in the region of the Black Sea (i.e., the Pontus Euxinus). Ovid's response to the barbarian peoples among whom he was exiled is intriguing because, notwithstanding its possible literary antecedents,[6] the poet responds with the cultural superiority of the Latin educated elite toward the uncivilized and uneducated tribes of the empire (*Tr.* 3.10.1–4; 3.14.46–52; 4.1.94; 5.7.50–74; 5.12.57–58). Ovid experiences geographical and social isolation living among the barbarian tribes: "Weary I lie among these far away people in this far away place" (*Tr.* 3.3.12–13); "A Roman will wander among Sarmatian shades, a stranger forever among barbarians" (*Tr.* 3.3.63). According to Ovid, the hostile climate of Tomis makes the barbarian tribes even more repulsive and loathsome in their appearance and drinking habits (*Tr.* 3.10.21–24). In sum, Ovid considers that he is experiencing a living "death" among the barbarians[7]—specifically, the Bessi, Getae, Basternae, and Sauromatae (*Tr.*

---

5. For discussion of the various theories regarding Ovid's exile, see John C. Thibault, *The Mystery of Ovid's Exile* (Berkeley: University of California Press, 1964).

6. It is beyond the scope of this paper to discuss the truthfulness of Ovid's rhetoric concerning his exile and the accuracy of his depiction of "barbarian" culture at Tomis. Gareth D. Williams (*Banished Voices: Readings in Ovid's Exile Poetry* [Cambridge: Cambridge University Press, 1994] argues that Ovid borrowed motifs from Virgil's *Aeneid* in his description of Tomis and its inhabitants. Since Virgil was not describing "true" barbarians but rather the rugged life of primitive Italians in his epic poem, Ovid's rhetoric on this remote part of the empire in the Black Sea, Williams proposes, also cannot be trusted geographically or historically. For a more positive assessment of Ovid's "antibarbarian" rhetoric and its accuracy, see Jan Felix Gaertner, *Ovid, Epistulae Ex Ponto, Book 1* (Oxford: Oxford University Press, 2005). More generally, see P. J. Davis, "The Colonial Subject in Ovid's Exile Poetry," *AJP* 123 (2002): 257–73; Emma Dench, *From Barbarians to New Men: Greek, Roman, and Modern Perceptions of Peoples from the Central Apennines* (Oxford: Oxford University Press, 1995).

7. Whatever the cause of his exile, Ovid depicts his banishment to Tomis as a "living death." It is as if Caesar in his "merciful wrath" had sent him to the waters of the Styx (*Tr.* 1.2.60–66; cf. 5.2.74–76; *Pont.* 1.8.24–27; 2.3.43–44). He portrays his situation of exile from Rome as so desperate—"my earlier and harder death" (*Tr.* 3.3.56)—that a longing for actual death consumes him (3.2.23–24; *Pont.* 1.5.85–86): "Ah me! that I have so often knocked upon the door of my own tomb but it has never opened to me!" Indeed, the poet even cites his own epitaph as a measure of his determination to die (*Tr.* 3.3.73–76). Ultimately, however, Ovid concedes that he was more scared that if his death wish were granted, he would die as an exile buried in the dreaded soil of

2.187–200; 3.10.5–6; 4.6.47–48)—and observes, with justified paranoia,[8] that only the walls and closed gates of the fortress at Tomis keep the hostile tribes at bay (*Tr.* 3.14.41–42; 4.1.67–68; 5.10.27). Here we see in miniature the irrational mixture of fear, loathing, mockery, and superiority that the barbarians aroused in the Roman educated elite.

Notwithstanding, it would be unwise to assume that such feelings toward the barbarians were universal among the Romans or other people groups of the empire. It is debatable whether there was a uniformly superior attitude toward the nations on the part of the Romans. Erich S. Gruen's nuanced reading of how Roman writers depicted nations such as the Gauls and Britons points in a different direction.[9] Moreover, there was a

---

Tomis (*Pont.* 1.257–258; cf. 3.1.5–6): "Often I pray for death, yet I even beg off from death for fear that the Sarmatian soil may cover my bones."

8. An inscription at Pisa (DocsAug §69), recounting the death of Gaius Caesar (4 CE: *Res Gestae* 14; Suetonius, *Tib.* 23), speaks of the victories (military and diplomatic) of the heir-apparent of Tiberius over the barbarian threat in this manner: "Gaius Caesar, son of Augustus (father of his country, pontifex maximus, guardian of the Roman empire and protector of the whole world), after the successful completion of his consulship campaigning beyond the furthermost territories of the Roman people, and doing noble service to the state in thoroughly conquering or winning over extremely large and warlike tribes, sustained wounds in the public service, and thanks to that misfortune was snatched by cruel fates from the Roman people." A stone fragment in Rome (DocsGaius §43b), probably from Claudius's triumphal arch on the Via Flaminia (Dio Cassius, *Historiae Romanae* 60.22.1; cf. *RIC* 1², "Claudius," §§30, 44), honors Claudius "because he conquered and received the surrender of eleven British kings without loss and was the first to subject barbarian races beyond the Ocean to the sovereignty of the Roman people." Note, too, the paranoia of the (late) anonymous author of *On Military Matters* 6.1 (fl. 366–375 CE), who speaks thus of the constant barbarian threat: "it must be recognised that wild nations are pressing against and howling around the Roman empire on all sides, and treacherous barbarism, protected by natural locations, is attacking all along the frontiers." For selections of the text, see David Cherry, *The Roman World: A Sourcebook* (Oxford: Blackwell, 2001), §42.

9. On Roman attitudes to the "other," see Erich S. Gruen, *Rethinking the Other in Antiquity* (Princeton: Princeton University Press, 2011), 115–96. On enlightened Greek attitudes on the nobility of barbarians, see Edith Hall, *Inventing the Barbarian: Greek Self-Definition through Tragedy* (Oxford: Clarendon, 1989), 211–23; see the writings of H. C. Baldry, n. 11 *infra*. Some of the Roman love poets showed little interest in the Julio-Claudian military "jingoism" against the barbarian nations, preferring the delights of love to the imperial propaganda (e.g., Propertius, 3.4.13–18). See Carol U. Merriam, "'Either with Us or against Us': The Parthians in Augustan Ideology," *Scholia* 13 (2004): 50–70. However, see the venomous stereotyping of barbarians in

mixed response toward the barbarians among the Greek philosophers and Roman writers. There was, to be sure, an imperialistic agenda regarding the "Romanization" of subject peoples. Pliny the Elder, to cite one example, believed that *humanitas* should be imposed on the barbarian tribes. Italy, the "parent of all lands," was chosen by the gods

> to gather together the scattered realms and to soften their customs and unite the discordant wild tongues of so many peoples into a common speech so that they might understand each other, and to give civilisation to mankind (*humanitatem homini*), in short to become the homeland of every people in the entire world.[10]

However, a papyrus fragment of Antiphon's *On Truth* (P.Oxy. 52.3647) reveals a different ideological perspective regarding barbarians. The fragment speaks of the physical homogeneity of the human race based on nature as opposed to distinctions originating from social class and law, even though the latter divisions remain entrenched in the world.

> The laws of our neighbours we know and revere: the laws of those afar we neither know nor revere. Thus in this we have been made barbarians with regard to one another. For by nature we are in all respects similarly endowed to be barbarian or Greek. One may consider those natural facts which are necessary in all men and provided for all in virtue of the same facilities—in these very matters none of us is separated off as a barbarian or a Greek. For we may all breathe into the air by way of our mouths and noses, we laugh when we are happy in our minds and we cry when we are in pain, we receive sounds by our hearing and we see with our eyes by light, we work with our hands and we walk on our feet.[11]

Cicero's *Pro Fonteio* (Greg Woolf, *Becoming Roman: The Origins of Provincial Civilisation in Gaul* [Cambridge: Cambridge University Press, 1998], 61–62).

10. Pliny the Elder, *Nat.* 3.39, cited in Woolf, *Becoming Roman*, 57. On the Roman assimilation of the Carthaginians, see Statius, *Silvae* 4.5.45–48. Paul, however, speaks of his obligation of "love" to Greek and barbarian (Rom 1:14; cf. 13:8–10), thereby rendering unimportant differences of social class (12:16b) and law (3:29–30; 10:12; 11:18–20; 12:14–21; 14:1–15:7) in the body of Christ.

11. The text is cited in Hall, *Inventing the Barbarian*, 218–20. For discussion of the philosophers' deliberations, Greek and Roman, on the barbarians, see H. C. Baldry, "The Idea of the Unity of Mankind," in *Grecs et barbares*, ed. Hans Schwabl (Vandoeuvres/Geneva: Fondation Hardt, 1962), 169–204; Baldry, *The Unity of Mankind in Greek Thought* (Cambridge: Cambridge University Press, 1965). Inexplicably, New

Furthermore, it would be equally naive to assume that there was universal positive regard among certain barbarian tribes toward other barbarian tribes. In Sophocles's *Ajax* 1290–1299, Teucer, the son of the Greek Telamon by a barbarian mother, responds to Agamemnon's racial abuse of him with these savage words:

> Pitiful creature, how can you be so blind as to argue the way you do? Are you not aware of the fact that your father's father Pelops long ago was a barbarian, a Phrygian? That Atreus, your own begetter, set before his brother a most unholy feast made from the flesh of his brother's children? And you yourself were born from a Cretan mother, whose father found a stranger straddling her and who was consigned by him to be prey for the mute fish. So being of such a kind, can you reproach a man like me for my lineage?[12]

Are the internal divisions among the barbarians one of the reasons why Paul—or the letter's pseudonymous author—highlights the ethnographically paradoxical polarity of "Scythian" and "barbarian" when speaking of the unity of diverse people groups in Christ (Col 3:11)?

Rome and its provincial clients, however, promoted their own version of "reconciliation" between different barbarian peoples. In 68 CE, on the obverse of a denarius from Spain we see busts of Gaul and Spain facing each other, with a small Victory placed in between. Below Spain is placed a horn of plenty, whereas below Gaul is an oblong shield. The legend is "Concord of the Spains and Gauls," but this is to be understood within the imperialistic framework of the legend on the reverse side of the coin: "Victory of the Roman People."[13]

In sum, we are faced with a more complex ideological landscape that we first imagined in locating social attitudes toward the "marginalized" barbarians and, indeed, in discerning the state of interpersonal relations among the barbarian tribes themselves. When we come to discuss the iconographic representation of barbarians the situation is equally complex. This article will explore the rendering of barbarians on the Augustan arches, temple reliefs, and monuments at the sites of Pisidian Antioch,

---

Testament scholars have overlooked Baldry's comprehensive coverage of the positive attitudes toward the barbarians in the ancient sources.

12. Baldry, *Unity of Mankind*, 32.

13. David C. Braund, *Augustus to Nero: A Sourcebook on Roman History 31 BC–AD 68* (Totowa: Barnes & Noble, 1985), §290 (= DocsGaius §72c).

Rome, La Turbie, and Susa, moving from the Greek East to the Latin West for a representative selection of evidence on the issue. We will also look at several inscriptions from the Latin West to see what light they throw on relations between the barbarians and Rome: are the relations more nuanced and reciprocal than we initially imagine? Throughout we will make some tentative suggestions on how this visual and inscriptional material might relate to the Pauline literature. However, most crucially, a series of methodological considerations have to be aired beforehand if we are to understand in a nuanced manner the Augustan propaganda and how this might relate to the apostle's understanding of his indebtedness to Greek and barbarian (Rom 1:14; cf. Col 3:11).

First, visual images do not necessarily interpret themselves and would have provoked complex reactions in contemporary viewers. Thus we must study carefully the inscriptional and numismatic evidence relevant to the sites in the Greek East and Latin West in order to clarify and interpret the ideology conveyed. This means that we have to situate the inscription properly in its local and wider historical context, if there is sufficient evidence for unpacking the latter perspective. Moreover, the state of preservation of the visual image and of its accompanying inscription may also pose problems for the accurate interpretation of the ideological intent of the monument. In two of the case studies of Augustan triumphal monuments and arches (§§1, 3.1, 3.2), we will pay detailed attention to their inscriptions, as well as to other relevant inscriptions from elsewhere in the empire, with a view to discerning the Roman attitude to barbarians in triumphal contexts.

Second, visual images are placed on monuments that stand physically in relation to other monuments within the city, or indeed, have iconographic and historical connection with other monuments elsewhere in the empire. In other words, the whole issue of the use of sacred space must be explored, including the ideology that emerges when the interrelation between the sites of various monuments is studied. In this regard, we will explore the ideological connections between monuments and buildings at Rome depicting humiliated barbarians and captive barbarian children (§2.2), as well as the ideological and historical connections between the La Turbie monument (Monaco, France: §3.1) and the arch of Susa (south of Turin, Italy: §3.2).

Third, we need to ask who might be erecting the triumphal monuments and why. The intentions of provincial clients in erecting monuments in honor of the Roman ruler's subjugation of the barbarians might not capture the subtle nuances of Augustus's approach to the nations in the *Res Gestae* or, indeed, reflect the actual historical circumstances (§§1, 2.1). Even if Augustus's self-presentation in the *Res Gestae* is propagandist and duplicitous, assuming for the sake of argument that the Tacitean portrait of Augustus as understood by Ronald Syme[14] is fundamentally correct,[15] we have to ask what the advantage was for Augustus in projecting such an image over against the more traditional Roman portrait of military *virtus* ("manliness"). In sum, visual images in the ancient world communicated the legitimacy of power. In the case of Augustus, it also involved the imposition of power by military force, or enforced social change by the process of Romanization, or conciliation by diplomatic overtures initiated and received.[16] Only by considering holistically the intentions of those erecting the monument and the motivations of the person honored will we come

---

14. For the argument that Augustus's "restoration of the Republic" was a hypocritical façade and that Tacitus's dark version of the Augustan Principate is to be preferred to the omissions, half-truths, and lies of the *Res Gestae*, see Ronald Syme, *The Roman Revolution* (Oxford: Oxford University Press, 1939), 2–3, 322–25, 404–5. For Tacitus's evaluation of Augustus, see Syme, *Tacitus*, 2 vols. (Oxford: Oxford University Press, 1958), esp. 1:431–32; cf. Donald Reynolds Dudley, *The World of Tacitus* (London: Secker & Warburg, 1968), 76–78; Karl Galinsky, *Augustan Culture: An Interpretative Introduction* (Princeton: Princeton University Press, 1996), 77–79. On the untruthfulness of the *Res Gestae*, see Ronald T. Ridley, *The Emperor's Retrospect: Augustus' Res Gestae in Epigraphy, Historiography and Commentary* (Leuven: Peeters, 2003). For more balanced approaches to Augustus's *Res Gestae*, each incorporating the new restoration of *Res Gestae* 34.1, see John Scheid, *RES GESTAE DIVI AUGUSTI: Hauts Faits du DIVIN AUGUSTE* (Paris: Les Belles Lettres, 2007); Alison E. Cooley, *Res Gestae Divi Augusti: Text, Translation, and Commentary* (Cambridge: Cambridge University Press, 2009). For an incisive critique of Syme and his interpretative legacy on Augustan studies, see E. A. Judge, *The First Christians in the Roman World: Augustan and New Testament Essays*, ed. James R. Harrison, WUNT 229 (Tübingen: Mohr Siebeck, 2008), 314–45.

15. For more nuanced portraits of the Augustan Principate over against Syme, see J. A. Crook, "Political History, 30 BC–AD 14" and "Augustus: Power, Authority, Achievement," in *The Augustan Empire 43 BC–AD 69*, vol. 10 of *The Cambridge Ancient History*, ed. Alan K. Bowman and Edward Champlin, 2nd ed. (Cambridge: Cambridge University Press, 1996), 70–112, 113–46; Erich S. Gruen, "The Expansion of the Empire under Augustus," in Bowman and Champlin, *Augustan Empire*, 147–97; Judge, *First Christians*, 34–345.

16. See the discussion of Jaś Elsner, "Inventing Imperium: Texts and the Propaganda of Monuments in Augustan Rome," in *Art and Text in Roman Culture*, ed. Jaś Elsner (Cambridge: Cambridge University Press, 1996), 32–53.

to a more incisive appraisal of what is actually happening in the transaction of honor and, consequently, the meaning of the visual imagery on the monument. We turn now to our three case studies.

1. THE SEBASTEION AND THE *RES GESTAE* AT PISIDIAN ANTIOCH:
A CASE STUDY IN THE INTERSECTION OF ICONOGRAPHY AND EPIGRAPHY

The complex history of the archaeological excavation of the site of Pisidian Antioch has already been extensively discussed by scholars and is not germane to our focus.[17] Near to the two main streets of Pisidian Antioch is the Sebasteion. The imperial sanctuary is approached by the Tiberia Plateau, which culminated in twelve steps, above which stood the arch of Augustus, constructed in 2/1 BCE.[18] This served as a propylon to the sanctuary proper. Since the extensive 1924 expedition of the University of Michigan, led by Francis W. Kelsey, the stairs and pavement had almost entirely disappeared by the next excavation, led by Stephen Mitchell and Marc Waelkens in 1982. The residents of nearby Yalvaç had removed the stones for their own building projects, with the result that by 2004 the foundations of the arch of Augustus were no longer to be found.[19] Thus our discussion of the remains of the arch of Augustus will be confined to a selection of the iconography documented in David Robinson's 1926

---

17. David M. Robinson, "Roman Sculptures from colonia Caesaria (Pisidian Antioch)," *Art Bulletin* 9 (1926): 5–69; Cornelius C. Vermeule, *Roman Imperial Art in Asia Minor* (New Haven: Belknap Press of Harvard University Press, 1963), 78–79; Stephen Mitchell and Marc Waelkens, *Pisidian Antioch: The Site and Its Monuments* (London: Duckworth, 1998), 146–47; B. B. Rubin "(Re)presenting Empire: The Roman Imperial Cult in Asia Minor, 31 BC–AD 63" (PhD diss., University of Michigan 2008), 38–44; Rubin, "Ruler Cult and Colonial Identity: The Imperial Sanctuary at Pisidian Antioch," in *Building a New Rome: The Roman Colony of Pisidian Antioch (25 BC–300 AD)*, ed. Elaine K. Gazda and Diana Y. Ng (Ann Arbor: Kelsey Museum of Archaeology, 2011), 33–60, esp. 41–44; Adrian John Ossi, *The Roman Honorific Arches of Pisidian Antioch: Reconstruction and Contextualization* (PhD diss., University of Michigan, 2010), 14–107. The important work of K. Tuchelt, "Bermerkugen zum Tempelbezirk von Antiochia ad Pisidiam," in *Beiträge zur Altertumskunde Kleinasiens: Festschrift für Kurt Bittel*, ed. Rainer Michael Boehmer and Harald Hauptmann (Mainz: von Zabern, 1983, 501–22) was unavailable to me.
18. For the dating, see Ossi, *Roman Honorific Arches*, 21.
19. Ibid., 15. For the dramatic contrast between the archaeological remains present at the site in 1924 and 2004, see Rubin, "Ruler Cult," 40 fig. 3.7 and 48 fig. 3.17.

pioneering article,[20] with the pictorial evidence sourced from the Kelsey Museum Archives, the original pieces now being at the Yalvaç Museum. The upper section of the Augustan arch is the best preserved since the lower section had disappeared long before the Michigan excavations.

On the frieze on the western outer face of the Augustan arch and in the spandrels over the archways of the monument, there was rich and complex iconography that articulated the Augustan ideology of rule. First, there was inscribed a *sidus Iulium*, the apotheosis sign of his adoptive father, Julius Caesar.[21] The dedicatory inscription to Augustus on the arch bears the same message of Caesar's apotheosis and Octavian's adoption into the Julian family with the title "son of god."[22]

Second, the frieze contained a Capricorn, the astrological sign prophetically associated with Augustus's birth (Suetonius, *Aug.* 94.12; Dio Cassius, *Historiae Romanae* 56.25.5; Manilius, *Astronomica* 507–509).[23] Given that his birth sign on September 23–24 was in reality Libra (Manilius, *Astronomica*, 4.547–552), Augustus must have chosen Capricorn for other reasons.[24] Rather than it being a case, as some scholars have argued, of Augustus preferring his conception date to his birth date,[25] we should ask why Augustus's clients in Pisidian Antioch, who erected the monument, decided to emphasize the Capricorn motif. It is worth remembering that the iconography of the arch of Augustus interacts ideologically with the text of the *Res Gestae* at the same site. Capricorn was associated with

---

20. Robinson, "Roman Sculptures." For Robinson's two pictorial reconstructions of the arch, see Rubin, "Ruler Cult," 36 fig. 3.2 and 38 fig. 3.5.

21. Ossi, *Roman Honorific Arches*, 300 fig. 131 (Kelsey Museum Archives 7.1453).

22. The inscription, datable to 2/1 BCE, is as follows (Ossi, *Roman Honorific Arches*, 21): Imp. Caes[ari. di]vi.[f. a]ugusto. ponti[f]ici. m[axim]o cos. x[iii. trib] un[iciae] potestatis. xxii. [im]p. xiiii. p[. p.] ("For the imperator Caesar Augustus, son of a god, pontifex maximus, consul for the thirteenth time, with tribunician power for the twenty-second time, imperator for the fourteenth time, father of the country").

23. Rubin, "Ruler Cult," 43 fig. 3.9; Ossi, *Roman Honorific Arches*, 300 fig. 128.

24. For discussion, see Tamsyn Barton, "Augustus and Capricorn: Astrological Polyvalency and Imperial Rhetoric," *JRS* 85 (1995): 33–51; Emma Gee, *Ovid, Aratus and Augustus: Astronomy in Ovid's Fasti* (Cambridge: Cambridge University Press, 2000); Paul Rehak, *Imperium and Cosmos: Augustus and the Northern Campus Martius* (Madison: University of Wisconsin Press, 2006), 71–73.

25. Barton ("Augustus and Capricorn," 34, 36, 39, 42, 47) argues that ancients were more flexible about birth signs than moderns, choosing what was the most appealing sign personally.

Western Europe—especially Spain, Gaul, and Germany—the area that the (then) Octavian had controlled before Actium (31 BCE).[26] A new age had dawned with the end of the winter solstice traditionally associated with Capricorn.[27] Capricorn now ruled the entire world through Augustus as its savior, since he and his family members—as his Greco-Phrygian and Roman clients at Pisidian Antioch gratefully acknowledged—had conquered the barbarian peoples on the edge of the empire. Thus the appearance of the Capricorn in the iconography of the arch synchronized with the motif of the "conquest of the nations," as we will see below, in the *Res Gestae* (3.1–2; 4.3; 25–33; cf. the Latin preface).

Third, over the archway of the western facade are placed two kneeling bound captives in the spandrels. One is nude, one is partially draped, and their precise identification been debated by scholars.[28] Charles Brian Rose has proposed that Hadrian's arch, built as the ornamental city gate of Pisidian Antioch, had copied motifs already present on the arch of Augustus.[29] It is possible that the two Hadrianic standard-bearing barbarians, one from Gaul and the other from Parthia, had been previously placed on the eastern facade of the Augustan arch.[30] Thus, if Rose is correct, the "conquest of the nations" motif is visually present on both the eastern and western facades of the arch.

Fourth, naval iconography (ship prows, the ram of a warship, tritons, the god Poseidon) pointed symbolically to Augustus's famous victory at

---

26. Manilius, *Astronomica* 4.791–796: "You, Capricorn, rule all that lies beneath the setting sun and all that stretches thence to touch the frozen north, together with the peoples of Spain and of wealthy Gaul; and you, Germany, fit only to breed wild beasts, are claimed by an uncertain sign." Cf. Horace, *Odes*, 2.17.19–20.

27. Tamsyn Barton, *Ancient Astrology* (London: Routledge, 1994), 40. Rubin ("(Re)presenting Empire," 38–39) states: "While not a symbol of victory in itself, this Capricorn is probably intended to signify that Augustus' rise to power was preordained in the stars."

28. Mitchell and Waelkens, *Pisidian Antioch*, 162 fig. 113 (partially draped captive); Rubin, "Ruler Cult," 43 fig. 3.12 (nude captive), 99 fig. 5.19a (partially draped captive).

29. Charles Brian Rose, "The Parthians in Augustan Rome," *AJA* 109 (2005): 21–75. On the arch of Hadrian at Pisidian Antioch, Ossi, *Roman Honorific Arches*, 108–185; Ossi, "The Arch of Hadrian and Sabina at Pisidian Antioch: Imperial Associations, Ritual Connections, and Civic Euergetism," in Gazda and Ng, *Building a New Rome*, 85–108.

30. Ossi, *Roman Honorific Arches*, 302 fig. 133 (Kelsey Museum Archives 7.1613); 302 fig. 134 (Kelsey Museum Archives KR110.04).

Actium.³¹ Winged figures of victory, of a quasi-supernatural character, feature with garlands on the spandrels of the western face (nude males) and on the eastern face (draped females).³² Combining Hellenistic and sacral elements in the iconography, the divinely sanctioned nature of Augustus's rule is powerfully emphasized.³³ This is reinforced by the presence of other prominent deities on the arch, variously identified by scholars.³⁴ In the sanctuary proper, the inscriptional dedication of the Sebasteion underscores the superintendence of Augustus's rule by Jupiter.³⁵ Last, several large statues, each 2 m high, crowned the top of the arch, representing Augustus and his family. A headless statue most likely represents Augustus as Zeus,³⁶ while another statue perhaps depicts the Roman ruler pinioning a barbarian captive.³⁷

What portrait of victory emerges from the Augustan triumphal arch at Pisidian Antioch? There is little doubt, as Adrian John Ossi argues,³⁸ that the Augustan arch at Pisidian Antioch is a "visual *Res Gestae*." It does not just commemorate a single victory like the other Augustan arches.³⁹ Its ideological sweep embraces Augustus's ancestry, birth, triumviral years, divinely sanctioned rule from Actium onward, and continuing maintenance of the borders of Rome against the unruly peoples. What is significant is that his clients in the city have erected the arch and, as its inscription demonstrates (*supra* note 22), they are conveying an honorific

---

31. Ibid., 76. For the tritons, see Ossi, "Arch of Hadrian," 97 fig. 5.15a (Kelsey Museum Archives 7.1391).

32. Ossi, *Roman Honorific Arches*, 80–81. For victory figures, Rubin, "Ruler Cult," 43 fig. 3.10 (Kelsey Museum Archives 7.1139).

33. Ossi, *Roman Honorific Arches*, 83.

34. Ibid., 84–86. For the local god Mên Askaênos, see Rubin, "Ruler Cult," 43 fig. 3.13.

35. Rubin ("[Re]presenting Empire," 63) renders the incomplete inscription thus: IOVI • OPT • MAX | AUG • ET • GEN • COL | [*vacat*] EVEI ("To Jupiter Optimus Maximus | Augustus and the Genius of the Colony | [ ] the son of Eueius"). Rubin (ibid., 55–71) argues that the Latin dedication was a collaborative effort on the part of Italian colonists with the local Greco-Phrygian elite, one of whom is mentioned on the inscription ("Eueius"). He observes that Augustus functions as an intermediary—having the same "godlike" status as the Olympian deities—between Jupiter and the genius of the Colony, Pisidian Antioch.

36. Rubin, "Ruler Cult," 58 fig. 3.23 (Kelsey Museum 7.1432).

37. Ibid., 43 fig. 3.14 (Kelsey Museum 7.1434).

38. Ossi, *Roman Honorific Arches*, 71–72.

39. Ibid., 71–72.

accolade to their imperial benefactor for bringing the city so much prosperity and prestige in Asia Minor.[40] This is certainly not a case of "Romanization" imposed on conquered provincials, but rather an integration of indigenous Hellenistic and Roman elements in honor of the benefactor of the world.[41] But how does the iconography of Augustus's triple arch intersect with the *Res Gestae* located somewhere near the site of the Sebasteion?

The motif of the "conquest of the nations" is central to the *Res Gestae*.[42] Announced first in the preface to the *Res Gestae*, the motif is handled with great skill as far as its ideological impact in the inscription. In terms of Augustus's strategy of conquest, Augustus waged wars by land and sea against foreign nations (*Res Gestae* 3.1; 4.3), pardoning only those whom he "could safely pardon" (3.2). His preferred policy, however, was more "to preserve than to destroy" the peoples of the nations (3.2; cf. 13). The most extensive discussion of the nations occurs in *Res Gestae* 25–33. The passage is a masterful example of Augustus's geopolitical categorization of the Roman Empire by which he spotlights his exemplary virtue.[43]

After securing victory over Rome's internal enemies at Actium and Sicily (*Res Gestae* 25), Augustus pursued world conquest (26–27). Simultaneously, Augustus stabilized the Roman Empire by establishing military colonies (28), reversing the humiliating losses to the Parthians (29), and pushing into the territory of the Pannonian peoples in order to create a buffer against barbarian invasion (30). In contrast to the militarism of the previous section (26–30), *Res Gestae* 31–33 presents the diplomatic strategies by which Augustus secured the loyalty of conquered peoples to Rome: engaging various royal embassies, protecting suppliants seeking refuge, and meeting noble ambassadors. Importantly, Augustus emphasizes twice the unprecedented nature of these diplomatic contacts with the peoples (31.1, 32.3). Indeed, the highly exotic names of these peoples and their rulers would have dazzled Augustus's Roman audience with the extent of the empire (27, 32–33). Thus, by means of this rich portrait of the military

---

40. Ibid., 58.

41. Note the insightful comment of Ossi (ibid., 56): the arch "stands as an attempt to integrate the multicultural population, not by turning Greeks and Phrygians into Romans, but by melding aspects of each cultural tradition into a new provincial culture."

42. See the first-rate discussion of Davina C. Lopez, *Apostle to the Conquered: Reimagining Paul's Mission*, Paul in Critical Contexts (Minneapolis: Fortress, 2008), 86–113.

43. E. A. Judge, "On Judging the Merits of Augustus," in Judge, *First Christians*, 241.

and diplomatic pacification of the peoples, the *Res Gestae* draws attention to two of the pivotal Augustan virtues—*virtus* (25–30) and *clementia* (31–33)—upon which the expansion of the Roman Empire depended (34.2). This "grand narrative" of empire is a story about the virtuous Augustus ensuring the dominance of his house by victory on the battlefield (30.1; cf. 1.1; 2).[44]

How does the message of the *Res Gestae* interact with the iconography on the triple arch leading up to the Sebasteion at Pisidian Antioch? In the case of the triple arch, the local Greeks and Phrygians from Pisidian Antioch worked with the Roman elite in the colony to effect a fusion of indigenous and imperial ideologies, with a view to honoring the Julio-Claudian ruler as the world benefactor, and to secure his blessing as the intermediary between the Roman gods and the colony. It is significant that the fusion of Greco-Phrygian and Roman culture revealed on the triple arch relegated the barbarians to the margins of the Roman Empire in the Greek East. There was no sense that *clementia* ("mercy") rather than military *virtus* ("manliness") might be a preferable policy in handling the unruly and uncivilized barbarian peoples in some cases. The ideological subtlety of Augustus's handling of the barbarian nations as depicted in the *Res Gestae*—by *virtus* and *clementia* equally—is drowned out by the military jingoism of Augustus's clients, Roman and Greco-Phrygian, at Pisidian Antioch.

The thematic connection between the triple arch and the *Res Gestae* regarding the fate of the barbarian nations under the Augustan hegemony finds an unexpected dialogue partner with the writings of the apostle Paul. The apostle displays an intense interest in the nations within the ambit of God's covenantal and electing grace in Christ (e.g., Rom 3:27–4:25; 9:22–26; 11:7–24; 15:7–12; Gal 3:1–4:11, 24–31; Eph 2:11–22). In contrast to the Roman and indigenous elite at Pisidian Antioch, Paul considered himself to be equally indebted to "Greek and barbarian" (Rom 1:14),[45] emphasizing how the root of Jesse extended his messianic grace to the gentile peoples (15:7–12), and how Greeks and Jews, barbarians and Scythians were all embraced in Christ (Col 3:11). Moreover, Paul

---

44. Horace refers indirectly to the "god-like" triumphs of Augustus: "To achieve great deeds and to display captive foeman to one's fellow-citizens is to touch the throne of Jove and scale the skies" (*Ep.* 1.17.33–34).

45. For an insightful analysis of this little-discussed verse, see Robert Jewett, *Romans: A Commentary*, Hermeneia (Minneapolis: Fortress, 2007), 130–32.

would have encountered popular stereotypes of barbarians, similar to those he saw at Pisidian Antioch, elsewhere in the eastern Mediterranean cities that he visited during his missionary outreach.[46] Undoubtedly, in considering his shift in mission from the Greek East to the Latin West (Rom 1:9–10, 13, 15b; 15:25–29), the apostle had to grapple with how to shift hardened Roman attitudes of superiority toward the barbarian nations, as much as toward the Jews (Rom 11:17–21; 14:10). The preponderance of triumphal arches in the Greek East and Latin West, with their iconography of humiliated barbarians, testified to the challenge he faced.

But what of the wider semantic domains associated with the "nations" in Augustan ideology? Do they have any relevance for Paul's writings? Of particular interest is how Augustus boasts about the result of the diplomatic encounters with various embassies and kings (*Res Gestae* 32.3): "And while I have been leader very many other peoples have experienced the good faith [*fidem*; πίστεως] of the Roman people." Edwin Ramage discusses the interrelation of *fides* ("faith") and *iustitia* ("justice"),[47] citing the evidence of Livy and Cicero in this regard.[48] He observes that Romans "viewed *fides* as the foundation of *iustitia*."[49] In the case of international diplomacy in the *Res Gestae*, "Augustus' sense of justice is triggering the

---

46. The evidence of Corinth and nearby Isthmia, for example, is ambiguous, reflecting both indigenous and barbarian motifs. See Vermeule (*Roman Imperial Art*, figs. 27–30) for captive barbarians on Corinthian sculptures and panel reliefs, but they postdate Paul (*Roman Imperial Art*, 83, 87: 160–170 CE). In the museum of Corinth I saw another small (undated) captive barbarian statue on exhibition: could this be a first-century-CE example? See Harrison, "More Than Conquerors," 4 fig. 2. A Roman arch, hurriedly built and of poor workmanship, was erected for Nero's visit to the Isthmian Games and his proclamation of freedom from taxation for the province Achaia (67 CE: SIG^3 814). However, the triumphal arch at Isthmia, symbolic of the greatness of the Roman Empire, did not possess any sculpture, let alone barbarian reliefs. See Timothy E. Gregory and Harrianne Mills, "The Roman Arch at Isthmia," *Hesperia* 53 (1984): 407–45. It is important to realize that indigenous motifs still appeared on the local triumphal arches. Pausanias 2.3.2 refers to an arch over the Lechaion Road at Corinth, with sculptures of the gods of Acrocorinth on its top. See Charles M. Edwards, "The Arch over the Lechaion Road at Corinth and Its Sculpture," *Hesperia* 63 (1994): 263–308. In sum, there is no contemporary evidence of barbarian reliefs at Corinth, and indigenous motifs still appeared, as was the case with Pisidian Antioch.

47. Edwin S. Ramage, *The Nature and Purpose of Augustus' "Res Gestae"* (Stuttgart: Steiner, 1987), 45–46, 89–90.

48. Ibid., 90.

49. Ibid., 46.

fides (32.3) that attracts legations from the ends of the world."⁵⁰ What is intriguing here for Pauline scholars is the link in Romans between "justice" (δικαιοσύνη), "justification" language (δικαιόω), and faith (πίστις: 3:22, 26, 28, 30; 4:5, 9, 11, 13; 5:1; 9:30; 10:4, 6, 10) and the incorporation of the "nations" into the people of God. Is this overlap of motifs between Augustus and Paul merely the collision of different "symbolic universes"? Or is Paul implicitly highlighting for his Roman auditors how the God of Israel graciously summons the nations to himself in comparison to the justice attracting the barbarian tribes to be loyal to Rome and Augustus? The question is difficult to answer with certainty, but it again underscores the rich intersection of the "nations" motif in Paul's writings with the *Res Gestae*. This warns us against an exclusive concentration on the iconographic evidence at the expense of a critical analysis of the accompanying epigraphic evidence, as stimulating a backdrop as the visual evidence might be for Pauline scholars.

2. Monuments at Rome Commemorating Augustus's Triumph over the Barbarians: A Case Study in the Intersection of Iconographic and Numismatic Evidence

2.1. The Triple Arch at the Roman Forum

The single-bay Actian arch of Augustus, erected in 29 BCE, will not be discussed due to the continuing controversy concerning its location and its relation to the later triple arch of Augustus.⁵¹ The triple arch of Augustus in the Roman Forum, near the temple of Divus Julius, commemorated the conquest of the Parthians and pointed to Augustus as a worthy successor of Augustus.⁵² This was erected in 19 BCE in honor of the recovery of the

---

50. Ibid., 46. For a wider discussion of the Roman semantic domain of *fides* ("faithfulness"), *pietas* ("piety"), and *iustitia* ("justice") and how it relates to Rom 1:17, see Benjamin Evans Holdsworth, "Reading Romans in Rome: A Reception of Romans in the Roman Context of Ethnicity and Faith" (PhD diss., Durham University, 2009), 167–210, 260–74. For the first major study of πίστις ("faith") against its Greco-Roman and Pauline context, see B. Cueto, "The Concept of ΠΙΣΤΙΣ in Greco-Roman Context and Its Impact on Paul's Writings" (PhD diss., Dallas Theological Seminary, 2012, forthcoming Paternoster Press, 2016).

51. See Robert Alan Gurval, *Actium and Augustus: The Politics and Emotions of Civil War* (Ann Arbor: University of Michigan Press, 1995), 8, 36–46.

52. For discussion, see Leicester B. Holland, "The Triple Arch of Augustus," *AJA*

spoils and standards from Parthia through the diplomacy of Augustus (*Res Gestae* 29.2; Dio Cassius, *Historiae Romanae* 54.8.4; cf. 51.19; Suetonius, *Aug.* 21.3). We know about its design from the reverse side of an Augustan denarius (*RIC* I², "Augustus," §§131–37). Augustus surmounts the triple arch in a four-horse chariot, flanked by a Parthian on the left and right, holding, respectively, a standard and an aquila and bow. Significantly, even though Augustus's achievement was entirely diplomatic, the iconography of Augustus on the arch is presented in triumphal terms. In sum, as we saw with the triple arch of Pisidian Antioch and the *Res Gestae* (§1), the visual image of military subjugation may well not correspond to historical reality. The same may be said of the image of the Parthian, depicting Augustus's diplomatic triumph, on the cuirass of the famous statue of Augustus at the villa of Livia at Prima Porta. There we see at the very center of the composition the Parthian king handing over the legionary standards to another cuirassed figure, most likely in this case to be the god Mars, but another possibility is that he a representative of the Roman legions.[53]

2.2. The Interrelation of Monuments and Sacred Space in Relation to "Barbarian" Motifs

The interrelation of monuments and sacred space in the city of Rome also conveyed symbolic messages about the ruler and his conquest of the barbarian tribes. Three examples will suffice. First, a few hundred meters away from the site of the *Res Gestae*, which highlighted Augustus's domination of the nations (3.1–2; 4.3; 13; 25–33), was Agrippa's monumental map displaying the extent of the Roman Empire and its peoples.[54] The portrait of Augustus as the conqueror and appeaser of the nations in the Latin inscription is thereby underscored by the map's visual commemoration of the size of the Roman Empire.

---

50 (1946): 52–59; Andrew Wallace-Hadrill, "Augustus' Parthian Honours, the Temple of Mars Ultor and the Arch in the Forum Romanum," *Papers of the British School at Rome* 66 (1998): 71–128; Rose, "Parthians in Augustan Rome," 21–75; Filippo Coarelli, *Rome and Environs: An Archaeological Guide* (Berkeley: University of California Press, 2007), 79–81; Fred S. Kleiner, *A History of Roman Art*, 2nd ed. (Boston: Wadsworth, 2010), 64.

53. Paul Zanker, *The Power of Images in the Age of Augustus* (Ann Arbor: University of Michigan Press, 1990), 189, 190 fig. 148a, 191 fig. 148b.

54. Richard Hingley, *Globalizing Roman Culture: Unity, Diversity and Empire* (London: Routledge, 2005), 79.

Second, the modest house of Augustus on the Palatine was located near a model of Romulus's hut,[55] underscoring Augustus's status as the "new Romulus," the traditional founder of Rome, along with Aeneas.[56] Significantly, the house was next to the sacred precinct where Augustus would soon erect a temple to Apollo. Lightning struck the grounds after Augustus had acquired the house, prompting him to demonstrate his piety to his patron deity, Apollo, by erecting a temple on the site (Velleius Paterculus, *Historiae Romanae* 2.81.3; Dio Cassius, *Historiae Romanae* 49.15.5; Suetonius, *Aug.* 29.3).[57] Apollo was the deity who had given Augustus victory over Sextus Pompeius at Naulochos in 36 BCE and over Antony and Cleopatra at Actium in 31 BCE.[58] Consequently, not only was Apollo honored with the temple next to Augustus's house, but also within Augustus's house itself there was a wall painting of Apollo with his lyre.[59]

More important for our purposes, the motif of the conquest of the barbarian nations was used in the iconography of the other (and oldest) Apollonian temple at Rome, the so-called temple of Apollo Sosianus, located

---

55. Charles Gates, *Ancient Cities: The Archaeology of Urban Life in the Ancient Near East and Egypt, Greece and Rome* (London: Routledge, 2003), 337; Mary Beard et al., *A History*, vol. 1 of *Religions of Rome* (Cambridge: Cambridge University Press, 1998), 189–92; Susan Walker, "The Moral Museum: Augustus and the City of Rome," in *Ancient Rome: The Archaeology of the Eternal City*, ed. Jon Coulston and Hazel Dodge (Oxford: Oxford University School of Archaeology, 2000), 61–75, esp. 62–64. On the house of Augustus on the Palatine, see Irene Iacopi, *The House of Augustus: Wall Paintings* (Rome: Electa, 2008); Galinsky, *Augustan Culture*, 187–89.

56. Horace, *Saec.* 41–60; Suetonius, *Aug.* 7.2.

57. See the Villa Albini relief of Apollo, Diana, and her mother, Latona, being received by the winged figure of Victory at the site of the Palatine—so Galinsky proposes (Galinsky, *Augustan Culture*, figs. 122 117). Diana was also Augustus's patron deity, as the presence of Apollo with his lyre and Diana on her stag on the Prima Porta statue shows (Donald C. Earl, *The Age of Augustus* [New York: Crown, 1968], 192; cf. Zanker, *Power of Images*, 190–91 figs. 148a and 148b).

58. Virgil's portrait of Augustus as divinely elect is underscored when the gods (Apollo, Neptune, Venus, Minerva) fight at Augustus's side and help him to defeat the Egyptian forces with their loathsome gods and commanders (Virgil, *Aen.* 8.678–681). See also Propertius (*Elegies* 4.37–68), who portrays Phoebus Apollo as delivering divine help to Augustus. On the importance of Apollo to Augustus, see John F. Miller, *Apollo, Augustus and the Poets* (Cambridge: Cambridge University Press, 2009). On the Palatine temple to Apollo and its relation to Actium, see Virgil, *Aen.* 8.704–706; Propertius 4.6. For an excellent source-based discussion of the Palatine temple to Apollo, including its design and activities, see Cooley, *Res Gestae Divi Augusti*, 184–85.

59. Galinsky, *Augustan Culture*, pl. 5b.

nearby in the southern end of the Campus Martius (i.e., the Circus Flaminius). Gaius Sosius, the consul of 32 BCE, had began two years earlier the reconstruction of the temple that, at the time of its restoration, was called the temple of Apollo Medicus. But the progress of the temple's redevelopment was interrupted by the civil war and was temporarily stalled by Sosius's political support of Antony. When Gaius Sosius switched his alliance to Augustus after Antony's defeat in 31 BCE and was reconciled with the victorious Princeps, Augustus dedicated the temple of Apollo Sosianus sometime afterward.[60] This was the temple in which, according to the Julian foundation myths, Augustus was divinely conceived as the son of Apollo (Suetonius, *Aug.* 5; 94.4, 6; cf. Dio Cassius, *Historiae Romanae* 45.1). The frieze on the external pediment of the temple depicts the battle of Theseus and Hercules against the Amazons, recalling the battle of the Amazons that was rendered on the base of the victory monument erected at Actium.[61] On the interior frieze block of the temple, however, two northern barbarian captives, possibly Illyrians and part of Augustus's 29 BCE triple triumph (*Res Gestae* 4.1; 30.1), are shown sitting on a parade float (*feculum*), hands bound behind their backs, ready to be hoisted in midair for exhibition in Augustus's triumphal procession.[62] In sum, it is evident from the Apollonian temples on the Palatine and the Campus Martius that Augustus, as the new founder of Rome, kept the barbarian hordes at bay from the capital of the empire—whether it be the threat posed by the Egyptians or by the Illyrians—through the agency of his patron deity, Apollo.

Third, in the Campus Martius was set the *horologium Augusti*, the giant sundial designed by the astrologer Facundus Navius.[63] This monument,

---

60. Galinsky (ibid., 215) notes that Cn. Caesar, consul of 431 BCE, had dedicated this earlier Apollonian temple. Undoubtedly, this link of the temple with Augustus's adopted family would also have influenced Augustus's own rededication of the temple.

61. Edward Champlin, *Nero* (Cambridge, MA: Belknap Press of Harvard University Press, 2003), 141. On the external frieze, see Eugenio La Rocca, *Amazzonomachia. Le sculture frontonali del tempio di Apollo Sosiano* (Rome: De Luca Editore, 1985).

62. See Keith Bradley, "On Captives under the Principate," *Phoenix* 58, nos. 3–4 (2004), pl. 1; Zanker, *Power of Images*, 70 fig. 55. On the Augustan temple of Apollo on the Palatine, see Galinsky, *Augustan Culture*, 188–89, 215–19, 277–99, 314. Galinsky (*Augustan Culture*, fig. 168) also points to another Augustan relief showing the defeat of barbarians—on this occasion depicting a battle between the Romans and the Gauls—that possibly belonged to the temple of the Dioscuri at Rome.

63. Additionally, see Ammianus Marcellinus, *Res Gestae* 17.4.12; Strabo, *Geogr.* 17.805; Pliny the Elder, *Nat.* 30.6.71.

dedicated to the Sun (*CIL* 6.709), was placed between the *ara Pacis Augustae* and the (later) *columna Antonini Pii*. The symbolic importance of the monument is seen in the inscription accompanying the sundial: *Aegypto in potestatem populi Romani redacta Soli donum dedit* (*CIL* 6.702: "On the occasion of Egypt's submission to the power of the Roman people he gave a gift to the Sun").[64] The sundial celebrates Augustus's victory at Actium (31 BCE) that secured peace in the Greek East, whereas the *ara Pacis Augustae*, strategically placed nearby, eulogizes Augustus's establishment of peace in the Latin West.[65] Notwithstanding the peace and fertility motifs of the *ara Pacis*, Rose has argued that the two male children in foreign dress on the north and south friezes are respectively Gallic and (royal) Bosporan captives from the barbarian tribes.[66] A similar motif is commemorated on an aureus from Lugdunum that shows a bearded and cloaked barbarian holding up a small child stretching out its arms to Augustus.[67] The different interactions posited in the visual imagery—barbarians holding up children in submission to the ruler and the ruler bringing up captive barbarian in his own family—points to the complexity of the negotiated outcomes, symbolically and in actuality, for the conquered barbarian tribes.

We might ask how this carefully calculated positioning of triumphal monuments and temples, each underscoring the all-encompassing victory of the Roman ruler over the nations, could have been countered by Paul in his Letter to the Romans. Unexpectedly for Romans familiar with the iconography of the triumphal arches and temples at Rome, Paul portrays the love of Christ (Rom 8:35a, 37b, 39b) as the only power able to preserve believers through tribulation (v. 35). It provides them eschatological victory over cosmic enemies imperiling the soul and body (Rom 8:37b–39; cf. 5:9). As Robert Jewett observes,[68] the aorist participle ἀγαπήσαντος in

---

64. Cited, in abbreviated form here, in Carole Elizabeth Newlands, *Playing with Time: Ovid and the Fasti* (Ithaca, NY: Cornell University Press, 1995), 24.

65. Ibid., 24. On the *ara Pacis Augustae*, see Zanker, *Power of Images*, 172–83; Gates, *Ancient Cities*, 339–42.

66. Charles Brian Rose, "Princes and Barbarians on the Ara Pacis," *AJA* 94 (1990): 453–67. Contra Orietta Rossini (*Ara Pacis*, new. ed. [Rome: Electra, 2010], 48–79), who posits imperial family members.

67. For the numismatic reference and picture, see Ann L. Kuttner, *Dynasty and Empire in the Age of Augustus: The Case of the Boscoreale Cups* (Berkeley: University of California Press, 1995), 187.

68. Jewett, *Romans*, 549; Leon Morris, *The Epistle to the Romans*, Pillar New Testament Commentary (Grand Rapids: Eerdmans, 1988), 340.

Rom 8:37b, refers to a "single act of love" (cf. 8:30). It denotes Christ's timely death for the ungodly enemy (5:6, 8, 10a). The submissiveness of the defeated barbarians and their rough treatment at the hands of their captors portrayed on the triumphal arches and temple reliefs contrasts markedly with the way that believers participated in their benefactor's unsurpassed victory on their behalf.

Why, then, does Paul use the ὑπέρ-compound in verse 37 (ὑπερνικῶμεν), and what would it have signified for Roman auditors familiar with the imperial propaganda of victory?[69] Jewett and C. E. B. Cranfield point to a variant of a famous maxim of Menander for the clarification of the word's meaning: "to be victorious [νικᾶν] is good [καλόν], but to be super-victorious [ὑπερνικᾶν] is bad [κακόν]."[70] The idea conveyed by ὑπερνικᾶν is that the victory achieved is excessive in its scope: consequently the victor is marked as a "super-victor" among vastly inferior victors.[71] In using the ὑπέρ-compound, Paul pivots the total superiority of Christ's soteriological victory over against all other victors in history, whether human or cosmic. In Paul's view, therefore, the triumph of the Julian house over its political opponents at Rome and its victories over the barbarian threat to the empire, articulated on the arches and temple reliefs, was in reality a passing sideshow (see 1 Cor 2:7–8; 7:31b).

3. Augustus's Conquest of the Alpine Tribes: A Case Study in the Intersection of Iconography and Epigraphy at the Sites of La Turbie and Susa

3.1. La Turbie (Monaco)

The monument at La Turbie to Augustus's pacification of the Alpine tribes (*Res Gestae* 26.3) in 16–14 BCE was erected in 7/6 BCE.[72] It was origi-

---

69. Jewett's concise discussion (*Romans*, 549–50) of the imperial background pertaining to Rom 8:37 is outstanding.

70. Ibid., 548–49; C. E. B. Cranfield, *Romans 1–8*, ICC (Edinburgh: T & T Clark, 1975), 441.

71. Jewett, *Romans*, 549; F. F. Bruce, *The Epistle of Paul to the Romans: An Introduction and Commentary*, TNTC (Leicester: Inter-Varsity Press, 1963), 181.

72. For discussion of the monument, see Jules Formigé, *Le Trophée des Alpes: La Turbie* (Paris: Centre Nationale de la Recherche Scientifique, 1949); Philippe Casimir, *Le Trophée d'Auguste à la Turbie* (Marseille: Tacussel, 1932); Gilbert Charles Picard, *Les trophées romains: Contribution à l'histoire de la religion et de l'art triomphal de*

nally 50 m high and still dominates the environs today at 35 m.[73] The west face of the monument's first podium was nearest to the entrance and the Roman road, having the most complete fragments of its iconography and inscription.[74] The second podium, by comparison, is very incomplete, but probably had statuary (eagles) in the corners.[75] Both podiums were surmounted by a circular colonnade of twenty-four Doric columns—four of which survive—with a frieze decorated with military symbols.[76] James Bromwich observes that the niches, originally twelve, are still visible between the columns and posits that statues of Augustan generals filled them.[77] On top of this, a cone roof supported a trophy, which, according to Jules Formigé,[78] was a statue of Augustus.

On either side of the inscription on the first podium are reliefs of two small winged Victories presenting their crowns to Augustus.[79] Also there are two reliefs of Alpine tribe members, each depicting a male captive squatting with his hands bound behind his back, accompanied by a female seated at his side with hands crossed at the front. These are placed to the right and left of the victory inscription, with the captives squatting under a cruciform-shaped trophy "tree," from which hang their weapons,

---

Rome (Paris: de Broccard, 1957), 291–301; Nicole Candace Hartshorn, "Images of Power: The Augustan Trophy of the Alpes as a Roman Visual Narrative and Commemoration" (MA thesis, California State University, 2006); Sophie Binninger, *Le Trophée d'Auguste à la Turbie* (Paris: Patrimonie, 2009). On the history of restoration of the monument, with photographs, see ibid., 18–37. See, too, Formigé's reconstruction of the monument (*Le Trophée des Alpes*, pl. 51); cf. Casimir, *Trophée d'August*, 46. For a general discussion of the arches of early imperial Gaul, see Fred S. Kleiner, *The Arch of Nero in Rome: A Study of the Roman Honorary Arch before and after Nero* (Roma: Bretschneider, 1985), 40–50.

73. James Bromwich, *The Roman Remains of Southern France: A Guidebook* (London: Routledge, 1993), 271.

74. Formigé, *Trophée des Alpes*, 47–64.

75. Ibid., 65.

76. Formigé (ibid., 68–69) lists the following: a cuirass, a wild boar, a bull, horns, a skull, and a ship's prow (alluding to Augustus's naval battle on Lake Constance: 15 BCE). For a picture of the frieze, on the entablature above the columns, as well as one of the niches between the columns, see ibid., fig. 7.

77. Bromwich, *Roman Remains*, 274.

78. Formigé, *Trophée des Alpes*, 74.

79. For a picture, see Binninger, *Trophée d'Auguste*, 50.

shields, and tunics.[80] The fragments of the captive reliefs have been reconstructed—consisting of ninety-eight pieces on the left, sixty-three on the right[81]—from the stereotyped renderings of bound captives found at Carpentras, Saint-Rémy, and Orange.[82] It is worth remembering, if Formigé and Bromwich are correct, that the statues of Augustus and his generals dominate architecturally over the "captive" reliefs, thereby accentuating the symbolism of Augustus's total triumph over the barbarians.[83] Nicole Candace Hartshorn also observes that, in contrast to the female captive on the right, whose eyes are directed toward the male captive, the female captive on the left looks defiantly upward toward the trophy tree and its spoils—a testimony to the intense struggle required by the Roman forces to overcome the Alpine tribes.[84]

Formigé reconstructed the inscription, consisting of 145 fragments, from its reproduction in Pliny the Elder (*Nat.* 3.20.136–138). Sophie Binninger argues that Pliny did not see the original inscription but more likely had consulted the official documents in the imperial archives at Rome.[85] The inscription, listing the forty-four Alpine tribes conquered by Augustus,[86] is set out below:

To Imperator Caesar Augustus,
son of god,

---

80. For a picture, see Ferris, *Enemies of Rome*, 40 fig. 16; Binninger, *Trophée d'Auguste*, 50.

81. Bromwich, *Roman Remains*, 273.

82. See the helpful picture in Binninger (*Trophée d'Auguste*, 50) contrasting the existing fragments on the left with the reconstituted relief in marble on the right. Additionally, see Formigé, *Trophée des Alpes*, 52–54 and pl. 47.

83. As evidence for the possibility of a statue of Augustus crowning the monument, Formigé (*Trophée des Alpes*, pl. 51) notes that a fragment of a bronze statue has been discovered. However, Formigé's assertion that two captives also adorned the cone roof—argued on the basis of an analogy with Trajan's trophy—is possible but unprovable (ibid.).

84. Hartshorn, *Images of Power*, 49–50.

85. Binninger, *Trophée d'Auguste*, 51. On the inscription, see Formigé, *Trophée des Alpes*, 54–64. For pictures of Mommsen's and Formigé's rendering of the inscription, see Casimir, *Trophée d'Auguste*, 56, 61.

86. Casimir (*Trophée d'Auguste*, 63–114) provides an excellent historical exposition of each of the tribes. On the geographical spread of the tribes, see Formigé, *Trophée des Alpes*, 60–61. Strabo (*Geogr.* 4.32) mentions an Augustan altar, location unknown, which is inscribed with the names of sixty Gallic tribes.

pontifex maximus,
imperator 14 times,
in his 17th year of his tribunician power.
The senate and the Roman people [erected this monument],
in memory of the fact that under his orders,
and under his auspices, all the people of the Alps,
from the Upper Sea to the Lower,[87]
have been brought under the command of (the) Roman people.[88]
Names of Alpine peoples conquered:
Trumpilini, Camunni, Venostes, Vennonetes,
Isarci, Breuni, Genaunes, Focanates.
The four Vindelician nations:
Cosuantes, Rucinates, Licates, Catenates,
Ambisontes, Rugusci, Suanetes, Calucones,
Brixentes, Leponti, Viberi, Nantuates, Seduni,
Veragri, Salassi, Acitavones, Medulli, Ucenni,
Caturiges, Brigiani, Sogionti, Brodionti,
Nemaloni, Edenates, Esubiani, Veamini, Gallitae,
Triullati, Ectini, Vergunni, Eguituri, Nemeturi,
Oratelli, Nerusi, Velauni, Suettri.

Pliny adds his personal addendum: "I have not included the twelve non-belligerent states of the Cottiani, nor those that were controlled by the Italian municipalities under the *Lex Pompeia*" (*Nat.* 3.20.138).

There is little doubt from this inscription and from the *Res Gestae* that the conquest of the Alpine peoples was, in Roman perception, a "just war" (cf. *Res Gestae* 26.3: "without waging unjust war on any people"). Under Augustus's orders (*eius ductu*) and under his "godlike" auspices (*auspiciis que*; cf. *Res Gestae* 30.2; Tacitus, *Ann.* 2.26; Livy 28.12), the conquests of the barbarian tribes were carried out. There is no suggestion here of an ill-considered or arbitrary decision on the part of Augustus. He alone had the right to consult the gods through the interpretation of omens (*Res Gestae* 4.2; cf. pontifex maximus ["High Priest"], La Turbie inscription, *supra*), procuring their favor and thereby winning victories by means of his generals.[89] The same point is made about Augustus's auspices on the

---

87. Respectively, the Adriatic and Tyrrhenian Seas.

88. Casimir (*Trophée d'Auguste*, 57) translates loosely: "submit to Roman laws" (*se sont soumis aux lois romaines*).

89. P. A. Brunt and J. M. Moore, eds., *Res Gestae Divi Augusti: The Achievements of the Divine Augustus* (Oxford: Oxford University Press, 1967), 44.

Gemma Augusta, where he is depicted in the guise of Jupiter, lituus in hand, greeting the victorious Tiberius.[90] Consequently, the Alpine peoples are placed under the providential ordering of the Roman gods and under the command of the Roman people (*sub imperium p.r.*). Thus the iconography of the La Turbie monument powerfully substantiates the message of the inscription.

Notwithstanding Augustus's imposition of Roman rule upon the Alpine tribes, the Roman ruler became a patron to the barbarian kings who had accommodated themselves to Roman rule and had become his *amici* ("friends"). Consequently, as Pliny notes, Augustus did not declare war on them because they had demonstrated that they were not hostile to Rome. The twelve Cottianae cities were indebted to their king, Marius Julius Cottius, for their preservation. Cottius, the first century BCE ruler of the Ligurian tribes, had made peace with Julius Caesar, but for a while had maintained independence in the face of Augustus's onslaught against the Alpine tribes. However, Cottius relented, submitted, and was named prefect of the twelve tribes—*pace*, fourteen tribes in the Susa inscription *infra* (§3.2)[91]—in his region by Augustus for his loyalty as an *amicus* ("friend"). As we will see, Cottius, in reciprocation of this honor, honored Augustus with a triumphal arch at his capital Segusio in 8 BCE (modern Susa, Italy).

In sum, what we witnessing in Pliny's brief addendum to the inscription is the conciliatory approach that Augustus adopted toward some barbarian tribes (see *Res Gestae* 26.4, 31–33) because of the establishment of *amicitia* ("friendship"). This stands in contrast to the iconography of humiliated nations on the La Turbie monument and the "just" war ideology articulated in the inscription. But caution is required lest we overstate the social significance of what is happening here. The Cottianae cities have become an exemplum of the benefits that compliance with Rome brings in contrast to those who do not submit to Roman rule. This result had propagandist value for the Roman cause in Gaul. Consequently Cottius became an honored figure in Roman literature (Pliny the Elder, *Nat.* 3.20; Pliny the Younger, *Ep.* 3.1.10; Ammianus Marcellinus, *Res Gestae* 15.10.2, 7; Ovid, *Pont.* 4.7). Once again we see how critical it is to bring the inscription accompanying the monument into dialogue with its iconography, as

---

90. Zanker, *Power of Images*, 230–31 fig. 182.
91. On the differences between Pliny's rendering of the La Turbie inscription and the Susa inscription, see J. Prieur, "Les arcs monumentaux dans les Alpes occidentals: Aoste, Suse, Aix-les-Bains," *ANRW* 12.1:454–55.

well as its attendant historical circumstances, lest we overemphasize the brutality of Roman imperialism or naively play down its reality (*Res Gestae* 26–30).

3.2. Susa (South of Turin, Italy)

The Augustan arch at Susa (ancient Segusio), datable to 9/8 BCE from its inscription, has no pediment or sculpture in the spandrels.[92] Its famous sculptured frieze wraps around all four sides of the immense rectangular arch, which was erected on the road leading to the Alpine crossing to Gaul.[93] It commemorates the signing of a treaty of friendship between Augustus, the ruler of Rome, and Marcus Julius Cottius, the son and successor of King Donnus, the ruler of fourteen small tribes in the Cottian Alps (*Res Gestae* 26.3).

The iconography is the best preserved of any triumphal arch in Italy. On the east side of the relief is depicted the act of submission of the Alpine tribes,[94] whereas on the north side we see the Roman ritual of the *souvetaurile* being performed.[95] In this sacred ceremony, a pig, sheep, and bull were sacrificed to Mars in order to bless and purify the land. In the middle of the west side of the relief is rendered the pivotal scene for our purposes, namely, the signing of the peace treaty.[96] Two people are seated face-to-face before a table: Augustus is seated prominently to the left and is easily recognizable due to his distinctive hairstyle, whereas Cottius sits opposite the Roman ruler on the right. The third person behind the table, Émile Espérandieu suggests,[97] is a representative of the cities, with Roman

---

92. Émile Espérandieu, *Recueil general des bas-reliefs de la Gaule romanine* (Ridgewood: Greg Press, 1965 [Fr. orig. Paris 1907]), 1:15–20; Prieur, "Les arcs monumentaux," 442–75, esp. 451–59. Kleiner, *Arch of Nero*, 32–33; Anna Maria Cavargna Allemano, "Il fregio dell'arco di Susa espressione locale di arte provinciale romana," in *Arco di Susa Eretto da Marco Giulio Cozio in Onore di Cesare Ottaviano Augusto (8 a.C—1992 d.C): Monografia per il Bimillenatio*, ed. G. Fabiano, Segusium 31 (Torino: Società di Ricerche e Studi Valsusini, 1991), 207–33; Kleiner, *History of Roman Art*, 93–95. Ermanno Ferrero (*L'Arc d'Auguste à Suse* [Turin: Société d'archéologie et des beaux-arts, 1901]) was unavailable to me.

93. Espérandieu, *Recueil general*, 15; Kleiner, *History of Roman Art*, 93 fig. 7.5

94. Espérandieu, *Recueil general*, 16 "Face est" (single plate).

95. Ibid., 18 "Face nord" pl. 1, 19–20 "Face nord" pls. 2–4.

96. Ibid., 16 "Face oust" pls. 1–2; Kleiner, *History of Roman Art*, 93 7.6 (top relief).

97. Espérandieu, *Recueil general*, 17.

lictors nearby holding their fasces. Finally, on the south side of the relief, we see the ceremony of lustration closing the ceremony of the signing of the peace treaty.[98]

The bronze inscription, originally inserted in the attic of the arch, celebrates the establishment of the *pax Augusta* as follows:

> To Imperator Caesar Augustus,
> son of god,
> pontifex maximus,
> in his 15th year of his tribunician power,
> imperator 13 times,
> Marcus Julius Cottius, son of King Donnus,
> prefect of the states which are written underneath:
> > *Segovii, Segusini, Belaci, Caturiges, Medulli,*
> > *Tebavii, Adanates, Savincates, Egdinii Veaminii,*
> > *Venisami, Iemerii, Vesubianii, Quadiates*
> > and the states which have been under that prefect.[99]

What are we to make of the dynamics of power being enacted in the iconography of the arch and its inscription? Is this just another instance of the enforced "Romanization" of barbarian subjects? It is clear from the inscription that the erection of the arch in honor of Augustus is an act of reciprocation to the Roman ruler for his preservation of the fourteen Alpine states and for the honoring of their king who, although now a subject of Augustus, has been appointed as an imperial prefect. Ossi's conclusion is apt:

> The inscription makes it clear that the arch was built at the behest of the tribal communities in honor of their new ally, rather than as an imperially-ordered sign of military dominion. The arch commemorates a change in political status, for which the residents were indebted to Augustus, and the preserved decoration of the arch reflects this primary purpose.[100]

---

98. Ibid., 16 "Face sud" pl. 1, 17–18 pls. 2–4.

99. *CIL* 5.7231. For a (still) useful exposition of the inscription, see Giuseppe Ponsero, *Piccolo Cenno Sovra L'Arco Trionfale di Cesare Ottaviano Augusto Existente Nella Citta di Susa* (Torino: Dalla Tipografia Mussano, 1841), 21–32, reproduced in Fabiano, *Arco di Susa*, 95–106.

100. Ossi, *Roman Honorific Arches*, 64.

3.3. Latin West Inscriptions Revealing the Dynamic of Barbarian Indebtedness

A similar picture emerges when we concentrate on other inscriptions from the Latin West dealing with the barbarians, especially those from Gaul and Spain. A few examples will suffice. An inscription from the city of Vaison in Narbonnese Gaul unveils the rituals of indebtedness existing between the Gallic tribe of the Vocontii, living in Vaison-la-Romaine, and their Roman patron, Burrus, the praetorian prefect of Claudius and Nero (51–62 CE: Tacitus, *Ann.* 51–62). Burrus, a native of this wealthy Romanized city, had ensured the continuance of imperial favor to his fellow citizens and was recompensed with this public honor on a stone.

> The Vocontii of Vaison (set this up) in honour of their patron Sextus Afranius Burrus, son of Sextus, of the tribe Voltinia, military tribune, procurator of the empress, procurator of Tiberius Caesar, procurator of deified Claudius, prefect of the Praetorian guard, honoured with the insignia of a consul. (DocsGaius §259)

However, the transaction of indebtedness not only occurred between the Gallic barbarian clients and imperial patron but was also expressed in reciprocal rituals of gratitude between the imperial patron and his barbarian clients. We gain a sense of "obligation" on Claudius's part to the loyal Gallic tribes in Narbonnese and Transalpine Gaul in his oration—recorded on a bronze tablet found at Lyons—on the admission of Gallic citizens to Roman offices (48 CE): "When my father Drusus was subduing Germany, it was they who by their tranquility provided undisturbed and profound peace in his rear."[101]

Moreover, imperial senators in their military careers ensured that they created relationships of indebtedness with the barbarians, pivoting compliant tribes over against the more contumacious tribes, in order to establish peace within the provinces. This is particularly evident in the senatorial career of Plautius, consul in 45 and 74, the extent of which spanned five Principates and which included a legateship in Spain. A striking vignette of one particular stage of that career is recounted in an

---

101. For a translation of the speech (DocsGaius §369; cf. Tacitus, *Ann.* 12.23–25), see Allan Chester Johnson et al., eds., *Ancient Roman Statutes* (Austin: University of Texas Press, 1961), §175.

honorific inscription (post-74 CE) found on a stone near ancient Tibur, a town twenty miles to the east of Rome. Adopting a policy of "divide and conquer" in the province of Moesia, Plautius created strong ties of obligation to Rome and to himself with several barbarian kings from the Balkans by returning to them their sons and brothers, who had formerly been captured by the Sarmatian tribes. In the case of the Sarmatians, however, their tribes are ruthlessly crushed and subjected to the Roman people. The honorific decree outlines Plautius's achievements in this manner:

> To Tiberius Plautius Silvanus Aelianus, son of Marcus, of the tribe Aniensis, pontifex, priest of Augustus, one of the board of three directors of the Mint, quaestor of Tiberius Caesar, legate of the fifth legion in Germany, praetor urbanus, legate and member of the staff of Claudius Caesar in Britain, consul, proconsul of Asia, propraetorian legate of Moesia, in which he transported more than 100,000 of the trans-Danubians, with their wives and children and chiefs and kings to be tribute-paying subjects; he crushed a rising of the Sarmatians at its outset, although he had dispatched a large part of his army to the expedition against Armenia; he transported kings hitherto unknown and hostile to the Roman people to the river bank which he was guarding to pay homage to the Roman standards; he restored their sons to the kings of the Bastarnae and Rhoxolani and to the king of the Dacians his brothers, who had been rescued or captured from the enemy; from some of them he took hostages; by these means he both assured and extended the peace of the province, driving the king of the Scythians from the siege of Heraclea of the Chersonese, which lies beyond the Dnieper.[102]

Finally, a Spanish inscription throws additional light on the indebtedness of the barbarian tribes to their Roman overlords because of the reciprocally binding nature of the client-patron relationships established in each case. It is worth remembering that Paul intended to go to Spain after visiting the Romans (Rom 15:24a, 28), with Roman house churches acting both as his financial patron (15:24b) and prayer partner (15:31-32) in his mission to the geographical extremity of Europe in the Latin West. Thus the profuse use of the language of "indebtedness" in Romans not well only may have had theological import but also reflected the social and political realities with which the Roman overlords and their Spanish subjects

---

102. DocsGaius §228. For the full translation, see S. J. Miller, *Inscriptions of the Roman Empire AD 14–117*, LACTOR 8 (London: Carfax, 1971), §42.

were intimately familiar. What is intriguing about this Augustan edict (15 BCE) on two bronze tablets, issued at Norbonne and found in northwestern Spain in 1999, is the Roman release from obligation and, conversely, the imposition of obligation on, respectively, the compliant Spanish tribe (the Paemeiobrigenses) and the noncompliant Spanish tribe (the Aiiobrigiaecini). It shows how the language of "indebtedness" and "obligation"—referring here to the obligation to provide taxation and manpower to the Romans—functioned socially and politically in the Latin West well before Paul projected a visit to Hispania after ministering at Rome.[103]

---

103. A more muted portrait of imperial "obligation" and "indebtedness" emerges if we consider the Latin inscriptions from central Spain. As Robert C. Knapp argues (*Latin Inscriptions from Central Spain* [Berkeley: University of California Press, 1992], 413), "Contact with the military and imperial civil personnel was probably as sporadic and ephemeral as the epigraphy suggests; the area presumably paid its taxes and was left alone." However, there is still sufficient evidence of loyalty being exercised by Spanish clients toward their Republican and imperial patrons and of *fides* ("faithfulness") on the part of the patrons toward their clients. An inscription (Knapp, *Latin Inscriptions*, §91) states: "The Bastetanian people saw to it that (this monument) be set up to Lucius Porcius in recognition of his excellent administration of the province." Since no L. Porcius ever was a governor of Spain, Knapp (*Latin Inscriptions*, 80) argues that "the interpreter was thinking of M. Porcius Cato, who was consul and proconsul in Spain in 195–194 BC." There are also two inscriptions honoring the Roman ruler with this formula (*Latin Inscriptions*, §§117, 174): "This altar is made sacred to the divine spirit of Caesar in response to his safety and victory." But, again, there is uncertainty regarding the dating of the inscriptions: while the lettering in each case points to an early date of composition (first to second century CE), the formula belongs to a later period (third to fifth century CE). Additionally, freedmen are honored for holding a post on the six-man board in charge of the worship of the emperor (*Latin Inscriptions*, §119 [second century CE]; §296 [191 CE]). Furthermore, the town councillors of the Spanish town Complutum in Madrid province (*Latin Inscriptions*, §120 [late first century–early second century CE]) decree that Gaius Nonius Sincerus could erect an honorific statue and inscription to his father, Cnaeus Nonius Crescens, for being chief "magistrate" of the town and "flamen of Rome and Augustus." Last, the Spanish tribes continued to dedicate to native gods (e.g., Velicus, Deus Togatus) and to local gods covered by Roman names (e.g., Nymphae, Deus Maximus). But they also showed *fides* to the traditional Roman deities (e.g., Jupiter, Mars) and to the gods who protected the imperial house (i.e., Mars Augustus [second century CE; *Latin Inscriptions*, §116], Pantheus Augustus [second century CE; §119]. For discussion of the deities, with the provision of an index, see *Latin Inscriptions*, 405–7, 471. In sum, the geographical isolation of central Spain precluded—in comparison to other Spanish regions and their major cities (e.g., Augusta Emerita)—intimate and regular access to the imperial networks, with the result that central Spain maintained a

The edict is reproduced below:

Imperator Caesar Augustus, son of the deified, in his 8th year of tribunician power, and as proconsul proclaims.
"I have learned from all of my deputies who have been in charge of the province across the Duero river that the fortress-dwelling Paemeiobrigenses, who belong to the Susarri people, remained loyal when all the rest were in revolt. Therefore I present them all with perpetual exemption from obligations; and as for the lands and boundaries which they possessed when my deputy Lucius Sestius Quirinalis governed this province, I order them to possess these lands without any dispute.
To the advantage of the fortress-dwelling Paemeiobrigenses, who belong to the Susarri people, to whom I had previously given exemption from all demands, I put back in their place the fortress-dwelling Aiiobrigiaecini, who belong to the Gigurri people, with the consent of the community itself; and I order the fortress-dwelling Aiiobrigiaecini to perform every public obligation with the Susarri."
Decided at Narbo Martius on 14 and 15 February, in the consulship of Marcus Drusus Libo and Lucius Calpurnius Piso.[104]

---

strong indigenous culture politically and religiously. Notwithstanding, there was sufficient exchange with imperial Rome in central Spain for the proper expression of obligation and indebtedness in the Latin inscriptions, both at the divine and human level. See also the important discussion of Leonard A. Curchin, *The Romanization of Central Spain: Complexity, Diversity and Change in a Provincial Hinterland* (London: Routledge, 2003). It is also worth remembering that the iconography of the Iberian Peninsula (Spain) differs from the relentless imagery of Roman victory and barbarian defeat found on the Augustan arches of southern France. The Augustan propaganda adopts a subtler and less imperialistic approach in Iberia. William E. Mierse (*Temples and Towns in Roman Iberia: The Social and Architectural Dynamics of Sanctuary Designs from the Third Century BC to the Third Century AD* [Berkeley: University of California Press, 1999], 124) notes that the militaristic relief decoration of the theater at Augusta Emerita alludes to Augustus's victory at Actium and not to his conquests on the Iberian Peninsula. We have to be sensitive, therefore, to the subtle differences in antiquity between conventions (i.e., expressions of obligation and indebtedness) and iconography (i.e., the depiction of victory over barbarians) city by city, region by region, and province by province.

104. M. G. L. Cooley, ed., *The Age of Augustus*, LACTOR 17 (Cambridge: Cambridge University Press, 2003), §M27. The Latin text is found in Géza Alföldy, "Das neue Edikt des Augustus aus El Bierzo in Hispanien," *ZPE* 131 (2000): 171–205. The literary evidence also confirms the *cost* of the indebtedness to Augustus envisaged by his Spanish military clients. The dedication of clients to Augustus "in the fashion of the Spaniards" (Dio 53.20) meant in the case of the Spaniards "to vow one's life for

Mostly, however, from the Roman and barbarian viewpoint, relations of indebtedness to the Roman ruler are much less complicated than the edict above. On the base of a golden statue of Augustus at the Forum of Augustus at Rome, datable to after 2 BCE (*Res Gestae* 24.2), the pacification of Further Spain, Baetica, is attributed to the benefits and care of Augustus as the benefactor of the world.

> To Imperator Caesar Augustus, father of his country, Further Spain, Baetica, because through his beneficence (*eius beneficio*) and perpetual care (*perpetua cura*), the province has been pacified. 100 pounds of gold.[105]

What light do the rituals of mutual "indebtedness" and "obligation"— evinced in the La Turbie, Susa, Vaison, Lyons, Tibur, Norbonne, and Further Spain inscriptions (*supra* §§3.1–3)—throw on Paul's attitude toward the barbarians? Clearly, Paul is inverting to some extent the rituals of obligation and indebtedness of the Latin West. In a remarkable social, pastoral, and evangelistic strategy, Paul says he is indebted to culturally and educationally diverse groups (Rom 1:14a: ὀφειλέτης εἰμι), whether Greek or barbarian. The self-conscious cultural superiority of Greeks toward the barbarian tribes is relativized in Paul's mutual obligation to both groups.[106] For Paul, the believer is indebted to no one (Rom 13:8: Μηδενὶ μηδὲν ὀφείλετε), except for the "debt" of love to all, articulated in

---

the leader and not to survive him if he perished in battle" (Galinsky, *Augustan Culture*, 328, citing on 426 n. 115 the following sources as confirmation: Valerius Maximus, *Facta et Dicta Memorabilia* 2.6.11; Caesar, *Bell. gall.* 3.22). Also, as a religious expression of indebtedness, Dio Cassius (*Historiae Romanae* 55.10a.2) mentions that in 2 BCE Lucius Domitius Ahenobarbus erected an altar of Augustus on the banks of the Elbe upon "establishing a friendly alliance with the barbarians."

105. Braund, *Augustus to Nero*, §44 (= DocsAug §42). Note the "benefactor" inscriptions to Augustus, Tiberius, and Claudius, set out respectively below: "Divine Augustus Caesar, son of god, imperator of land and sea, the benefactor and saviour of the whole world, the people of the Myrians" (DocsAug §72); "Tiberius Caesar, divine Augustus, the son of the divine Augusti, imperator of land and sea, the benefactor and saviour of the whole world, the people of the Myrians" (DocsAug §88); "Euphanes, son of Charinus, a Rhodian, the present *stephanephorus* and priest of divine Augustus … has dedicated from his own resources this statue of the saviour and benefactor of all mankind" (DocsGaius §135).

106. On Greek attitudes to the barbarians, see Hall, *Inventing the Barbarian*; Harrison, *Greeks and Barbarians*. On Roman attitudes to the barbarian, see Ferris, *Enemies of Rome*.

the Old Testament (Lev 19:18 LXX) and fulfilled in the Jesus tradition (Rom 13:8-10; cf. Matt 22:36-40; Mark 12:28-34).[107]

It is worth remembering that Paul's citation of Lev 19:18b includes the wider context of the LXX passage, an important hermeneutical dimension to the New Testament exegesis of Old Testament texts that C. H. Dodd highlighted many years ago.[108] The "love of neighbor" spoken of in Lev 19:18b is prefaced by a series of social motifs that are regularly punctuated by the concluding formula "I am the LORD" (vv. 10b, 12b, 14b, 16b, 18b).[109] There is concern for the poor and the stranger (vv. 9-10), honesty in human relations (vv. 11-12), a refusal to exploit the weak (i.e., one's neighbor, the hired man, or people with disabilities: vv. 13-14), justice in the courts and the necessity of neighborliness (vv. 15-16; cf. 35-36a), and a refusal to hate or seek revenge (vv. 17-18a). Given that love in the ancient Near East is community-related and expresses family solidarity, the "love command," as Erhard Gerstenberger argues, "refers to the shared connection and mutual responsibility of human beings living in a community of faith. The fact that Lev 19:34 fully includes the foreigner within the community shows the new dimension given to the old familial ethos."[110] The rationale for this wide-ranging social expression of covenantal holiness (Lev 19:2) originates with Israel's indebtedness to God for his exodus liberation of the Israelites, as well as their empathetic remembrance of the harsh experience of captivity before their liberation from Egypt (19:33-35):

---

107. Note the comment of John E. Hartley (*Leviticus*, WBC 4 [Dallas: Word, 1992], 318) regarding Jesus's use of Lev 19:19 (Matt 22:36-40; Mark 12:28-34): "Jesus took this commandment, elevated it as the second of the two great commandments, and expanded the circle of 'an acquaintance' to include all fellow humans, particularly anyone in need."

108. C. H. Dodd, *According to the Scriptures* (London: Collins, 1952), 74-133. Gordon J. Wenham (*The Book of Leviticus*, NICOT [Grand Rapids: Eerdmans, 1979], 274) writes: "In its original context Lev 19:18 epitomises and expresses the principles governing all the laws that surround it. Love for one's neighbour comes out in not stealing from him, or lying to him, or cheating him in business."

109. Erhard S. Gerstenberger (*Leviticus*, OTL [Louisville: Westminster John Knox, 1996], 262) observes: "The concluding formula solemnly underscores the norms imparted in these verses."

110. Ibid., 272.

When an alien lives with you in your land, do not ill-treat him. The alien living with you must be treated as one of your native-born. Love him as yourself, for you were aliens in Egypt.... I am the LORD your God, who brought you out of Egypt.

However, whereas the Levitical text confines "love of neighbor" to internal community relations in covenantal Israel, Paul's indebtedness of love ranges both outside the believing community ("Owe nothing to *anyone*, except...," Rom 13:8a) and inside the believing community ("to love *one another*," 13:8b). Paul's subsequent references to external persecution and internal harmony underscore this dual perspective (Rom 13:14, 16a, 17-21).[111]

Furthermore, the believer is justified before God by grace (Rom 4:4: κατὰ χάριν) and not by "works" of indebtedness (4:4: κατὰ ὀφείλημα). The dynamic of divine grace (Rom 4:1-25)—expressed in love through the Spirit (5:5: ἡ ἀγάπη τοῦ θεοῦ; 12:9a: ἡ ἀγάπη ἀνυπόκριτος; cf. 13:8-10)— explains why the apostle challenged the denigration and stereotyping of the "barbarian" in mid-50s Rome.[112] The consequences for social relations within the body of Christ were immediate: the "strong" were obligated to put up with the failings of the "weak" (Rom 15:1: Ὀφείλομεν δὲ ἡμεῖς), and the gentile was obligated to the Jew in beneficence to the poor (15:27: ὀφειλέται εἰσὶν αὐτῶν). But in Rom 1:14 the apostle spells out what this obligation meant for the believer's mission to the marginalized people groups *outside of* the body of Christ. His decision would enable his house churches to embrace not only the peoples from barbarian tribes with

---

111. For a fine discussion of Rom 13:8-14 in its LXX perspective, see Mark A. Seifrid, "Romans," in *Commentary on the New Testament Use of the Old Testament*, ed. G. K. Beale and D. A. Carson (Grand Rapids: Baker Academic, 2007), 682-84.

112. This contrasted with the Roman understanding of "obligation" (*officium*) to the gods, one's family, state, and patrons (Jewett, *Romans*, 132). Indissoluble ties of honor, piety, and reciprocity defined each of these relationships. The βάρβαροι were excluded in each instance until Claudius's admission of the chieftains of Long-haired Gaul to the Roman Senate in 47 CE, though by that time Narbonnese Gaul and Baetica in Spain had already produced senators and equestrian officials for the Senate. For Roman auditors hearing Rom 1:14 for the first time, the social implications of what Paul was saying would have been confronting because of the open-ended and nondiscriminatory nature of the obligation envisaged.

whom the Romans had patronal relations but also those tribes whom the Romans had punished for their noncompliance.[113]

4. Conclusion

In this essay we have attempted to chart the importance of the intersection of archaeological, iconographic, numismatic, and inscriptional evidence, where it is available, in discussing the meaning of the visual evidence pertaining to barbarians in the cities of the Greek East and Latin West. Moreover, the importance of the interrelation between honorific monuments and the sacred spaces of the city has also to be considered for the ideology and symbolism that is conveyed. Where these intersections and interrelations are taken seriously, we have demonstrated that, in the case of the visual evidence relating to barbarians, significant pathways for the social and theological interpretation of Paul's letters are opened up. The interpretative vistas provided by these new pathways enable us to appreciate once again the radical social implications of Paul's gospel in its first-century Greco-Roman context.

Bibliography

Alföldy, Géza. "Das neue Edikt des Augustus aus El Bierzo in Hispanien." *ZPE* 131 (2000): 171–205.
Baldry, H. C. "The Idea of the Unity of Mankind." Pages 169–204 in *Grecs et barbares*. Edited by Hans Schwabl. Vandoeuvres/Geneva: Fondation Hardt, 1962.
———. *The Unity of Mankind in Greek Thought*. Cambridge: Cambridge University Press, 1965.
Barton, Tamsyn. *Ancient Astrology*. London: Routledge, 1994.
———. "Augustus and Capricorn: Astrological Polyvalency and Imperial Rhetoric." *JRS* 85 (1995): 33–51.

---

113. Paul's enlightened stance toward barbarians had no impact in shifting hardened official attitudes within the Christian bureaucracy of the later empire. Note the comment of Annalina Caló Levi (*Barbarians on Roman Imperial Coins and Sculpture* [New York: American Numismatic Society, 1952], 4): "Neither in coins nor in official sculpture did the advent of Christianity cause any change in the conception of the barbarian. He appears until the end as a sign of the victory or of the victorious power of the emperor over his military enemies."

Beard, Mary, John N. North and Simon Price, eds. *A History.* Vol. 1 of *Religions of Rome.* Cambridge: Cambridge University Press, 1998.

Binninger, Sophie. *Le Trophée d'Auguste à la Turbie.* Paris: Patrimonie, 2009.

Bradley, Keith. "On Captives under the Principate." *Phoenix* 58 (2004): 298–319.

Braund, David C. *Augustus to Nero: A Sourcebook on Roman History 31 BC–AD 68.* Totowa: Barnes & Noble, 1985.

Bruce, F. F. *The Epistle of Paul to the Romans: An Introduction and Commentary.* TNTC. Leicester: Inter-Varsity Press, 1963.

Brunt, P. A., and J. M. Moore, eds. *Res Gestae Divi Augusti: The Achievements of the Divine Augustus.* Oxford: Oxford University Press, 1967.

Casimir, Philippe. *Le Trophée d'Auguste à la Turbie.* Marseille: Tacussel, 1932.

Cavargna Allemano, Anna Maria. "Il fregio dell'arco di Susa espressione locale di arte provinciale romana." Pages 207–33 in *Arco di Susa Eretto da Marco Giulio Cozio in Onore di Cesare Ottaviano Augusto (8 a.C–1992 d.C): Monografia per il Bimillenatio.* Edited by G. Fabiano. Segusium 31. Torino: Società di Ricerche e Studi Valsusini, 1991.

Champlin, Edward. *Nero.* Cambridge, MA: Belknap Press of Harvard University Press, 2003.

Cherry, David. *The Roman World: A Sourcebook.* Oxford: Blackwell, 2001.

Coarelli, Filippo. *Rome and Environs: An Archaeological Guide.* Berkeley: University of California Press, 2007.

Cooley, Alison E. *Res Gestae Divi Augusti: Text, Translation, and Commentary.* Cambridge: Cambridge University Press, 2009.

Cooley, M. G. L. ed. *The Age of Augustus.* LACTOR 17. Cambridge: Cambridge University Press, 2003.

Cranfield, C. E. B. *Romans 1–8.* ICC. Edinburgh: T&T Clark, 1975.

Crook, J. A. "Political History, 30 BC–AD 14." Pages 70–112 in *The Augustan Empire 43 BC–AD 69.* Vol. 10 of *The Cambridge Ancient History.* Edited by Alan K. Bowman, Edward Champlin, and Andrew Lintott. 2nd ed. Cambridge: Cambridge University Press, 1996.

———. "Augustus: Power, Authority, Achievement." Pages 113–46 in *The Augustan Empire 43 BC–AD 69.* Vol. 10 of *The Cambridge Ancient History.* Edited by Alan K. Bowman, Edward Champlin, and Andrew Lintott. 2nd ed. Cambridge: Cambridge University Press, 1996.

Cueto, B. "The Concept of ΠΙΣΤΙΣ in Greco-Roman Context and Its Impact on Paul's Writings." PhD diss., Dallas Theological Seminary, 2012, forthcoming Paternoster Press.

Curchin, Leonard A. *The Romanization of Central Spain: Complexity, Diversity and Change in a Provincial Hinterland.* London: Routledge, 2003.
Dauge, Yves Albert. *Le barbare: recherches sur la conception romaine de la barbarie et de la civilisation.* Collection Latomus 176. Brussels: Latomus, 1981.
Davis, P. J. "The Colonial Subject in Ovid's Exile Poetry." *AJP* 123 (2002): 257–73.
Dench, Emma. *From Barbarians to New Men: Greek, Roman, and Modern Perceptions of Peoples from the Central Apennines.* Oxford: Oxford University Press, 1995.
Dodd, C. H. *According to the Scriptures.* London: Collins, 1952.
Dudley, Donald Reynolds. *The World of Tacitus.* London: Secker & Warburg, 1968.
Edwards, Charles M. "The Arch Over the Lechaion Road at Corinth and Its Sculpture." *Hesperia* 63 (1994): 263–308.
Ehrenberg, Victor, and A. H. M. Jones. *Documents Illustrating the Reigns of Augustus and Tiberius.* 2nd ed. Oxford: Clarendon, 1983.
Elsner, Jaś. "Inventing Imperium: Texts and the Propaganda of Monuments in Augustan Rome." Pages 32–53 in *Art and Text in Roman Culture.* Edited by Jaś Elsner. Cambridge: Cambridge University Press, 1996.
Espérandieu, Émile. *Recueil general des bas-reliefs de la Gaule romanine.* Vol. 1. Ridgewood: Greg Press, 1965.
Ferrero, Ermanno. *L'Arc d'Auguste à Suse.* Turin: Société d'archéologie et des beaux-arts, 1901.
Ferris, Iain M. *Enemies of Rome: Barbarians through Roman Eyes.* Stroud: Sutton, 2000.
Formigé, Jules. *Le Trophée des Alpes: La Turbie.* Paris: Centre Nationale de la Recherche Scientifique, 1949.
Gaertner, Jan Felix, ed. and trans. *Ovid, Epistulae Ex Ponto, Book 1.* Oxford: Oxford University Press, 2005.
Galinsky, Karl. *Augustan Culture: An Interpretative Introduction.* Princeton: Princeton University Press, 1996.
Gates, Charles. *Ancient Cities: The Archaeology of Urban Life in the Ancient Near East and Egypt, Greece and Rome.* London: Routledge, 2003.
Gee, Emma. *Ovid, Aratus and Augustus: Astronomy in Ovid's Fasti.* Cambridge: Cambridge University Press, 2000.
Gregory, Timothy E., and Harrianne Mills. "The Roman Arch at Isthmia." *Hesperia* 53 (1984): 407–45.

Gruen, Erich S. "The Expansion of the Empire under Augustus." Pages 147–97 in *The Augustan Empire 43 BC–AD 69*. Vol. 10 of *The Cambridge Ancient History*. Edited by Alan K. Bowman, Edward Champlin, and Andrew Lintott. 2nd ed. Cambridge: Cambridge University Press, 1996.

———. *Rethinking the Other in Antiquity*. Princeton: Princeton University Press, 2011.

Gurval, Robert Alan. *Actium and Augustus: The Politics and Emotions of Civil War*. Ann Arbor: University of Michigan Press, 1995.

Hall, Edith. *Inventing the Barbarian: Greek Self-Definition through Tragedy*. Oxford: Clarendon, 1989.

Harrison, James R. "'More Than Conquerors' (Rom 8:37): Paul's Gospel and the Augustan Triumphal Arches of the Greek East and Latin West." *Buried History: The Journal of the Australian Institute of Archaeology* 47 (2011): 3–20.

———. "Paul's 'Indebtedness' to the Barbarian (Rom 1:14) in Latin West Perspective." *NovT* 55 (2013): 311–48.

Harrison, Thomas, ed. *Greeks and Barbarians*. Edinburgh: Edinburgh University Press, 2011.

Hartley, John E. *Leviticus*. WBC 4. Dallas: Word, 1992.

Hartshorn, Nicole Candace. "Images of Power: The Augustan Trophy of the Alpes as a Roman Visual Narrative and Commemoration." MA thesis, California State University, 2006.

Hingley, Richard. *Globalizing Roman Culture: Unity, Diversity and Empire*. London: Routledge, 2005.

Holland, Leicester B. "The Triple Arch of Augustus." *AJA* 50 (1946): 52–59.

Holdsworth, Benjamin Evans. "Reading Romans in Rome: A Reception of Romans in the Roman Context of Ethnicity and Faith." PhD diss., Durham University, 2009.

Iacopi, Irene. *The House of Augustus: Wall Paintings*. Rome: Electa, 2008.

Jewett, Robert. *Romans: A Commentary*. Hermeneia. Minneapolis: Fortress, 2007.

Johnson, Allan Chester, Paul Robinson Coleman-Norton, Frank Card Bourne, and Clyde Pharr, eds. *Ancient Roman Statutes*. Austin: University of Texas Press, 1961.

Judge, E. A. *The First Christians in the Roman World: Augustan and New Testament Essays*. Edited by James R. Harrison. WUNT 229. Tübingen: Mohr Siebeck, 2008.

———. *A History of Roman Art: Enhanced Edition*. Boston: Wadsworth, 2010.
Kleiner, Fred S. *A History of Roman Art*. 2nd ed. Boston: Wadsworth, 2010.
———. *The Arch of Nero in Rome: A Study of the Roman Honorary Arch before and after Nero*. Rome: Bretschneider, 1985.
Knapp, Robert C. *Latin Inscriptions from Central Spain*. Berkeley: University of California Press, 1992.
Kuttner, Ann L. *Dynasty and Empire in the Age of Augustus: The Case of the Boscoreale Cups*. Berkeley: University of California Press, 1995.
Levi, Annalina Caló. *Barbarians on Roman Imperial Coins and Sculpture*. New York: American Numismatic Society, 1952.
Merriam, Carol U. " 'Either with Us or against Us': The Parthians in Augustan Ideology." *Scholia* 13 (2004): 50–70.
Mierse, William E. *Temples and Towns in Roman Iberia: The Social and Architectural Dynamics of Sanctuary Designs from the Third Century BC to the Third Century AD*. Berkeley: University of California Press, 1999.
Miller, S. J. *Inscriptions of the Roman Empire AD 14–117*. LACTOR 8. London: Carfax, 1971.
Mitchell, Stephen, and Marc Waelkens. *Pisidian Antioch: The Site and Its Monuments*. London: Duckworth, 1998.
Morris, Leon. *The Epistle to the Romans*. Pillar New Testament Commentary. Grand Rapids: Eerdmans, 1988.
Oliver, J. H. "Epigramma magni momenti: *IG* IX, 1135." *GRBS* 8 (1967): 238–39.
Ossi, Adrian John. "The Roman Honorific Arches of Pisidian Antioch: Reconstruction and Contextualization." PhD diss., Univerisity of Michigan, 2010.
Picard, Gilbert Charles. *Les trophées romains: Contribution à l'histoire de la religion et de l'art triomphal de Rome*. Paris: de Broccard, 1957.
Ponsero, Giuseppe. *Piccolo Cenno Sovra L'Arco Trionfale di Cesare Ottaviano Augusto Esistente Nella Citta di Susa*. Torino: Dalla Tipografia Mussano, 1841, 21–32. Reproduced as pages 95–106 in *Arco di Susa Eretto da Marco Giulio Cozio in Onore di Cesare Ottaviano Augusto (8 a.C—1992 d.C): Monografia per il Bimillenatio*. Edited by G. Fabiano. Segusium 31. Torino: Società di Ricerche e Studi Valsusini, 1991.
Prieur, J. "Les arcs monumentaux dans les Alpes occidentals: Aoste, Suse, Aix-les-Bains." *ANRW* 12.1:454–55.

Rehak, Paul. *Imperium and Cosmos: Augustus and the Northern Campus Martius.* Madison: University of Wisconsin Press, 2006.
Ridley, Ronald T. *The Emperor's Retrospect: Augustus' Res Gestae in Epigraphy, Historiography and Commentary.* Leuven: Peeters, 2003.
Robinson, David M. "Roman Sculptures from colonia Caesaria (Pisidian Antioch)." *Art Bulletin* 9 (1926): 5–69.
Rocca, Eugenio La. *Amazzonomachia: Le sculture frontonali del tempio di Apollo Sosiano.* Rome: De Luca Editore, 1985.
Rose, Charles Brian. "The Arch of Hadrian and Sabina at Pisidian Antioch: Imperial Associations, Ritual Connections, and Civic Euergetism." Pages 85–108 in *Building a New Rome: The Roman Colony of Pisidian Antioch (25 BC–300 AD).* Edited by Elaine K. Gazda and Diana Y. Ng. Ann Arbor: Kelsey Museum of Archaeology, 2011.
———. "The Parthians in Augustan Rome." *AJA* 109 (2005): 21–75.
———. "Princes and Barbarians on the Ara Pacis." *AJA* 94 (1990): 453–67.
Rubin B. B. "(Re)presenting Empire: The Roman Imperial Cult in Asia Minor, 31 BC–AD 63. PhD diss., University of Michigan, 2008.
———. "Ruler Cult and Colonial Identity: The Imperial Sanctuary at Pisidian Antioch." Pages 33–60 in *Building a New Rome: The Roman Colony of Pisidian Antioch (25 BC–300 AD).* Edited by Elaine K. Gazda and Diana Y. Ng. Ann Arbor: Kelsey Museum of Archaeology, 2011.
Scheid, John. *RES GESTAE DIVI AUGUSTI: Hauts Faits du DIVIN AUGUSTE.* Paris: Les Belles Letters, 2007.
Seifrid, Mark A. "Romans." Pages 607–95 in *Commentary on the New Testament Use of the Old Testament.* Edited by G. K. Beale and D. A. Carson. Grand Rapids: Baker Academic, 2007.
Smallwood, E. Mary. *Documents Illustrating the Principates of Gaius, Claudius and Nero.* Cambridge: Cambridge University Press, 1967.
Syme, Ronald. *The Roman Revolution.* Oxford: Oxford University Press, 1939.
———. *Tacitus.* 2 vols. Oxford: Oxford University Press, 1958.
Thibault, John C. *The Mystery of Ovid's Exile.* Berkeley: University of California Press, 1964.
Tuchelt, K. "Bermerkugen zum Tempelbezirk von Antiochia ad Pisidiam." Pages 501–22 in *Beiträge zur Altertumskunde Kleinasiens: Festschrift für Kurt Bittel.* Edited by Rainer Michael Boehmer and Harald Hauptmann. Mainz: von Zabern, 1983.
Vermeule, Cornelius C. *Roman Imperial Art in Asia Minor.* Cambridge, MA: Belknap Press of Harvard University Press, 1963.

Walker, Susan. "The Moral Museum: Augustus and the City of Rome." Pages 61–75 in *Ancient Rome: The Archaeology of the Eternal City*. Edited by Jon Coulston and Hazel Dodge. Oxford: Oxford University School of Archaeology, 2000.

Wallace-Hadrill, Andrew. "Augustus' Parthian Honours, the Temple of Mars Ultor and the Arch in the Forum Romanum." *Papers of the British School at Rome* 66 (1998): 71–128.

Wenham, Gordon J. *The Book of Leviticus*. NICOT. Grand Rapids: Eerdmans, 1979.

Williams, Gareth D. *Banished Voices: Readings in Ovid's Exile Poetry*. Cambridge: Cambridge University Press, 1994.

Woolf, Greg. *Becoming Roman: The Origins of Provincial Civilisation in Gaul*. Cambridge: Cambridge University Press, 1998.

Zanker, Paul. *The Power of Images in the Age of Augustus*. Ann Arbor: University of Michigan Press, 1990.

Contributors

Bradley J. Bitner (Ph.D. 2013, Macquarie University, Sydney) is currently Tutor in New Testament and Greek at Oak Hill College, London. Recent publications include *Paul's Political Strategy in 1 Corinthians 1–4: Constitution and Covenant* (Cambridge: Cambridge University Press, 2015).

Alan Cadwallader is Senior Lecturer in Biblical Studies at the Australian Catholic University, Canberra. Recent publications include *Colossae in Space and Time* (coeditor; Vandenhoeck & Ruprecht), *Where the Wild Ox Roams* (editor; SheffieldPhoenix), and *Fragments of Colossae* (ATF Press).

Malcolm Choat is an Associate Professor in the Department of Ancient History at Macquarie University, Sydney, and Macquarie University Ancient Cultures Research Centre. His current research includes projects on scribal practice in documentary papyri, the rise and development of monasticism in Egypt, and questions of authenticity and forgery in the papyri.

James R. Harrison studied Ancient History at Macquarie University and graduated from the doctoral program in 1997. Professor Harrison is the Research Director at the Sydney College of Divinity and an Honorary Associate of Macquarie University Ancient History Department. His recent publications include *Paul's Language of Grace in Its Graeco-Roman Context* (Mohr Siebeck, 2003) and *Paul and the Imperial Authorities at Thessalonica and Rome* (Mohr Siebeck, 2011).

Brigitte Kahl received her Th.D. (1983) and Dr.sc.theol. (1987) from Humboldt University in Berlin, where she taught Ecumenical Bible Studies and New Testament (1989–1997). She served as a Professor of Biblical Theology and Exegesis at Paderborn University (1997–1998), prior to becoming a Professor of New Testament at Union Theological Seminary in New York (1998–). Her most comprehensive publication on visual exegesis thus far is *Galatians Re-imagined: Reading with the Eyes of the Vanquished* (Augsburg Fortress, 2010).

Julien M. Ogereau (Ph.D. 2014) studied Theology, New Testament, and Early Christian Studies at the Sydney College of Divinity and Macquarie University. He is currently a Research Associate with the Exzellenzcluster Topoi B-5-3 at Humboldt-Universität zu Berlin. He is also a Honorary Research Associate withMacquarie University and the 2015 Junior Research Fellow of the Macquarie University Ancient Cultures Research Centre. Recent publications include *Paul's Koinonia with the Philippians* (Mohr Siebeck, 2014).

Paul Trebilco (Ph.D. 1987) studied Theology at the University of Otago, New Zealand, and completed his Ph.D. at the University of Durham in the United Kingdom. He is currently Professor of New Testament Studies in the Department of Theology and Religion, University of Otago. His recent publications include *The Early Christians in Ephesus from Paul to Ignatius* (Mohr Siebeck, 2004) and *Self-Designations and Group Identity in the New Testament* (Cambridge University Press, 2012).

L. L. Welborn (Ph.D. 1992) studied New Testament and Early Christianity at Vanderbilt University and the University of Chicago and is currently Professor of New Testament and Early Christianity at Fordham University. Recent publications include *Paul, the Fool of Christ: A Study of 1 Corinthians 1–4 in the Comic-Philosophic Tradition* (T&T Clark, 2005) and *An End to Enmity: Paul and the "Wrongdoer" of Second Corinthians* (de Gruyter, 2011).

Index of Primary Texts

Old Testament

Genesis
1:28	139, 142
3–4	119
3:6	142
4:9–10	145
4:11–12	145
4:17	145
4:21–22	145
4:23–24	145
10:8–12	145

Exodus
1–16	119
1:14 16	119
16:18	231
19:4	128
20:4–5	111

Leviticus
19:2	309
19:10	309
19:11–12	309
19:12	309
19:13–14	309
19:14	309
19:15–16	309
19:16	309
19:18	309
19: 33–35	309
19:34	309
19:35–36	309

Numbers
16:32	119

Deuteronomy
5:8–9	111

Deuterocanonical Books

1 Maccabees
9:14	61

Ancient Jewish Writers

Josephus, *Bellum judaicum*
4.241	228

Philo, *De virtutibus*
173–74	227
174	228

Philo, *De somniis*
155	228

New Testament

Matthew
9:35	3
10:11	3
22:36–40	308

Mark
6:56	3
12:28–34	309

Luke		5:10	297
8:1	3	8:30	297
13:22	3	8:35	296
16:20–21	193	8:37	296, 297
		8:37–39	296
Acts		8:39	296
13:1–14:24	13	9:22–26	290
17:2	17	9:30	292
17:16	112	10:4	292
17:16–34	18	10:6	292
18:1–18	96	10:10	292
18:7	97	10:12	281
18:12–17	95, 96	11:7–24	290
19	101	11:17–21	291
19–20	265	11:18–20	281
19:23–40	266	12:9	310
19:35	5	12:14–21	281
20:15	121	12:16	281
20:17	121	13:8	308, 310
20:26	265	13:8–10	281, 309
20:33	265	13:14	310
20:34	265	13:16	310
20:35	265	13:17–21	310
		14:1–15:7	281
Romans		14:3	227
1:9–10	291	14:10	227
1:13	291	15:1	310
1:14	281, 283, 290 308, 310	15:7–12	290
1:15	291	15:24	305
3:22	292	15:25–29	292
3:26	292	15:27	310
3:27–4:25	290	15:28	305
3:28	292	15:31–32	305
3:29–30	281	16:1	97
3:30	292	16:23	20, 97, 98
4:1–25	309, 310		
4:4	310	1 Corinthians	
4:5	292	1–6	157
4:9	292	1:14	97
4:11	292	1:22	264
4:13	292	1:26	227–28
5:1	292	1:26–28	193, 226
5:6	297	1:26–29	20
5:8	297	1:27–28	227
5:9	296	2:7–8	297

4:8–13	32	4:24–31	290
4:9–13	227		
4:12	228	Ephesians	
6:4	227	1:3–14	29
6:20	229	1:13	264
7:20–21	193	2:11–22	290
7:21	229	4:25	264
7:22	229	4:28	264
7:31	297	4:29	264
8	230	4:30	264
8:9	230	5:4	264
8:14	231	5:5–8	34
8:15	231		
9:24–27	23, 159, 184	Philippians	
9:27	23	2:3–8	265
10:7	24	2:5–8	15
10:14–22	24	4:12	228
11:1–16	183	4:22	34
11:17–34	193		
11:22	203, 229, 230	Colossians	
11:29–30	230	1:2	32
11:30	203, 229	1:7	266
11:33	230	2:15	61
12:2	24	2:18	61
12:3	24	3:11	282, 290
15:32	60	3:15	61
16:9	267	3:1–17	30, 115
16:11	227	3:1–4:6	32
16:19	266	3:11	283
		3:22–25	34
2 Corinthians		4:12–13	266
1:8	266	4:13	32
2	98	4:15–16	32
2:5–8	21		
4:8–9	32	1 Thessalonians	
6:3–10	32	2:9	228
7	98	4:17	119
7:12	21	5:10	227
8:9	3		
10:10	227	1 Timothy	
11:27	228	4:7–10	60
		6:11–12	60
Galatians			
3:1–4:11	290	2 Timothy	
4:14	227	4:6–8	60

2 Timothy (cont.)
   4:20   121

Philemon
   22   266

1 Peter
   2:18   34

Revelation
   1–3   120
   1:2   131
   1:9   118, 131
   1:11   131
   1:12   131
   1:19   131
   2–3   9
   2:13   137
   3:14   32
   3:14–22   32
   3:17   228
   5:6   132
   5:8   132
   5:13   135
   7:1–3   135
   8:18–24   133
   8:19   133
   9:20–21   117
   10:2   135
   10:5   135
   10:6   135
   11:18   117
   12   117, 128, 132, 133, 137
   12–13   137
   12:1–5   118, 119
   12:2   133
   12:3–4   131
   12:4   118
   12:4–5   118, 131
   12:5   119, 132
   12:6   118
   12:7–9   118, 131
   12:8   118
   12:9   118, 119, 131 137, 142
   12:12   117, 118, 135, 141
   12:12–13   131
   12:13–16   131
   12:13–17   117, 133
   12:14   118, 119, 128
   12:14–15   119
   12:15   118
   12:15–17   116, 117
   12:16   115, 116, 117, 119, 120, 121, 122, 135, 141, 142, 143, 144
   12:17   118, 132, 144
   12:18   111
   13:1   135
   13:2   118, 137
   13:3–4   118, 132
   13:7   132, 140
   13:8   132
   13:10   132
   13:11   135
   13:14   131
   14:7   135
   18:11–13   140
   21   137
   21–22   119
   22:1   137
   22:1–2   145
   22:1–5   143
   22:3   137

Early Christian Literature

Gregory of Nyssa, *De pauperibus amandis*
   1, PG 46:457   220

Jerome, *Epistulae*
   121   61

John Chrysostom, *Homiliae in Epistulam I ad Corinthios*
   21.5, PG 61:176   210

Tertullian, *Adversus Valentinianos*
   7   33

INDEX OF PRIMARY TEXTS

Greco-Roman Literature

Alciphron, *Epistulae parasiticae*
24	189
24 [3.60.1]	202
24 [3.60.1]	202
24 [3.60.3]	202, 203

Ammianus Marcellinus, *Res Gestae*
14.6.25	201
15.10.2	301
15.10.7	301
17.4.12	295

Anonymous, *On Military Matters*
6.1	280

Apollodorus, *Bibliotheca*
1.6.1–2	139

Appian, *Bella civilia*
2.48	220
2.120	201

Appian, *Bellum jugurthinum*
41.5	205

Appian, *Historia romana*
1.6–13	239

Apuleius, *Metamporhoses*
1.6–7	189
3.26	205
9.12	204
10.18–33	203
10.19	203
10.23	203
10.25–27	203
10.28	203
10.33	203

Aristophanes, *Plutus*
552–554	194

Aristotle, *Poetica*
1449a30	223

Aristotle, *Politica*
1253a2–3	3
1255b19–20	3
1252b28–29	3
1252b31–53a1	3
1321b	3

Athenaeus, *Deipnosophistae*
54e	195

Aulus Gellius, *Noctes Atticae*
10.3.5	228

Ausonius, *Griphus ternarii numeri*
36–37	54

Caesar, *Bellum civile*
1.35	205
3.20–21	220

Caesar, *Bellum gallicun*
3.22	308

Cicero, *De domo suo*
5	206
6	206
7	206
53	206
54	206
13	207
89	207, 194

Cicero, *De haruspicum responso*
1.41	4

Cicero, *De oratore*
2.236	223

Cicero, *De republica*
1.31	205
2.40	194

Cicero, *Epistulae ad Atticum*
 5.13.1 266
 6.8.1 266
 6.8.4 266
 12.32.2 220
 14.9.1 220
 15.17.1 220

Cicero, *In Catilinum*
 4.14–17 194

Cicero, *Pro Flacco*
 18 216

Cicero, *Pro Lege manilia*
 2.4–6 260
 5.11 260
 6.14–19 260

Cicero, *Pro Murena*
 1 194

Cicero, *Pro Sestio*
 1 206
 2 207
 53 . . . . 206, 207
 57 207
 65 207
 78 . . . . 206, 207
 81 206
 85 . . . . 206, 207
 96–97 205
 106 207
 126 207
 127 207

Demosthenes, *In Midiam*
 211 195

Demosthenes, *Orationes*
 21.185 228
 21.198 228

Dio Cassius, *Historiae Romanae*
 41.37–38 220
 42.29–33 220
 45.1 295
 49.15.5 294
 51.19 293
 53.20 307
 54.8.4 293
 55.10a.2 308
 56.25.5 286
 60.22.1 280

Dio Chrysostom, *Orationes*
 7.1–103 212
 7.81 212
 7.104–152 212
 7.105–106 212–13
 7.107 213
 7.109–138 213
 7.125 212
 7.130 213
 7.133 213
 7.138 214
 31.121 . . . . 55, 61

Epictetus, *Diatribai*
 3.9.14 227
 3.22.45 228
 4.8.25 227

Hesiod, *Theogonia*
 132–138 139
 154–186 139
 453–506 139
 616–735 139
 820–885 139

Horace, *Carmina*
 1.2.50–53 277
 1.12.33–60 277
 1.35.25–40 277
 1.37 277
 3.3.37–48 277
 3.5 277
 3.14 277
 4.2.33–36 277–78
 4.5.25–36 278

4.14	278	Lucian, *Somnium*	
4.15	278	3	224
Horace, *Carmen saeculare*		Manilius, *Astronomica*	
41–60	294	4.547–552	286
54–60	278	507–509	286
		4.791–796	287
Horace, *Epistulae*			
1.17.33–34	290	Martial, *Epigrammaton*	
2.1.250–257	278	1.92.5–9	200
		1.92.10	200
Horace, *Epodi*		10.5	189
9	278	10.5.3–12	200
Horace, *Satirae*		Menander, *Dyskolos*	
1.8	221	284–286	195
Livy, *Periochae*		Nonnos, *Dionysiaca*	
16	54	12	139
28.12	300	29–32	139
Lucian, *Cataplus*		Ovid, *Ex ponto*	
20	228	1.257–258	280
		3.1.5–6	280
Lucian, *De mercede conductis*		4.7	301
24	229		
		Ovid, *Tristia*	
Lucian, *Demonax*		1.3.7.51–52	5
57	55	1.5.69–70	4–5
		2.121–154	279
Lucian, *Gallus*		2.187–200	279–80
1	228	2.207–215	279
		2.225–236	278
Lucian, *Hermotimus*		2.240	279
81	229	3.3.12–13	278
		3.6.32	279
Lucian, *Necyomantia*		3.10.1–4	279
21	231	3.10.5–6	280
		3.10.21–24	279
Lucian, *Piscator*		3.14.41–42	279
34	229	3.14.46–52	279
		4.1.67–68	280
Lucian, *Saturnalia*		4.1.94	279
19, 20, 31, 38	228	4.2.1–74	278
		4.6.47–48	280

Ovid, Tristia (cont.)
5.7.50–74	279
5.10.27	280
5.12.57–58	279

Paulus, *Digest*
25.3.4	210

Pausanias, *Graeciae descriptio*
2.3.2	291
10.4.1	4

Phaedrus, *Fabulae Aesopiae*
1.1.13–14	224
1.15.9–10	224
2.6.1	224
3.13.14–15	224
3. Prologue 34–37	224

Phaedrus, *Philogelos*
43	226

Philostratus, *Vita Apollonii*
4.22	25

Philostratus, *Vitae sophistarum*
25	59

Plato, *Phaedrus*
234E	227

Plato, *Respublica*
364A	228

Plato, *Theaetetus*
176C	227

Pliny the Elder, *Naturalis Historia*
3.20	301
3.20.136–138	299
3.20.138	300
3.39	281
30.6.71	295

Pliny the Younger, *Epistulae*
3.1.10	301

Plutarch, *Vitae*
Cic. 49.2	228
Luc. 23.1	54, 55

Plutarch, *Moralia*
830D–831A	203

Pollux, *Onomasticon*
3.66	129
5.163	129

Propertius, *Elegiae*
2.10	278
3.4	278
4.6	278
4.37–68	294
3.4.13–18	280

Pseudo-Quintilian, *Declamationes maiores*
9	58

Pseudo-Quintilian, *Declamationes minores*
260.13	54
260.24	54, 59
279.8	59
287.8	58
302	58
305.8	59
305.16	59
317.11	59
382.2	59

Pseudo-Sallust, *Epistulae*
2.5.1	205

Quintilian, *Institutio oratoria*
6.1.23	209
6.3.8	223

INDEX OF PRIMARY TEXTS

Sallust, *Bellum catilinae*
36.4	206
36.5	206
37.1–3	205–06
37.7	206
37.8	206

Sallust, *Historiae*
1.44	227

Seneca the Elder, *Controversiae*
1.1	208
1.1.14	199
1.2.4	56
2 pref. 2	59
3 pref.	208
3 pref. 12–13	59
10.4	208
10.4.1	209
10.4.2	208, 209
10.4.4	209
10.4.6	209, 211
10.4.7	209
10.4.8	211
10.4.9	209
10.4.10	210
10.4.11	210
10.4.12	210
10.4.13	210
10.4.14	210
10.4.15	210
10.4.16	210
10.4.17–18	210
10.4.18–25	209
10.4.20	199
10.4.22	211
10.4.24	211

Seneca the Younger, *De clementia*
2.6.2	209
2.6.3	199

Seneca the Younger, *De ira*
3.18.1	228

Seneca the Younger, *Epistulae morales*
7	55
22.1	59
30.8	59
37	56
70.20	59

Servius, *In Vergilii Aeneidem commentarii*
3.67	54

Sophocles, *Ajax*
1290–1299	282

Strabo, *Geographica*
4.1.5	4
12.8.15	265
14.1.24	265
17.805	295

Statius, *Silvae*
4.5.45–48	281

Suetonius, *Divus* Augustus
5	295
7.2	294
21.3	293
29.3	294
44	53
94.4	295
94.6	295
94.12	286

Suetonius, *Divus Claudius*
18.2	192

Suetonius, *Divus Julius*
26	59
39	58

Suetonius, *Divus Tiberius*
23	280

Tacitus, *Annales*
2.6	300
4.62	53

Tacitus, Annales (cont.)
12.23–25	304
12.43	192
13.50–51	259
14.42	211
14.42–45	192, 211
14.45	211
51–62	304

Tacitus, Dialogus
39.4.12	259

Tacitus, Historiae
1.4	194, 211

Valerius Maximus, Facta et Dicta Memorabilia
2.4.7	54
2.6.11	308
9.2.1	228

Velleius Paterculus, Historiae Romanae
2.81.3	294

Virgil, Aeneid
8.678–681	294
8.704–706	294

Virgil, Vita Aesopi
1	225
2	225
4–7	225
15	226
18	225
27	225
31	225
38	226
38–64	226
41	226
55	225
65	226
69	225
77b	225

Vitruvius, De architectura
1	131
5	131

Inscriptions and Papyri

Année épigraphique
1971.45	33

Bulletin épigraphique
1970.584	48

Ascough, *Associations in the Greco-Roman World*
§§1–7	18
§§47–59	18
§§147–58	31
§§317–318	36
§§319–29	36

BCH 11 (1887)
§11	53

BGU
2.447	76–77

Braund, *Augustus to Nero*
§44	308

CIG
2900	49

CIL
4.9839	218
4.9932	218
5.7231	303
6.67	33
6.702	296
6.709	296
6.6215	34
6.6216	34
6.9824	33
6.10250	33
6.29791	33

INDEX OF PRIMARY TEXTS

Cooley, *The Age of Augustus*			*IGRR*	
§M27			3.1056	258
			4.868	49
Cottier, *Customs Law of Asia*	256–67		4.869	49
			4.870	48
Crawford, *Roman Statutes*				
§25	170		IKorinthKent	
			§226	96
DocsAug			§232	20
§42	308			
§69	280		*IMT*	
§72	308		1498	49
§88	308			
			Inscription of Augustus, Spain	307
DocsGaius				
§43b	280		Johnson, *Ancient Roman Statutes*	
§135	308		§175	304
§228	305			
§259	304		Kastor the pugilist, Colossae	57
§369	304			
			Knapp, *Latin Inscriptions from Central Spain*	
Harvey, *Roman Lives*				
§55	34		§91	306
			§116	306
IEphesos			§117	306
1a.7.2	4		§119	306
1a.8	4		§120	306
1a.18	5, 192, 215		§174	306
1a.22	5, 6		§296	306
1a.24B	5			
1a.22	5		Lattimore, *Greek and Latin Epitaphs*	
1a.23	5, 6		299	217
1a.27	5, 56, 100–01			
2.212	5		LBW	
2.430	6		1693b	48
2.728	5			
3.730	5		Miller, *Inscriptions of the Roman Empire*	
5.1606	5		§42	305
6.2034	5			
7.1.3025	182		Naldini, *Il cristianesimo in Egitto*	
			§4	73
IG				
II² 3297	6		*NewDocs*	
IX 1135	278		5:95–99	101
			5:107	101

INDEX OF PRIMARY TEXTS

NewDocs (cont.)
5:108–9	101
6:112–32	75
7:31–32	80
10:110–13	4

MAMA
4.168	70
6.40	48, 51
6.41	48
6.42	58
6.47	52
6.48	52
6.154	52

OGI
2.458	99
2.484	215–16

Ossi, *Roman Honorific Arches*
21	287

P.Bas.
1.16	73–74

P.Gen. Inv.
108	84

P.Mich.
2.121	80
5.241	80
5.250	80
5.251	80

P.Oslo
3.98	77–78

P.Oxy.
1.43v	81
1.99	79
3.405	71
3.413	189, 223
34.2719	80
52.3647	281

P.Ryl.
3.457	71

P.Vars.
2	189

Res gestae divi Augusti
Latin preface	287
1.1	290
2	290
3.1	289
3.1–2	286, 293
3.2	289
4.1	295
4.2	300
4.3	286, 289, 293
13	289
14	280
24.2	308
25	289
25–30	289
25–33	286, 289, 293
26–27	289
26–30	289, 302
26.3	297, 300, 302
26.4	301
27	289
28	289
29	289
29.2	293
30	289
30.1	295
30.2	300
31–33	290, 301
31.1	289, 290
32–33	289
32.3	289, 291, 292
34.2	290

Sebasteion 288

SB
8. 9902	84
10.10728	7
16.12497	74–75

24.16000	82–83	59	169
		75–76	177
SEG		80–82	167
25.118	49	80–89	157
26.121	4	82–89	166
28.848	49	94–99	168
29.301	20	126–128	174
51.1573	192	168–176	175
57.332	23	215–221	174
57.1384–85	30	230	177
59.237	49	258	166

Head, *Greek Coins of Ionia*

SIG	
2.684	192
2.801	95

§§233–34	6
§235	6
§242	6
§254	6
§259	6
§262	6
§§264–65	6
§268	6
§§270–72	6
§§276–77	6
§§280–81	6
§291	6
§§298–99	6
§§301–3	6
§306	6
§§308–9	6

Stauber, *Steinepigramme*
1.02.15.01   58

Stroud, *The Sanctuary of Demeter and Kore*
§127   24

von Aulock, *Münzen und Städte Phrygiens*
§§586–588   48

Coins

Amandry, *Le monnayage*

pl. Xb	173
pl. XIa	173
pl. XXIIf	174
pl. XIIIb	173
pl. XIIId	173
pl. XIIIg	173
pl. XVI	175, 182
pl. XXI	179
9–10	164
19–22	174
24–26	157
34	174
35	166
43–55	173
55–69	175

Knapp and MacIsaac, *The Coins*
116–120   168

RIC 1²
"Augustus," §§131–37   293
"Claudius," §§30, 44   280

RPC 1

1–5	164
16–17	163
146	169
245–257	166
264–266	172
§258	180
§1116	179

RPC 1 (cont.)

§1134	173
§1136	173
§1140	173
§1141	173
§1143	173
§§1149–50	169
§§1151–71	175
§1158	176
§§1201–2	57, 180
§1204	174
§1238	180
§1253	179
§1271	174
§1283	179
§1646	179

RPC 1 Supp 1

§2891	50

von Aulock, *Münzen und Städte Phrygiens*

§§83–94	49
§545	50
§547	50
§§586–588	48

Terracotta Lamps

Oscar Broneer, *Terracotta Lamps*

§633	20

Index of Modern Authors

Abrahamsen, Valerie Ann 14
Abramenko, Andrik 190, 196, 232
Adams, Edward 34
Adamsheck, Beverley 23
Aicher, Peter J. 36
Aitken, Ellen Bradshaw 113
Alcock, Susan 191, 232
Aldrete, Gregory S. 33
Alföldy, Geza 196 232, 307, 311
Alkier, Stefan 152
Allemano, Anna Maria Cavargna 302
Alston, Richard 67, 70, 85
Alsup, John E. 119, 149
Amandry, Michel 15, 22, 50, 63, 154–57, 161, 164–69, 173–78, 186
Amerling, Walter 10, 94, 104
Andreau, Jean 248–49, 251, 254, 258–59, 263, 267
Andronikos, Manolēs 17
Archibald, Zosia H. 28
Armisen-Marchetti, Mireille 56, 62
Arnaoutoglou, Ilias 9, 37
Arnold, Clinton E. 13, 49, 62
Ascough, Richard S. 9, 16–18, 28, 37, 103, 105, 107, 249, 266, 267, 271
Asgeirsson, Jon Ma 115, 149
Ashbrook, Susan 89
Ashby, Thomas 35
Atkins, Margaret 189, 239, 241–42
Atkinson, K. M. T. 263–64, 267
Attridge, Harold W. 163
Aufrecht, Walter E. 68
Aulock, Hans Silvius von 48, 50, 62
Aune, David E. 118, 145
Avi-Yonah, Michael 11

Badian, Ernst 252, 261 267
Bagdikian, Anita 156, 186
Bagnall, Roger S. 67–68, 70, 72, 76–77, 82, 85, 197–98, 233
Bakker, Jan Theo 35
Bakirtzis, Charalambos 14
Balch, David L. 113, 138, 145, 241
Baldry, H. C. 280, 311
Baldwin, Barry 193, 223, 233
Balabanski, Vicky 117, 146
Baldry, H. C. 281–82
Balz, Horst 145
Balzat, Jean-Sébastien 180–81, 184
Bammer, Anton 28
Bang, Peter F. 251, 259, 268
Barclay, John M. G. 95, 109, 255, 268
Barker, Don 71, 85
Barrandon, Nathalie 260, 261, 268
Barton, Carlin 58
Barton, Tamsyn 286, 287
Basore, John W. 209, 233
Bauckham, Richard 103, 105
Baysal, H. H. 51, 52, 62
Beacham, Richard C. 48
Beale G. K. 310
Beard, Mary 33, 294, 312
Becatti, Giovanni 222, 233
Bellinger, Alfred R. 163, 186
Beloch, Julius 220, 233
Bendemann, Reinhard von 2, 37
Benjamin, Anna S. 49, 62, 211, 214
Benjamin, Walter 211, 214, 233
Benner, A. R. 202, 233
Bérard, François 105, 246, 250, 268
Best, E. E. 201, 233

-335-

Betti, Fabio 36
Betz, Hans Dieter 230, 233
Bietak, Manfred 67
Bilgin, M. 32
Binder, Donald D. 10
Binninger, Sophie 298, 299, 312
Bisel, Jane 221, 233
Bisel, Sarah 190, 192, 221, 233
Bitner, Bradley J. 21, 22, 151–87, 170
Black, Clifton C. 114, 149
Bloomquist, Gregory 114
Blum, Irene 122, 124, 144, 146
Bodel, John 89–91, 93, 104–5, 108, 190–91, 221, 233, 246–47, 250, 268
Boehmer, Rainer Michael 285, 316
Bogaert, Raymond 215, 233, 248, 268
Bol, Renate 121–22, 126–27, 129, 146
Bolden, Ron 152
Bonaria, Marius 193, 233
Bonner, Stanley F. 206, 233
Bormann, Lukas 14
Bornkamm, Günther 229, 230, 233
Bouley, E. 47, 62
Bourne, Frank Card 314
Bousquet, Jean 250, 268
Bowersock, G. W. 7, 205, 234
Bowman, Alan K. 69, 74, 85, 197, 234, 240, 254, 258–59, 268, 284, 314
Bradley, Keith 193, 234, 295, 312
Brandt, Olof 35
Branham, R. Bracht 231, 234
Braund, David C. 215, 234, 282, 308, 312
Brélaz, Cédric 14
Brescia, G. 58, 63
Bresson, Alain 250–51, 253, 268
Breytenbach, Cilliers 13, 17, 23, 29, 266–67, 268
Brocke, Christoph vom 17, 152
Bromwich, James 298, 299
Broneer, Oscar 20, 23, 159
Brookins, Timothy A. 20, 184
Bruce, F. F. 297, 312

Brunt, P. A. 189, 190, 194–96, 206, 208, 214–15, 219–20, 234, 258–61, 268, 300, 312
Buckler, William 48, 52
Burke, Trevor I. 177
Burnett, Andrew 15, 50, 63, 153, 156–58, 162–65, 176
Burns, Thomas S. 70, 86
Burrell, Barbara 5, 6, 37
Byrne, Maurice A. 11
Cadwallader, Alan 4, 30, 32, 41–66, 267–68
Cain, Hans-Ulrich 121, 124, 130, 143, 146
Calder, William 48, 52, 105
Capasso, Luigi 192, 234
Capdetrey, Laurent 8, 37
Camilleri, Valeria Giulia 31
Canavan, Rosemary 30, 113, 115–16, 146
Cansever, Meltem 25
Carlsen, Jesper 50, 63
Carson, D. A. 310
Carson, R. A. G. 163
Carlsson, Susanne 50, 63
Carson, R. A. G. 154
Carter, Michael 20, 45, 47, 61, 63
Cascio, Elio Lo 258
Casey, Patrick J. 153
Casimir, Philippe 297–300, 312
Castelli, Elizabeth A. 55, 63
Cavargna Allemano, Anna Maria 302, 312
Cébeillac-Gervasoni, Mireille 8, 37
Chamberland, Guy 53, 63
Champlin, Edward 223, 236, 240, 284, 295, 312, 314
Chancey, Mark A. 11, 163
Chaniotis, Angelos 47, 63, 247
Chankowski, Véronique 250, 269
Charlesworth, James H. 104
Cherry, David 280, 312
Childe, V. Gordon 7, 37
Choat, Malcolm 67–88, 68, 73, 84, 86
Claridge, Amanda 33

Clarke, Andrew D. 20, 97, 105, 156–57, 160, 181
Cloud, Duncan 194, 234
Coarelli, Filippo 35, 293, 312
Cohoon, J. W. 213, 234
Coleman, Kathleen M. 45, 63
Coleman-Norton, Paul Robinson 213, 235, 314
Coles, Revel A. 79, 86
Collart, Paul 14, 15
Collins, Adela Yarbro 137–38, 146
Collins, John J. 109
Concannon, Cavan W. 20–21, 41, 57–58, 63, 159–60, 168
Connolly, Peter 8, 37
Constantakopoulou, Christy 266, 273
Cook, B. F. 105
Cook, John 215, 234
Cook, John Granger 103, 105
Cooley, Alison E. 89, 93, 246, 269, 284
Cooley, M. G. L. 307, 312
Cornell, Timothy J. 7
Corte, Matteo Della 218, 234
Cottier, M. 28, 256, 257–60, 262, 263, 269
Cotton, Hannah M. 10, 217, 240
Coulston, Jon 35, 294, 317
Coupry, Jacques 15
Cowey, James M. 76, 86
Cox, Sherry C. 190, 192, 234
Cranfield, C. E. B. 297, 312
Crawford, Michael 90, 107, 163, 166, 170, 269
Croix, G. E. M. de Ste. 192–93, 212, 234
Crook, J. A. 190, 240, 260, 273, 284, 312
Crossan, John Dominic 113, 146
Crowther, C. V. 269
Cueto, B. 292, 312
Cunningham, I. C. 193, 234
Cuno, James 43, 63
Curchin, Leonard A. 307, 313
Czerny, Ernst 67
D'Andria, Francesco 31, 51, 62
Dally, Ortwin 121, 123–24, 146
Daly, Lloyd W. 193, 223, 226, 234

Danker, Frederick W. 37
Dauge, Yves Albert 277, 313
Davies, John K. 28, 247, 250–51, 253, 269
Davidson, Gladys R. 154
Davis, P. J. 279, 313
Day, John 213, 235
Dean, L. R. 19
DeConick, April D. 115, 149
De Coulanges, Fustel 7, 37
Deissmann, Adolf 37, 72, 86, 105, 269
Demougin, Ségolène 263, 269
Dench, Emma 279, 313
DeSilva, David 114–15, 146
Despinēs, Giōrgos 17
Dessau, Hermann 263, 273
Dignas, Beate 249–50, 269
Dinahet, Marie-Thérèse Le 254, 271
Dmitriev, Sviatoslav 9, 38
Dobbins, John Joseph 33, 249
Dodd, C. H. 309, 313
Dodge, Hazel 8, 35, 37, 294, 317
Domergue, Claude 47, 62
Dörner, Friedrich Karl 215, 235
Dondin-Payre, Monique 9, 38, 269
Ducrey, Pierre 15
Dudley, Donald Reynolds 35, 284, 313
Duman, Bahadir 30
Duncan-Jones, Richard 199, 235, 254, 257, 269
Dunn, James D. G. 61, 63
Dutch, Robert S. 156, 159–60, 184
Eadie, John W. 70
Earl, Donald C. 294
Eck, Werner 69, 217, 235
Edson, Charles F. 17
Edwards, Catharine 35
Edwards, Charles M. 291, 313
Edwards, Douglas R. 123, 146
Edwards, Katharine May 22, 156, 157, 177, 186
Ehrenberg, Victor 313
Ehrhardt, Norbert 121, 123, 146
Eisen, Ute E. 90, 113

INDEX OF MODERN AUTHORS

Elliott, J. Keith	177	Fröhlich, Pierre	9, 38
Elliot, Neil	36	Futrell, Alison	48, 63
Elsner, Jaś	153, 284, 313	Gaertner, Jan Felix	279, 313
Emmel, Stephen	68	Gagniers, J. des	32, 48
Enagonios, Hermes	46	Galinsky, Karl	284, 294–95, 313
Engelmann, Helmut	255, 269	Gardner, Percy	156, 185
Engels, Donald W.	22, 186, 203, 235	Garielsen, Vincent	28
Erdkamp, Paul	262, 269	Garland, Robert	223, 235
Espérandieu, Émile	302, 313	Garnsey, Peter	195–96, 199, 215, 219, 235–36, 241
Evans, Craig A.	99, 105, 151		
Ewald, Björn Christian	35	Gaselee, S.	204, 236
Fabiano, G.	303, 315	Gates, Charles	8, 38, 68, 86, 294, 313
Fairweather, Janet A.	207, 235	Gathercole, Simon	106
Fantham, Elain	214, 235	Gauley, Steven W.	68
Faraone, Christopher A.	23	Gauthier, Philippe	8, 38
Feissel, Denis	14, 105	Gazda, Elaine K.	285, 287, 316
Ferrary, J. L.	269	Gebhard, Elizabeth R.	19, 187
Ferrero, Ermanno	302, 312	Gee, Emma	286, 313
Ferris, Iain M.	277, 299, 312	Gempf, Conrad	144, 150
Ferguson, Everett	94, 107	Gemünden, Petra von	112
Finkielsztejn, Gérald	264, 269	Gerber, Albrecht	25, 270
Finley, M. I.	4, 6, 38, 194–95, 206, 208, 215, 219, 233, 235–36, 251, 269	Gerber, Christine	113
		Gerstenberger, Erhard S.	309
Fishwick, Duncan	186	Geva, Hillel	11
Fitzgerald, John T.	248	Gibson, Elsa	94, 106
Fleming, Rebecca	213	Gill, David W. J.	96–97, 106, 144, 150
Fleming, Stuart J.	154, 235	Glotz, Gustave	7, 38
Fobes, Francis H.	202, 235	González, Julian	170
Forbis, Elizabeth	8, 38	Goodman, Penelope J.	70, 86
Formigé, Jules	297–98, 313	Goodrich, John K.	98, 106
Forstner-Müller, Irene	67	Gordon, Arthur E.	93, 105, 106
Foss, Pedar William	33	Gotter, Ulrich	68
Fotopoulos, John	158	Gounarē, Emmanouela G.	15
Fox, Harry Bertram Earle	156, 186	Gounaris, Georgios G.	15
Frank, Tenney	248, 261, 270	Grant, Mary	223, 236
French, David	11	Greaves, Alan M.	123, 146
Frey, Jean-Baptiste	10	Grégoire, Henri	245, 270
Friedländer, Ludwig	200, 235	Gregory, Timothy E.	19, 291, 313
Frier, Bruce W.	72, 75–77, 85, 197, 198, 220, 235	Grey, Cam	189, 198, 236
		Grossschmidt, Karl	56–57, 64
Friesen, Steven J.	5, 9, 22, 27, 96–98, 102, 105, 152, 158, 165, 168, 187, 196–97, 203, 229, 239–41, 255, 270	Gruen, Erich S.	261, 270, 280, 284, 314
		Guardia, R. La	165
		Guizza, F.	52
Friesinger, Herwig	56, 65	Günther, Wolfgang	146
Frija, Gabrielle	8, 11, 38	Gurval, Robert Alan	292, 314

INDEX OF MODERN AUTHORS

Habel, Norman C. 117, 146
Haelst, J. van 73, 86
Hahn, Johannes 68
Halfmann, Helmut 50, 63
Hall, Edith 280–81, 308, 314
Hallet, Christopher 146
Hammond, Mason 11
Hamon, Patrice 9
Hanson, John Arthur 48
Hardie, Alex 201, 236
Hardin, Justin K. 13
Harding, Mark 226, 242
Harl, Kenneth W. 163, 170
Harland, Philip A. 9, 28, 37, 52, 103, 105
Harlow, Daniel C. 109
Harrill, J. Albert 229, 236
Harris, William V. 190–91, 193 195–200, 215, 236, 250, 257, 259, 261, 262, 270
Harrison, James R. 1–40, 101, 112–13, 122, 146, 266, 270, 271, 279–317
Harrison, Thomas 277, 308, 314
Hartley, John E. 309, 314
Hartshorn, Nicole Candace 298, 299, 314
Harvey, Brian K. 34
Harvey, Susan Ashbrook 108
Hasenohr, Claire 262, 272
Hatzfeld, Jean 262, 265, 270
Hauptmann, Harald 285, 316
Haynes, I. 262
Head, Barclay Vincent 6, 22, 28
Heckel, Waldemar 11
Hellerman, Joseph 16
Hellholm, David 112
Hemer, Colin 9
Henderson, John 193, 236
Hendrix, Holland L. 17, 29
Henten, Jan Willem van 106
Herda, Alexander 124, 147
Hermansen, G. 220, 236
Herrmann, Peter 147
Herzog, Irmela 35
Heuchert, Volker 153, 157, 163
Hicks, E. L. 24

Hillard, T. W. 28
Hills, Julian Victor 34
Hinard, François 191, 236
Hingley, Richard 293, 314
Hitchner, Bruce 259
Hock, Ronald F. 223, 236
Hoff, Michael C. 155
Hogarth, David George 25
Hohlfelder, Robert L. 11, 23
Holdsworth, Benjamin Evans 292, 314
Holland, Leicester B. 292, 314
Hölscher, Tonio 111, 147, 153
Holum, Kenneth G. 10, 11
Hombert, Marcel 75 86,
Hopkins, Keith 190–91, 193, 197, 221, 236, 262
Hornum, Michael B. 46, 47, 64
Horsley, G. H. R. 27, 101, 106, 113, 147
Horst, Pieter Willem van der 91, 94, 104, 106
Horster, Marietta 8, 38
Howgego, Christopher J. 15, 64, 153, 157–58, 161–62, 164, 166, 176–77, 186
Hoyo, Toni Ñaco del 261
Hueber, Friedmund 28
Huechert, Volker 15, 153, 158, 170
Hugueney, Jeanne 220
Hultin, Jeremy F. 264, 270
Humann, Carl 31
Hunter, David G. 89, 108
Huttner, Ulrich 29, 49, 52–53, 64
Iacopi, Irene 294, 314
Ibrahim, Leila 23
Ierardi, Michael 158, 171
Imhoof-Blumer, Friedrich 156, 185
Iplikçioğlu, Sıtkı İsa Bülent 26
Jashemski, Wilhelmina 221, 233
Jackson, John 211, 237
James, Sarah A. 165, 168
Jameson, Fredric 214, 237
Jeal, Roy 114–15, 147
Jenkins, Gilbert K. 28
Jenkyns, Richard 4, 36, 38
Jensen, Robin M. 147

INDEX OF MODERN AUTHORS

Jewett, Robert   34, 36, 103, 106, 290, 296-97, 314
Johnson, Allan Chester   304, 314
Johnson, Gary J.   106, 270
Jones, A. H. M.   8, 38, 258, 261, 270, 313
Jones, Christopher P.   47, 212, 237, 245
Jones, Nicholas F.   18
Jones, Tom B.   161
Jongman, Willem M.   197, 237
Jordan, D.   23
Jördens, A.   69, 70, 86
Joshel, Sandra R.   217, 237, 254, 270
Judge, E. A.   1, 28, 35, 38, 73, 87, 152, 227, 232, 237, 266, 271, 284, 289, 314
Kah, Daniel   76, 86
Kahl, Brigitte   111-13, 136-37, 139, 142, 145, 147
Kant, Laurence H   106
Kanz, Fabian   56, 57, 64
Kardos, Marie-José   263, 271
Karlsson, Lars   50, 63
Karwiese, Stefan   28
Kaster, Robert A.   208, 237
Katsari, Christina   163, 171-72, 250, 272
Kearsley, R. A.   27, 30
Keegan, Peter   218, 237
Keil, J.   263, 271
Kent, J. H.   19, 96, 97, 106, 169
Keppie, Lawrence   106
Ker, Walter C. A.   200, 237
Kidson, Lyn   28, 259, 271
King, Helen   191, 234
King, Martin Luther   192
Kirbihler, François   260-61, 263-64, 271
Kirchhoff, Adolf   24
Klauck, Hans-Josef   229, 237
Kleiner, Fred S.   293 302, 315
Kleiner, Gerhard   123, 147, 298, 302
Kloft, Hans   196, 237
Kloppenborg, John S.   9, 39, 103-7, 249, 271
Knapp, Robert C.   168-69, 306, 315
Kneissl, Peter   217, 235
Knibbe, Dieter   26, 256, 269
Koch, Daniel   35
Koch, Dietrich-Alex   104, 107
Koester, Craig R.   107
Koester, Helmut   14, 27, 28, 137, 146, 148, 264, 266, 271
Koet, Bart J.   104, 137
Kolb, Anne   69
Konakçi, Erim   30
König, Jason   56, 64
Kontokosta, A. C. Hrychuk   46, 47, 64
Koukouli-Chrysanthaki, Chaido   14
Kraemer, Ross S.   94, 95, 107
Krapinger, Gerot   45, 58, 64-65
Krause, Jens-Uwe   198, 237
Kraybill, J. Nelson   140, 148
Kreitzer, Larry   32, 112, 148, 151, 155
Krentz, Edgar   60, 64
Krinzinger, Fritz   56
Kroll, John H.   155, 167
Krüger, Julian   67, 79, 80, 81, 87
Kruger, Michael J.   71, 87
Kühnert, Barbara   189, 238
Kullberg, Jesper Blid   50, 63
Kunzl-Snodgrass, Annemarie   111
Kuttner, Ann   134, 148, 296, 315
Labarre, Guy   11, 254, 271
Ladstätter, Sabine   28
Laet, Siegfried J. de   256-57, 271
Lafond, Yves   8, 37
Lambers, Karsten   35
Lambros, Paulos   15
Lamoine, Laurent   8, 37
Lampe, Peter   35, 91, 102, 107-8, 229-30, 238
Lanciani, Rodolfo   190, 221, 238
Landes, Christian   47, 62
Landvogt, Peter   251, 271
Lapaulus, Étienne   15
Lattimore, Richard   216, 217, 238
Laubry, Nicolas   105
Laubscher, Hans Peter   222, 238
Laum, Bernhard   24, 248-49, 271
Laurence, Ray   214, 238
Lavedan, Pierre   220, 238
Lehmann, Clayton Miles   10, 11
Lemerle, Philippe   14

Levene, D. S. 206
Levi, Annalina Caló 313, 315
Levick, Barbara 11, 107, 171, 262, 265, 269, 271
Levine, Lee I. 10
Lewin, Ariel 11
Lewis, David 46, 64
Lewis, Peter 152
Liebengood, Kelly D. 248, 271
Lifshitz, Baruch 10
Ligt, Luuk de 169, 197, 238
Lindemann, Andreas 227, 238
Lintott, Andrew 190, 240, 260, 273, 312, 314
Litinas, Nikos 80, 87
Liu, Jinyu 9, 39, 249, 271
Llewelyn, Stephen R. 101
Loane, Helen J. 251, 271
LoCascio, Elio 197, 237
Longenecker, Bruce W. 1, 2, 39, 102, 107, 232, 238, 248 255, 272
Lopez, Davina 113, 129, 135, 147, 289
Lotz, John Paul 28
MacDowall, David W. 154, 164–66, 186
MacIsaac, John D. 168, 169
MacMullen, Ramsay 90 92, 107, 190–91, 194, 217, 220–21, 228, 238, 246, 252, 272
Macro, A. D. 215–16, 238
Maderna, Caterina 126, 148
Madigan, Kevin 90, 107
Maggi, Giuseppe 190, 238
Magie, David 8, 39, 215, 238
Maier, Harry O. 111, 113–17, 123, 148
Maischberger, Martin 121–22, 124, 143, 146, 148
Maiuri, Amedeo 219, 238
Malherbe, Abraham J. 223, 238
Malkin, Irad 266
Mann, Christian 55, 57–58, 64
Marchal, Joseph A. 15
Marcus, Joyce 7, 39
Marcus, Lars 35
Martin, Dale B. 163, 255, 272
Martin, Josef 209, 239

Martin, Victor 84, 87
Martzavou, Paraskevi 18
Mason, H. J. 203, 238
Matthews, John F. 258, 272
Mattusch, Carol C. 165
Mayer, Emmanuel 255
Mazar, Benjamin 11
Mazar, Eliat 11
McHugh, Michael P. 94, 107
McLean, Bradley Hudson 89, 92–95, 107, 246, 271
Meeks, Wayne A. 1, 3, 39, 230, 238
Meggitt, Justin J. 1, 97, 107, 154, 191–93, 195–96, 200, 214, 239, 255, 272
Meritt, B. D. 19, 39, 190
Merkelbach, Reinhold 58
Merriam, Carol U. 280, 315
Meshorer, Ya'akov 11
Meskell, Lynn 43, 64
Metcalf, William E. 162
Meyer, Elizabeth A. 217, 239, 252, 272
Meyer, Fredreick G. 221, 233
Meyers, Eric M. 11
Mierse, William E. 307, 315
Migeotte, Léopold 8, 39, 249, 272
Millar, Fergus 90–91, 107, 189, 204, 239
Miller, John F. 294
Miller, S. J. 305, 315
Mills, Harrianne 291, 313
Millis, Benjamin W. 165, 180–81, 184
Minnen, Peter van 75, 78, 87
Miranda, E. 52
Mirau, Neil A. 68
Misgav, Haggai 94, 108
Mitchell, Stephen 11, 163, 171–72, 250, 260, 272, 285, 287, 315
Mitternacht, Dieter 35
Momigliano, A. D. 7, 39, 251, 272
Monson, Andrew 68, 87
Moon, Warren G. 134, 149
Moore, J. M. 300
Morizot, P. 262
Morley, Neville 189–93, 198, 203, 206, 232, 239

INDEX OF MODERN AUTHORS

Morris, Ian   191, 197, 216, 237, 239, 248, 251, 258, 273
Morris, Leon   296, 315
Morstein-Marx, Robert   192, 194, 239
Mowery, Robert L.   13
Moxnes, Halvor   112, 148
Müller, Christel   262, 272
Müller, Wolfgang   67, 72, 78, 87
Mumford, Lewis   7
Murphy-O'Connor, Jerome   11, 27, 54, 64, 95–96, 108
Naldini, Mario   73, 87
Nash, Ernest   35
Nasrallah, Laura S.   16, 17, 229, 239
Nawotka, Krzysztof   148
Netzer, Ehud   10–11
Newlands, Carole Elizabeth   296
Ng, Diana Y.   285, 287, 316
Niang, Aliou Cissé   113, 148–49
Nicolet, Claude   261–62, 272
Nigdelis, Pantelis   17, 18
Nijf, Onno M. van   9, 39, 249, 255, 257, 259–60, 264, 272
Nobbs, Alanna   226, 242
Nongbri, Brent   71, 87
Norêna, Carlos F.   35
Nützel, J. M.   132
Oakes, Peter   14, 33, 36
O'Brien, Peter T.   29
Ogereau, Julien M.   1, 16, 245–75
Økland, Jorunn   156, 158, 181–83
Okunak, M.   132
Oliver, J. H.   278, 315
Olsson, Birger   10, 35
Osborne, Robin   189–90, 192, 194–95, 198, 239, 241–42
Osiek, Carolyn   90, 107, 114, 149, 192, 241
Ossi, Adrian J.   13, 285–88, 303, 315
Oster, Richard   26–28, 151–52
Özdoğan, Mehmet   43, 64
Packer, James E.   33, 35, 39, 219, 239
Pailler, Jean-Marie   47, 62
Palagia, Olga   46, 64
Panagopoulou, Katerina   266, 273
Panetta, Marisa Ranieri   33
Pangle, Thomas L.   3
Papageorgiadou-Bani, Harikleia   171
Papakonstantinou, Zinon   58
Parker, Andrew   60, 64
Parkin, Anneliese R.   189, 198–99, 209–10, 236
Parkins, Helen M.   8, 214, 238
Parrish, David   8, 39
Paul, George M.   158, 171
Perry, B. E.   193 223–24, 239
Petitmengin, Pierre   105
Pettegrew, David K.   19, 168
Pfanner, Michael   121, 124, 130, 143, 146
Pfitzner, Vic   40, 60, 64
Pflaum, H.-G.   49, 64
Pharr, Clyde   314
Picard, Gilbert Charles   297, 315
Pickering, S. R.   73
Pietsch, W.   55, 64
Pilhofer, Peter   14
Pitts, Andrew W.   71
Plümacher, Eckhard   267, 268
Pollini, John   134, 149, 151
Ponsero, Giuseppe   303, 315
Ponting, Matthew   258
Portefaix, Lilian   14
Porter, Stanley E.   23, 71
Posluschny, Axel   35
Platner, Samuel Ball   35
Pleket, H. W.   196, 239, 248, 251, 253, 261, 273
Plümacher, Eckhard   267
Préaux, Claire   75
Prell, Marcus   190, 193–95, 198, 200, 240
Price, Jonathan J.   94
Price, Martin   158
Price, S. R. F.   39 108, 112–13, 149
Prieur, J.   301–2, 315
Pucci, Giuseppe   250
Purcell, Nicholas   190, 198, 201, 203, 240
Ramage, Edwin S.   23, 291
Ramsay, W. M.   11–13, 49, 245, 273
Rapoport, Amos   67, 87

INDEX OF MODERN AUTHORS

Rathbone, Dominic   69, 85, 258, 260, 266, 273
Ratté, Christopher   46
Rawson, Elizabeth   52, 65, 190–91, 240, 242, 260, 273, 286
Redford, Donald B.   68, 87
Reed, Jonathan L.   113, 146
Rehak, Paul   286, 316
Reiser, Marius   151–52
Reynolds, Joyce Maire   103, 108
Revell, Louise   51, 65
Rhoads, David   116, 149
Rich, John   4, 33, 39, 70, 88
Richardson, John   260, 273
Richardson, Lawrence   33
Richardson, Peter   36
Richardson-Hay, Christine   56, 65
Ricl, Marijana   217, 240
Ridley, Ronald T.   284, 316
Riesner, Rainer   96, 108
Rife, Joseph L.   23
Riggs, Christina   68–69
Ripollès, Pau   50, 63, 156
Ritti, Tullia   31, 47, 52, 65
Rives, James   108
Rizakis, A. D.   165
Robbins, Vernon K.   114–15, 149
Robert, Louis   26, 46–48, 65, 245–47, 253, 273
Robinson, Betsey A.   180
Robinson, David M.   12, 285–86, 316
Robinson, Edward   28
Robinson, O. F.   219, 220, 240
Rocca, Eugenio La   295, 316
Rogers, Guy MacLean   27, 56, 65, 100, 108
Rohden, Paulus de   263, 273
Rohrbaugh, Richard L.   2–4, 7, 40
Rolfe, J. C.   206, 240
Roloff, Jürgen   119, 149
Romano, David Gilman   240
Rose, Charles Brian   287, 293, 296, 316
Rosen, Ralph M.   45, 63
Rossing, Barbara   117, 119, 149
Rossini, Orietta   296

Rostovtzeff, Michael Ivanovitch   250–51, 261, 273
Rotroff, Susan I.   155
Rousset, Denis   105
Routledge, Carolyn   68, 88
Rowlandson, Jane   78, 88
Rubin, B. B.   13, 285–88, 316
Runesson, Anders   10
Rupprecht, Hans-Albert   68, 88
Rusten, Jeffrey   193, 234
Sabloff, Jeremy A.   7, 39
Safrai, Shmuel   108
Safrai, Zeev   108
Saller, Richard   89, 91, 108, 197, 217–18, 237, 240, 248, 251, 258, 273
Salomies, O.   269
Salmeri, Giovanni   250–51, 253
Salmon, J. B.   22
Samaran, C.   245, 273
Sampley, J. Paul   16, 60, 64, 224, 236
Samuel, Deborah H.   73
Sánchez, David   113, 149
Sarrazanas, Clément   14
Sasel-Kos, Marietta   22
Saunders, R.   28
Scanlon, Thomas   58, 65
Schäfer, Christoph   265, 273
Scheid, John   284, 316
Scheidel, Walter   196–97, 199, 236–37, 240–41, 248, 251, 258, 273
Scherrer, Peter   28, 263, 274
Schiesaro, Alessandro   223, 241
Schmalz, Geoffrey C. R.   18
Schmeller, Thomas   230, 241
Schneider, Gerhard   145
Schneider, Rolf Michael   130, 149
Scholer, David M.   232, 237
Schowalter, Daniel N.   22, 158, 165, 168, 187, 203, 240
Schröter, Jens   268
Schwartz, Joshua   108
Schwarzer, Holger   136, 149
Scobie, Alexander   200, 219–20, 241
Scranton, Robert   23
Sear, Frank   51, 65

INDEX OF MODERN AUTHORS

Seesengood, Robert Paul 60, 65
Seifrid, Mark A. 310, 316
Seim, Turid Karlsen 112
Selal, C. 32
Sève, Michel 15, 105
Shapiro, Alan 111, 150
Sharp, Michael 69, 88
Shaw, Brent D. 217, 218, 240–41
Shaw, Joseph W. 2
Sidebotham, Steven E. 262, 274
Sigismund, Marcus 163
Sijpesteijn, Pieter Johannes 74, 84, 88
Silvestrelli, Francesca 50, 62
Sjoberg, Gideon 6, 40
Slingerland, Dixon 96, 108
Sluiter, Ineke 45, 63
Small, Alastair 186
Smallwood, E. Mary 316
Smith, R. R. R. 46
Snodgrass, Anthony 111
Snyder, Graydon F. 95, 108
Sorek, Susan 10
Spawforth, A. J. S. 23, 165, 167, 181
Stambaugh, John E. 8, 40
Standhartinger, Angela 113
Stansbury, Harry A. 20
Stanton, Graham N. 99, 108
Stauber, Josef 58
Steen, Jesper 35
Stefanidou-Tiveriou, Theodosia 17
Stein, Wilma Olch 23
Steinby, Margareta 35
Stern, Ephraim 11
Stewart, Andrew 134, 149
Strachan, Lionel R. M. 169
Strocka, Volker Michael 121, 124–25, 130, 149
Stöger, Hannah 35
Strootman, Rolf 54, 65
Stroud, R. S. 19, 24
Sullivan, J. P. 201, 241
Sullivan, Richard 11
Sutherland, C. H. V. 163
Swift, E. H. 173
Syme, Ronald 263, 274, 284, 316

Tabbernee, William 89–91, 94–95 245, 274
Tannenbaum, Robert 103, 108
Taussig, Hal 113, 147
Teixidor, J. 258, 274
Theissen, Gerd 1, 227–29, 241, 255, 274
Thibault, John C. 279, 316
Thierfelder, Andreas 193, 241
Tiwald, Markus 2, 37
Toalster, P. 13
Tomlinson, Richard 69, 88
Tomson, Peter J. 108
Toner, J. P. 196, 241
Too, Yun Lee 208, 237
Trainor, Michael 30, 32, 267–68
Tran, Nicolas 9, 249, 254–55, 269, 274
Travaglini, Adriana 31
Trebilco, Paul 20, 28, 89–109, 144, 150, 264, 267
Treggiari, Susan M. 215–16, 241
Trell, Bluma L. 158
Trinkl, E. 55, 65
Tröster, Manuel 54, 65
Tuchelt, K. 285, 316
Unnik, W. C. Van 11
Unwin, James R. 20
Uro, Risto 115, 149
Ustinova, Yulia 46, 65
Verboven, Koenraad 199, 241
Verhoef, Eduard 15
Vermeule, Cornelius C. 285, 291, 316
Veyne, Paul 199, 222, 241, 255
Vielhauer, Philipp 264, 274
Ville, Georges 46, 65
Vitelli, Giovanna 35
Vivenza, Gloria 258
Voutyras, Emm 17
Waele, Ferdinand J. de 192, 241
Waelkens, Marc 13, 285, 287, 315
Walbank, Mary E. Hoskins 22, 156, 158, 171, 176, 186
Walker, Susan 294, 317
Wallace-Hadrill, Andrew 4, 33, 70, 88, 191–92, 196, 219, 241, 293, 317
Walters, James C. 22, 158, 187

Walton, Steve	265, 274
Waltzing, Jean-Pierre	249, 274
Wankel, Hermann	26
Watson, Duane F.	115, 149
Watson, Nick J.	60, 64
Weber, Georg	53, 65
Weber, Patrick	15
Weber, Wilhelm	49
Weidemann, Thomas	57, 65
Weiler, Ingomar	215, 240, 242
Weiss, Adolf	227–28
Weiss, Alexander	98, 109
Weiss, Johannes	227–28, 242
Weiss, Peter	157, 167
Weiss, Ze'ev	10
Weissenrieder, Annette	112, 150
Welborn, L. L.	2, 20, 40, 98, 109, 157, 160, 189–242
Welch, Katherine E.	50, 65
Wendt, Friederike	112
Wenham, Gordon J.	309, 317
West, Allen B.	19, 179
White, Adam	184
Whittaker, C. R.	189–90, 192–94, 198, 242, 274
Whittaker, Dick	262
Wiemken, Helmut	193, 223, 242
Wierschowski, L.	262
Wilkes John	247, 250–51, 253, 269
Williams, Charles K.	219
Williams, Gareth D.	279, 317
Williams, Hector	23
Williamson, George	163
Wilson, Andrew	254, 259, 268
Wilson, Stephen G.	9, 103, 107
Winkler, John J.	204, 225, 242
Winter, Bruce W.	21, 169, 171, 229–30, 242
Winterbottom, Michael	208, 242
Wiplinger, Gilbert	25
Wiseman, J. R.	22
Wiseman, T. P.	228, 242
Wissowa, G.	274
Witke, Edward Charles	191, 242
Wlach, Gudrun	25
Wood, John Turtle	24
Woodhead, A. G.	90, 109, 247, 274
Woolf, Greg	35, 190–91, 193, 196, 199–201, 204–9, 214, 235, 242, 281, 317
Wörrle, M.	269
Yamauchi, Edwin M.	8, 40
Yavetz, Zvi	189, 194, 216, 219, 242
Yeo, Khiok-Khng	158
Yiftach-Firanko, Uri	78, 88
Yilmaz, Salim	31, 47
Zabehlicky, Heinrich	265
Zaccagnini, Carlo	259, 270
Zangenberg, Jürgen K.	109, 152, 163
Zanker, Paul	40, 111–12, 130, 133–34, 150, 153, 293–94, 296, 301, 317
Zannis, Angelos G.	13
Zeitz, Heinrich	224, 243
Zervos, O. H.	219
Zimmermann, Carola	13, 29, 249, 275
Zimmermann, Norbert	28
Zingale, L. Migliardi	78, 88
Ziskowski, Angela	175
Zoller, C.	13
Zuiderhoek, Arjan	8, 40, 52, 65, 190, 243, 261, 275

www.ingramcontent.com/pod-product-compliance
Lightning Source LLC
Chambersburg PA
CBHW031704230426
43668CB00006B/101